The Face of Tutankhamun

Christopher Frayling is Professor of Cultural History and head of the faculty of Humanities at the Royal College of Art. An historian, a critic and an award-winning broadcaster, he is well known for his work on BBC Radio 4, Channel 4 and BBC2 television, most recently writing and presenting the series *The Face of Tutankhamun*. He has published numerous books and articles on aspects of cultural history, including *Spaghetti Westerns* (1980) and *Vampyres* (1991).

Professor Frayling is a trustee of the Victoria and Albert Museum, Chairman of the Visual Arts Panel of the Arts Council of Great Britain, and a member of the Arts Council. He is currently writing a biography of Sergio Leone for Faber.

He is married and lives in Bath and London.

Christopher Frayling

The Face of Tutankhamun

ff

faber and faber

LONDON · BOSTON

First published in 1992
by Faber and Faber Limited
3 Queen Square London WC1N 3AU

Photoset by Parker Typesetting Service, Leicester
Printed in England by Clays Ltd, St Ives plc

Christopher Frayling is hereby identified as author of this
work in accordance with Section 77 of the Copyright, Designs
and Patents Act 1988

A CIP record for this book is available from the British Library

ISBN 0-571-16845-0

For Helen, with love

CONTENTS

'. . . to feel oneself as a European in command, almost at will, of Oriental history, time and geography; to institute new areas of specialization; to establish new disciplines; to divide, deploy, schematize, tabulate, index, and record everything in sight (and out of sight) . . . and, above all, to transmute living reality into the stuff of texts, to possess (or think one possesses) actuality mainly because nothing in the Orient seems to resist one's powers: these are the features of Orientalist projection entirely realized in the *Description de l'Egypte*, itself enabled and reinforced by Napoleon's wholly Orientalist engulfment of Egypt by the instruments of Western knowledge and power . . .'

Edward Said, *Orientalism* (1978)

'On this Friday, October 9th, he noted his arrival at Suez, and observed that he had as yet neither gained nor lost. He sat down quietly to breakfast in his cabin, never once thinking of inspecting the town, being one of those Englishmen who are wont to see foreign countries through the eyes of their domestics . . .'

Jules Verne,
Around the World in Eighty Days (1873)

'The foot was not shrunk or shrivelled, or even black and unsightly, like the flesh of Egyptian mummies, but plump and fair, and, except where it had been slightly burnt, perfect as on the day of death – a very triumph of embalming . . . I wrapped up this relic of the past in the remnants of the old linen rag which had evidently formed a portion of its owner's grave clothes, and put it away in my Gladstone bag, which I had bought at the Army and Navy Stores – a strange combination, I thought.'

Henry Rider Haggard, *She* (1887)

'Before the close of the year 1922 the name of the ancient Egyptian king, Tutankhamen, may have been familiarly known to a couple of hundred Egyptologists and students of Egyptology in the world, and perhaps five hundred more persons might have remembered that they had heard or read of him at some time or another. Now his name is familiar to thousands throughout the world, far more familiar indeed than the greatest names in Egyptian history, the Thotmes and the Ramses. A curious fact, because he was a most undistinguished and ephemeral monarch . . . It may be that the general interest in this discovery is due largely to the human love of tales of buried treasure and the desire to gloat over gold and precious stones, as a cynic has observed. But we may also attribute it, at least partially, to higher motives, to the human love of the wonderful, and to the stirring of the imagination that is caused by such a revelation of ancient days as this. Fairy tales seem outdone; we see in existence the ancient splendour of Ormuz and of Ind, of Cairo and Baghdad that we read of, as children, in the stories of Sinbad and of Aladdin. Two benevolent djinns in the persons of Lord Carnarvon and Mr Carter seem to have revealed to us, by a touch of their wands, the ancient Pharaoh . . . preserved as by magic with his royal state about him until these latter days, for us to behold him and wonder.'

H. R. Hall (Deputy Keeper of Egyptian Antiquities, British Museum), in *Wonders of the Past* (1925)

'The trick is not to get yourself into some inner correspondence of spirit with your informants . . . but to figure out what the devil they think they are up to.'

Clifford Geertz, *On the Nature of Anthropological Understanding* (1976)

PREFACE

Many books have been written about Tutankhamun, the 18th Dynasty boy-pharaoh who ruled Egypt probably from 1333 to 1323 BC. The touring exhibitions of the fabulous treasures found in his tomb that visited Europe and America in the 1960s and 1970s stimulated scores of them, and in the past few years alone three major works have been published: Nicholas Reeves's *The Complete Tutankhamun* (1990), H. V. F. Winstone's *Howard Carter and the Discovery of the Tomb of Tutankhamun* (1991) and, especially, the magisterial study by T. G. H. James, *Howard Carter: The Path to Tutankhamun* (1992). These books have been written by Egyptologists or specialists in the history of archaeology, and they are concerned with the history of the pharaoh and his times, or with the story of the archaeological excavation which began in November 1922, led by Lord Carnarvon and Howard Carter, exactly seventy years ago.

This book is not written by an Egyptologist, and it is not primarily about either ancient Egypt or archaeology. It is by a cultural historian, and its twin aims are to examine the extraordinary impact of the discovery of the tomb, and the ways in which that discovery was received and interpreted by the general public in the 1920s – and has been since. The Face of Tutankhamun, so to speak, rather than Tutankhamun himself.

No archaeological discovery has ever captured the public imagination in the same way, or to the same extent, and this book seeks to explore the reasons why. It has been written in the belief – to paraphrase Edward Said – that the wider cultural impact and the reception of the 'wonderful things' found in that tomb can tell us much more about the Occident than about the Orient, both in the 1920s and today. And it is, I believe, the first book to deal with this surprisingly neglected aspect of the story.

The first part of *The Face of Tutankhamun* traces and examines in detail the impact of the discovery. Then – in their own words, sometimes from unpublished sources – the main participants relate what it was like to take part in the great excavation. This is followed by a series of influential short stories of the time, set in and around archaeological digs and the world of Egyptology, several of them exciting variations on the 'curse of the mummy' theme. A section on the 1920s craze for Tutmania leads on to three examples of writing about Tutankhamun today. One concerns the blockbusting exhibitions of the last thirty years, another the popular image of ancient Egypt, and the third the sorry state of the boy-king's mummy, as it lies in the tomb where it was originally buried some 3,000 years ago.

Together, these essays, extracts and stories

present a series of perspectives on the discovery of the tomb of Tutankhamun as a social and cultural phenomenon, and as an aspect of popular culture from the 1920s to the present day. They mix fact and fiction, as did popular reactions to the news of the finding of the treasure.

The archaeologist Howard Carter could never understand what all the fuss was about. After all, the discovery was mainly of interest, he thought, to specialists in Egyptology. This book looks at the fuss, and at why it happened in the ways it did.

ACKNOWLEDGEMENTS

The Face of Tutankhamun accompanies a major five-part BBC television series of the same title, which I have written and presented. I would like to thank Roy Davies, Derek Towers and David Wallace, Sue Coley and Anne Miller, John Howarth and David South, Anthony Wornum, Peter Thorn, Eric Fever and Andy Bates, and especially Sylvia Van Kleef (who helped to research some wonderful things), all of whom were involved in the production and filming of the series. The many exciting adventures we had while making *The Face of Tutankhamun* would fill another, very different, book. At times, these adventures almost succeeded in challenging my healthy cynicism about 'the curse of the pharaohs'. They included: the lights abruptly going out when I first mentioned the curse while standing over Tutankhamun's glass-topped sarcophagus deep within the tomb itself; the sound packing up, for no apparent reason, when I started my commentary next to the gold portrait mask of the pharaoh, in the Egyptian Museum in Cairo; the director suffering a sudden trouble with the gall-stones (the illness which Howard Carter himself suffered in the early 1920s) midway through the shoot; the snapping of the main cable holding up the elevator in the Cairo hotel where we were staying, and its dramatic fall for twenty-one floors with the director and the

presenter still in the elevator; a very nasty respiratory attack – I stopped breathing for several seconds, as though my vocal cords had sandpaper lids on them – after a day's filming in a tomb shaft full of dried bat droppings; virtually the entire crew getting conjunctivitis after we had filmed a night-time sequence in the Valley of the Queens about some Edwardian Egyptologists and artists who tried to raise the ghost of Akhnaton, and who attributed *their* subsequent attacks of acute conjunctivitis (or 'trachoma') to the revenge of the heretic king himself. And so on.

For believers in 'the curse', this would all doubtless count as hard evidence; for myself, I prefer to believe that the causes had more to do with the Egyptian climate in April, the microclimate inside the tombs, the power supply (we were sometimes plugged into a wiring system originally installed by Howard Carter, just after the turn of the century), eccentric ideas about machine maintenance, sheer coincidence, and – where more mundane manifestations of 'the curse' were concerned – the caterers, than with the wrath of Tutankhamun. But there's no persuading some people. I simply can't fathom why Victorian and Edwardian Britons went to Egypt *for the healthy climate*.

I would also like to thank Dr Donald P. Ryan, Project Director of the Pacific Lutheran University Valley of the Kings project, who, in inimitable style, took us around the sites of Howard Carter's early experiences as an archaeologist and actually persuaded me to go down a deep crevice ('Don't look down, Christopher') in a 367-foot cliff, in search of the cliff-tomb prepared for Queen Hatshepsut (which Carter studied in 1916). Also Dr Mohamed Ibrahim Bakr, the Chairman of the Egyptian Antiquities Organization, and Romany Helmy, who made it all possible. Back home, Richard Humphries of the Tate Gallery, John Styles of the Victoria and Albert Museum, Dr Gillian Naylor and Susannah Handley of the Royal College of Art, David Butters of the Swaffham Museum, Professor Jeffrey Richards of the University of Lancaster and Donald Knight, historian of the British Empire Exhibition at Wembley – all provided help and support. So too did Dr Javomir Malek of the Griffith Institute in Oxford, and the great Egyptologist T. G. H.

James (ex-British Museum). This book is a long way away from their scholarly interests, but it was very good of them to be so encouraging about it. John Carter and Rosalind Berwald generously permitted me to consult and publish extracts from manuscripts in their care. The staff in the Bodleian Library, the British Library, the Griffith Institute, the National Art Library, the Royal College of Art Library and at Highclere Castle were always friendly and efficient. And the fashion designer Erté (Romain de Tirtoff) reminisced with me about Paris in the mid-1920s, shortly before he died.

Most of all, I would like to thank my wife, Helen, who lived through this project – at a difficult time – who word-processed the text, and who literally saved my life in Egypt. I couldn't possibly have written the book without her.

Christopher Frayling
Luxor and Bath, April 1992

THE MAIN EVENTS

1866	26 June	George Herbert, 5th Earl of Carnarvon, born at Highclere Castle.
1874	9 May	Howard Carter born in west London.
1891	September	Carter arrives in Egypt for the first time, employed by the Egypt Exploration Fund as an assistant draughtsman on a survey team, initially at Beni Hasan and Deir el-Bersha.
1892	February	Carter starts work at El-Amarna, under the Egyptologist and 'father of modern archaeology' Flinders Petrie, who gives him his first experience as an excavator.
1893	October	Carter starts nearly six years of work at El-Deir el-Bahari, copying works of art from the walls of the mortuary temple of Queen Hatshepsut.
1900	1 January	Carter takes up his appointment as Inspector of Monuments of Upper Egypt (organizing a 'system for the protection of tombs'), reporting to the French-administered Antiquities Service.
1902	January	Carter combines his duties as Inspector with excavation work for retired American lawyer and sponsor of archaeological digs Theodore Davis, some of it in the Valley of the Kings.
1904	1 January	Carter is transferred as Inspector from Upper to Lower Egypt.
1905	8 January	An affray at the Serapeum, the tomb of the sacred bulls in Saqqara, indirectly leads to Carter's resignation, and a period of working as a 'gentleman dealer' in antiquities and a freelance painter.

1907	autumn	Lord Carnarvon, who has been visiting Egypt to convalesce off and on since 1903, is granted permission to excavate in the Theban necropolis (or 'the Tombs of the Nobles').
1909	spring	Carnarvon and Carter join forces for 'exploration at Thebes'.
1912		Publication of the book *Five Years' Exploration at Thebes, 1907–11*.
1912	16 February	Theodore Davis is quoted as declaring, 'The Valley of the Tombs is now exhausted.'
1914	June	Davis's concession to dig in the valley is handed over to Carnarvon.
1917	autumn	The 'systematic' search by Carnarvon and Carter for the lost tomb of the pharaoh begins in earnest.
1922	4 November	The first stone step is uncovered.
	5 November	The steps are cleared.
	23 November	Carnarvon arrives in Luxor.
	26 November	First view of 'wonderful things' in the antechamber of the tomb of Tutankhamun.
	29 November	Official opening of the antechamber and inner room or annexe.
	30 November	First press report in *The Times*.
	7–18 December	Assembly of excavation team, with help from the Metropolitan Museum in New York.
	27 December	The first object, 'a painted wooden casket', is removed from the tomb.
1923	10 January	Announcement of Carnarvon's agreement with *The Times*.
	30 January	First of Harry Burton's photographs of the interior of the tomb published.

17 February   Official opening of the burial chamber.

25 February   Controversy in the American press about 'who owns the name' of Tutankhamun.

c.6 March   Carnarvon bitten by a mosquito.

5 April   Death of Carnarvon.

6 April   Sir Arthur Conan Doyle interviewed about 'the curse'.

7 April   Collectors of Egyptian antiquities reported to be 'in a panic'.

14 May   First artefacts leave by hand-propelled railway and steam barge for Cairo.

1924   21 January   Lenin dies in the Soviet Union and is subsequently embalmed in an 'ancient Egyptian' way.

12 February   Official lifting of the granite lid of the quartzite sarcophagus.

13 February   Carter leads his team in a 'strike'.

15 February   Lockout at the tomb.

12 April   Carter leaves England for his American lecture tour.

23 April   Official opening of the British Empire Exhibition at Wembley.

1925   13 January   Fresh concession to continue work on the tomb is finally renegotiated with the Egyptian government.

28 April   Opening in Paris of the Exposition Internationale des Arts Décoratifs et Industriels Modernes: the high point of the Art Deco style, partly influenced by Tutmania.

28 October   First view of the mummy of Tutankhamun, as the lid of the third ('inner') coffin is raised.

	11 November	Post-mortem of the mummy commences.
1930	10 November	The last artefacts are taken out of the tomb.
1932	spring	The last objects are railed and shipped to Cairo.
1934	undated	Director of the Metropolitan Museum Herbert Winlock concludes his extensive list of so-called 'Victims of the Curse'.
1939	2 March	Carter dies at 49 Albert Court, South Kensington.
	6 March	Carter is buried at Putney Vale cemetery, south London, beneath a plain gravestone.

The Face of Tutankhamun

Can You See Anything?

In her introduction to Howard Carter and Arthur Mace's book *The Discovery of the Tomb of Tutankhamen*, written just nine months after Carter first opened the tomb of the boy pharaoh in the Valley of the Kings, Lady Burghclere (Lord Carnarvon's sister Winifred) wrote:

'If it is true that the whole world loves a lover, it is also true that either openly or secretly the world loves Romance. Hence, doubtless, the passionate and far-flung interest aroused by the discovery of Tut-ankh-Amen's tomb, an interest extended to the discoverer, and certainly not lessened by the swift tragedy that waited on his brief hour of triumph. A story that opens like Aladdin's Cave and ends like a Greek myth of Nemesis cannot fail to capture the imagination of all men and women who, in this workaday existence, can still be moved by tales of high endeavour and unrelenting doom.'

Hers was one of the more perceptive comments about the cultural impact of the great discovery, written during its aftermath. First Aladdin's Cave; then Nemesis.

Howard Carter had cleared the stone steps leading down to the tomb on 5 November 1922. The next day he had sent his patron and sponsor, George Edward Stanhope Molyneux Herbert, 5th Earl of Carnarvon, a coded telegram to the family estate of Highclere Castle, near Newbury: 'AT LAST HAVE MADE WONDERFUL DISCOVERY IN VALLEY STOP A MAGNIFICENT TOMB WITH SEALS INTACT STOP RE-COVERED SAME FOR YOUR ARRIVAL STOP CONGRATULATIONS ENDS.'

Carnarvon's first inclination had been to respond coolly, with the words: 'POSSIBLY COME SOON'. He had been involved with Carter's excavation work off and on for about thirteen years, and there had been many false alarms during that time. Carter himself, or rather his horse, had stumbled on what he had thought was an intact royal tomb, just in front of the Temple of Queen Hatshepsut, as long ago as 1898. He had proudly invited the Egyptian Prime Minister, Mustafa Pasha, the British Resident and Consul-General Lord Cromer (a man so powerful that he was known in Cairo circles as 'the Lord'), and other notables to the grand public revelation of 'the mystery behind the masonry' three years later, only to discover that some nine months of digging with a small army of workmen had revealed a completely empty space beyond the door. 'A cursory examination,' Carter wrote, 'proved that there was *nothing*. I was filled with dismay.' It was an awful moment for a young, self-taught archaeologist who was determined – too determined on this occasion – to make a name for himself, a moment he was to remember right up to the end of his life. But Carnarvon also knew that in more recent years Howard Carter had been adopting what he called a 'systematic and exhaustive approach' to the whole business of finding an undiscovered and intact royal tomb in the Valley of the Kings. The approach had involved taking a 2½-acre triangle of ground in the centre of the valley, the reference points being the tombs of Rameses II, Merneptah and Rameses VI, dividing it up on a grid system derived from plans for artillery barrages in the First World War, and clearing away the heaps of debris and stone chippings right down to the bedrock. As Carter said, 'In 1917, our real campaign in the valley opened', a campaign (he chose the word judiciously) which lasted for five long years, and which initially produced very little beyond a few fragments of pottery and flakes of limestone. 'Interesting,' Carter added ruefully, 'but unexciting'. When Carnarvon heard of the 'Wonderful Discovery', in November 1922, he may have paused to reflect on all the research money he had been pouring into Carter's work in the valley over the years (a workforce of up to 100 men and three foremen; total cost so far in the region of £35,000), but he must have quickly realized that this was the moment they had both been waiting for.

Then, as now, archaeology was popularly thought to be just a matter of tombs and treasures and exciting things like that. Carnarvon himself had once said to the Egyptologist Percy Newberry that he would prefer to find an unrifled tomb than win the Derby; as one of the very few people in Britain who was actually in a position to make the choice, he wasn't being merely rhetorical when he said it. Ambrose Lansing, an Assistant Curator of the Egyptian Department at the Metropolitan Museum of Art, wrote in 1923:

'We once had the pleasure of entertaining Rudyard Kipling at the headquarters of our Expedition in Thebes. He described the life of the field archeologist very happily by saying, "It furnishes a scholarly pursuit with all the excitement of a gold prospector's life!" That goes far towards explaining why a sporting gentleman like the . . . Earl of Carnarvon was willing to spend money and so many discouraging years looking for an unplundered tomb in the Valley of the Kings.'

Maybe, at the beginning of November 1922, the sporting gentleman had backed a winner. Fragments of materials from Tutankhamun's funeral ceremony had been found nearby back in 1907, which seemed to suggest that he was connected with that particular part of the valley. Maybe this was *the* winner.

Lord Carnarvon's second telegram read 'PROPOSE ARRIVE ALEXANDRIA 20th', and on 23 November he reached Luxor with his daughter Lady Evelyn Herbert. There were still some heart-stopping moments for Carter. The seals on the door showed clearly that the tomb had already been opened twice, over 3,000 years before; and some broken pots among the rubble bore the names of several pharaohs in addition to Tutankhamun. Might this be 'a cache rather than a tomb' – a collection of royal mummies, walled up to protect them from tomb-robbers – and a plundered one at that? But by 26 November the 30-foot sloping passageway leading down into the tomb had been cleared, and a second sealed doorway revealed. Carter's published description of what happened next was to become a classic in the history of archaeological literature, and the most often quoted passage in the best-selling book from which it came:

'The decisive moment had arrived. With trembling hands I made a tiny breach in the upper left-hand corner . . . candle tests were applied as a precaution against possible foul gases, and then, widening the hole a little, I inserted the candle and peered in. Lord Carnarvon, Lady Evelyn and Callender [Arthur Callender, known as 'Pecky', a retired railway engineer and old friend of Carter's] standing

anxiously beside me to hear the verdict. At first I could see nothing, the hot air escaping from the chamber causing the candle flames to flicker, but presently, as my eyes grew accustomed to the light, details of the room within emerged slowly from the mist, strange animals, statues and gold – everywhere the glint of gold. For the moment – an eternity it must have seemed to the others standing by – I was struck dumb with amazement, and when Lord Carnarvon, unable to stand the suspense any longer, inquired anxiously, "Can you see anything?" it was all I could do to get out the words, "Yes, wonderful things." Then, widening the hole a little further, so that we both could see, we inserted an electric torch.'

Actually, like so many of the well-known stories associated with the discovery of Tutankhamun's tomb, the one about 'wonderful things' – compiled in the summer of

1923 – didn't happen quite as reported. Carter's own notes, presumably written that same evening of Sunday, 26 November, are more prosaic.

'It was some time before one could see; the hot air escaping caused the candle to flicker, but as soon as one's eyes become accustomed to the glimmer of light, the interior of the chamber gradually loomed . . . with its strange and wonderful medley of extraordinary and beautiful objects. Lord Carnarvon said to me, "Can you see anything?" I replied to him, "Yes, it is wonderful." I then with precaution made the hole sufficiently large for both of us to see. With the light of an electric torch as well as an additional candle, we looked in. Our sensation and astonishment are difficult to describe . . . the first impressions suggested the property-room of an opera of a vanished civilization.'

Lord Carnarvon's version, written for an article in *The Times*, gives another account of Carter's words. In reply to the question, 'Well, what is it?' the archaeologist says, 'There are some marvellous objects here.' A further reminiscence by Carnarvon tells it yet another way: 'Mr Carter . . . did not say anything for two or three minutes, but kept me in rather painful suspense. I thought I had been disappointed again, and I said, 'Can you see anything?' 'Yes, yes,' he replied. 'It is wonderful.'

The most famous version, from Volume 1 of the book *The Discovery of the Tomb of Tutankhamun*, was in fact written by Arthur Mace, an Associate Curator of Egyptian Art at the Metropolitan Museum in New York, a distant cousin of Carter's mentor and hero the

Egyptologist Flinders Petrie, and a specialist in the handling and conservation of delicate materials. Mace had been one of the first to join the super-group of specialists working on the tomb from December 1922 onwards. He based *his* version on Carter's notebooks and conversations, and reconstructed them into a thrilling narrative with 'literary help' (as Carter put it) from 'my dear friend Mr Percy White the novelist, Professor of English Literature in the Egyptian University'. White, who had nearly thirty novels to his credit, had most recently written a semi-autobiographical romance called *Cairo*. The transformation of 'it is wonderful' or 'there are some marvellous objects here' into the much more memorable 'Yes, wonderful things', and indeed of all Carter's instant impressions into a story which could almost have been written by Rider Haggard (for the setting) or Conan Doyle (for the suspense), was to be a key stage in the present-

ation of the discovery to a public which knew and probably cared very little about the finer points of archaeological research.

When he tried to write without literary help and advice, Carter's prose sometimes tended to be over-ripe, and to bear the stamp of an autodidact who wanted to appear a 'scholar'. But with the book as with the tomb, he was good at picking the best specialist talent. Together Mace, White and Carter push the story along like an elegant and well-written locked-room mystery.

Howard Carter once recalled that if he hadn't become an archaeologist, he could have made a competent detective – not the Sherlock Holmes kind, making stunning deductions followed by the well-known (if apocryphal) put-down, 'Elementary, my dear Watson', but the kind who painstakingly sifted all the evidence and then arranged the clues to come to careful conclusions: a craftsmanlike detective rather than an inspirational one. *The Discovery of the Tomb of Tutankhamun* remains the great detective story of the 1920s, with the added attraction of an adventure-story setting about 'a vanished civilization'.

Mace, White and Carter describe the moment of discovery as if it suddenly comes into focus on a stage, or through a camera lens, or on the screen of a cinema: the flickering candle, the blurred image of gold, the viewer's eyes gradually growing accustomed to the light in the total immersion of the tomb. For a second, Carter thought he was looking at wall paintings carved in relief; then, as he adjusted focus, he realized these were three-dimensional *things* – sculptures and statues and domestic artefacts. And he couldn't believe his eyes. It was this spectacle, captured in the light of candle-as-magic-lantern (the apt image used by Antonia Lant), which struck him 'dumb with amazement'.

Lord Carnarvon was much moved by the image as well, but in a different way. When interviewed by *The Times*, he tended to make comparisons not with other Egyptian antiquities but with modern, everyday things: nice clothes, fine furniture, expensive jewellery, a Derby winner. He had become involved in archaeological excavations nineteen years before, literally by accident. One of his expensive passions (in addition to horse-racing and photography) had been motoring: he had owned several cars in France before they were even allowed on the roads in England, and when they were, he was one of the first to register his ownership. In 1903 he'd had a spectacular motoring accident in Germany, which led to his move – on doctor's orders – to where

the climate was said to aid recovery, and his discovery of another absorbing pastime: the excavation and collection of Egyptian antiquities. Although by 1922 Lord Carnarvon had become a well-known collector (with Carter sometimes acting as his dealer) and although, unlike other gentlemen-amateurs of the time, he liked to supervise operations on site (rather than from a floating gin-palace on the Nile), it was scarcely surprising that his reaction to the discovery tended to be expressed in terms of modern-day 'wonderful things' and valuable consumer durables. Some of the early reports of his excitement (tailored to the presumed interests of the readership) tended to make tomb number 62 sound like an ancient version of the Burlington Arcade. In what he called the 'extreme and somewhat fascinating' public interest in the discovery – which had reached epidemic proportions in Europe and America by Christmas 1922 – he spotted a whole series of entrepreneurial possibilities. Perhaps the spectacle would strike the public 'dumb with amazement' as well.

Carnarvon appears to have been something of a film buff as well as someone who enjoyed dining with film moguls, and on 24 December he wrote to Howard Carter about the most effective ways of selling the story to the various mass media. One section of this letter (cited by Thomas Hoving) was headed 'Cinema', and it included an outline script, for the benefit of film companies which had already started the bidding, in seven sections. The 5th Earl's scenario went like this:

i. *The approach to the limestone Valley of the Kings* or Biban el-Muluk, 3 miles to the

Lord Carnarvon at rest.

west of Luxor, on the opposite bank of the Nile, and its elaborate necropolis: across the Nile, past the gigantic windswept and now silent Colossi of Memnon and the magnificent terraced mortuary temple of Queen Hatshepsut at El-Deir el-Bahari (or 'the northern monastery'), over the Theban cliffs and into the valley itself. A 'panoramic' section.

ii. *The history of the excavation* and of earlier, less spectacular, explorations at Thebes from 1907 onwards. This film footage (which 'we can get up') would be followed by the discovery of Tutankhamun's tomb itself some 13 feet below a well-known tourist attraction, the entrance to the tomb of Rameses VI – of all unlikely places! – and the uncovering of the steps and the two sealed doorways.

iii. *The contents of the corridor and the first chamber*, illuminated with powerful electric lamps, with the mysterious sealed door beyond, guarded by two life-sized figures of a king in black, facing each other like sentinels, with the protective sacred cobra upon their foreheads.

iv. *The official opening of the tomb* – a restaging of the ceremony which took place on 29 November 1922, in the presence of Lady Allenby [the High Commissioner himself was far too busy coping with the rise of Egyptian Nationalism], the Governor of the Province, the chief of police, Carnarvon and his daughter, and Mr Arthur Merton of *The Times*, whose report, published the following day, was the first to attract the attention of the world's press: 'An Egyptian Treasure – Great Find at Thebes'.

v. *A look at the treasures*, including the three gilded couches, the guardian statues, the four dismantled chariots, 'the finest fabrics' and the spectacular golden throne ('one of the most marvellous pieces of furniture that has ever been discovered'), plus other treasures yet to be unearthed.

vi. *The unveiling of the mummy*, which, it was assumed, would have been found in its sarcophagus and coffins by the time the film was made.

vii. *A strong and uplifting ending . . .*

Within months the Hollywood Goldwyn Picture Company Ltd (which was competing at that stage with Pathé) had padded out the Earl's outline to include proposed sequences showing 'the essence and idea of Ancient Egypt, including the Pyramid and the Sphinx' and a dramatized version of 'the wonderful ceremonies attendant upon the interment of a dead Pharaoh, with living people chosen from living Egyptians looking like those from Tutankhamen's time'. In a period when exotic

feature-length documentaries, not to mention biblical epics with parallel stories set in the present, were packing them in, this could well become, in the Goldwyn representative's words, 'one of the biggest and most profitable events in film history'.

Although the event never happened (one can just imagine the star-studded première at Grauman's Egyptian Picture Theatre in Los Angeles, which had been built in 1922), the actual footage of the excavation and the dismantling of the tomb was to be filmed by official photographer Harry Burton, who was seconded to the project from the Metropolitan Museum's Egyptian Expedition. The Carnarvon and Goldwyn letters reveal how remarkably aware the project's sponsor was of the wider cultural implications of the discovery: beyond the specialized world of Egyptologists, archaeologists and museum people was a vast public (especially in England, France, Germany and America) ready, willing and even eager to consume the images, styles and artefacts of ancient Egypt. A public which Lady Burghclere was to describe as 'all men and women who, in this workaday existence, can still be moved [the 'still' is interesting] by tales of high endeavour and unrelenting doom'.

On 13 February 1923 the *New York Times*, under the headline 'Use Telescope to Get Pictures', reported that a film company ('not American') had tried to take pictures of the tomb from a distance 'with the aid of a telescope'. Following 'warm discussions' with Howard Carter, the company eventually made peace with the team of discoverers, who were to be seen 'posing all over the place before the cameras of the latest arrivals'. Three days later, the London *Times* reported that 'definite arrangements for the official film of the excavation are not yet completed. The matter is receiving Lord Carnarvon's close attention.' In the end, the rights were kept by the archaeologists – using, it was said, equipment provided by Sam Goldwyn.

The first priorities on the ground were, of course, to record, photograph, draw, map, transport and conserve the many thousands of individual objects which were found in the tomb. Howard Carter and his hand-picked super-group of experts (Arthur Mace, Harry Burton, 'Pecky' Callender, the chemist Alfred Lucas, the Egyptologists Percy Newberry, Alan

Gardiner and James Henry Breasted, and the architectural draughtsmen Walter Hauser and Lindsley Foote Hall) set new standards of professionalism and scholarship in this work. When the tomb was first opened, Lord Carnarvon wrote optimistically and somewhat naïvely of the 'weeks of work' facing Carter. In fact, the complete clearance of the tomb took almost *ten years* and the resulting paper documentation fills a substantial room at the Griffith Institute in Oxford to this day.

A routine was quickly established for the antechamber, the first room to be studied. Each object or group of objects was given a reference number and photographed *in situ*, with and

and usable. Then, each object was removed to one of the 'laboratory tombs' – Rameses XI became a storeroom, Seti II a conservation workshop and photographic studio, while tomb number 55 became a darkroom – for cleaning and conservation work before being rephotographed against a neutral background and transported by makeshift hand-propelled railway and shipped up the Nile by steam barge to Cairo. No wonder there were moments when Carter wondered whether 'there was more to be done than any human agency could accomplish'. The sheer scale of the operation, the sheer number of 'wonderful things', like the completeness of the tomb – which, it transpired, had been robbed within a few years of Tutankhamun's burial in 1323 BC, a time when artefacts and paintings were of much less interest to tomb-robbers than perfumes and other exotic unguents – were quite without precedent.

without the number in shot. Harry Burton's pictures (a number of which appear in this book) were lit with two electric lamps, one fixed and one portable (rather than magnesium flares, which took ages to disperse) – often in difficult conditions – and they have been called 'among the finest archaeological photographs ever made'. Each object was then located on a ground plan, and Carter or Mace wrote a brief description of it on a numbered record card, sometimes with a pencil or ink drawing to help with identifying details and visual characteristics. Carter's own drawings, done on the spot and at great speed, are always clear, accurate

Everywhere the Glint of Gold

Beyond these first priorities, there was the question of how to handle what the *Daily Express* was quick that autumn of 1922 to call 'Tutankamun Ltd': the presentation of this specialized material to the non-specialized world. For, following the influential *Times* article of 30 November 1922, the discovery of Tut's tomb rapidly became a major cultural phenomenon, or, to use a 1920s word, a 'craze'. The craze touched every aspect of design, from the 'Tutankamen Rag', played by the palm court orchestra in the ballroom of the Winter Palace Hotel, Luxor, to the interiors of new self-consciously opulent French trans-atlantic liners (the huge *fumoir* of the *Normandie* was surrounded by 6-metre lacquered panels covered in Egyptian-style bas reliefs), from the latest lines in Egyptian-inspired garments, furniture, interior designs and fashion accessories in London, Paris, Berlin and New York – smart young women such as Lady Elizabeth Bowes-Lyon (now the Queen Mother) simply *had* to include a Tut-inspired outfit embroidered with ancient motifs in their honeymoon trousseaus – to buildings, shop windows or even factories. In Paris Cartier produced a new range of Egyptian jewellery in precious metals (as he predicted, on 8 February 1923, 'the discovery of the tomb will bring in some sweeping changes in fashion in jewellery'); Van Cleef and Arples competed with brooches and bracelets depicting vultures, Anubis dogs, baboons and assorted scenes from the 'Egypt of the Pharaohs' in sapphires, rubies, emeralds and onyx; Leon Bakst unveiled his 'Isis' collection; Jean Dunand designed lacquered neck pieces with brightly coloured geometrical motifs; a perfume from Ramsès of Cairo called 'Secret de Sphinx' came on to the market; Gustave Miklos produced dog sculptures in gilt bronze and coloured

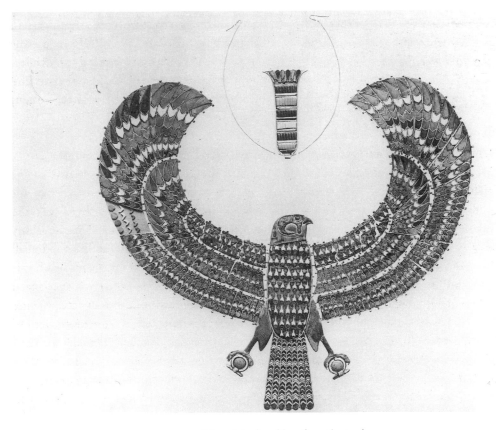

The original necklace from the tomb.

metals (based on the ritual couches discovered in the antechamber); and the *Folies Bergère* popularized the Egyptian-style ostrich-feather fan with 'Tutenkhamen's Follies'.

The *New York Times* on 7 February 1923 reported that 'businessmen all over the world are pleading for Tut-Ankh-Amen designs for gloves, sandals and fabrics', in an article which advanced the opinion that the painted wooden portrait bust found in the antechamber was really 'like a modern woman's dress dummy, called, I believe, by dressmakers an Arabella or tailor's mannekin used for trying on and fitting garments'. How appropriate, therefore, that the garment trade should be so interested. A fortnight later, the headline was 'Egypt Dominates Fashion Show Here – Designs Copied From Luxor Pictures Decorate Many Suit Models – Prize Wrap Has Hathor – Tomb Vogue Will Prolong Bobbed Hair'. The Egyptian trend was 'on' before the discovery, said the report, but now it had become a *fashion*. A fashion for new styles of garments (with low waists, wraps around the hips and fabrics falling to the ankles), and a fashion for Egyptian colour combinations and motifs. Then, hot on the heels of the Hathor wrap, the Luxor gown and even the Carnarvon frock, it was the turn of 'Pharaoh's Sandals', which 'May Set New Style'. One of the 'members of staff' at the excavation site was reported as saying, 'When the king's sandals have been restored they will be among the most wonderful articles among these extraordinary works of art, and I fully expect that in a few years' time we shall see our smartest ladies wearing footwear more or less resembling and absolutely inspired by these wonderful things ...' Sure enough, a 'New

60 New Spring Styles in 60 Regal Stores from Coast to Coast

New Egyptian Sandal

In Patent Leather, Brown Russia Calf And White Kid

The Egyptian Style Influence is reflected in this decorative Sandal with its perforated instep, strap and collar. The petal-shaped cutout design suggests the Lotus flower, and the straps are fastened by the new Isis buckle.

Egyptian Sandal' in patent leather, with an 'Isis' buckle, was quick to appear. And on 25 February – under the headline 'Tut-Ankh-Amen Art to Sweep New York – Much Traffic in Name – Trade-mark Is Sought for Hats, Dolls, Toys, Parasols, Jewelry and Cigarettes' – there was a story about patent lawyers asking the $64,000 question of the moment: 'Who owns the name of Tut-Ankh-Amen?' It was a question that had first been asked on the night of 30 November 1922, the night the news first broke on an unsuspecting world, and 'It may flood the Federal courts with litigation for years to come'. Apparently, claims for the exclusive commercial use of 'Tut, Tut-tut and Two-Tank and other variations' had been filed all over the place; even for the brand name 'ushabti' to label a type of tiny doll patterned after the small wooden shabti figures (intended to do manual work on the pharaoh's behalf in the next world) found in the tomb. Another company went for the name 'Tutankham' – a cunning mixture of Tut and Omar Khayyam – instead. The New York fashion house of Lefkowitz and Pitofsky had, it was reported on 21 February, been quick off the mark when it cabled Lord Carnarvon, offering him no less than \$100,000 for the exclusive right to reproduce 'garments, embroideries and colorings on all apparel found in the tomb'. When they didn't get a reply, they had upped the figure to \$230,000; but Carnarvon did not bother to acknowledge either of the cables (if indeed he received them). By 18 July the *New York Times* was concluding that the surprise

THE TUTANKHAMEN OVER-BLOUSE

4½ gns.

JESSETTE LTD.
29 SLOANE STREET S.W.

New original designs can be had in all white, white embroidered black, navy and Egyptian colours, in heavy crêpe de Chine. Any size made to order. The above design is an exact reproduction of the hieroglyphic of the king, from the tomb at Luxor.

These are designed and entirely made by hand in our own workrooms.

Big Season in the silk trade could be credited to Tutankhamun: 'Dry-Goods – Men Hear Egyptian Find Lifted Dull Silk Trade to High Record; Craze Spreads Overnight'. 'The exploration of an old tomb,' commented a Silk Association representative, 'furnished the necessary setting to change the vogue to a riot of designs and colour combinations.'

On 1 April a *Vogue* editorial, entitled 'The Mode Has a Rendezvous by the Nile', had predicted that New York would follow Paris in the new *mode à l'égyptienne*. New Yorkers could therefore expect draped and pleated dresses, headbands, pyramid and scarab motifs, and a boost to the perfume and cosmetics trades very distantly derived from the use of aromatics and make-up in ancient Egypt.

Original figures used to illustrate popular fashion magazines of the 1920s.

This wasn't the first time that *haute couturiers* had turned to Egypt (the excavations of the 1890s had, for example, stimulated a less dramatic 'revival'); indeed, Parisian designers were claiming that they had foreseen the trend of 1923 at least one season *before* the publicity surrounding discovery of Tutankhamun's tomb. But it was being more aggressively marketed this time round.

'Long before King Tutankhamen threw aside his sand bedclothes, only to find himself confronted with a modern lady affecting an Egyptian silhouette . . . Paris had pulled its skirts up in front, had flattened its silhouette in back, and taken far more kindly, we feel sure, to open work, non-supporting sandals than did those waferlike ladies who troop so stiffly around the friezes of the tomb. And just because some *couturiers* anticipated the Egyptian influence over a year ago, all the excitement about Madame Tutankhamen's frocks leaves Paris the least little bit indifferent . . . But she doesn't mind admitting that it is also due in part to the royal resurrection itself, for Paris dearly loves a keen interest in its clothes. Pleating was never better – and that's Egyptian. Tiered skirts are seen – and they are Egyptian. But we aren't to be *entirely* Egyptian this year. The Modern World would rather exchange places with Tutankhamen himself, than forsake the various smart artifices that are the epitome of advanced civilization.'

A follow-up *Vogue* article, on 'The Kohl Pots of Egypt', enlarged on the cosmetics theme by turning the *mode à l'égyptienne* into a soft-focus male fantasy (straight out of the *Arabian Nights*). From kohl pots to flesh pots, so to

charmingly feminine atmosphere. The plastered walls are bright with designs copied direct from nature by no mean artist . . . Nubian slaves lead the Queen to her bath, a marble-lined tank sunk in the floor and filled with the amber-toned water of the Nile. Her skin glistens with the glow of health as the slaves polish limbs whose grace and symmetry, poise and undulating movements are almost a lost art to the Western civilizations . . . Now comes the emphasizing of the charms of features and expression. In cunning pots of pale porphyry reposes the antimony preparation known as kohl. This black cosmetic, applied to the rims of the eyelids with a pointed reed, increases the size and brilliance of the Queen's eyes till they shine like polished agates . . .'

speak.

'Among the marvellous treasures found in the tomb of Tutankhamen were many intimately connected with the daily lives of those who occupied this palatial [sic] house of the dead. These included wigs, toilet accessories, and a Queen's robe, which, we are told, was exquisitely embroidered with semiprecious stones arranged in a diamond shape . . . It was probably the very gown worn by Ankhenasaton, the beautiful daughter of that religious reformer, the famous Akhenaton . . . Let us softly pull back the tapestry which hangs before the portal of Ankhenasaton's bedchamber, and, with the privilege of the unseen, watch her prepare for the duties of the day. In the pale light of dawn, the room has a

But by mid-July – the date of the Dry-Goods conference reported by the *New York Times* – *Vogue* was already cautioning that 'so much attention has been drawn to Egypt's influence on our frocks that the mode is becoming self-conscious about it'. *Becoming*? As fashion historian Micki Forman suggests, the mode had been pretty 'self-conscious' from the word go. And *Vogue* had been ever so slightly sniffy about it, ever since the April editorial – perhaps because the magazine was beginning to promote American-originated garments (rather than American derivatives) and styles which came from the 'Modern World' of nearer home. But for a short time at least, 'Madame Tutankhamen's frocks' had been added to *Vogue*'s repertoire of dream and fantasy images.

Meanwhile, in England the *Daily Express* of 9 March 1923 was breathlessly announcing, 'The Tutankhamen hat has arrived.' It could be viewed at Liberty's in Regent Street, where 'old Egyptian patterns borrowed from the British Museum have been adapted to headgear'. Four pictures of models wearing variations on the hat – 'as Pharaoh wore them?' – were printed side by side with pictures of the bridesmaids chosen for the royal wedding which was to take place on 26 April. At the same time, the *Illustrated London News* observed – in an article printed opposite a full-page picture of the royal wedding cake – 'Egyptian and modern styles share the honours where bridal gowns are concerned this spring.' Four days later the *Express* reported that 'Egyptian Fashions Make New Furnishing Vogue – as the season advances there is no doubt that the trend will grow':

'Dove-grey walls, soft and mystic and yet light in their effect, provide a fitting background to the black and gold lacquer cabinet. The most interesting feature of this type of room, however, is the recess, which has been treated in a novel way. A panel of blue and gold embroidery with a warm black frame is placed on the wall of the alcove, where narrow lines of black paint throw up the soft-grey background. The box ottoman, which fits snugly into the space and could be made inexpensively by the local carpenter, is covered with Chinese blue and gold embroidery . . . A plentiful supply of cushions is required for rooms of this type [especially] the novel pear-shaped cushion of black velvet with golden embroidery . . . An oriental floor vase completes the Eastern effect.'

No matter that the room looked Chinese-moderne; it just had to be *Egyptian*.

This was followed, on 21 March under the headline 'Luxor-y!', by a photograph of 'Miss Desirée Welby, one of the débutantes of the season, wearing an Egyptian dress of her own design', and, incidentally, sitting on an Egyptian-style throne while wearing a home-made pharaonic head-dress. The *Daily Mail* had jumped on the old Egyptian bandwagon by 16 April, with an article entitled 'Summer Fashions – Luxor influence reported this season', in which it was noted that 'even the bathing dresses have a distinct Egyptian style'. An accompanying photograph showed a model wearing a heavily strapped one-piece 'Tutankhamen' bathing costume in 'terracotta stockinette'. On the same day, the *Morning Post* reported an 'Egyptian vogue in women's wear', and gave particular prominence to 'Tutankhamen skirts and three-piece suits, specimens of which in variegated colours and Egyptian design attract rather by daring originality than actual artistic merit'.

The Times had been one of the first to spot the way things were going in England when on 23 January, in an article about mid-season evening gowns, it had glimpsed the deathless 'Mummy wrap':

'There is also the draped fabric frock which seems to presage a return to the tight waist. It is based on the swathings of the priestess mummy in the British Museum, and heralds what the treasures of Luxor may suggest for evening wear. The dress, the effect of which was beautiful, was low-waisted, and tied in front with a long sash, but the swathings were tight almost to discomfort . . . the original mummy swathings were decidedly not designed for movement!'

Later in the season, ran another report, the models displaying the 'mummy wrap' by teetering down the cat-walk looked as though they 'might have stepped from the walls of Tutankhamen's tomb'. The reporter presumably hadn't noticed that the shapely goddesses depicted on the north and south walls of the burial chamber are not in fact mummies at all.

As James Stevens Curl rightly observes in his recent study of *The Egyptian Revival*:

'The furnishings and other contents of the pharaoh's mausoleum were of such superlative design and quality that they became models almost overnight, and not only for rare artefacts. Modern publicity ensured a widespread following for the Nile style. Fashionable ladies wore Egyptianizing "Cleopatra" earrings, while their aspiring sisters contented themselves with less perfect jewellery: designers like Pierre Legrain produced Egyptian chairs; and Egyptian motifs appeared on objects from ashtrays to cinemas . . . The discovery of the tomb of Tutankhamun and the publicity given to the marvellous furnishings stimulated a new phase in the Nile style. The impact of film spectaculars also helped to popularize the style as never before. The great Paris Exposition Internationale des Arts Décoratifs et Industriels Modernes in 1925 also stimulated a new style now known as Art Deco that was unquestionably influenced by certain elements of the Egyptian Revival, notably the corbelled openings, the highly coloured geometrical ornament, and the pyramidal composition . . .'

It should be added that when Art Deco designers made reference to such Egyptian motifs, they tended to abstract from them – in bright colours, often presented within triangles – and to combine them with elements from other sources: Egyptian and Mayan are sometimes difficult to distinguish. Martin Battersby, in *The Decorative Twenties*, concludes that it was, above all, the opulent over-the-top quality of the Tutankhamun artefacts which made them such a rich source of inspiration at the time:

'The sheer quantity of gold objects, and in particular the gold coffins [after autumn 1925], made an immediate appeal to the imagination of the general public, while the furniture and personal belongings of the young king, which had escaped the plundering of tomb-robbers, spanned the centuries between and made him more real and understandable than the shrivelled and painted mummies of subsequent pharaohs which were all that the majority of people associated with ancient Egypt.

For a time the beautiful objects, elegant to the point of decadence, were a source of inspiration to designers as photographs appeared in periodicals and newspapers . . . [In London] a new furniture store exhibited reproductions of all the furniture found in the tomb.'

The phrase 'the Egyptian Revival' had, of course, been used before of moments in the history of design. The main difference between the 1923–5 revival and the two previous ones of note was, precisely, the fresh impetus given to it by the mass media of newsprint, photography and the cinema.

Up until the era of 'Tutmania', the influence of the Nile style had, on the whole, been confined to the worlds of collectors, connoisseurs, art lovers and private interior decorators. It had been around in Europe since Roman times, and had been part of a continuous, if sometimes eccentric, tradition of sorts since the early Renaissance. It often took the form of individual decorative motifs, such as obelisks and hieroglyphics, gleaned from travellers' tales and objects in private collections. But it took Napoleon Bonaparte's expedition of 1798, and the subsequent publication of the ten-volume *Description de l'Egypte,* to turn an antiquarian interest into a *style* for the first time. The style was, as Patrick Conner's *The*

Inspiration of Egypt puts it, part of the 'cult of the exotic, which exploited Egyptian motifs for the sake of their connotations of extravagance and outlandish mystery'. Like a luxuriously bound edition of *The Arabian Nights*. The poet Robert Southey, in his *Letters from England* (1807), evoked some choice examples:

'Everything now must be Egyptian, the ladies wear crocodile ornaments, and you sit upon a Sphinx in a room hung round with mummies, and the long black lean-armed long-nosed hieroglyphicized men, who are enough to make the children afraid to go to bed. The very shopboards must be metamorphosed into the mode, and painted in Egyptian letters, which, as the Egyptians had no letters, you will doubtless conceive must be curious . . .'

One of the best-known buildings in London to use the new Egyptian style in a *complete* way was the Egyptian Hall in Piccadilly, a museum of spectacular and magical and curious objects, finished in 1812. W. Leigh Hunt visited the Egyptian Hall in 1861, as part of his *Saunter through the West End*, and he found the combination of showbiz and Egyptiana a bit too much to take:

'Egyptian architecture will do nowhere but in Egypt. There, its cold and phony ponderosity ("weight" is too pretty a word) befits the hot, burning atmosphere and shifting sands. But in such a climate as this, it is worth nothing but an uncouth assembly. The absurdity, however, renders it a good advertisement. There is no missing its great lumpish face as you go along.

It gives a blow to the mind, like a heavy practical joke.'

This mixture of *Arabian Nights* fantasy, conjuring up perfumed images of 'the Orient', and over-coloured exoticism did not last very long as a style. By 1812, the year of the Egyptian Hall, novelist Maria Edgeworth could put into the mouth of her trend-following character Mr Soho (in *The Absentee*) the crushing verdict: 'Egyptian hieroglyphic paper, with the *ibis border* to match! The only objection is, one sees it *everywhere* – quite antediluvian – gone to the hotels even . . .'

The second Egyptian revival of the nineteenth century (in Britain, at any rate) had more to do with the Bible than the exotic. A combination of large-scale, heavily detailed history paintings in Old Testament settings (by such artists as William Holman Hunt, David Wilkie, Thomas Seddon, Edwin Long, Frederick Gooddall and Edward Poynter) and the promotion of conventionalized, flat Egyptian ornament in preference to over-decorated Victoriana – by design reformers and design educators, with their 'grammars of ornament' – gave the Nile style a far less frivolous set of connotations. The concern, as Patrick Conner continues, was now 'more with abstract principles of colour and pattern than with adopting specific motifs'. True, it was still a question of viewing ancient Egypt through a Western European prism (instead of extravagance and mystery, the Old Testament and missionary zeal – neither of which had overmuch to do with the realities of a developing Islamic society), but at least the lessons of early archaeology and anthropology were beginning to have an effect.

Meanwhile, in France, in the second half of the nineteenth century, the mysteries of Egypt were associated with a less prosaic and severe set of images. Parisian painters and poets, wallowing in what Mario Praz has called 'the romantic agony' and in the 'fabulous richness of the Oriental background', retold the histories of the ancients as exotic tales of courtesans, tyrannical queens and 'sexual cannibals' such as Cleopatra. The Sphinx's inscrutable smile was reinterpreted as something to do with she-vampires and their willing victims. 'The Orient' meant the sensuality of another place, although it was best enjoyed at home in Paris.

But following the discoveries of November 1922, the Egyptian style reached the high street for the very first time. From previous revivals, it retained the *connotations* of luxury, exoticism, sensuality, mystery and even – as we shall see – a touch of the Old Testament. But the big difference this time round was the mechanical reproduction of the image and the object, and the publicity machines used to promote them.

Mass-produced accessories and ornaments made of bakelite and plastic, with hieroglyphics, winged discs, scarab beetles, obelisks, nude goddesses and assorted stepped forms, appeared in the shops next to Tut-related tins, cigarette packets and other ephemera. In 1924 Huntley and Palmer issued a biscuit tin in the shape of a funeral urn, with ancient Egyptians bearing gifts all around the sides; a rival firm, Dunmore & Sons, preferred a multi-faceted tin with a portrait of a 1920s-looking pharaoh on the lid, for containing mummy-coloured confectionery. Luxor toilet requisites ('preferred by fastidious women') launched a new advertising

slogan: 'Have you, *too*, discovered Luxor?' The music-hall 'discovered' the sand-dance, performed to vaguely 'Oriental' up-tempo music by rubber-limbed burlesque artists in red tarbooshes; thus ex-soldiers in the audience who had been stationed at Abassia during the war had the opportunity both to enjoy being reminded of the desert setting and to express their scorn for the native inhabitants at the same time. Cinemas, such as, in the London area alone, the Kensington Cinema (1926), the Carlton, Upton Park (1929), the Luxor, Twickenham (1929), the Astoria, Streatham (1930), and the Carlton, Essex Road (1930), were built with temple façades or 'daring Egyptian decorative schemes' within. A hastily concocted film (now lost) called *Tut-ankh-Amen's Eighth Wife* was released, and, in the *Sketch Magazine*, the irrepressible cartoon dog Bonzo appeared in a special coloured portrait by George E. Studdy showing his surprised reaction to a row of mummified cats in a glass case (actually the British Museum's collection).

'Even Bonzo', ran the caption, 'becomes interested in the discoveries in that Egyptian tomb.' Perhaps to compete with him, a firm in Mount Vernon, USA, produced a creature called 'Tut's pup', who, according to the *New York Times* of 25 February 1923, was 'an elongated dog which is being sold with a rhyme telling of the dog that followed Tut about and protected him, and urging the owner to take the dog to bed with him for protection' – a *very* long way away from the jackal god Anubis!

The boy-pharaoh seemed to be both ancient and modern at the same time. Ancient, in the obvious sense that – in the words of *The Times* leaders of 1 December and 16 February – 'he reigned and died more than thirteen centuries before our era ... in days so distant', '... five hundred years later did Homer sing ... at the first glimmering of European civilization'. Modern, in the sense that he died so young (between seventeen and twenty years old, Carter eventually estimated, like all those young

The Carlton Cinema, Essex Road, London N1

soldiers in the trenches of Flanders) and, by a very 1920s telescoping of time, seemed to incarnate the very essence of modernism. The *New York Times*, under the headline 'Like Casualties from the Trenches', reported on 10 February 1923:

'As the objects have been brought out, spectators have remarked that from the manner in which they were bandaged and transported with almost tender care on the stretcher-like trays, they reminded one of casualties being brought out of the trenches or casualty clearing stations. As a matter of fact, great quantities of surgical bandages, cotton wool and surgical safety pins are actually being used.'

Taking up the theme, a caption to one of the reprinted illustrations from Carter's *The Discovery of the Tomb of Tutankhamen* read:

'Looking like a severely wounded man after treatment in a casualty ward – one of the sentinel statues of Tutankhamen being packed for removal . . .' Shortly after the *New York Times* piece, the *Manchester Guardian* quoted Harry Burton as saying that Tutankhamun must have been a dapper, as well as an outdoorsy young ruler and soldier, 'a man of fashion, scrupulously exact in the fit and hang of his garments . . .' Tut was young, he was hip, and he evidently liked to surround himself with the latest luxury items: his funerary arrangements were like being buried with your favourite Type 35 2-litre Bugatti racer.

Avant-garde artist Wyndham Lewis celebrated this paradox by naming his pet dog 'Tut', and by writing provocative articles about the connections between modern art and the research conducted by G. Elliot Smith into ancient funeral ceremonies and mummification. Fernand Léger turned his attention from machines to pyramids and tomb paintings, René Clair (with Man Ray and Marcel Duchamp) included a camel in a sequence showing a Parisian funeral cortège as part of the film *Entr'acte* (1925), while the sculptor Alberto Giacometti, with his brother Diego, made a plaster table lamp (with the light concealed in the central vase) directly based on the lotus-like calcite lamp found in the burial chamber. The painter C. R. Nevinson declared of the discoveries, 'The modern artist has been trying to get back to the intelligence of the Egyptian in a different form. European civilization for the last 200 years has been nothing but a terrible decadence as compared with the Egyptians . . . we are losing not only our craftsmen, but our mentality'. Nevinson supported the idea of a delegation of avant-garde artists and art critics visiting Luxor, to 'appraise the importance' of the artefacts to the modern world. The significance of pre-perspective and the flat depiction of the figure would be high on the agenda.

Critic Clive Bell, though, was not so sure. 'I do not regard the art of the Tutankhamen period as at all of first-rate importance or as representing an important period in Egyptian art,' he was quoted as saying by the *Westminster Gazette* on 7 February 1926. 'So far as we who are not archaeologists are concerned, we would rather have two or three small objects from the 4th Dynasty or earlier than any amount from the Tutankhamen period [2575 BC during the Old Kingdom or before, as opposed to 1323 BC, 18th Dynasty, during the New Kingdom]. Most modern artists,' he asserted, 'would agree.'

Robert Graves and Alan Hodge, in their book *The Long Weekend*, evoked the impact of these 'wonderful things' on London society by stressing the point about 'the modernist spirit':

'The discovery . . . was given typical Twentyish publicity. Ancient Egypt became the vogue – in March 1923 the veteran Professor Flinders Petrie lectured on Egypt to an entranced Mayfair gathering. Replicas of the jewellery found in the Tomb, and hieroglyphic embroideries copied from its walls were worn on dresses; lotus flower, serpent, and scarab ornaments in vivid colours appeared on hats. Sandy tints were popular, and gowns began to fall stiffly in the Egyptian style. Even the new model Singer sewing machine of that year went

Pharaonic, and it was seriously proposed that the Underground extension from Morden to Edgware, then under construction, should be called Tutancamden, because it passed through Tooting and Camden Town. Cambridge students staged an Egyptian rag, raising from the dead Phineas, the purloined mascot of University College, and awarding him an honorary Blue. A secret tomb (a subterranean public lavatory) was prepared in Market Square, and undergraduates appeared at the appointed hour, wearing towels like Egyptian slaves. At the cry of "Tut – and – Kum – in", the dead Phineas arose. The lost tribes of Cleopatra then appeared and performed the "Cam-Cam".'

The simultaneous discoveries by archaeologist Sir Leonard Woolley at Ur of the Chaldes in Mesopotamia (today's Iraq), discoveries which included – in Woolley's immortal words – 'where Abraham and his family lived' and apparent evidence for the accuracy of the legend of the Flood, although they sometimes grabbed the headlines when the Tut story went quiet, just didn't manage to capture the public imagination to the same extent. The late Victorians would have revelled in the discovery of material evidence for the Old Testament stories. But the post-war generation of the early 1920s had other things on its collective mind. Graves and Hodge went on to speculate:

'Serious archaeologists were surprised that so much popular interest greeted the [Tutankhamun] discovery, which had done no more than fill up a small gap in comparatively recent Egyptian history, while so little could be beaten up for far more interesting, ancient and beautiful discoveries in the Mesopotamian cities of Ur, Nineveh and Carchemish, and in the Indus valley. The fact was that Tutankhamen, who had succeeded his revolutionary father-in-law the Pharaoh Akhenaton, seemed somehow to embody the modernist spirit: whereas the Mesopotamians were boringly ancient . . . Bible-reading was out of fashion.'

The contrast, conclude Graves and Hodge, was between age and youth, between Victorianism and modernism, between Old Testament morality and, frankly, treasure or *gold*. Literally, the golden calf. Everywhere the glint of gold, as Carter observed by the flickering light of his candle, in a phrase which could have provided the punch-line to countless newspaper advertisements for jewellery at the height of Tutmania. When the *New York Times* first reported the discovery, on 1 December 1922, it did so under the headline 'Gem-studded relics in Egyptian tomb amaze explorers', adding the next day, 'Recent find in Egypt valued at £3,000,000', and on 4 December, 'Americans going to Egypt can see the great discovery at Thebes . . . the intrinsic value of which is estimated at $15,000,000.' There wasn't yet a brand of confectionery called 'All Gold' in 1923, but a Mackintosh's Toffee magazine campaign in Britain more than adequately filled the gap:

When Tutankhamen's tomb was found
By excavators underground
Unearthed appeared alongside Tut
A tin of Mummified de Luxe.

It was a theme later taken up, amazingly, by a tinned meat company which was very struck by the state of preservation of Tutankhamun's food put aside for the next world, stored in pottery jars. This followed a *Daily Mail* report that, 'The finding of canned beef 3,350 years old in Tutankhamen's tomb is admitted by cold-storage experts to be a record. Mr Raymond, hon. secretary of the British Cold Storage Association, says the record, so far as cold storage is concerned in this country, stands at eighteen years.' The clear conclusion was that the Egyptians must have known a thing or two about preservation.

Small wonder that Evelyn Waugh wrote so dismissively of the whole phenomenon of Tutmania in one of his travel essays called *Labels* (1929), compiled after visits to Bodell's Hotel in Port Said and the Mena House Hotel in Cairo.

'The romantic circumstances of the Tutankhamen discovery were so vulgarized in the popular press that one unconsciously came to regard it less as an artistic event than some deed of national prowess – a speed record broken, or a birth in the Royal Family . . . The fact that a rich and beautiful woman, even though living very long ago, should still require the toilet requisites of a normal modern dressing table was greeted with revelations of surprise and delight and keenly debated controversies in the press about the variable standards of female beauty. The fact that idle men, very long ago, passed their time in gambling and games of skill was a revelation. Everything of "human" interest was extensively advertised, while the central fact, that the sum of the world's beautiful things had suddenly been enormously enriched, passed unemphasized and practically unnoticed.'

A few years earlier in Hollywood, Cecil B. De Mille, a keen student of 'human-interest' stories of all descriptions, had begun preparing his epic version of *The Ten Commandments* for Paramount Studios. When he first broached the subject to Adolph Zukor, in autumn 1922, the studio chief was profoundly unimpressed:

' "Old men wearing table cloths and beards?" he said. "Cecil, a picture like that could ruin us. How much will it cost?"

"A million dollars," De Mille replied. "Just think of it, we'll be the first studio in history to open and close the Red Sea."

"Or maybe," said Zukor, "the first director to open and close Paramount".'

But De Mille was convinced that a mixture of religious epic, special effects, a parallel 'story of sin' set in the present day (which would, in fact, take up the lion's share of screen time), Victorian morality contrasted with fashionably Egyptian opulence, not to mention a risqué version of the Golden Calf orgy filmed in two-strip colour, would have just what it took to provide 'mass appeal'. Rudolph Valentino had scored a terrific hit with *The Sheik* two years before; this new project would have *Arabian Nights* style sequences 'designed to set flappers blushing' (as one newspaper wrote of *The Sheik*), the Old Testament *and* Tutankhamun. De Mille ordered the Cairo offices of the Lasky Company to get hold of written and visual material on the discovery, and took a lot of persuading not to make King Tut himself (rather than

Ramses II, the pharaoh who chased the Israelites out of Egypt).

The Times of 19 February 1923 quoted the New York press as saying: 'In private houses, hotels, subways, suburban trains, theatres and in Wall Street, everywhere one goes one hears constantly of the great Pharaoh and his treasures, and the light which is about to be thrown upon a historical mystery'. And what exactly was this mystery? Nothing less than the mystery of 'the Pharaoh whose armies perished in the Red Sea when pursuing the Israelites'. Clearly, the pre-publicity for *The Ten Commandments* and the impact of Howard Carter's discovery had become hopelessly – and, from Cecil B.'s point of view, productively – confused. The film opened in December 1923; it cost $1½ million and grossed $4.

De Mille was to return to the ancient Egyptian theme in 1934 with *Cleopatra*, which owed less to Victorian paintings and more to the Art Deco style, and which – visually to link a story that actually happened between 51 and 30 BC to one that happened over 1,200 years earlier – began and ended with the great stones of a royal tomb opening and closing. The camp goings-on which occurred between the entry into the tomb and its sealing were, it was implied, reconstructed from the kinds of artefacts which archaeologists had discovered in the Valley of the Kings.

Actually, the 'historical mystery' of the possible connection between Tutankhamun and Moses had filled the correspondence columns of the serious press ever since the first reports of the discovery. On 21 February 1923 a correspondent to *The Times* in London had felt

compelled to point out that Moses was *not* hidden in the bulrushes near Thebes in Upper Egypt (the bulrushes were in *Lower* Egypt); the real question for 'us Bible students' was whether either of the pharaohs Akhenaton or Tutankhamun was 'the spiritual father of Moses'. This led to assorted rural vicars writing in to discuss whether the evidence contained in the tomb 'fitted in well' with the Bible story; whether 'Moses was dead long before Tutankhamen was born ... I'd like to know which of the dates is correct, the biblical or the Egyptian?' (there seemed to be a discrepancy of about 150 years), and why everyone was confusing Akhenaton (whose monotheism was at least analogous to Christianity, in a primitive sort of way) with Tutankhamun (whose worship of the old Theban god Amun eventually led to the branding of Akhenaton as a 'heretic'). The Egyptologist Arthur Weigall added to the confusion on 13 October 1923, at the start of his lecture tour around America on the subject of Tutankhamun and his times, when he was reported by the *New York Times* as speculating:

'It is probable that the opening of the inner tomb will reveal that Tutankhamen was the Pharaoh of the Exodus and clear up many obscure points in Biblical lore. It also may show that the Jews were migrating to Palestine from Egypt and met Moses and said, "Come on and let's go into this good trade territory in the East." I rather think it may be something interesting like that. Jolly interesting if it were.'

Professor Flinders Petrie, in that lecture to 'an entranced Mayfair gathering' on 21 March 1923 – as quoted in *The Times* – was on equally speculative form when he opined to the assembled ladies that the golden couches found in the antechamber weren't Egyptian at all but 'Babylonian in origin'. The couches had, apparently, been imported from Babylon to Thebes in several pieces and been merely *constructed* in Egypt.

Seeking to explain the atmosphere of speculation, confusion and well-intentioned dottiness which seemed to surround news of the discovery in the minds of educated people, on 6 April 1923 *The Times* offered the thought: 'All the world, more especially the English-speaking world, rejoiced in Lord Carnarvon's success [and] read with wonder of the treasures he had found. They felt, however dimly, that a new world had been revealed to them, that the whole range of their thoughts and feelings had been enlarged ...' It was quite natural, continued *The Times*, for 'the English-speaking world' to relate this mind-expanding experience to the Bible, and to the history *they* knew. This was a useful way into the 'unusual significance of that age'; the splendid artistic treasures had perhaps led to far too much emphasis on the 'outward significance' of the *present* age.

Sooner or later, all the hype, the speculation, the excitement and the madness surrounding Tut were bound to get in the way of the painstaking work of scholarship and conservation which Carter and his team were trying to continue, often in sweltering conditions, in the Valley of the Kings itself. It was equally inevitable that when it did, there would be an almighty collision.

It happened midway through the first season's clearance of the tomb, around the time of the official confirmation, in February 1923, that the boy pharaoh's mummy *was* still inside his magnificent gold coffin – an announcement which significantly increased the eagerness of journalists, tourists and official visitors to see for themselves, by fair means or foul. Arthur Mace wrote from Luxor, 'Archaeology plus journalism is bad enough, but when you add politics it becomes a little too much.'

Charles Breasted (James's son and at that time a journalist himself), who was present as the antechamber and the burial chamber were cleared, added that:

'The discovery of Tutankhamen's tomb – the most romantic and thrilling story of archaeological exploration and discovery since Schliemann's revelations at Troy and those of Sir Arthur Evans in Crete – broke upon a world sated with First World War conferences, with nothing proved and nothing achieved, after a summer journalistically so dull that one English farmer's report of a gooseberry the size of a crab apple achieved the main news pages of the London Metropolitan dailies. It was hardly surprising, therefore, that the Tutankhamen discoveries should have received a volume of world-wide publicity exceeding anything in the history of science. Almost overnight Carter and Carnarvon became international figures. Their fame brought with it a host of unaccustomed and extraordinarily harassing problems.'

Just as Carter and Carnarvon were the last of the Edwardian 'explorers' who saw the political, social and economic contexts of archaeological work in Egypt changing around them – between the time their partnership began in earnest in 1909 and the spring of 1923 – so, Breasted suggested, they found themselves at the centre of a new phenomenon, the growth of 'world-wide publicity'. He continued, from personal experience:

'Carter was suddenly faced with the most enormous and difficult task which had ever confronted a field archaeologist, and with an inundation of visitors such as Egypt had not experienced since the Persian invasion . . . The seasonal volume of mail at the Luxor post office was doubled and trebled. The telegraph office at the station was completely buried under a deluge of newspaper despatches. Tourist shops quickly sold out their stocks of cameras and films, and of books on the history of Egypt. The two leading hotels of Luxor set up tents in their gardens, where many guests were fortunate to be accommodated for a single night on army cots. Each day the hordes of visitors swarmed across the river and into The Valley, where they gathered around the pit at the opening to Tutankhamen's tomb . . .'

Howard Carter was to take up the story, from his point of view, in *The Discovery of the Tomb of Tutankhamen*:

'The tomb drew like a magnet. From a very

early hour in the morning the pilgrimage began. Visitors arrived on donkeys, in sand-carts, and in two-horse carts, and proceeded to make themselves at home in the valley for the day. Around the top of the upper level of the tomb there was a low wall, and here they each staked out a claim and established themselves, waiting for something to happen. Sometimes it did, more often it did not, but it seemed to make no difference to their patience. There they would sit the whole morning, reading, talking, writing, photographing the tomb and each other, quite satisfied if at the end they could get a glimpse of anything. Great was the excitement, always, when word was passed up that something was to be brought out of the tomb. Books and knitting were thrown aside, and the whole battery of cameras was cleared for action and directed at the entrance passage. We were really alarmed sometimes that the whole wall should give way, and a crowd of visitors be precipitated into the mouth of the tomb.'

The net result was that a difficult job became even more difficult. Carter's reaction, even when recollected in tranquillity, reads like a *cri de coeur*:

'Surely, the claims of archaeology for consideration are just as great as those of any other form of scientific research, or even – dare I say it? – of that of the sacred science of money-making itself. Why, because we carry on our work in unfrequented regions instead of in a crowded city, are we to be considered churlish for objecting to constant interruptions? I suppose the reason really is that in popular opinion archaeology is not work at all. Excavation is a sort of super-tourist amusement, carried out with the excavator's own money if he is rich enough, or with other people's money if he can persuade them to subscribe it, and all he has to do is to enjoy life in a beautiful winter climate and pay a gang of natives to find things for him . . . The serious excavator's life is frequently monotonous and . . . quite as hard-working as any other member of society.'

It didn't help, he added, when tourist agencies all over the world insisted on advertising 'a trip to Egypt to see the tomb', when what they should have been advertising was a trip to see a group of long-suffering archaeologists going about their daily business . . .

The Light of Publicity

While Howard Carter and his team tried to remove the artefacts from the tomb to the nearby 'laboratory tombs' on wooden stretchers and thence by the Décauville hand-railway along the 5½-mile stretch of bumpy sand to the Nile, during the precious weeks before April when the heat was still bearable, they discovered that, in Carter's words, 'No power on earth could shelter us from the light of publicity.' Relations with the press had started off badly when Lord Carnarvon signed a contract with *The Times*, publicly announced on 10 January – 'The Tomb of the King – Contract Given to *The Times*' – which granted the Thunderer exclusive access to all the official stories emanating from the tomb and added that any other journalist, 'including Egyptians', would have to negotiate their use of this exclu-

Hand-drawn 'photograph' of the excavation.

sive material through the offices in Printing House Square, London, and Gresham House, Cairo. This seemed like a great idea at the time: *The Times* had an honourable tradition of covering archaeological issues and could perhaps act as a buffer or press agent between Carter's team and the world's press. But it infuriated the Egyptian newspapers, who started casting doubts on the ability of the Englishmen to 'protect and preserve Egypt's heritage', and it encouraged rival British newspapers (notably the *Daily Express* and the *Daily Mail*), as well as the *New York Times*, to make as much mischief as they possibly could. While *The Times* printed regular reports by their correspondent Arthur Merton (a friend of Carter's), bylined, as they rather smugly put it, 'Valley of the Kings, by runner to Luxor', other newspapers had to content themselves with secondhand stories, on-the-spot accounts of

the tense atmosphere surrounding the stone parapet at the opening of the tomb, gossip more or less overheard in the bar at the Winter Palace Hotel, historical surveys by London-trained Egyptologists, moral panics about tomb desecrations and slighted Egyptian officials and, on one bizarre occasion, a photograph of some cotton wadding used to protect the objects in transit which was mistaken for a mummy's shroud. When the two life-sized wooden guardian figures were carried into the daylight from within the antechamber, some newspapers referred to them as giant black monkeys. Perhaps that is how they looked, wrapped up for transit, and yet good photographs of them *in situ* had already appeared in *The Times* on 30 January, for those who were prepared to use their eyes.

Another line, this time calculated to stir up American readers, was to claim that the team from the Metropolitan Museum were not amused by the thought that their hard work simply provided acres of copy for the London *Times*. On 14 March Arthur Mace angrily wrote to the *Morning Post* on behalf of his colleagues that they were quite content with Carnarvon's agreements with a single British newspaper, adding 'Our interest in the tomb is purely scientific ... we deeply resent being exploited in this way by irresponsible mischief-makers.' Six days later Sir John Maxwell of the Egypt Exploration Society, an associate of the Carnarvons, let rip in *The Times* with a letter written on the notepaper of the Winter Palace:

'The ridiculous situation created by these bickerings, imaginary slights, &c, has afforded some amusement to the guests in the Winter Palace Hotel, who have been lost in wonderment at this mountain made out of a molehill. The moles have been busy, have worked hard, and displayed an energy worthy of a better cause ...'

Then there was the question of ownership of the treasures: should they be 'shared' between Lord Carnarvon and the Egyptian Government, as had become the convention in the late nineteenth century, or should they all go as of right to the Cairo Museum, as seemed more politic during the period of Egypt's struggles to become an independent state in fact as well as in name? When *this* question became thoroughly entangled with statements by Nationalist politicians and commentators about the presence of colonialist agents masquerading as scientists on Egyptian soil, the battlelines became even more confused.

There were complaints from Printing House Square that unscrupulous journalists were deliberately arousing 'anti-British sentiment among the Mohammedans'. This was particularly mischievous, *The Times* added, perhaps a trifle disingenuously, because although, as was well known, Lord Carnarvon was solely interested in the love of learning and science, it was only too easy to persuade the 'Mohammedans', especially those of Nationalist persuasion, that there was some secret ulterior motive behind the excavation. The Egyptians had always had mixed feelings about their pre-Islamic past and couldn't understand why, if there was no ulterior motive spelled *Gold*, anyone would go to such lengths to discover and excavate valuable antiquities. So *The Times*'s rivals could easily get hold of that juicy anti-British quotation, especially if they insisted on spreading unfounded stories about Lord Carnarvon's intention to take the pharaoh's mummy back home with him to England. Howard Carter was greeted one morning with the spectacle (which must surely be unique) of the *Daily Express* reporter supporting the Egyptian Nationalists in their case against a member of the oppressive ruling class of Britain. Towards the end of the season, the anger of the British press (except *The Times*) reached the point where some newspapers refused to mention Carter or Carnarvon by name − which may have been particularly irksome to Carter, since in November and December even *The Times* had tended to attribute everything to Carnarvon ('Lord Carnarvon's wonderful discovery'), on the grounds that he who paid the piper must also have discovered the tune, while on 22 December the *New York Times* had referred to him as 'the

American Egyptologist'.

The feud between the archaeologists and the press if anything worsened during the second season (1923–4), when Howard Carter alone had to handle a situation for which he could scarcely have been less temperamentally suited, responding to the official request 'all press or no press' by apparently agreeing and then appointing Arthur Merton an honorary member of the archaeological team (from which privileged position he simply continued to file his exclusive reports to the The Times in London). Soured relations with local and international newspapers, mixed with the volatile political situation, were eventually and inexorably to lead in February 1924 to the first lockout in the history of archaeological excavation and thence to the law courts in Cairo – a sad story which has been recorded in admirable detail by T. G. H. James, in *Howard Carter: The Path to Tutankhamun* (1992) and by H. V. F. Winstone in *Howard Carter and the Discovery of the Tomb of Tutankhamun* (1991). Suffice to say that the biggest row was over the question of whether the much put-upon wives of members of the super-group could have their own private view, after the official lifting of the granite lid of the sarcophagus on 12 February 1924. The newly appointed Minister of Public Works in Egypt, Morcos Bey Hanna – a well-known Nationalist who had been imprisoned for treason and almost hanged by the British a few years before – had taken a deep dislike to Howard Carter as a person, as an Englishman and as a walking symbol of colonialism. The Minister responded to Carter's request for a private view by forbidding him to allow the wives into the burial chamber – why should

they be allowed in, he argued, before the wives of senior Egyptian politicians, and even cabinet ministers? – and by sending a mounted column of armed policemen to ensure that his instructions were carried out. Carter, so furious that he was said to be scarcely in control of himself, responded by going on strike, leaving the heavy lid of the sarcophagus dangling on a temporary arrangement of ropes and pulleys, and publicly complaining of 'the impossible restrictions and discourtesies of the Egyptian Public Works Department', which had led the team as a protest to 'refuse to work any further upon their scientific investigations'. The press had a field day. Here *was* something to write home about. Amid headlines such as 'Locked out at Luxor', 'The Tomb Isn't Yours', 'Discourtesies', 'Tomb Locked Against Mr Carter', 'Ultimatum to Mr Carter', *The Times* wrote a strong editorial in Carter's defence, openly criticizing the 'ungentlemanly' behaviour of the regime towards the ladies, while Carter himself determined to take legal action against the Egyptian Government. This in turn led to a telegram from Ramsay MacDonald at 10 Downing Street which read: URGE CARTER ON HIGHEST AUTHORITY TO STOP LEGAL PROCEEDINGS. MAKE AMICABLE ARRANGEMENT WITH EGYPTIAN AUTHORITIES. Characteristically, Carter continued to insist, 'I will fight on.' It took the fall of the Nationalist Government, the cancellation of the agreement with *The Times* and the abandonment by the Carnarvon Estate of any share in the treasures – all of which took several months of valuable excavation time – to re-establish a workable relationship between all concerned.

Even today, officials connected with the

antiquities of Egypt, as well as many of the inhabitants of the town of Qurna near the Valley of the Kings, tend to treat the discovery of the tomb of Tutankhamun as a 'tainted' subject: tainted by association with the last days of British power, by folk memories of Howard Carter's bad behaviour and by the fact that the project happened to take place during a watershed period in the relationships of foreign archaeologists with the host Egyptian government. As one official said to me in April 1992, 'We don't like Tutankhamun, and we haven't liked him since 1922. We know he's popular with tourists. Fine. But to us his treasures have always left a sour taste. Something to do with imperialism.'

So the collision between the demands of Tutmania in the West, Nationalist politics in Egypt and excavation work in the Valley of the Kings has had an enduring legacy. What is less well known is that when Howard Carter was back home in England, just before embarking on a major lecture tour in the United States of America in the spring of 1924, he encountered a classic example of Tutmania at first hand, and immediately tried to put a stop to it.

In the Amusements Park area of the British Empire Exhibition, which was opened by King George and Queen Mary in the new Wembley Stadium on 23 April – St George's Day – 1924, nestling between the Flying Machine ('captive aeroplanes on a wheel – great speed and an illusion of flying – price 6d'), Jack and Jill ('up the hill in basket chairs, and a chute to the bottom – price 6d'), the Whirl of the World ('two-seater cars on a floor composed of 15-foot discs revolving in opposite directions – price 6d') and the Safety Racer ('race between

two cars each holding 22 people – price 1s') was a very special attraction: Tut-ankh-amen's Tomb ('Reproduction of tomb of the Egyptian king recently discovered at Luxor by Lord Carnarvon and Mr Howard Carter – price 1s 3d, children 8d').

This attraction had been publicly announced in *The Times* and other newspapers (without reference to the fact that it was to be located in the Amusements Park) two months before:

'A complete replica of the tomb of Tutankhamen has been completed for the British Empire Exhibition at Wembley. The work has been carried out by Mr W. Aumonier, the Architectural Sculptor, who evolved all the reproductions from photographs. The work was superintended by Mr A. Weigall, ex-Inspector General of Antiquities in Egypt. The contents will be arranged in Wembley in exactly the same positions in which they were found at Luxor. The tomb has been dug out of the ground.'

Having bought their tickets, visitors entered a long, low and white construction, got up to resemble the rock cliffs of Thebes, and were shown, by a gentleman in a red tarboosh, full-colour and full-sized facsimiles of the contents of the antechamber. Then, having turned left and seen the antechamber from another perspective, they walked down a corridor and were shown the golden shrine and stone sarcophagus (unopened, of course). Then, along another corridor to the exit and the joys of the Flying Machine. The organizers were particularly proud of this exhibit:

'TUTANKAMEN'S TOMB RECONSTRUCTED AT

WEMBLEY. HOW IT HAS BEEN
CONSTRUCTED ON THE SAME LINES AS THAT
IN THE VALLEY OF THE KINGS.

Situated at almost the extreme end of the
main avenue running from the gardens through
Toy Town, the reconstruction of the Tomb at
Luxor is proving one of the Amusements Park's
chief attractions. Here the visitor can take an
inexpensive journey to Upper Egypt, and visit
by proxy what has become famous as the most
exclusive spot in the world. Through the skill
of Mr Weigall and Mr William Aumonier, the
tomb and its contents have been faithfully
reproduced. The three ceremonial couches, the
mannequin figure, the guardian effigies,
resplendent in black and gold, the many
caskets, the lotus vases and the shrine itself all
are faithfully reproduced. By the ingenious
method of forming a walk in what in the actual
tomb would be solid rock, the confined space is
dealt with conveniently and the visitor views
the object as though framed in a picture . . .'

The replicas in the tomb had, apparently,
been made by William Aumonier with the help
of twelve skilled craftsmen, and had taken six
months to produce in a studio off the Tottenham Court Road, 'from photographs and
sketches Mr Arthur Weigall took at Luxor'.
The 'smallest hieroglyphics were reproduced so
faithfully that they could be read by Egyptologists'. And it was estimated, said the publicity, that gold and gold-leaf worth nearly
£1,000 had been used to colour the shrine and
couches.

So why, after all the preparation, wasn't this
'inexpensive journey to Upper Egypt' part of
the 150-acre exhibition site proper (to the west

of the 40-acre Amusements Park or 'Pleasure
City'), with its buildings and tents and galleries
devoted to all of Britain's 'Dominions,
Colonies, Protectorates and Mandated Terri-
tories'? After all, Ceylon was represented by a
facsimile of the Temple of the Tooth at Kandy,
India by a steel and ferro-concrete pavilion 'in
seventeenth-century Moghul style', Palestine
(sharing with Cyprus) by a themed shopping
bazaar, and Canada by, of all things, a
sculpture of H. R. H. the Prince of Wales
modelled in butter. And the entire exhibition's
logo, by J. C. Herrick, of a flat, one-
dimensional lion standing on three parallel
lines, was said to be 'in the ancient style': historian Jonathan Woodham has recently written
that the lion motif was directly influenced 'in
design terms' by the discovery of
Tutankhamun's tomb. Two of these lions,
interpreted in stone, stood guard outside the
British Government Pavilion, as if it was an
ancient temple, and they were said by the *Illustrated London News* to 'reduce those around
Nelson's Column to mere kittens'.

Certainly, the higher purposes of the Exhibition – in the Prince of Wales's own words, to
put over the message to all the peoples of the
Empire that they should be 'in no wise slothful
stewards, but that they should work unitedly
and energetically to develop the resources of
the Empire for the benefit of the British race,
for the benefit of those other races which have
accepted our guardianship over their destinies,
and for the benefit of mankind generally' –
such purposes could credibly be represented by
Lord Carnarvon's great discovery and Howard
Carter's work (with back-up from an Egyptian
work-gang) in making sense of it.

EXIT

GOLDEN SHRINE
SHEWING STONE SARCOPHAGUS

CORRIDOR

CORRIDOR

ANTE CHAMBER WITH
COUCHES AND FIGURES

STEPS TO
PASSAGE

CORRIDOR

ENTRANCE

TICKET OFFICE

The answer was, above all, that Britain's relationship with Egypt had become highly complex and ambiguous: the exhibition brief didn't cover ex-Protectorates which had been granted semi-independence (following a period, since the First World War, of both active and passive resistance on the part of the Wafd, or official Nationalist Party, and others) and which were about to come, briefly, under the 'veiled protection' of the British authorities again. At a time when the tomb itself was locked up, because of a highly publicized clash of wills between the Egyptian Minister of Public Works and a British archaeologist, it would have been tactless, to say the least, to present a facsimile of that same tomb as a symbol of 'Egypt' (surprisingly, none of the publicity mentioned that the Wembley version represented the *only* way of seeing the Tutankhamun treasures in context, following the events of February 1924). And in any case, said the official brochure, 'Not all the attractions of the Amusements Park are frivolous. For those of a serious turn of mind, there are many fascinations which must cause the visitor to give a gasp of admiration.'

This splendid replica was one of them.

The *Connoisseur* magazine tended to agree. The remarkable monument on display at Wembley was a fine example of pride in craftsmanship and skill in imitation; it was, said the *Connoisseur*'s critic, 'encouraging to be able to add that all the reproductions had been made by *British workmen* under Mr Aumonier's direction'. During a period of art history when the *Morning Post* was gleefully quoting an academic sculptor to the effect that young Henry Moore's early work was 'quite without taste',

Preparing a replica for the Wembley exhibition.

and most probably Bolshevik to boot, it made a refreshing change to see *well-made sculpture* at an international exhibition. Forget about those avant-garde artists who were attempting to harness Tutankhamun to their cause; this was more like it.

The modernists were less than impressed by such arguments, or indeed by the Wembley Empire Exhibition as a whole. They found most of the examples of contemporary work (such as, within the Palace of Arts, the modern rooms 'decorated in the style of 1924' – following a competition launched in *Country Life* magazine – by Lord Gerald Wellesley and Mr Trenwith Wells) to be both insular and aloof from the most exciting developments in Europe. Evelyn Waugh, writing five years later, reckoned that the decision to locate Tutankhamun's tomb in the Exhibition had been a particularly retrograde step: 'In the mind of the public, the tomb became a second Queen's Doll's House full of "quaint" and "amusing" toys'. He might have added that even doll's houses had only relatively recently come to be treated as toys rather than design guides and adult ornaments.

When he got to hear about it, Carter was absolutely furious. The day before the Exhibition opened, when Carter had just arrived in New York for his lecture tour, the *Daily Express* ran the headline 'Carter's Wembley Bombshell – Attempt to Close the Pharaoh's Tomb'. What had happened was that Wembley Amusements Ltd had received a writ from Carter's London solicitors, stating that the archaeologist 'objects to the wood and plaster replica of the tomb in the Amusements Park . . . on the grounds that it violates certain copyrights held by him'. The replica of the tomb *must* have been constructed, alleged Carter in documents recently unearthed by H. V. F. Winstone, using 'plates and letterpress', the rights to which were controlled by him. If Wembley Amusements would concede this fact, then Carter would be prepared to superintend the design of another replica which, unlike the version put together by Messrs Aumonier and Weigall it was implied, would be 'a real and worthy representation'. The day after their shock headline, when other newspapers were waxing eloquent about plans for the gala opening of the Exhibition, the *Daily Express* quoted one of the partners in the firm of solicitors to the effect that Howard Carter's intention was 'to make it clear to the public that he accepts no responsibility for the exhibits and reserves his rights to the record of the work'.

Like the controversy about the copyright in the name of 'Tutankhamen' in America, which began the very night the news of the discovery broke, this action was about who *owned* a series of images which seemed to have entered the public bloodstream. Where Carter was concerned, apart from the distinct possibility that a side-show in an amusements park would be far from a 'worthy presentation' and might do damage to his professional reputation (always a subject on which he was prickly, as a self-taught archaeologist who didn't belong to the right clubs), there was the added irritation that Arthur Weigall, the project's consultant, had crossed swords with him many times in the past (in Egypt), and had made a nuisance of himself earlier that year as special correspondent for the *Daily Mail* in the Valley of the Kings. So the phrasing of the writ, that the facsimile based on copyright photographs should immediately be 'withdrawn from public gaze', in fact covered a multitude of sins.

Wembley Amusements had little difficulty in proving that Tut-ankh-amen's Tomb was based on photographs and reference materials obtained or produced by Arthur Weigall, photographers working for the *Daily Mail* and others, and the case was dismissed. But it remains interesting as an example of an archaeologist trying, against all the odds, to 'contain' the cultural impact of his discoveries, and specifically of Howard Carter's volatile state of mind at the time, confronted by the excesses of Tutmania.

Today it is impossible to check how 'worthy' the facsimiles actually were, since, after the second season of the Wembley Empire Exhibition from May to October 1925 (when, as the official brochure advertised, 'the approach to this replica of the famous Luxor tomb is very greatly improved and is made by way of a sandy desert road between rows of palm trees'), the various attractions from the Amusements Park were sold off to other fun fairs such as those at Blackpool and Southend. Occasionally, there are reported sightings, but so far they have proved to come from other strange and exotic 'Egyptian' entertainments – distant relatives of the Egyptian Hall opened in London way back in 1812.

As Howard Carter wrote, looking back on the events of 1922–5, once the dust had settled: 'One must suppose that at the time the discovery was made, the general public was in a state of profound boredom with news of reparations, conferences and mandates, and craved for some new topic ... The idea of buried treasure is one that appeals to most of us.' And he recalled the reaction of the first visitors to look upon the golden coffin in the burial chamber, the most spectacular of all the pieces of buried treasure: 'Each had a dazed, bewildered look in his eyes, and each in turn, as he came out, threw up his hands before him, an unconscious gesture of impotence to describe the wonders that he had seen ...'

By then it seemed that Lady Burghclere had been very perceptive when, in her introduction to the first volume of Carter, Mace and White's best-selling book, she referred to the story of the discovery as a latter-day version of 'Aladdin's Cave', with its treasure and its magic lamp.

Into the Valley of Death

Lady Burghclere had added that if the public's excitement was first stimulated by a story of 'Aladdin's Cave', it was sustained by 'a Greek myth of Nemesis', for the treasure seemed to be guarded by an evil genie and its first victim was, according to the popular press, none other than Lord Carnarvon himself.

Robert Graves and Alan Hodge agreed:

'But that was not all: a month after the principal discoveries Lord Carnarvon, the leader of the expedition, suddenly died. A mosquito had bitten him, near the entrance to the tomb, and the bite turned poisonous. Almost everyone agreed that his death was due to the Pharaoh's anger at having his rest disturbed. A well-known Egyptologist declared that a curse was undoubtedly responsible, though Howard Carter, the deputy leader, laughed at the idea and continued to excavate. Conan Doyle, the creator of Sherlock Holmes, was asked for his opinion ... During the next few years, several other members of Lord Carnarvon's expedition died, from natural causes, and each time the rumours of the Pharaoh's curse were revived.'

Evelyn Waugh was more damning: '... after the discovery came the death of Lord Carnarvon, and the public imagination wallowed in superstitious depths.'

Just as the excavation story, even as reported in *The Times*, was beginning to be demoted from the front page, and to require a specialized knowledge of Egyptology on the part of readers to explain its significance, the demise of Lord Carnarvon (which could be reported by *all* the newspapers) gave it both a new 'angle' and a new lease of life. What happened was this. On or about 6 March 1923, perhaps in the Valley of the Kings, perhaps in the town of Luxor or in Aswan (the accounts differ), the fifty-seven-year-old Lord Carnarvon was bitten on the left cheek by a mosquito. While shaving with his cut-throat razor, in his suite of rooms at the Winter Palace Hotel, he accidentally scraped the top off the small pimple which had formed and it started to become inflamed. It was immediately treated with iodine – Carnarvon was particularly susceptible to insect bites and, according to his doctor, always travelled with an extensive medicine chest – but his temperature rose during the day to 101°F and his daughter Evelyn insisted that he go to bed. He was very run-down anyway, following the official opening of the burial chamber, angry exchanges with the press and with Howard Carter, and the realization of the sheer extent of the work which lay ahead, and his health had never been robust; but a couple of days in bed seemed to revive his spirits. He even felt well enough to travel to Cairo, where he registered at his favourite hotel, the Continental. Lady Evelyn supervised the arrangements, in the hope that her father would receive proper medical attention there. The Egyptologist Alan Gardiner met him, as he later recalled in the book *My Working Years*:

'[It] was the culmination of a season of both excitement and sorrows. He might, perhaps, have recovered from the mosquito bite which he got in Luxor if he had taken better care of himself . . . [He] came down to Cairo and invited me to dine with him at the Mohammed Ali Club. He expressed himself very tired and despondent but insisted on going to a film. There he said that his face was hurting him and

I begged him to go back to his hotel, the Continental. But no, he would see the film to a finish, and he was never out of doors again . . . despite the presence of the best doctors in Cairo.'

The doctors strongly advised him to remain in bed this time, and to be very careful about what he ate and drank – advice which he coolly swept aside as he continued to drink wine shipped over from the cellars at Highclere Castle. But his neck glands had swollen up, his whole face was beginning to ache and his temperature had risen to 104°F.

Lady Evelyn wrote to Carter (in Luxor) on 18 March, in a letter quoted by T. G. H. James: '. . . the old Man is *very* seedy himself and incapable of doing anything . . . He feels just *too* rotten for words . . . Oh! the worry of it all and I just can't bear seeing him really seedy. However, there it is. I've made a point of making rather light of it to most people as I don't want an exaggerated account in the papers.'

An urgent telegram followed, saying that the situation was becoming critical. In the absence of penicillin, the blood poisoning had developed into pneumonia, and, despite Lady Evelyn's attempts to put the press off the scent, the story by now was all over the British newspapers. Howard Carter rushed to his patron's bedside, Carnarvon's son Lord Porchester was summoned from a polo game and immediately sailed from Meerut in India, Lady Carnarvon took off from England – the technical details of the flight were turned into high drama on the front pages – and the patient was reported as saying, 'I have heard the call. I am preparing.' Just before two o'clock in the morning on 5

April he died. Carter wrote in his diary the simple sentence, 'Lord Carnarvon dies, 2 a.m.', and issued the statement, 'This tomb has brought us bad luck.' The body was embalmed in Cairo, before being taken to England and buried on Beacon Hill – a burial place of the ancient Britons – overlooking Highclere.

In its 'Appreciation' on 30 April, *The Times* wrote: 'None, henceforth, can stand by that grave without recalling the unstinted labour, the steady devotion which wrought that triumph, the work of the true Englishman, sportsman, student, artist and above all great-hearted gentleman who will be laid today beneath the turf of his own native hillside.'

This 'latest conquerer of the East' would be 'as closely associated in the future with the treasure of ancient Egypt as a former Lord Elgin is connected with the Elgin Marbles in the British Museum'. Such was the interest in the departure of the 'last of the noble patrons of Egyptology' that it relegated the latest news of the illness of Lenin in the Soviet Union to the bottom of the page.

The Pharaoh Awakes

The death of Lord Carnarvon provided the press with a whole series of ready-made 'angles' on the discovery of the tomb of Tutankhamun, angles which had the great advantage of being cobblable together at home rather than in the sweltering heat of the Valley of the Kings. In popular fiction, and in the writings of fashionable occultists, ancient Egypt had long been associated with potent forms of magic, strange mystical forces and,

above all, curses. Translations of the Egyptian guidebook to the next life, the so-called *Book of the Dead* (actually *The Book of Going forth by Day*), and of tomb inscriptions had sold surprisingly well in the late nineteenth century, and made a tidy income for museum curators working in departments of Egyptian antiquities. They may have been intended for scholarly consumption, but that wasn't how they were always consumed. Such books reinforced the popular image of ancient Egypt as a kingdom obsessed with dead things and magic spells.

With the development since the 1860s of Egyptology as an academic discipline, centred on philology and language, interest in the spiritual aspects of ancient Egypt had become increasingly marginalized by the professionals, and had tended to resurface within popular culture and within the world of 'the occult'. While Egyptologists deciphered, and artists and designers increasingly detached the *look* of Egypt from its spiritual context, other groups tried to keep alive (or fan the dying embers of) the old Neo-Platonic or Hermetic traditions in some very strange ways. Since they weren't too concerned about classical scholarship, or dining at the high tables of Oxbridge colleges, or even about the established Church, they saw no problem in deriving nourishment from pre-Christian, pre-Greek and above all pre-materialist philosophy, as they interpreted it. And while the discipline of Egyptology became more exclusive, so these groups became all the more attractive, partly because they could present themselves as being beleaguered as well. What did it matter if the disciples couldn't read hieroglyphics? The Hermetic tradition had predated the deciphering of the Rosetta Stone by a very long time.

Within the new occult establishment, Helena Petrovna Blavatsky had founded the Theosophical Society (an earlier name had been the Brotherhood of Luxor) in September 1875 after attending a lecture delivered in New York City entitled 'The Lost Canon of Proportion of the Egyptians' by a man who claimed personal acquaintanceship with ancient 'elements' – in the spectacular forms of jackal- and hawk-headed creatures as seen on tomb walls – which inhabited fire, water, air and earth and which 'can be mischievous but can also help mankind'. Such elementals weren't allegorical, said the lecturer, they were *real*. Would it not be a good thing, thought Madame Blavatsky in a moment of inspiration, 'to form a society for this form of study'? Her massive 1,900-page book *Isis Unveiled* (1877) gave a clear idea of why such notions exercised a strong fascination in the era of Charles Darwin and the new social theory:

'If modern mentors are so much in advance of the old ones, why do they not restore to us the lost arts of their post-diluvian forefathers? Why do they not give us the unfading colours of Luxor – the Tyrian purple; the bright vermilion and dazzling blue which decorate the walls of this place and are as bright as on the first day of their application? The indestructible cement of the pyramids . . .'

The answer, available to the select few who were prepared to rise above the dull world of the everyday, was as clear and bright as the polychrome decoration on the pillars of the temple at Luxor:

'. . . many are those who, infected by the mortal epidemic of our century – hopeless materialism – will remain in doubt and mortal agony as to whether, when man dies, he will live again, although the question has been solved by long-gone generations of sages. The answers are these. They may be found on the time-worn granite pages of cave-temples, on sphinxes, propylons and obelisks . . . except the initiates, no one has understood the mystic writing.'

As James Webb adds, in his study *The Occult Underground*, 'It may be doubted whether any but the initiates knew what a propylon was.'

Theosophy enjoyed something of a revival in the years following the First World War, when, to many bereaved families, the question, 'Will he live again?' had a particular urgency, and when Madame Blavatsky's society began to move up-market, into social worlds which, through Freemasonry and Rosicrucianism, already had Egyptian obsessions of their own, Theosophy's membership of the occult establishment made it seem positively respectable (to say the least) compared with the activities of well-publicized occultists such as the 'Great Beast' himself, the 'Black Magician' and 'King of Depravity', Aleister Crowley. Crowley had graduated through the complicated ranks of the Hermetic Order of the Golden Dawn in London, but his epiphany had occurred in March 1904, near the galleries of the Boulak Museum in Cairo (the predecessor of today's Egyptian Museum, situated some way outside the centre of Cairo). It was from there, over a three-day period, that his Holy Guardian Angel, Aiwass, was said to have dictated to him

The Book of the Law, preparing the way for the Age of Horus and containing the axioms, 'Do what thou wilt shall be the whole of the Law' and 'Every man and every woman is a star.' His *Confessions* refer to this event as the climax of his life:

'On some day before March 23rd, Ouarda [in real life, his wife, Rose] identified the particular god with whom she was in communication from a stele in the Boulak Museum, which we had never visited. It is not the ordinary form of Horus but Ra-Hoor-Khuit. I was no doubt very much struck by the coincidence that the exhibit, a quite obscure and undistinguished stele, bore the catalogue number 666. But I dismissed it as an obvious coincidence.

March 19th. I wrote out the ritual and did the invocation with little success. I was put off, not only by scepticism and the absurdity of the ritual, but by having to do it in robes at an open window on a street at noon. She allowed me to make the second attempt at midnight.

March 20th. The invocation was a startling success. I was told that "the Equinox of the gods had come"; that is, that a new epoch had begun. I was to formulate a link between the solar-spiritual force and mankind . . .

March 23rd to April 7th. I made inquiries about the stele and had the inscriptions translated into French by the assistant curator at Boulak. I made poetic paraphrases of them.'

Following the events in the Valley of the Kings of November 1922, one of Crowley's magical children, who went by the name of Frater Achad (in real life Charles Stansfeld Jones), wrote a very strange little book called *The Egyptian Revival*, in which he described 'the underlying reason for public interest in the Tomb of Tutankhamen':

'. . . in order, if possible, to discover the hidden causes it will be necessary for us to make a brief survey of the Egyptian Current of Thought from the earliest times to the present day. We do not find the public interest centred alone in the treasures found in the tomb of Tutankhamen, but in nearly every instance reference is made to his immediate predecessor King Amenhatep IV, or to use his more familiar title King Khu-en-Aten [actually Akhenaton] . . . After his death, Tutankhamen is said to have re-established the old order and the worship of Amen-Ra in place of that of Aten. What was the cause of this controversy, and what is its bearing on the thought of the present day?'

The answer, for those who had ears to hear, was that the discovery heralded a major revival of the 'influence of the Ever-coming son, the Crowned Child, Lord of the New Aeon', or the Cycle of Aquarius, and in addition helped to explicate (always explicate, for some reason, rather than explain) the meaning of the Tarot pack.

The artefacts and relics of ancient Egypt had by then become, in the esoteric publications of both the occult underground and the occult establishment, a kind of celestial lightning conductor (carrying 'the Egyptian Current of Thought', in capitals) which magically linked adepts to the thoughts of the older gods, and illuminated the path for those who were prepared to reject the 'hopeless materialism' of the age and the strictures of the established Church. Positive thinking, with lots of footnotes and esoteric references to the Hermetic tradition. These magicians and magi and clairvoyants ('clair' is scarcely the first word which springs to mind when examining their output) had developed a relationship to objects on display in the Egyptian galleries of museums similar to that of an acquaintance of Jean François Champollion in the 1820s who had found an easier way of deciphering the Rosetta Stone: he stared at the stone, waited for enlightenment to strike and then said whatever came into his head. Sometimes, the adepts didn't even have to visit museums; they simply had to look at their mantelpieces, on which were displayed the sad trophies of a visit to the Theban Necropolis.

In 1895 Henry Morton Stanley recorded an 'inventory of articles purchased by a gentleman in the portico of the Ramesseum', from one of the local souvenir-sellers who catered to his strange obsession with the Egyptian Current of Thought: 'Three men's heads, one woman's head, one child's head, six hands large and small, twelve feet, one plump infant's foot, one foot minus a toe, two ears, one part of a well-preserved face, two ibis mummies, one dog mummy . . .' It was, he added, a trade 'such that will make old people think of *their* graves and Atheists thoughtful'.

In the related world of popular mystery fiction, ancient Egypt had been associated since the 1880s (at least) with various recurring stories: the story of the artefact excavated from a tomb, brought back to England's green and pleasant land, and endowed with magical (usually nasty) powers; the story of the artefact which encourages its new owner to dream himself back into ancient times – often with 'less-

ons' for the present day; the story of the mummy in the museum, usually the British Museum, which comes back to life and wreaks havoc on its disturbers; the story of an ancient princess who is let out of the bottle by mistake and either falls in love or turns into a harpy; the story of a royal mummy who is deliberately reincarnated by a gang of initiates; and – the most relevant of all – the story of an archaeologist who lives to regret the day he had the temerity to open an ancient tomb: he should have read the sign over the door.

Short stories in the monthly fiction magazines of the time, such as the *Belgravia*, the *Cornhill* and *Pearson's*, and full-length novels such as E. and H. Heron's *The Mystery of Baelbrow* (1899), Guy Boothby's *Pharos the Egyptian* (1900) and *The Curse of the Snake (1902)*, Bram Stoker's *The Jewel of Seven Stars* (1903), George Griffith's *The Mummy and Miss Nitocris* (1906) and Algernon Blackwood's *The Nemesis of Fire* (1908), as well as the adventure stories of Henry Rider Haggard – notably *She* (1887), *The Yellow Girl* (1908) and *Smith and the Pharaohs* (1920) – and Sax Rohmer – *The Brood of the Witch Queen* (1918) and *She Who Sleeps* (1928), about a confidence trick involving a famous archaeological dig – gradually and steadily added new variations or twists to the basic pattern. The popular interest in archaeology and Egyptology and in the activities of occult societies involving well-known names combined to give these works of fiction a wide readership. The authors found the mysterious proper names, and the magic spells, in academic books written by philologists and museum curators: far from repaying the compliment, professional Egyptologists moved further and further away from the 'Egypt' of the high-street bookshop.

So when Lord Carnarvon died – it was alleged in mysterious circumstances – a repertoire of ready-made explanations immediately presented themselves to the popular press and authors of popular novels. Even before his death, on 24 March 1923 the *Daily Express* reprinted a letter to the *New York World* in which the veteran novelist Marie Corelli remarked that she had forewarned Carnarvon of his fate. Marie Corelli had specialized since the mid-1880s in visionary romantic novels which involved much speculation about 'the spiritual regions' and railed against 'the paganism of the age', such as *The Sorrows of Satan* (1895), which was made by D. W. Griffith into a melodramatic film in 1925, shortly after her death.

'PHARAOHS GUARDED BY POISONS? LORD CARNARVON WARNED BY MARIE CORELLI.

Miss Marie Corelli sees the hand of Pharaoh rather than the bite of a mosquito in the illness of Lord Carnarvon. The novelist . . . says that she wrote to Lord Carnarvon expressing the wish that nothing unfortunate would chance to him in the pursuit of his discoveries. She adds, "I cannot but think some risks are run by breaking into the last rest of a king of Egypt whose tomb is specially and solemnly guarded, and robbing him of his possessions. According to a rare book I possess, which is not in the British Museum, entitled *The Egyptian History of the Pyramids* (translated from the original Arabic by Vattier, Arabic Professor to Louis XVI of France), the most dire punishment follows any rash intruder into a sealed tomb.

The book . . . names 'divers secret poisons enclosed in boxes in such wise that those who touch them shall not know how they come to suffer'. That is why I ask, Was it a mosquito bite that has so seriously affected Lord Carnarvon?"'

The society palmist and 'seer' Velma also claimed (in a book published after the event) that Lord Carnarvon had been warned before returning to Luxor for the last time – on this occasion in a private consultation. In *My Mysteries and My Story* he wrote:

'Lord Carnarvon had more than an ordinary interest in the occult. He was keen that I should keep nothing back . . . "I see great peril for you," I told him [after the consultation]. "Most probably – as the indications of occult interest are so strong in your hand – it will arise from such a source."

His interest aroused, he discussed the excavations in the Valley of the Kings. "Whatever happens," he said, "I will see to it that my interest in things occult never gets so strong as to affect either my reason or my health . . ."'

Not so very long after asking Velma the very reasonable question, 'Is it preposterous rot to think of the influence of all these old priests still surviving today?' the 5th Earl of Carnarvon was dead.

The well-known clairvoyant Count Louis Hamon, known as Cheiro, made a similar revelation in his book *Real Life Stories* (1934). Apparently, an ancient Egyptian sorceress – 'the seventh daughter of the King Atennaten', Princess Makitaten no less – had been kind enough to transmit the warning to him through a species of automatic writing:

'It was to the effect that on his arrival at the tomb of Tut-Ank-Amen [Lord Carnarvon] was not to allow any of the relics found in it to be removed or taken away. The ending of the message was "that if he disobeyed the warning he would suffer an injury while in the Tomb, a sickness from which he would never recover, and that death would claim him in Egypt".

Rightly or wrongly I sent this warning to Lord Carnarvon. The letter reached him as he was leaving England. He read it over to one of his companions, the Hon. Richard Bethell, and to a close friend of Admiral Smith Dorrien, whose letter relating these facts I have in my possession. Lord Carnarvon, as all his friends know, was an extremely strong-headed obstinate type of Englishman . . . [He said,] "If at this moment of my life all the mummies of Egypt were to warn me I would go on with my project just the same." It is common knowledge what happened.'

The reference to the taboo surrounding sacred 'relics' found in the tomb links Cheiro's story to another aspect of the case, which the newspapers had covered *before* Carnarvon's death, and which again links the coverage of the curse of Tutankhamun to the world of popular fiction. On 24 February 1923, in an attempt to scotch wild press rumours about his intention to transport the pharaoh's mummy to a museum in England or Cairo, Lord Carnarvon had written to *The Times*:

'At the present moment, King Tutankhamen rests, to the best of our belief, where he was originally placed. When the time comes to ascertain whether it *is* the mummy of the King, I personally and those associated with me are most anxious that arrangements should be made to leave his body in the sarcophagus in its present resting place . . . I may say that I have not yet discussed the point, nor do I view with favour the somewhat unwholesome and morbid taste which some people seem to enjoy of looking at mummies exposed in glass cases in museums.'

Earlier in the month, at the height of the rumours in the press, a correspondent to *The Times* had hit home with the stirring comparison between the corpse of the pharaoh and that of the late Queen herself:

'I wonder how many of us, born and brought up in the Victorian era, would like to think that in the year, say, 5923, the tomb of Queen Victoria would be invaded by a party of foreigners who robbed it of its contents, took the body of the great Queen from the mausoleum in which it had been placed amid the grief of the whole people, and exhibited it to all and sundry who might wish to see it? The question arises whether such treatment as we should count unseemly in the case of the great English Queen is not equally unseemly in the case of King Tutankhamen.'

Ten days later, Sir Henry Rider Haggard strongly supported this argument – in another letter to *The Times*, of 13 February – by suggesting that as a precaution for all time the king's mummy should be sealed up 'with concrete' in one of the chambers of the great pyramid. Rider Haggard had been shown around the recently discovered tomb of Nefertari by the young Howard Carter in March 1904, when he was doing research for a series of articles about ancient Egypt for the *Daily Mail*, one of which had been about 'the treatment accorded to the bones of Pharaohs by those who drag them from the grave'. He had also, according to his private diary entry for 31 March 1917 – a reminiscence – undergone a mysterious 'experience with the mummy which is now in the Norfolk Museum at Norwich', an experience which took place in West Kensington and contributed to the story of *She*, which he happened to be writing at the time (the mummy in question had probably been placed in the museum courtesy of the Egypt Exploration Society). In November 1922, with his unrivalled track-record for producing both adventure stories *and* non-fiction pieces about the land of the pharaohs, he had 'suggested to *The Times* that I should go out for them to write about this business, but found that they had already completed their arrangements'. So, when he wrote his letter, he could expect to command some respect:

'Now, the minor Pharaoh, Tutankhamen, is to be added to the long list of more illustrious "dug-outs". Presently he, too, may be stripped and, like the great Rameses and many another monarch very mighty in his day, laid half-naked to rot in a glass case of the museum at Cairo, having first been photographed as he came from the embalmer's bath. Yes, to rot, for thus exposed I doubt whether any of them will last another century; and meanwhile to be made the butt of the merry jests of tourists of the baser sort, as I have heard with my own

ears. Is this decent? Is this doing as we would be done by? Or, to put it more strongly, when we remember what was the faith of these men, Pharaohs or peasants, and that the disturbance of their tombs and bodies was the greatest horror by which they were obsessed, is it not an outrage and one of the most unholy? Examine them by all means; X-ray them; learn what we can of history from them . . . but then hide them away again for ever, as we ourselves would be hidden away.'

Professor Flinders Petrie, the venerable and eccentric Egyptologist, found the suggestion about the pyramids quite ridiculous, and replied angrily to a reporter from the *Westminster Gazette*:

'I see no reason why the remains of the Pharaohs should be cemented up in the great Pyramids so that no-one should see anything more of them. Besides, why spoil the Great Pyramid? . . . It's no good sentimentalizing about the one-hundredth of the remains when the ninety-nine-hundredths have been wrecked by the Egyptians themselves.'

The solution to the long-term future of the mummies was to build a special museum at Thebes (where the climate was good for conservation) and, just in case any light-fingered visitor might get ideas, to police it with 'a garrison of some fifty armed men'. Easy.

This was a view which in principle found favour with Sir John Maxwell, a man not noted for his tact, who wrote to *The Times* on 20 March:

'If public opinion in this matter is genuine, then, to be consistent, all bodies of the rich and poor alike should be recommitted to the earth, and all national museums should take steps to return their mummies to Egypt for reinterment. But it might be as well to remind good people at home that at all museums on a Bank Holiday the crowd dearly loves its mummy! As regards Egyptian sentiment, it would be absurd to contend that now the Egyptians have any feelings in the matter at all.'

Clearly the professionals held very different views about treating dead bodies as objects of study – or 'material', or texts – to writers of fiction and most general readers. On the whole, to judge by the correspondence columns in spring 1923, the balance of opinion was that the archaeologists were transgressing a deeply felt taboo, and they would surely pay for it. Like Doctors Faustus, Frankenstein and Jekyll – all of them deeply embedded within popular mythology – the scientists who dug in the sand would be destroyed by the results of their researches, because they had gone *too far*.

In this sense, the curse of the pharaohs embodied – in metaphorical form – a popular response to what was seen as a serious transgression: the 'amateurs' had no direct access to the closed world of Egyptologists, so instead they tended to resort to occult explanations, which were so much more attractive and easy to understand.

And when the news of Lord Carnarvon's death broke, in the first instance it was to the writers of fiction, rather than to the professional archaeologists, that the popular newspapers turned. Sir Arthur Conan Doyle was by that time one of the leading lights in the spiritualist movement: 'My one aim in life,' he was shortly to write, 'is that this great truth, the return and communion of the dead, shall be brought home to a material world which needs it so badly.' At the beginning of April 1923, he was about to embark on his second mission to the United States, promoting the cause of spiritualism. There were said to be about a million people in the States who styled themselves spiritualists, and Doyle fervently hoped that he could improve on that number as a result of his efforts and his talents as an orator. His first mission, starting in April 1922, had concentrated on the eastern seaboard. This time he would go coast to coast, starting at Carnegie Hall. Conan Doyle's well-known beliefs, combined with the fact that he had written two of the great 'mummy' stories some thirty years before, during the heyday of Sherlock Holmes – *The Ring of Thoth* (1890) and *Lot No. 249* (1892) – made him an obvious commentator on the curse. As he stepped down the gangplank of the SS *Olympic* in New York, on Friday, 6 April, he duly obliged. According to the *Morning Post*:

'He was inclined to support to some extent the opinion that it was dangerous for Lord Carnarvon to enter Tutankhamen's tomb, owing to occult and other spiritual influences. He said, "An evil elemental may have caused Lord Carnarvon's fatal illness. One does not know what elementals existed in those days, nor what their form might be. The Egyptians knew a great deal more about these things than we do."'

Maybe, he added, this was yet more 'material evidence' to persuade a materialistic age of the existence of spirits on the other side.

The following day, Conan Doyle elaborated on his theory to the *Daily Express*. Apparently, and despite what the newspapers were saying, the pharaoh's curse had claimed not just one victim but *two*. The second was an ex-reporter for the *Daily Express* called Fletcher Robinson, who was an old friend of Conan Doyle's, going back to Sherlock Holmes days. Robinson had shown the author around Dartmoor in 1901, when he was preparing *The Hound of the Baskervilles*, and put him up in his home at Ipplepen (where the handyman went by the name of Harry Baskerville). He may even have helped to write the book, for Doyle in his dedication wrote, 'This story owes its inception to my friend, Mr Fletcher Robinson, who has helped me both in the general plot and in the local details.' Twenty-two years later, Conan Doyle linked his friend's demise with that of Lord Carnarvon. Robinson's death, which had happened a long time before Carnarvon's, was nevertheless:

'. . . caused by Egyptian "elementals" guarding a female mummy, because Mr Robinson had begun an investigation of the stories of the mummy's malevolence. "It is impossible to say with absolute certainty if this is true," said Sir Arthur to me today. "If we had proper occult powers we could determine it, but I warned Mr Robinson against concerning himself with the mummy at the British Museum. He persisted, and his death occurred . . . I told him he was tempting fate by pursuing his enquiries . . . The immediate cause of death was typhoid fever, but that is the way in which the elementals guarding the mummy might act. They could have guided Mr Robinson into a series of such circumstances as would lead him to contract the disease, and thus cause his death – just as in Lord Carnarvon's case, human illness was the *primary* cause of death."'

But what, asked the intrepid reporter, about other archaeologists working in the Valley of the Kings? Why had *they* not been struck down by the spiritual guardians of the tomb? The reply was characteristically assured and very British: 'It is nonsense to say that because "elementals" do not harm everybody, therefore they do not exist. One might as well say that because bulldogs do not bite everybody, therefore bulldogs do not exist!'

On the evening of 6 April Rider Haggard was giving a talk to an audience of Rotarians in Hastings. During question time, he took the opportunity to lay into Conan Doyle's ideas about the curse of the pharaohs, and his comments were duly published under the headline 'Black Magic' in the following morning's *Daily Mail*:

'All this nonsense about Lord Carnarvon having been brought to his end by magic is dangerous nonsense. Dangerous because it goes to swell the rising tide of superstition which at present seems to be overflowing the world. Do you suppose that God Almighty would permit a Pharaoh, who after all was only a man with a crown on his head, to murder people by magical means, thousands of years after his own death, and let loose what people in spiritualist circles call an "elemental", which I take to mean a devil? If that can happen, let us abandon all hope, for indeed we are in the hollow of the hand of darkness . . .'

If the *Morning Post* turned to Conan Doyle and the *Mail* to Rider Haggard, the *Daily Express* went one further by commissioning a major article from Algernon Blackwood, author of numerous short stories, as the paper put it, 'of the dream world and the mystic'. His first collection, *The Empty House and Other Ghost Stories*, had appeared in 1906. The article was headlined 'Superstition and the Magic Curse' and was printed two days after Rider Haggard's contribution. Having discussed the difficulties experienced by scientists when trying to find a sensible way into the vexed subject of magic or the supernormal, and the great gulf which seemed to exist between professionals and amateurs in this field, he went on:

'The popular interest in so-called Egyptian magic stimulated by the recent tragedy to an excavator has again proved that there are numerous intelligent persons who think that such higher states of consciousness, with their corollary of higher knowledge and strange powers, have been possible in the past, and are still accessible today. The ancients, they claim, favoured a line of enquiry foreign to our present day mental attitude. The gulf, however, between such persons and those who are merely superstitious remains, I think, unbridgeable. In this particular instance the methods by which Egyptian magicians are thought to have protected their dead from violation seem to be secret poison [the Corelli thesis] or a curse [the Conan Doyle thesis]. If poison, one would ask how this poison could be confined in its attack to a single individual only. If a curse, the whole question of thought, now so much in the public mind, comes under survey. A curse is a violent and concentrated strain of thought of which ordinary minds are, fortunately, hardly capable ... The power of thought, the effectiveness of suggestion, are today established for any open-minded person. Both easily escape the label of superstition. But to credit an Egyptian magician of several thousand years ago with sufficient thought power to kill a man today is to lay a heavier burden upon a "curse" than it can bear ...'

There was one more great author in this extended family. He had written the first well-known Egyptian mummy story (in the English language, anyway) way back in November 1845: it was called *Some Words with a Mummy* and concerned the experimental application of electric current to a 3,000-year-old cadaver. Unfortunately, Edgar Allan Poe had been dead for nearly three-quarters of a century, and all attempts to get in touch with him since had proved fruitless. Not to be put off by this, the *New York Times* completed the pantheon by running a front-page story on 30 June with the headline 'P. L. Poe Ill Like Carnarvon – Following Visit to Tut-ankh-Amen's Tomb':

'Following his return from Tutankhamen's tomb, Philip Livingston Poe, kin of Edgar Allan Poe, has been in a serious condition at his home here from streptococcus poisoning, Mrs Poe says. Mr and Mrs Poe had been back in Baltimore about two months when, a week ago last Monday, Mr Poe was stricken with illness that quickly developed into pneumonia, as happened in the case of Lord Carnarvon in Egypt. Ever since the Poes returned from their tour friends have been jokingly warning them of the "mummy's curse". The joking wore off, however, when Mr Poe became ill . . .'

In general, the mystery writers and popular novelists who were interviewed by the press helped to promote an aura of 'the uncanny' around the story of the excavation, and in particular around the death of Lord Carnarvon – an aura which was already more than half-way there. They developed the connection (which seemed to 'fit') between Tutankhamun and the curse which has survived to the present day, even eclipsing public interest in the wonderful objects which were removed from the tomb. And, as they did so, stories began to appear in popular newspapers about strange artefacts which bore hieroglyphic messages protecting the tomb from intruders across the ages, artefacts which were being 'suppressed' by professional Egyptologists. Such stories added the necessary ingredient of a conspiracy to the proceedings: not only was the opening of the tomb dangerous; the Egyptologists knew it and they were trying to hide the fact. The first of these stories concerned 'an ordinary clay tablet', said to have been found over the entrance of the tomb, which Lord Carnarvon had had the temerity to remove in order to substitute his own family's coat of arms. The hieroglyphics on the clay tablet looked something like this:

or like this:

The first passage reads: 'As to anyone who would violate my body which is in the tomb and who shall remove my image from my tomb, he shall be hateful to the Gods, and he shall not receive water on the altar of Osiris, neither shall he bequeath his property to his children for ever and ever.' The second passage reads: 'As to him who desecrates my dwelling or who shall damage the tomb and who shall violate my body, the Ka of Ra will be disgusted with him and he will not bequeath his property to his children, his heart shall never rest during his lifetime, neither shall he receive water in the necropolis. His soul will be destroyed for ever, for this land is broad and knows no bounds.'

When the inscription said to have been found over the entrance to Tutankhamun's tomb was decoded by a 'well-known Egyptologist', it read more like Marie Corelli than anything from ancient Egypt: 'Death shall come on swift wings to whoever toucheth the tomb of Pharaoh.' In other words, the inscription was nothing less than the 'curse of Osiris' itself, which originated with the older gods and about which so many stories had been written – a curse so powerful that it could travel across 3,000 years.

According to a self-styled student of the occult and amateur archaeologist who offered this information to the papers, this tablet had been dislodged and catalogued by Howard Carter, and then erased from the written record and buried in the sand, since the excavators were 'worried that the Egyptian labourers would take it seriously' and that this could disrupt the work schedule.

Then there was the spell incised on a reed torch decorated with gold foil which was discovered at the entrance of the Treasury: 'It is I who hinder the sand from choking the secret chamber, and who repel that one who would repel him with the desert flame. I have set aflame the [?desert], I have caused the path to be mistaken. I am for the protection of Osiris.'

This torch had stood in front of the life-sized statue, carved in wood and covered with resin, of the black Anubis dog, guardian of the chamber. Again, the story was put about that the spell had contained an extra line which had been excised from the written record: '. . . And I will call all those who cross this threshold into the sacred precincts of the King who lives for ever.'

Another story, arising from the Marie Corelli revelations that there were 'divers secret poisons' hidden in sealed tombs, had it that

Carnarvon must really have cut himself on some sharp object, or opened some infected box, and that the offending artefact had been quietly removed from the inventory of the find, or else neutralized in some way. It seems to have been widely accepted that 'curses', like elaborate booby traps, were a common feature of ancient tombs. Actually, both were extremely rare, and in the case of 'curses' (which were probably written to deter potential tomb-robbers, or crooked maintenance men, but which, if so, do not seem to have been too effective) the very few documented examples tend to date from the 5th Dynasty (Old Kingdom) and the 13th Dynasty (Middle Kingdom), or, respectively, 1,000 and 500 years before Tutankhamun and 4,000 years before the invention of academic archaeology. Where Tutankhamun's tomb is concerned, there is no evidence at all that any 'clay tablet' was ever found, the extra line added to the mild symbolic spell on the torch (which *does* exist) was pure fabrication, while the poisoned object materialized only in the world of sensational novels.

But embellishment and conspiracy were the order of the day. On 6 April 1923 the *Daily Mail* printed a story about the dreaded mosquito which 'may have previously settled on embalming fluids found buried with Tutankhamen'. To this the Egyptologist Professor Percy Newberry replied, 'In the valley itself there are no mosquitoes, so that the poisonous bite must have occurred at Luxor.' On the same day, the *Daily Express* started the ball rolling on a story about 'Lord Carnarvon's Last Hours – Sudden Failure of Lights'. As the 5th Earl breathed his last, at two o'clock in the morning, 'suddenly all the electric lights in the Cairo Hospital went out, leaving them all in complete darkness. After a lapse of a few minutes the lights came on again, only to go out abruptly. This curious occurrence was interpreted by those anxiously awaiting news as an omen of evil.'

In the next few weeks, the 'Lights' story generated more and more detail: it wasn't just the hospital lights but the entire electricity supply of Cairo, all four grids, which failed for five minutes, at the moment of death. Lord Allenby was said to have launched an immediate inquiry, under the chairmanship of the head of the Cairo Electricity Board, which concluded that there was 'no technical explanation whatsoever'. It must surely have been an example of the vengeance of King Tut.

Then there was Lord Carnarvon's beloved three-legged terrier bitch, named Susie, who at exactly two in the morning in the grounds of Highclere let out a long howl and dropped down dead. This story seems to have originated with no less a source than Lord Porchester, the 6th Earl, who had left Susie with the family when he set off for army service in India.

In his early years working among the antiquities of Egypt, Howard Carter himself seems to have romanced about the existence of 'the curse of the pharaohs' as T. G. H. James has discovered. In January 1900, when showing a visitor around the recently studied tomb of Amenophis II, Carter was quoted as saying that the pharaoh's mummy was 'probably protected . . . by a curse pronounced in the band of hieroglyphics around the top of the sarcophagus upon any marauding hands'. He may have been trying to impress the visitor (a Mrs Andrews), or he may have been adding drama to the occasion – he did sometimes embroider details in this way. Either way, there is no evidence for *this* curse either on or off the sarcophagus, and even if there had been, Carter could not have read it.

By the time of the great discovery, Carter was much more experienced in his dealings with impressionable members of the public and he seems to have shed most of the romantic ideas he took with him to Egypt when he was a young man. He still had a tendency to embroider, on occasions, if press reports are to be believed. On 19 April 1924 he told a *New York Times* reporter about 'a novel of travel which some literary man of the time had written to entertain Tut-ankh-Amen on his pilgrimage through the lower world' (no such 'novel' had in fact been found); during the angry period of lockout, he had made heated remarks about 'certain documents' unearthed during the discovery which shed controversial light on the biblical story of the Exodus (documents which didn't exist); and in later life he apparently liked to spin an entertaining yarn about going off in search of the lost tomb of Alexander the Great – on one occasion he even claimed to have found it, but added, 'The secret will die with me.' But where the curse of Tutankhamun was concerned, he had no time at all for romance. On 4 October 1924 he was quoted thus by the *New York Times*:

'He said he had not the slightest belief that any occult influence was responsible for the death of Lord Carnarvon, and that he had no fears for himself in that direction. "It is rather too much to ask me to believe that some spook is keeping watch and ward over the dead Pharaoh, ready to wreak vengance on anyone who goes too near," Carter said.'

On a later occasion, he wrote a more elaborate rebuttal (quoted by T. G. H. James) which shows that he had thought a great deal about the public's interest in the curse and its origins:

'The sentiment of the Egyptologist . . . is not one of fear but of respect and awe. It is entirely opposed to the foolish superstitions which are far too prevalent among emotional people in search of "psychic" excitement. It is not my intention to repeat the ridiculous stories which have been invented about the dangers lurking in ambush, as it were, in the Tomb, to destroy the intruder. Similar tales have been a common feature of fiction for many years, they are mostly variants of the ordinary ghost story, and may be accepted as a legitimate form of literary amusement. But there is another and a serious side to this question which calls for protest. It has been stated in various quarters that there are actual physical dangers hidden in Tut-Ankh-Amen's tomb – mysterious forces, called into being by some malefic power, to take vengeance on whomsoever should dare to pass its portals. There was probably no place in the world freer from risks than the Tomb. Scientific research had proved it to be sterile . . . all sane people should dismiss such inventions with contempt.'

Carter could be much more blunt than this when he chose. A favourite riposte in later life was, 'The answer is spherical and in the plural . . . And as a matter of fact the word "Osiris" referred to the deceased. And by the way, I am still alive.' If there *was* any curse, he wrote in his notebook, it took the form of 'Messrs Creepy, Crawly Biteum and Co.', the company of nasty insects which bit him when he was camping out in the desert.

Most of the other professional Egyptologists and museum curators interviewed at the time agreed with Carter. Herbert Winlock, who was appointed Director of the Metropolitan Museum in 1932, even compiled, as a kind of parlour game, a chart of all the 'Victims of the Curse, according to the Newspaper Reporters' in 1934, in order to have a *statistical* reply to those papers who claimed to have found yet more 'victims'. By the time he compiled this, the tally was certainly impressive: Carnarvon's half-brothers Aubrey and Mervyn; an X-ray specialist on his way to analyse a mummy; Arthur Mace; the French Egyptologist Georges Bénédite, who fell over when visiting the tomb;

Carnarvon's secretary, the Hon. Richard Bethell, and his father, Lord Westbury; a child who was run over by Lord Westbury's hearse at the funeral; Prince Ali Fahmy Bey, who had entered the tomb and was subsequently murdered at the Savoy Hotel in London; a manual attendant at the British Museum who dropped dead while labelling some objects from the tomb; a lecturer in archaeology from Leeds; and the Egyptologist Arthur Weigall. Winlock's chart sets out to demonstrate that the linking of these deaths to each other and to the opening of the tomb was fallacious. No objects from the tomb had found their way into the British Museum; Arthur Weigall, much to his own chagrin, was 'not allowed into the tomb except with the public'; if Prince Ali Fahmy Bey was ever in the tomb, 'it was as a tourist'; 'if tourists are subject to the curse, it should be remembered that a large number of them are elderly people travelling to Egypt for their health'; Arthur Mace – a sick man anyway, with heart, chest and stomach problems (exacerbated by several years of 'breathing cloth dust' in confined spaces) – died of pleurisy and pneumonia; and so on. The chart then shows that most of the people who *were* there when the tomb was opened (twenty out of twenty-six to be precise) were still in sound health.

Looking back, we can extend Winlock's list well beyond 1934. Of those closest to the excavation, Howard Carter died in 1939, the photographer Harry Burton in 1940, Alfred Lucas in 1945, Percy Newberry in 1949, Alan Gardiner in 1963, Douglas Derry (who was in charge of Tut's post-mortem) in 1969 and Lady Evelyn in 1980. Their *average* age at the

time of death was 76.3. But as T. G. H. James has sensibly written of such well-known facts:

'. . . the idea of a curse suited the popular image of ancient Egypt . . . To counter the excesses of such melodramatic beliefs by the invocation of common sense and the production of contrary evidence is a hopeless procedure. The idea of a curse is in a sense needed by many people to satisfy a kind of deep-seated expectation of supernatural evil.'

Part of the problem was that although most Egyptologists spoke out against the idea of a curse of the pharaohs, there were some who were prepared to give newspapers exactly what they wanted. Prominent amongst them was Arthur Weigall, ex-Chief Inspector of Antiquities for the Luxor region, ex-colleague of Carter (they never got on) and now freelance special correspondent for the *Daily Mail*. On 20 March 1923 – before Carnarvon's death – H. V. Morton wrote in the *Daily Express* (under the double headline 'Lord Carnarvon Poisoned – Is Pharaoh at Work?'):

'More than one authority believes that if we could go back a few thousand years and consult an ancient Egyptian magician we would find him a very disappointing person, whose stock-in-trade was an unconvincing mass of Mumbo Jumbo designed to impress the ignorant. Still, the fact remains that there's a strange atmosphere . . . I was riding back from the tomb of Tutankhamen with a friend the day after it had been opened. Inside the dark chamber, faced by the blue and gilt foot of the gigantic coffin, we had apparently both experienced the same eerie feeling. "Something will happen, you mark my words," he said. "Tutankhamen will get even with us for disturbing him!" "Do you honestly believe that?" I asked him. "Well, only half and half!" he replied.'

The friend was Arthur Weigall and what he actually said to H. V. Morton, when *Lord Carnarvon*, rather than the two friends, entered the tomb, 'in a very gay mood, and uttering several jocular remarks', was, 'If he goes down in that spirit, I give him six weeks to live!' And, of course, six weeks later Lord Carnarvon was dead. In summer 1923 Weigall published his book *Tutankhamen and Other Essays*, designed, like several other hastily compiled books by prominent Egyptologists, to cash in on the craze. It contained a chapter on 'the malevolence of ancient Egyptian spirits', full of juicy anecdotes about evil spirits, sinister omens and haunted artefacts, and ended on the teasing line, 'I have heard the most absurd nonsense talked in Egypt . . . but at the same time, I try to keep an open mind on the subject.' And in April 1926, when a blemish or scab discovered by Dr Douglas Derry of the Cairo Medical School on the left cheek of Tutankhamun's mummified face was said by the *Morning Post* to be in 'exactly the same position' as the fatal mosquito bite which killed Carnarvon, Weigall weighed in again. In point of fact, no one had revealed *any* evidence as to the 'exact' position of the mosquito bite, but the story, 'Curse of the Pharaohs – Uncanny Incidents', provided an excellent opportunity for 'the famous Egyptologist' to retell the old stories from his book. And to tease the readers with: 'While I cannot exactly say that I subscribe in believing the efficacy of

such curses, I must admit that some very strange things – call them coincidences if you will – have happened in connection with the Luxor excavations.'

It may also be more than coincidental that Weigall's interest in the curse should originate with Lord Carnarvon (rather than himself) entering the tomb, because, it has been suggested by T. G. H. James, his remarks – which helped fuel the 'curse' story as much as, if not more than, the comments of popular mystery writers – were made in the heat of the moment when he himself was denied access. Weigall was in an unusually uncomfortable position in early 1923. He knew a great deal about Egyptology (unlike most of the journalists in Luxor), he even knew Carter and Carnarvon from of old, and yet, since he didn't work for *The Times*, he had to be content with looking in on the discoveries from the parapet outside – just like everyone else. A letter to Carter in January (two days after Weigall started his contract with the *Mail*) begged him to be more open with friendly journalists and to encourage Carnarvon to renegotiate the deal with *The Times*. When neither of these things happened, Weigall hung around the tomb, taking photographs of the objects as they were removed on stretchers or of the tomb guards, in Arthur Mace's words, 'very fat and oily, and pretending to be a journalist only by accident so to speak'. Alfred Lucas later added, 'Having come to Luxor as a journalist to represent the *Daily Mail*, Mr Weigall was treated as a journalist, and not as an archaeologist, and he was not in the tomb during the opening ceremony, but outside, journalists being excluded, chiefly because there was not room for them . . .'

It may be that Weigall turned to the curse story with such a vengeance partly because he was upset at being excluded and wanted to get his own back, partly because he had little else to write about, and partly because it ensured him more column inches than any other major British Egyptologist at the time. There is also the possibility that he really *did* have an 'open mind' on the subject, but this is the least likely explanation. As we've seen, Weigall was to cross swords with Howard Carter yet again, in the following year, over the strange incident of the Wembley Amusements Park.

One of Weigall's favourite stories (which he trotted out, in book and article and interview form, off and on for nigh on three years) was the one about Howard Carter's canary. *This* may have started life with another eminent Egyptologist, James Henry Breasted of the University of Chicago, who had joined the team to evaluate the historical significance of the contents of the tomb. Carter, it appears, had brought with him a pet canary to keep him company in the Valley of the Kings in November 1922, at the start of the great season. Breasted elaborates:

'There are no song birds in Egypt, and the carolling of the canary was very pleasant, especially for the natives, who had never heard anything of the kind before and who came flocking for miles to hear it sing. They all said, "The bird will bring good fortune!" Not very long after this, Carter uncovered the first step of the flight of stairs leading down to the tomb of Tutankhamen . . . And they christened it "The Tomb of the Bird" . . . One day soon after the discovery Carter sent an assistant to fetch

something from his house, which happened to be empty, the servants having gone to the weekly market at Luxor. As the man approached the house he heard a faint, almost human cry. Then all was silent again – even the bird had stopped singing. Upon entering, he looked almost instinctively at the cage and saw coiled within it a cobra holding in its mouth the dead canary. News of this spread quickly and all the natives said, "Alas, that was the King's cobra, revenging itself upon the bird for having betrayed the place of the tomb, and now something terrible will happen!"'

The point was, on the golden portrait mask of the boy-king, as on his coffin-lids, perched on his forehead, was the divine cobra Wadjit, hooded and ready to spit fire and poison at the enemies of the pharaoh. And the cobra had eaten the bird, her first symbolic victim.

There are references to a canary belonging to Carter dating from a year *after* this supposed incident. He left the bird with Minnie Burton, the photographer's wife, for safekeeping when the season in the Valley of the Kings was over; she in turn handed it on to a bank manager in Luxor. So maybe the incident never happened, or maybe Carter took the trouble to buy a replacement canary. T. G. H. James inclines to the former view: 'It was a strange story, for it is hard to imagine how a cobra could have got through the bars of the cage. If they were so spaced that the snake could get in, surely the canary could have got out.'

When we were filming *The Face of Tutankhamun* we had the opportunity to put this to the test. A cobra was placed outside a normal-sized birdcage with bird inside, on the

steps of 'Castle Carter', at the entrance to the Valley of the Kings, and – before our very eyes – it reduced itself to the necessary width and slid through the bars. We only just managed to save the hapless bird. So the 'strange story' could have happened. Or it could have been another Egyptologist playing games with the press.

Henry Field, a young anthropologist fresh out of Oxford, was escorted around the tomb by Howard Carter in December 1925, with a letter of recommendation from Professor Breasted. As he looked in amazement at the gold coffin of the king, with his university tutor by his side, his mind was filled with fantasies about the curse. He recalled them vividly thirty years later, in his autobiography *The Track of Man*:

'[The tutor] and I were struck by the inscription over the door, "Death to those who enter". In the years to come the most lurid newspapers carried many stories describing the power of this curse. First Lord Carnarvon, the financier of the expedition, and then Howard Carter . . . and it was invariably pointed out that their deaths were the results of the ancient Egyptian curse. This I most emphatically do not believe. However, I do believe that there is much in existence that cannot be explained by any means known to us now . . . The owners of the Hope Diamond, for example, seem to have met with more than their normal share of ill-luck. Archaeology is riddled with legends, old and new. There is a story about Sir Bruce Ingram, long-time editor of the *Illustrated London News*, who was given a mummy's hand as a paperweight. The wrist was still bound with a copper bracelet set with a scarab. The hieroglyphs on the scarab, translated, proved to be, "Cursed be he who moves my body. To him shall come fire, water and pestilence." Several months later the editor's beautiful country house burned to the ground. It was rebuilt and a flood promptly swept through its ground floors. Sir Bruce did not wait for the pestilence. He sent the mummy's hand back to the Valley of the Kings. To call this superstition combined with coincidence is the easiest and also the most scientific way out. Nevertheless . . .'

This reminiscence, by a man who by the 1950s was well known in America and Britain as an academic and an anthropologist, is interesting for many reasons: first, there never was an inscription over the door, and even those who said there was never claimed it contained those words; second, Howard Carter died *sixteen years* after Lord Carnarvon; third, the story of the 'mummy's hand' was a staple of popular fiction in the 1920s; and finally, the legend of the house burning down was claimed by several other people as well ... It all goes to show that the specialists could be just as impressionable – and impressionistic – as the readers of popular newspapers who were condemned by Evelyn Waugh for wallowing in 'superstitious depths'. When they were writing for a non-specialized audience, that is.

Where the newspapers of the day were concerned, the curse story had one final fling, in March 1926, before being demoted from the front pages to more eccentric corners of the correspondence columns. On 28 March the *New York Times* ran the headline 'Sixth Tomb Hunter Succumbs in Egypt – Dr Mardrus Advances Theory of Strange Force'. The sixth 'tomb hunter' in question was Professor Georges Bénédite, director of the Egyptian antiquities section of the Louvre, who, it was claimed, had been 'closely connected with the discovery'. What made the story unusual was that Dr J. C. Mardrus, 'the Oriental scholar, translator of what is considered today the purest version of the *Arabian Nights* ... and known as one of the foremost living authorities on the Near East', was prepared, without ifs and buts, to attribute the Professor's death to mysterious forces, and to claim that his researches supported the thesis:

'He said he was neither an occultist nor a spiritualist, and made no claims to prophetic gifts, although his research work as an

Orientalist leads him to make a close study of the various branches of esoteric and secret sciences ... "This is no childish superstition which can be dismissed with a shrug of the shoulder," he said. "We must remember that the Egyptians, during a period of 7,000 years, in order to assure the calm of subterranean existence which was supposed to delight their mummies and prevent all attempts to disturb their rest, practised magical rites the power of which held no doubts for them. I am absolutely convinced that they knew how to concentrate upon and around a mummy certain dynamic powers of which we possess very incomplete notions."'

Dr Mardrus concluded by making a comparison with the Ark of the Covenant (or the 'Ark of the god Amun', as he called it) in the Old Testament, which 'struck down dead hundreds of priests who dared to approach it too closely. It must surely have been charged with an accumulation of forces unknown to us today.'

This, coming from a well-respected raider of the lost archives, led to a spirited editorial on 30 March ('Dr Mardrus might have been more profitably employed if he had found out of just what maladies his colleagues died, and just how old they were'), a letter from a vicar in Yonkers on 4 April ('We are still very much under the domination of the narrow, materialistic science of the past generation ... but we are rapidly rediscovering occult powers known for ages to Egyptian master-minds, and perfectly exemplified in the life of the Christ') and a long article in the *New York Times Magazine* on 11 April:

'There is a belief that a curse awaits the intruder [in an ancient tomb]. This is the idea that Sir Rider Haggard and his numerous imitators exploit in their tales of adventure. And there arises the question – what basis, if any, can be discovered for the hoodoo? . . . The theory of Dr Mardrus means that spirit, which dwells in living creatures, also haunts inanimate objects. And the theory is the more interesting because it emerges, not from the Protestant Fundamentalism of Tennessee, not from the Catholic Fundamentalism of Rome, but from the Critical Modernism of Paris. That mind affects matter and that matter affects mind are beliefs fairly to be described as universal.'

One aspect of matter affecting mind (or more particularly body) was the exposure of the archaeologists, for months and sometimes for years, to the artefacts shut up within the tomb:

'With every discovery, Tut's ire waxes warmer. As the archaeologist handles his food, fingers unguents which still yield fragrance, sniffs at perfumes, unfolds fabrics from the weaver's loom, abstracts jewels, catalogues pottery and sprays bouquets of flowers with liquid wax, Tut smiles. For Tut knows what kindly legacies have been left by the accomplished chemist whom he employed as his expert.'

Another aspect was the whole issue of auto-suggestion. There had been so much coverage of the curse in recent years that it would not have been surprising if some over-sensitive archaeologists had it on their minds as they tried to get on with the cleaning and conserving of contaminated objects. This aspect of the case had already featured in the columns of the *New York Times*, with a story on 12 September 1924 about the suicide in a taxi-cab of H. G. Evelyn White, a lecturer at Leeds University and a contributor to various American archaeological digs:

'Professor White was some years ago introduced by a monk into a secret room in an Egyptian monastry where he found and removed fragments of apocryphal books, some previously unheard of [!] and of inestimable value. His death Tuesday followed the suicide of a young music mistress who was infatuated with him, and at whose inquest he was to be the chief witness. At today's inquest, a letter in the dead man's handwriting was read, in which he said, "I know there is a curse on me, although I had leave to take those manuscripts to Cairo. The monks told me the curse would work all the same. Now it has done."'

Dr J. C. Mardrus, the most distinguished proponent of the 'dynamic powers' theory, and the only 'professional' who was prepared to be up-front about it – in public, at least – provides an interesting link between the two main manifestations of Tutmania in the public domain: the Egyptian style in art and design, and the mythology of the curse. For it was his then recent translation of the *Thousand and One Nights* which had stimulated the fashion designer Paul Poiret to mount his lavish 'Thousand and Second Night' event for the glitterati of Paris way back in June 1911. The invitation to this party, designed, like the event itself, by the painter Raoul Dufy, had promised, 'There will be not a cloud in the sky and there will exist nothing of what now exists.'

A contemporary account of the 'Thousand and Second Night', which took place in the garden and on the steps of a house in the avenue d'Antin, could almost be a catalogue of the visual clichés loosely associated with the Egyptian Revival of eleven years later; and the operative word is 'loosely', because both the geography and the iconography in fact came from all over the place.

'Orchestras sheltered in copses; there were parrots in trees studded with a thousand twinkling lights, pink ibis, multi-coloured cushions, calico mounted like an Eastern Bazaar, story-tellers, acrobats, artisans, miniature firework displays and delicate fountains in crystal bowls: nothing was forgotten, down to the thick carpets in the garden, muffling footsteps, so that the only sound was the rustling of the silks and satins of the costumes.'

Paul Poiret himself presided, dressed up as a Sultan.

When, in the mid-1920s, Poiret tried hard, but in vain, to revive the out-of-date elegance of pre-war Paris with his elaborate nightspot The Oasis (the garden was enclosed this time in an inflatable mosque-like dome made out of airship cloth), Dr Mardrus was regularly on the invitation list. The fixtures and fittings were inspired by a trip to North Africa in 1923, and the atmosphere was said to be 'anti-jazz and anti-Cubist'.

So, at the precise time when Mardrus was being interviewed about his eccentric views on the curse, he was also being fêted by the old guard of Parisian *haute couture*. Meanwhile,

all the rumours about the haunted tomb, and in particular about the dangers facing people who dared to remove magic objects from sacred places, were beginning to have an effect on collectors (perhaps of the kind met by Henry Morton Stanley at the turn of the century) in Britain. On 7 April 1923, under the headline 'Egyptian Collectors in a Panic – Sudden Rush to Hand over Their Treasures to Museums', the *Daily Express* reported:

'The death of Lord Carnarvon has been followed by a panic among collectors of Egyptian antiquities. All over the country people are sending their treasures to the British Museum, anxious to get rid of them because of the superstition that Lord Carnarvon was killed by the "ka" or double of the soul of Tutankhamen.'

Apparently, a small avalanche of parcels, containing the shrivelled hands, feet, ears and heads of mummies, as well as wooden, limestone and ceramic shabti figures and 'other relics from the ancient tombs' had been arriving on the doorstep of the British Museum with every post.

'Few of the parcels received at the museum bear the senders' names. The owners, in their eagerness to wash their hands of the accursed things, have tried to keep their identity secret. Statuettes that peer out of the corners of slanting eyes are responsible for many cases of "nerves" and the Museum is richer by several gifts of this sort – not much richer, however, for few of the pieces are valuable.'

The British Museum, continued the article, was something of a godsend to people who interpreted Carnarvon's death as 'confirmation of their fears', for it offered an easy means of 'shifting the liability to expert shoulders'. But these expert shoulders, or rather the curatorial staff in the Egyptian Department, were not too excited about this shower of unsolicited donations. Quite apart from the accessioning problem, they may perhaps have resented the fact that members of the public thought that they were 'shifting' the curse on to them – like a real-life version of M. R. James's ghost story *Casting the Runes* (1911).

'The Museum authorities are used to such liabilities, having harboured the coffin-lid of the powerful Priestess of Amen-Ra for years, but they are not at all grateful for the present flood of gifts. The museum weathered a similar storm years ago, when the story of the curse of the Priestess of Amen-Ra became public. Sufficient scare gifts were received to fill a large showcase.'

One story about the magic priestess which had been going the rounds concerned the photographer who attempted to take pictures of her coffin-lid. He'd locked the plates in his safe, but when he went to look at them some weeks later, 'The plates had become a thin brown powder.' The priestess evidently moved in mysterious ways, her wonders to perform.

Next to this front-page, seventy-line story was a succinct ten-line item, headed 'Work at the Tomb', about 'the preparation of the objects from the tomb of Tutankhamen for removal to Cairo', now under Mr Carter's direction. Harry Burton's photographs of the objects had not, it seemed, been turned into 'thin brown powder', and the hard end-of-

season work of classification, labelling, cleaning, conservation and transportation up-river to the museum would continue as if nothing untoward had happened. Evidently, the reporter could think of almost nothing to say, nothing sensational at any rate, about what was actually going on, day to day, in tomb 62 in the Valley of the Kings.

The Message of the Past

By the early 1930s the press, even *The Times*, had to all intents and purposes lost interest in the discoveries from the tomb of Tutankhamun. The much-publicized objects removed from the antechamber, the burial chamber and the treasury had by then been put on exhibition at the Cairo Museum (in display cases some of which remain unchanged to this day), so tourists could see for themselves; the last chamber (the inner room, or annexe) had been cleared by Christmas 1927; and conservation work on the remaining objects had long since ceased to seem worthy of a news story. After watching Howard Carter hard at work, sometimes alone, sometimes with a few associates, a visitor to the tomb in 1930 wrote, 'I pitied him, cooped up for years in the electrified darkness of the tomb.' On 2 February 1932 *The Times* succinctly reported, 'Mr Howard Carter's ten years' work on the tomb is ended.'

The first volume of *The Discovery of the Tomb of Tutankhamen* had been published in 1923, at the height of Tutmania, and it had been a great popular success. The third and, from the archaeological point of view, most useful volume was published in 1933 (largely written by Carter himself), and it attracted much less attention in the press and in book shops. Carter had originally intended to write a scholarly multi-volume account of the contents of the tomb, entitled *A Report upon the Tomb of Tutankhamen*, but after the last objects had been shipped to Cairo in spring 1932, he seemed to lack the energy, the confidence (always a problem in his dealings with Oxbridge-educated Egyptologists) and, perhaps, the inclination. So the *Report* was never written.

After his death, on 2 March 1939, of heart failure and Hodgkin's disease, at his flat at 49 Albert Court, overlooking the Royal Albert Hall, not a single senior Egyptologist, government official or museum curator attended his funeral. Of the journalists for whom he had provided (usually unwillingly, it has to be said) acres of copy for the five years following November 1922, none came to pay their respects. Only Bruce Ingram, editor of the *Illustrated London News*, the magazine which had been granted the right to publish tinted or coloured photographs of the discoveries, sent a floral tribute, and he was a friend of the family. Carter's funeral, at Putney Vale Cemetery in south London, with nine people in attendance, couldn't have been further removed from the magnificent burial customs of ancient Egypt, the study of which had occupied all of his adult life. The words on his plain gravestone were brief and to the point: 'Howard Carter, Archaeologist and Egyptologist, born 9 May 1874, died 2 March 1939'. In the same cemetery, nearby, there was a facsimile Egyptian temple, built for someone grander and better connec-

ted, with more reason to have a sense of posterity. Apart from an honorary degree from Yale University, which he received during his American lecture tour in 1924 and after which he was always billed on posters as 'Howard Carter, Hon. Sc.D.', he was given no academic or civil honours. Quite simply, after the death of Lord Carnarvon, there was no patron around to argue his case in the right social circles.

And yet, in the public eye, Howard Carter was (and still is, if we exclude Hollywood's Indiana Jones, who in part is based on him) the most famous archaeologist of all, the man who sought out and discovered Aladdin's Cave with its store of buried treasure. 'Can you see anything?' asked Carnarvon anxiously. '*Yes, wonderful things.*'

These wonderful things had kept the reading public, and the cinema-going public, and the fashion-conscious public, by turns amused and scared and entertained, in a very 'Twentyish' way – to use Robert Graves's word – at a time when they were sated with post-First World War conferences, and news of alarming developments in the Soviet Union and of instability in Weimar Germany. However, in reply to the question, 'Can you see anything?' different groups of people had evidently seen very different things.

The Egyptologists saw a new tomb which was almost intact, and thousands of artefacts within it which were in a remarkable state of preservation. Beyond that, the scholars weren't agreed among themselves about the significance of what they saw. Alan Gardiner, the philologist on the team (who mistrusted Carter's lack of interest in linguistic matters), later reflected that, 'The discovery has added very little to our knowledge of the history of the period. To the philologist the tomb was disappointing as it contained no written documents.'

When the super-group was first assembled, in December 1922, they confidently expected that the tomb would yield much historical data. James Henry Breasted thought that his brief, to sift through 'all the historical work', would turn out to be 'a staggering asssignment'. But in the event, there was very little 'historical work' to do, and he spent most of his time working on the seal impressions stamped on the various doors. The excavators had reckoned, for a brief time, that they had discovered a basketful of manuscripts; but the manuscripts turned out, disappointingly, to be pieces of Tutankhamun's underwear. As Carter observed, the tomb didn't even contain much information about Tutankhamun himself, beyond what was known from other written and visual sources already. In reply to the question, 'What have we found out?' he wrote, 'Remarkably little when you come right down to it', beyond the fact that he died and was buried. Tutankhamun was a minor pharaoh of the New Kingdom period (probably but by no means certainly on the throne from 1333 to 1323 BC), who died young – between seventeen and twenty years old, Carter reckoned – and during whose reign the political centre of Egypt returned from El-Amarna to Memphis, with Thebes becoming again the religious centre. It was also during his reign that the worship of Amun and the older gods (following the pharaoh Akhenaton's sustained attempt to ban them) was re-established, symbolized by his change of name, as a public figure, from

Tutankh*aten* to Tutankh*amun*. Apart from these facts – which were stretched to several chapters in the various books churned out in 1923, written by Egyptologists and curators who attributed more historical significance to the find than there turned out to be – as Carter wrote, 'The mystery of his life still eludes us: the shadows move but the dark is never quite dispersed.'

One reason why news of the discovery so rapidly turned into news of all sorts of other things may have been that there was so little history to write about. No documents to decipher, no 'texts' to appeal to the establishment of Egyptology. So the newly opened tomb became a void into which the obsessions of the day were unceremoniously pushed. But Alan Gardiner was in no doubt about the *visual* significance of the find:

'. . . as a revelation to the *artistic* achievement of the period, the discovery was quite unparalleled. Nothing like it had been discovered before . . . The fact that, after a superficial looting, it remained untouched for 3,000 years was probably due to a lucky chance. When, many years after Tutankhamen's burial, the hypogeum of Rameses the Sixth was being tunnelled out of the hillside above the tomb, the stone chippings from the excavation buried the entrance to Tutankhamen's much more modest sepulchre, which thus escaped. The value of the discovery to archaeology lies not only in the wealth of objects it revealed, but in the fact that these lovely things were recorded and preserved with such consummate skill.'

The tomb itself wasn't particularly exciting.

It seemed to have been constructed for some-one else (it's so much smaller than the other tombs of the pharaohs, and the only artwork there is is painted on to the walls of the burial chamber), which might suggest that Tutankhamun died unexpectedly or suddenly. But the quality, quantity and condition of the objects were 'quite unparalleled'.

This helps to explain why the purely visual impact of the discovery was so strong at the time – and since. Harry Burton's photographs, printed in black and white in *The Times* and coloured in the *Illustrated London News*, probably stimulated more interest than the captions and copy beneath them. 'Can you see anything?' Yes, a great deal – and artists, designers and craftspeople were among the first to react to the sight. In the fast-turnover worlds of fashion, fashion accessories and textiles, 'Tutankhamun Ltd' was well established by the spring of 1923. By later that year, avant-garde painters and sculptors were beginning to discuss the visual significance of the find, with its lessons for the present. By the late 1920s buildings inspired by Tutmania were beginning to appear. Whether as a contribution to the principles of art or, suitably modified, to the latest designs, or to the art directors of Hollywood films, it was, as Alan Gardiner said, 'the *artistic* achievement' which started the ball dancing.

And then, with Lord Carnarvon's death, the focus shifted away from the 'wonderful things' and on to the archaeologists who were digging for them. 'Can you see anything?' Yes, confirmation of popular attitudes towards ancient Egypt as a time and place when high priests went around incanting spells from *The Book of the Dead*, curses were inscribed over the door of every pharaoh's tomb and occult societies were born. Confirmation, if one wants to be cynical, of the well-known phrase or saying, 'When people cease to believe in God they don't believe in nothing, they believe in anything.' The spectacle was already there – in the form of popular novels, books about magic, academic texts taken up by Egyptomaniacs, and a folklore which went back to the Hermetic tradition – but that fateful mosquito bite propelled the curse of the pharaohs on to the front pages, where it has remained for nearly seventy years.

As far as the established Church was concerned, to judge by the correspondence columns the principal interest in the discovery was whether or not it confirmed the accuracy of Old Testament stories, and what light it shed on the history of Christianity. 'Can you see anything?' Yes, a biblical setting and another chance to draw attention to the growing consumerism of the West. Oddly enough, apart from a couple of contributions to the debate about whether or not mummies should be removed from their resting-places and put in glass cases, no one from the Church seems publicly to have questioned the moral right of archaeologists to do their research, and make their careers, in an ancient burial ground; perhaps they would have done if the burial ground had been a Christian one, or if Tutankhamun had not been associated with polytheism.

Howard Carter's favourite line about the wider cultural impact of the discovery came from Pope Pius XII: 'It is not an exhumation, it is a resurrection.' A resurrection which firmly established Egyptology as a discipline to be reckoned with (for the first few years after-wards, the financial contributions to arch-aeological digs and projects rose dramatically), which raised expectations – for better or worse, and most archaeologists today would say for worse – about the kinds of tombs and treasures which could well be unearthed in the future, which turned archaeologists and their patrons into celebrities and, above all, which stimulated an enormous amount of interest in the public domain. And yet the very public resurrection had little if anything to do with the religion, the culture or the society of the boy-pharaoh who lay in the tomb. Its most endur-ing monuments are several worlds away: in Paris the Art Deco jewels and pieces of furni-ture which are preserved in the Musée des Arts Décoratifs; in Berlin the sequence from Fritz Lang's masterpiece *Metropolis* (planned 1924, released 1926) where the robot Maria, repre-senting woman as pleasure machine in the

society of the future, performs an erotic Egyp-tian Deco-inspired dance, to amuse the dinner-jacketed guests in a city night-club; in Moscow the mummified corpse of the revolutionary leader Lenin, who died in January 1924 (after a long series of illnesses which had shared the front pages with Lord Carnarvon) and was subsequently preserved with an embalming fluid said to have been based on one 'used by the ancient Egyptians' so that he could be wor-shipped for ever in his glass-covered sarco-phagus within a mausoleum made of red Ukrainian granite and Karelian porphyry at the foot of the Kremlin wall in Red Square – as an icon of the Soviet Revolution or, as Stalin pre-ferred it, as the last pharaoh; in New York the skyscraping Chrysler Building, constructed in 1928–30, with its references to the Luxor Temple on the outside and its stylized lotus-flowers on the elevator doors inside; and in London the continuing fascination with the curse of Tutankhamun, embodied in a popular series of Hammer films made between 1959 and 1971, and in well-wrapped performances by character actors such as Boris Karloff and Christopher Lee.

In one sense this resurrection was a late, but classic, example of the phenomenon described by Edward Said as 'Orientalism': the pro-jection on to another culture, or the Other, of the system of thought, the values and concerns of an Occidental culture, first among the experts and specialists studying the alien cul-ture, then among the politicians actually administering it, and then within society as a whole. In this version of the story, the arch-aeologists and the museum establishment set the agenda, and the administrators of the

The discovery itself looked from the outside like one aristocrat entering the tomb of another aristocrat, with members of an exclusive club arguing among themselves about the significance of this remote encounter. In the absence of a 'lead' from members of the club, it was the outsiders, the newspapers, reflecting what might be called the popular Orientalism of novels, films, travel books and so on, with their conventions and their taboos, and the fashion industries, building on and adapting visual clichés which were already part of the currency, that set the pace. The relationship between academic Orientalism and its popular counterpart (or vice versa) was strengthened

'veiled protectorate' in Egypt made it stick. Meanwhile, the West continued to see itself – its best self – in the mirror of the East: in particular, the cultural history of Egypt was filtered through the domestic concerns, the 'common knowledge', of Europe and America. In another sense, the resurrection of Tutankhamun represents a challenge to this version, for the filtering process didn't begin and end with the experts – with the knowledge of the specialists setting and limiting the agenda – but rather within popular culture.

when some of the experts decided to join in. Howard Carter, on the other hand, tried to fight a rearguard action against 'Tutankhamun Ltd' at the Wembley Empire Exhibition of 1924 – but he lost the battle.

Eighteen months before this, Carter had taken his first, unfocused look through a hole made in the upper left-hand corner of the wall, at the end of the entrance corridor leading to the tomb: '. . . presently, as my eyes grew accustomed to the light, details of the room within emerged slowly from the mist, strange animals, statues and gold – everywhere the glint of gold. For a moment . . . I was struck dumb with amazement.' Then, three years later, he had raised the final coffin-lid and looked upon the royal mummy – the climax of the team's researches:

'The youthful Pharaoh was before us at last: an obscure and ephemeral ruler, ceasing to be the mere shadow of a name, had re-entered, after more than three thousand years, the world of reality and history! . . . The tomb had yielded its secret; the message of the past had reached the present in spite of the weight of time, and the erosion of so many years.'

But the message of the past which had reached the present wasn't at all the message he expected to receive. And the tomb's secret spread like wildfire.

In the Footsteps of Howard Carter

Howard Carter was born in London at 10 Richmond Terrace, off the Old Brompton Road, on 9 May 1874. He spent his childhood in the small market town of Swaffham in north-west Norfolk. His father, Samuel Carter, earned his living as a painter of animals – wild, domestic and agricultural – and as an illustrator for the *Illustrated London News*. Family tradition had it that Samuel made the original drawings for the Landseer lion sculptures at the foot of Nelson's Column in Trafalgar Square, but it has to be said that Carter family tradition sometimes tended to romanticize rather ordinary facts. Howard was the youngest of eleven children (eight of whom survived infancy), and it was partly because he was a weak, sickly child that he was sent to the country, to be brought up alone by two maiden aunts. His education there was minimal, beginning later than usual and ending at the age of fifteen when the need to contribute to the family economy became paramount. This gave Howard Carter something of an inferiority complex, which would haunt him – especially when he met Egyptologists from the university world – for the rest of his life. But some things he *did* inherit, in abundance: a good eye, the ability to draw, a love of natural history and, from his aunts, a Norfolk accent (which, by the mid-1920s, he had lost).

This section of *The Face of Tutankhamun* consists of selections from his previously unpublished notes towards an autobiography (some of them written in the mid-1930s, in exercise books), interspersed with extracts from contemporary writings by authors who crossed his path at the time. The unpublished notes are included by courtesy of John Carter, his great-nephew, and they have been transcribed as written.

I was born in London on the 9th of May 1874, at my father's town house in Earl's Court, which had a lovely garden full of animal pens for the purpose of study. But for reasons which were never explained to me, I was taken almost immediately to our house in Swaffham, Norfolk, in charge of a nurse.

I can hardly find any trace of my father in myself, except an inborn faculty for drawing, which unfortunately, in my case, was never fully cultivated. I work extremely hard when it pleases me, and when it does not, I am extremely idle. Although a lover of books my regret is that I never read sufficiently.

I have a hot temper and that amount of tenacity of purpose, which unfriendly observers sometimes call obstinacy and which nowadays, due to such of my idiosyncrasies, it pleases my enemies to term me as having 'un mauvais caractère'. Well! that I cannot help.

My father, an animal painter of no little fame, was the most powerful draughtsman I ever knew, particularly in the drawing of animals. He had an extraordinary knowledge of comparative anatomy and memory for form. He could depict any animal, in any action, foreshortened or otherwise, out of his head with the greatest ease, and be perfectly accurate both anatomically and specifically. However, if a son may criticize his father, this faculty was his misfortune, for by it he was not so obliged to seek nature as much as an artist should, hence his art became somewhat styled as well as period marked.

My mother, a most kindly woman, loved luxury. This liking I inherited, together with a terrible habit of neatness. I will keep my correspondence in the neatest order, but rarely write the necessary replies.

I was the youngest member of a large family, many brothers, and only one sister. They, when referring to me, always spoke of me as their 'younger' brother, using the adjective 'younger' more in the derogative sense than otherwise, and when speaking of themselves, always as 'senior brother'. Be that as it may, I received from them a good lot of training and at times, sixpenny or threepenny bits, if I allowed them to pick me up by my hair, or if I washed their paint brushes and scraped their palettes.

I have next to nothing to say about education. During my younger days I was a bad herniary case, and thus I was unable to go through the regular school training, or in sports such as other lads did and still do. Again, being the youngest of an artist family I had to start earning my living at the early age of fifteen. Nature thrusts some of us into the world miserably incomplete.

I loved anything connected with ornithology or entomology, but was never allowed to follow up seriously those studies as drawing and printing was considered the more profitable. Nevertheless, my holiday afternoons were spent in rambles about the country, watching the winning ways of insects and birds, their history and habits, and I fear these rambling propensities caused me to neglect the regular exercise of my profession.

Thus for a living I began by drawing in watercolour and coloured chalks, portraits of parrots, cats and snappy, smelly lapdogs. Although I was always a great lover of birds and animals, in fact, I was brought up with them, how I hated that particular species known as the lapdog.

Due to Lord and Lady Amherst of Hackney, to whom I owe an everlasting debt of gratitude for their great kindness to me during my early career. It was their Egyptian collection at Didlington Hall, Brandon, Norfolk, perhaps the largest and most interesting of its time in England, that gave me a premature longing for that particular country, for the purity of her blue sky, her pale aerial hills, her valleys teeming with accumulated treasures of age.

◻ ◉ ◻ ◉ ◻ ◉

Didlington Hall was a 10-mile walk from Swaffham, and the young Howard Carter spent much time there, drawing in the Egyptian collection (which included the very first mummy case to have been brought to England, in the early eighteenth century), and listening to stories about ancient Egypt and its archaeology.

Lord Amherst was an early and influential member of the Egypt Exploration Fund, set up in April 1882. The collection at Didlington entered popular mythology in the spring of 1886, when it was reported that 'among the wooden shabti figures is one with a charming expression which suggested to Rider Haggard the creation of *She*'. Rider Haggard was also a local man. His romantic adventure story of Kallikrates, a priest of Isis living in ancient Egypt who is loved in vain by Ayesha or *She-Who-Must-Be-Obeyed*, the beautiful queen of Kor who has discovered the secret of eternal life, was probably read by Howard Carter. In this extract from *She* (published 1887) Ludwig Horace Holly, an academic from Cambridge University, finds himself wandering around the labyrinths of the rock city of Kor. The style of the piece resembles the mature Howard Carter's and the climax – the 2,000-year-old Ayesha mourning over the body of her beloved Kallikrates, and cursing his loved one, the Princess Amenartas – is classic Rider Haggard.

My wearied body and overstrained mind awakened all my imagination into preternatural activity. Ideas, visions, almost inspirations, floated before it with startling vividness. Most of them were grotesque enough, some were ghastly, some recalled thoughts and sensations that had for years been buried in the *débris* of my past life. But, behind and above them all, hovered the shape of that awful woman, and through them gleamed the memory of her entrancing loveliness. Up and down the cave I strode – up and down.

Suddenly I observed, what I had not noticed before, that there was a narrow aperture in the rocky wall. I took up the lamp and examined it; the aperture led to a passage. Now, I was still sufficiently sensible to remember that it is not pleasant, in such a situation as ours was, to have passages running into one's bed-chamber from no one knows where. If there are passages, people can come up them; they can come up when one is asleep. Partly to see where it went to, and partly from a restless desire to be doing something, I followed the passage. It led to a stone stair, which I descended; the stair ended in another passage, or rather tunnel, also hewn out of the bed-rock, and running, so far as I could judge, exactly beneath the gallery that led to the entrance of our rooms, and across the great central cave. I went on down it: it was as silent as the grave, but still, drawn by some sensation or attraction that I cannot describe, I followed on, my stockinged feet falling without noise on the smooth and rocky floor. When I had traversed some fifty yards of space, I came to another passage running at right angles, and here an awful thing happened to me: the sharp draught caught my lamp and extinguished it, leaving me in utter darkness in the bowels of that mysterious place. I took a couple of strides forward so as to clear the bisecting tunnel, being terribly afraid lest I should turn up it in the dark if once I got confused as to the direction, and then paused to think. What was I to do? I had no match; it seemed awful to attempt that long journey back through the utter gloom, and yet I could not stand there all night, and, if I did, probably it would not help me much, for in the bowels of the rock it would be as dark at midday as at midnight. I looked back over my shoulder – not a sight or a sound. I peered forward down the darkness: surely, far away, I saw something like the faint glow of fire. Perhaps it was a cave where I could get a light – at any rate, it was worth investigating. Slowly and painfully I crept along the tunnel, keeping my hand against its wall, and feeling at every step with my foot before I put it down, fearing lest I should fall into some pit. Thirty paces – there was a light, a broad light that came and went, shining through curtains! Fifty paces – it was close at hand! Sixty – oh, great heaven!

I was at the curtains, and they did not hang

close, so I could see clearly into the little cavern beyond them. It had all the appearance of being a tomb, and was lit up by a fire that burnt in its centre with a whitish flame and without smoke. Indeed, there, to the left, was a stone shelf with a little ledge to it three inches or so high, and on the shelf lay what I took to be a corpse; at any rate, it looked like one, with something white thrown over it. To the right was a similar shelf on which lay some broidered coverings. Over the fire bent the figure of a woman; she was sideways to me and facing the corpse, wrapped in a dark mantle that hid her like a nun's cloak. She seemed to be staring at the flickering flame. Suddenly, as I was trying to make up my mind what to do, with a convulsive movement that somehow gave an impression of despairing energy, the woman rose to her feet and cast the dark cloak from her.

It was *She* herself!

She was clothed, as I had seen her when she unveiled, in the kirtle of clinging white, cut low upon her bosom, and bound in at the waist with the barbaric double-headed snake, and, as before, her rippling black hair fell in heavy masses down her back. But her face was what caught my eye, and held me as in a vice, not this time by the force of its beauty, but by the power of fascinated terror. The beauty was still there, indeed, but the agony, the blind passion, and the awful vindictiveness displayed upon those quivering features, and in the tortured look of the upturned eyes, were such as surpass my powers of description.

For a moment she stood still, her hands raised high above her head, and as she did so the white robe slipped from her down to her golden girdle, baring the blinding loveliness of her form. She stood there, her fingers clenched, and the awful look of malevolence gathered and deepened on her face.

Suddenly, I thought of what would happen if she discovered me, and the reflection made me turn sick and faint. But even if I had known that I must die if I stopped, I do not believe that I could have moved, for I was absolutely fascinated. But still I knew my danger. Supposing she should hear me, or see me through the curtain, supposing I even sneezed, or that her magic told her that she was being watched – swift indeed would be my doom.

Down came the clenched hands to her sides, then up again above her head, and, as I am a living and honourable man, the white flame of the fire leapt up after them, almost to the roof, throwing a fierce and ghastly glare upon *She* herself, upon the white figure beneath the covering, and every scroll and detail of the rockwork.

Down came the ivory arms again, and as they did so she spoke, or rather hissed, in Arabic, in a note that curdled my blood, and for a second stopped my heart.

'Curse her, may she be everlastingly accursed.'

The arms fell and the flame sank. Up they went again, and the broad tongue of fire shot up after them; then again they fell.

'Curse her memory – accursed be the memory of the Egyptian.'

Up again, and again down . . .

And so on. The flame rose and fell, reflecting itself in her agonized eyes; the hissing sound of her terrible maledictions, and no words of mine, especially on paper, can convey how terrible they were, ran round the walls and died away in little echoes, and the fierce light and deep gloom alternated themselves on the white and dreadful form stretched upon that bier of stone.

But at length she seemed to wear herself out, and ceased. She sat herself down upon the rocky floor, and shook the dense cloud of her beautiful hair over her face and breast, and began to sob terribly in the torture of a heart-rending despair.

'Two thousand years,' she moaned – 'two thousand years have I waited and endured; but though century doth still creep on to century, and time give place to time, the sting of memory hath not lessened, the light of hope doth not shine more bright. Oh! to have lived two thousand years, with my passion eating at my heart, and with my sin ever before me. Oh, that for me life cannot bring forgetfulness! Oh, for the weary years that have been and are yet to come, and evermore to come, endless and without end!

'My love! my love! my love! ... When wilt thou come back to me who have all, and yet without thee have naught? What is there that I can do? What? What? What? And perchance she – perchance that Egyptian doth abide with thee where thou art, and mock my memory. Oh, why could I not die with thee, I who slew thee? Alas, that I cannot die! Alas! Alas!' and she flung herself prone upon the ground, and sobbed and wept till I thought her heart must burst.

Suddenly she ceased, raised herself to her feet, rearranged her robe, and, tossing back her long locks impatiently, swept across to where the figure lay upon the stone.

'Oh Kallikrates,' she cried, and I trembled at the name, 'I must look upon thy face again, though it be agony. It is a generation since I looked upon thee whom I slew – slew with mine own hand,' and with trembling fingers she seized the corner of the sheet-like wrapping that covered the form upon the stone bier, and then paused. When she spoke again, it was in a kind of awed whisper, as though her idea were terrible even to herself.

'Shall I raise thee,' she said, apparently addressing the corpse, 'so that thou standest there before me, as of old? I *can* do it,' and she held out her hands over the sheeted dead, while her whole frame became rigid and terrible to see, and her eyes grew fixed and dull. I shrank in horror behind the curtain, my hair stood up upon my head, and whether it was my imagination or a fact I am unable to say, but I thought that the quiet form beneath the covering began to quiver, and the winding sheet to lift as though it lay on the breast of one who slept. Suddenly she withdrew her hands, and the motion of the corpse seemed to me to cease.

'What is the use?' she said gloomily. 'Of what use is it to recall the semblance of life when I cannot recall the spirit? Even if thou stoodest before me thou wouldst not know me, and couldst but do what I bid thee. The life in thee would be *my* life, and not *thy* life, Kallikrates.'

For a moment she stood there brooding, and then cast herself down on her knees beside the form, and began to press her lips against the sheet, and weep. There was something so horrible about the sight of this awe-inspiring woman letting loose her passion on the dead – so much more horrible even than anything that had gone before, that I could no longer bear to look at it, and, turning, began to creep, shaking as I was in every limb, slowly along the pitch-dark passage, feeling in my trembling heart that I had a vision of a Soul in Hell.

On I stumbled, I scarcely know how. Twice I fell, once I turned up the bisecting passage, but fortunately found out my mistake in time. For twenty minutes or more I crept along, till at last it occurred to me that I must have passed the little stair by which I descended. So, utterly exhausted, and nearly frightened to death, I sank down at length there on the stone flooring, and sank into oblivion.

When I came to I noticed a faint ray of light in the passage just behind me. I crept to it, and found it was the little stair down which the weak dawn was stealing. Passing up it I gained my chamber in safety, and, flinging myself on the couch, was soon lost in slumber or rather stupor.

■ ◉ ▣ ◉ ■ ◉

It was Lady Amherst who introduced the young Carter to the Eyptologist Percy Newberry, who in turn introduced him to Amelia Blandford Edwards, a popular novelist and founder of the Egypt Exploration Fund in London. The energetic Amelia Edwards, translator of *A Lady's Captivity Among Chinese Pirates* and author of the best-selling *The Patagonian Brothers*, *Barbara's History* and *Lord Brackenbury*, as well as travel books such as *Untrodden Peaks and Unfrequented Valleys*, is best known today for her book *One Thousand Miles Up the Nile* (1877), the chronicle of a river journey with several friends which took place in 1873–4.

'Miss Edwards,' wrote a critic, 'appears to have gone about the world open-eyed, and with note-book in hand, so vivid are some of her portraits.' The book was written, as she characteristically put it, because 'We cannot all be profoundly learned, but we can at least do our best to understand what we see.' It was Amelia Edwards – who, after the foundation of the Fund, campaigned tirelessly for the preservation of Egyptian monuments and, then, for women's suffrage – who gave Howard Carter his first proper job. As he recalled:

'I was sent to Egypt at the age of seventeen and a half, with a few pounds in my pocket but with a job as assistant draughtsman to the branch of the Egypt Exploration Fund [afterwards named the Egypt Exploration Society] called the Archaeological Survey of Egypt. During the summer before I left England, I did some preparatory work . . . in the British Museum . . . studying and copying the manuscripts, preserved in the Museum folios of Robert Hay, an explorer and patron of explorers who, during the first part of the nineteenth century, made a collection of "detailed and often minutely accurate drawings . . . of the Egyptian monuments".'

This extract from *One Thousand Miles up the Nile* is also concerned with the work of Robert Hay, and presents something of a contrast with Howard Carter's first experiences of Egypt. Amelia Edwards's party, including 'The Idle Man', 'The Painter' and herself, 'The Writer', has just recovered from a boat race with rival travellers aboard the *Bagstones*, and has recently visited the magnificent temple of Abu Simbel.

We now despaired of ever seeing a crocodile; and but for a trail that our men discovered on the island opposite, we should almost have ceased to believed that there were crocodiles in Egypt. The marks were quite fresh when we went to look at them. The creature had been basking high and dry in the sun, and this was the point at which he had gone down again to the river. The damp sand at the water's edge had taken the mould of his huge fleshy paws, and even of the jointed armour of his tail, though this last impression was somewhat blurred by the final rush with which he had taken to the water. I doubt if Robinson Crusoe, when he saw the famous footprint on the shore, was more excited than we of the *Philae* at sight of this genuine and undeniable trail.

As for the Idle Man, he flew at once to arms and made ready for the fray. He caused a shallow grave to be dug for himself a few yards from the spot; then went and lay in it for hours together, morning after morning, under the full blaze of the sun, – flat, patient, alert, – with his gun ready cocked, and a Pall Mall Budget up his back. It was not his fault if he narrowly escaped sunstroke, and had his labour for his reward. That crocodile was too clever for him, and took care never to come back.

Our sailors, meanwhile, though well pleased with an occasional holiday, began to find Abou Simbel monotonous. As long as the *Bagstones* stayed, the two crews met every evening to smoke, and dance, and sing their quaint roundelays together. But when rumours came of wonderful things already done this winter above Wady Halfeh – rumours that represented the Second Cataract as a populous solitude of crocodiles – then our faithful consort slipped away one morning before sunrise, and the *Philae* was left companionless.

At this juncture, seeing that the men's time hung heavy on their hands, our Painter conceived the idea of setting them to clean the face of the northernmost Colossus, still disfigured by the plaster left on it when the great cast was taken by Mr Hay more than half a century before. This happy thought was promptly carried into effect. A scaffolding of spars and oars was at once improvised, and the men, delighted as children at play, were soon swarming all over the huge head, just as the carvers may have swarmed over it in the days when Rameses was king.

All they had to do was to remove any small lumps that might yet adhere to the surface, and then tint the white patches with coffee. This they did with bits of sponge tied to the ends of

sticks; but Reïs Hassan, as a mark of dignity, had one of the Painter's old brushes, of which he was immensely proud.

It took them three afternoons to complete the job; and we were all sorry when it came to an end. To see Reïs Hassan artistically touching up a gigantic nose almost as long as himself; Riskalli and the cook-boy staggering to and fro with relays of coffee, brewed 'thick and slab' for the purpose; Salame perched cross-legged, like some complacent imp, on the towering rim of the great pschent overhead; the rest chattering and skipping about the scaffolding like monkeys, was, I will venture to say, a sight more comic than has ever been seen at Abou Simbel before or since.

Rameses' appetite for coffee was prodigious. He consumed I know not how many gallons a day. Our cook stood aghast at the demand made upon his stores. Never before had he been called upon to provide for a guest whose mouth measured three feet and a half in width.

Still, the result justified the expenditure. The coffee proved a capital match for the sandstone; and though it was not possible wholly to restore the uniformity of the original surface, we at least succeeded in obliterating those ghastly splotches, which for so many years have marred this beautiful face as with the unsightliness of leprosy.

What with boating, fishing, lying in wait for crocodiles, cleaning the colossus, and filling reams of thin letter paper to friends at home, we got through the first week quickly enough — the Painter and the Writer working hard, meanwhile, in their respective ways; the Painter on his big canvas in front of the Temple; the Writer shifting her little tent as she

listed.

Now, although the most delightful occupation in life is undoubtedly sketching, it must be admitted that the sketcher at Abou Simbel works under difficulties. Foremost among these comes the difficulty of position. The great Temple stands within about twenty-five yards of the brink of the bank, and the lesser Temple within as many feet; so that to get far enough from one's subject is simply impossible. The present Writer sketched the small Temple from the deck of the dahabeeyah; there being no point of view obtainable on shore.

Next comes the difficulty of colour. Everything, except the sky and the river, is yellow — yellow, that is to say, 'with a difference'; yellow ranging through every gradation of orange, maize, apricot, gold, and buff. The mountains are sandstone; the Temples are sandstone; the sandslope is powdered sandstone from the sandstone desert. In all these objects, the scale of colour is necessarily the same. Even the shadows, glowing with reflected light, give back tempered repetitions of the dominant hue. Hence it follows that he who strives, however humbly, to reproduce the facts of the scene before him, is compelled, *bon gré, mal gré*, to execute what some of our young painters would now-a-days call a Symphony in Yellow.

Lastly, there are the minor inconveniences of sun, sand, wind, and flies. The whole place radiates heat, and seems almost to radiate light. The glare from above and the glare from below are alike intolerable. Dazzled, blinded, unable to even look at his subject without the aid of smoke-coloured glasses, the sketcher whose tent is pitched upon the sandslope over against the great Temple enjoys a foretaste of cremation.

When the wind blows from the north (which at this time of the year is almost always) the heat is perhaps less distressing, but the sand is maddening. It fills your hair, your eyes, your water-bottles; silts up your colour-box; dries into your skies; and reduces your Chinese white to a gritty paste the colour of salad-dressing. As for the flies, they have a morbid appetite for water-colours. They follow your wet brush along the paper, leave their legs in the yellow ochre, and plunge with avidity into every little pool of cobalt as it is mixed ready for use. Nothing disagrees with them; nothing poisons them – not even olive-green.

It was a delightful time, however – delightful alike for those who worked and those who rested – and these small troubles counted for nothing in the scale ...

It was now the fifth day after our return from Wady Halfeh, when an event occurred that roused us to an unwonted pitch of excitement, and kept us at high pressure throughout the rest of our time.

The day was Sunday; the date February 16th, 1874; the time, according to *Philae* reckoning, about eleven a.m., when the Painter, enjoying his seventh day's holiday after his own fashion, went strolling about among the rocks. He happened to turn his step southwards, and, passing the front of the Great Temple, climbed to the top of a little shapeless mound of fallen cliff, and sand, and crude-brick wall, just against the corner where the mountain slopes down to the river. Immediately round this corner, looking almost due south, and approachable by only a narrow

ledge of rock, are two votive tablets sculptured and painted, both of the thirty-eighth year of Rameses II. We had seen these from the river as we came back from Wady Halfeh, and had remarked how fine the view must be from that point. Beyond the fact that they are coloured, and that the colour upon them is still bright, there is nothing remarkable about these inscriptions. There are many such at Abou Simbel. Our Painter did not, therefore, come here to examine the tablets; he was attracted solely by the view.

Turning back presently, his attention was arrested by some much mutilated sculptures on the face of the rock, a few yards nearer the south buttress of the Temple. He had seen these sculptures before – so, indeed, had I, when wandering about that first day in search of a point of view – without especially remarking them. The relief was low; the execution slight; and the surface so broken away that only a few confused outlines remained.

The thing that now caught the Painter's eye, however, was a long crack running transversely down the face of the rock. It was such a crack as might have been caused, one would say, by blasting.

He stooped – cleared the sand away a little with his hand – observed that the crack widened – poked in the point of his stick; and found that it penetrated to a depth of two or three feet. Even then, it seemed to him to stop, not because it encountered any obstacle, but because the crack was not wide enough to admit the thick end of the stick.

This surprised him. No mere fault in the natural rock, he thought, would go so deep. He scooped away a little more sand; and still the cleft widened. He introduced the stick a second time. It was a long palm-stick like an alpenstock, and it measured about five feet in length. When he probed the cleft with it this second time, it went in freely up to where he held it in his hand – that is to say, to a depth of quite four feet.

Convinced now that there was some hidden cavity in the rock, he carefully examined the surface. There were yet visible a few hieroglyphic characters and part of two cartouches, as well as some battered outlines of what had once been figures. The heads of these figures were gone (the face of the rock, with whatever may have been sculptured upon it, having come away bodily at this point), while from the waist downwards they were hidden under the sand. Only some hands and arms, in short, could be made out.

They were the hands and arms, apparently, of four figures; two in the centre of the composition, and two at the extremities. The two centre ones, which seemed to be back to back, probably represented gods; the outer ones, worshippers.

All at once, it flashed upon the Painter that he had seen this kind of group many a time before – *and generally over a doorway.*

Feeling sure now that he was on the brink of a discovery, he came back; fetched away Salame and Mehemet Ali; and, without saying a syllable to any one, set to work with these two to scrape away the sand at the spot where the crack widened.

Meanwhile, the luncheon bell having rung thrice, we concluded that the Painter had rambled off somewhere into the desert; and so sat down without him. Towards the close of the meal, however, came a pencilled note, the contents of which ran as follows:

'Pray come immediately – I have found the entrance to a tomb. Please send some sandwiches—A. M'C.'

To follow the messenger at once to the scene of action was the general impulse. In less than ten minutes we were there, asking breathless questions, peeping in through the fast-widening aperture, and helping to clear away the sand.

All that Sunday afternoon, heedless of possible sunstroke, unconscious of fatigue, we toiled upon our hands and knees, as for bare life, under the burning sun. We had all the crew up, working like tigers. Every one helped; even the dragoman and the two maids. More than once, when we paused for a moment's breathing space, we said to each other: 'If those at home could see us, what would they say!'

◨ ◉ ◨ ◉ ◨ ◉

The Painter's discovery turns out to be not a tomb (as they had all hoped) but a small chapel built on to the Great Temple. Amelia Edwards, far from being disheartened by this, muses about the sad state of Egyptian monuments in general:

'The tourist carves it all over with names and dates, and in some instances with caricatures. The student of Egyptology, by taking wet paper "squeezes", sponges away every vestige of the original colour. The "collector" buys and carries off everything of value that he can get; and the Arab steals for him. The work of destruction, meanwhile, goes on apace. There is no one to prevent it; there is no one to discourage it . . . The Louvre contains a full-length portrait of Seti I, cut out bodily from the walls of his sepulchre in the Valley of the Tombs of the Kings. The Museums of Berlin, of Turin, of Florence, are rich in spoils which tell their own lamentable tale. When science leads the way, is it wonderful that ignorance should follow?'

Tactfully, she omitted any British museums from her list, but the point was made. And six years later she helped to found the Egypt Exploration Fund, in order to do something about it. Howard Carter's arrival in Egypt, under the Fund's aegis, was very different. No champagne suppers, or boat races, or picnics in the desert for him; just some last-minute advice from his father – 'in Victoria station . . . with a last farewell, he gave me permission to smoke and presented me with a pound tin of suitable tobacco and a number of packets of OG cigarette papers as the train slowly rolled out of the station' – and a particularly uncomfortable rail journey from Boulak station in Cairo.

In due course we arrive at the railway station for Beni Hasan. Alighting from a dusty train, stiff and dirty after a long journey, does not fill one with enthusiasm. Later in the afternoon, with our impedimenta laden upon donkeys, we rode through the cultivated fields to the river, crossed over to the east bank in an antiquated native ferry boat and in the dark we climbed up to the rock terrace of the escarpment where the tombs are situated. There, as the twilight fell silently upon those dull-coloured rock cliffs, there was a look of gloom, an aspect of dreary

isolation, which gave rise to disturbed phantoms that sometimes haunt the wind on the eve of adventure.

We encamped in a spacious undecorated rock tomb chapel, ourselves including the Nubian cook, all in one chamber. The wee donkey, employed for bringing water and other supplies, was lodged in a small cave nearby.

It was my first acquaintance of Upper Egypt and camp life in a tomb. The life of an archaeologist was a very different affair in those days from what it is now, rough and ready, certainly not elaborate, but good enough for those who are not over-fastidious and certainly healthy, if only from the point of view of temperature. That warm, dry, motionless atmosphere with just one doorway for ingress and egress, light and air, created a strange sensation as I lay somewhat bewildered, trying to sleep on a roughly made palm-branch bed. It also has to be remembered that an archaeologist has to live where he can, not where he would.

But for me real sleep was out of the question. For most of the night I watched the brilliant starry heavens through the doorway, listened to the faint fluttering of the bats that flitter restlessly around the chamber, and in imagination called up strange spirits from the past until the first gleam of dawn, when, from sheer fatigue, I fell into a deep sleep.

It must have been at least an hour after sunrise that I woke, and became conscious of the glorious scene that was before me. The rock chamber in which we were encamped was high up on the slope of the cliffs, and from its doorway one saw the luxuriant Nile Valley stretched afar below. In the near distance, first came the edge of the tawny undulating desert plain. Then a little farther, arable land profuse of growing crops which in that early morning sunlight exuberate, rich and green, and then, intersecting its midst, was the Nile, like a silver ribbon, winding its way towards the Southern horizon where it melted into space.

Above the glorious horizon the pure blue heavens were flecked with tiny clouds, white as from the fleece of a lamb. It was a glorious panorama which made one forget that troubled and strange first night.

�«◎◘◎◘◎»

Howard Carter was employed as an assistant draughtsman to trace the tomb paintings of Beni Hasan, as part of the 'Archaeological Survey'. On the way there he had first met the great Egyptologist Flinders Petrie, who had impressed him mightily: 'as the son of an artist, what perhaps interested me most, besides the extent and precision of his knowledge, was his recognition and love of fine art.' And it was also the special qualities of the art on the walls at Beni Hasan which intrigued him: from his background, it was a subject on which he felt he was entitled to a point of view.

The immense dignity and restraint of Egyptian art struck me the moment I saw it. I realized that it was an art conventional to the utmost degree, yet while adhering strictly to rules and principles, it remained essentially faithful to the nature of the thing it portrayed.

Indeed, from the moment I began to study it, I was struck by the beauty of its line upon which it insists and, above all, its deep understanding in interpreting character. It was for

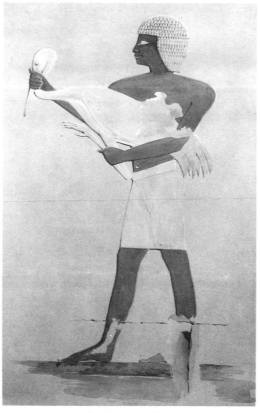

Copy of wall painting by Howard Carter.

that reason and for no other reason, that when I began my work at Beni Hasan, I was immensely disappointed with the method I was obliged to employ to copy that art, so dependent upon its purity of line.

Instead of copying those wall paintings, as anyone who practises the fine arts would do, to commence and finish a facsimile beside the original with a free hand, to my horror I found the modus operandi in force was to hang large sheets of tracing paper upon the walls and thus with a soft pencil trace the scenes upon them, no matter whether the scenes were painted in the flat, sculptured or in relief. No matter whether the wall surfaces were smooth or granular.

These completed tracings were then to be rolled up, transported to England, where they would be inked in with a brush and all inside the outlines of the figures filled in black like a silhouette; as it proved afterwards, often by persons without any knowledge of the origin of the drawing. These blackened tracings were then reduced to a very small scale by the process known as photo-lithography.

Needless to say, from an art point of view, the results were far from being satisfactory. However, I was young, it was my first experience and in the struggle for existence I had necessarily to obey and to carry out extraordinary methods of producing those beautiful Egyptian records, enhanced by the romance of an immense antiquity.

It is a common opinion that a tracing is an accurate method of rendering a copy of an original work of art, drawing or painting. As far as measurement goes, that might be so. But as tracings rarely if ever embody the character or understanding of the line traced, the original is thus dishonoured by its very soul left out. Especially of an art like that of the Egyptians that tolerates not a single line without care. Evidently the aim of the survey was more in mechanical exactitude than reproducing that ancient art in all its fairness.

Great was my joy when at last I was set to work upon making careful water-colour drawings of some of the more important details and scenes upon the walls of these tombs.

■ ◉ ■ ◉ ■ ◉

On one memorable occasion, Carter took time off to set out with a small group of colleagues, in search of the lost tomb of the pharaoh Akhenaton at El-Amarna. As a result of the excavation of El-Amarna by Petrie, Akhenaton was to become a cult figure in Egyptological circles – James Henry Breasted was to call him the first real personality in human history – and subsequently within popular culture: the question of the pharaoh's monotheism aroused particular interest, and Arthur Weigall was to write in 1923, 'By no other religion in the world is Christianity so closely approached as by the faith of Akhenaton.'

Early in the morning preceding Christmas Day, we mounted the Beduin Sheikh Sid's camels and, with some food stuffed in the saddle bags, some water in the zamzammia (water bottles) we started off upon the voyage of discovery. We crossed the plain of El Bershah, skirted along the base of the perpendicular cliffs of Sheikh Saïd that reach the river bank, where about noon we gained the open plain of El Amarna, where the picturesque ruins of the city of Akh-en-Aten lie bordering the palm groves that grow along the narrow strip of cultivated land. From there we trailed across the great open desert plain in a south-eastern direction, following the old beaten path of the *Budu*, at the far end of which, a large wide open valley situated at the south-eastern corner of the plain.

At the mouth, we struck an ancient road which led up the bed of the valley. This we followed over undulating ground for about an hour, when it took a sharp turn to the left, (eastward), and wound up a pass to the high plateau. On the barren boulder-bestrewn plateau, the tract of the ancient road was very clear, swept clear of all stones and obstacles, and in parts looking as if it had been made quite recently.

This road raised our hopes and excited us not a little. What could it really be? So conspicuous, why had it so long escaped archaeologists? These were the questions we asked ourselves, as we continued to follow it over hill and dale.

After two hours we reached some mounds of debris thrown from some ancient excavation. Here we dismounted, stiff and tired from the rolling gait of the camels. In the midst of these mounds were two extensive deep cuttings, not the tomb of Akh-en-Aten, but the famous Hat Nub quarries, their existence hitherto known only from records upon the monuments . . .

But oh! that camel – 'Ship of the Desert', Garmal, Hagîn or Dalul, 'Camelus dromedarius' of the genus *Tylopoda* (boss-footed), or whatever you may like to call him – where did not my body feel him? Fortunately, in the early morning, I had put several sheets of newspaper in my nether garments hence I was not so chafed as I might have been, nevertheless, I ached all over. The Beduins told me that camels live to a great age. Mine, I think, must once have formed part of the wealth of the patriarch Job, or maybe was one of the camels, laden with spices, that Joseph was sold by his brothers.

A camel's hump is said to vary in size according to the condition of the animal. My old beast must have been in excellent condition; he appeared to have a lump everywhere. He certainly had 'the hump', for no matter whether I put a pocket handkerchief in the saddle bag, or

took one out he grumbled inwardly with a gurgle and outwardly with a bubbling roar. I rode him astride, sometimes cross-wise, sometimes side-ways, but noways could I get used to his rolling side to side wobble. Do what I liked! he marched on! and if a tempting piece of green herbage allured him out of his path, he continued to walk on in this new direction simply because he was too dull to turn back into the right road of his own accord. Neither did he remind me of a scent bottle. In a word, I wished he had left his individuality at home – physically and temperamentally.

But I must not run down the poor beast too much, for he is most useful, has many good qualities, and one must remember that there is as much difference between a pack-camel and a riding-camel (hagîn), as between a thoroughbred race-horse and a cart-horse. His capacity for travelling long distances without water – owing to special structural modifications in the stomach – makes him specially valuable. His hair is woven into a variety of stuffs, used by the Bedu for clothing and tenting, and camel's milk forms an excellent and nutricious beverage. He kneels and rises at a given signal, but refuses to get up if over-laden. He may in other ways be stupid but he is very docile. He takes little heed of his master, still only partially domesticated; neither is he rendered serviceable by any cooperation on his own part, save extreme perseverance. However, he performs a very kindly act: when his rider is over-taken by a sand storm, he falls on his knees, stretches his head and long neck along the ground, closes his nostrils, and remains thus motionless, hence affording shelter for his rider, till the atmosphere clears.

With regard to beauty, the prettiest thing about him is the saddle with which the Bedu adorns him . . .

We were over twenty-five miles from Deir Bersha, and at least twelve miles from any kind of habitation. Our Bedu guides, who had walked on foot the whole way, and who had given a kindly leading hand to the camels whenever they had a difficult piece of ground to negotiate, suggested that we should sleep the night in the village of Haggi-Qaudîl.

We therefore decided that that was our best course, and to beg a night's lodging from W. M. Flinders Petrie, who had built a small mud house on the outskirts of that village, whence he was exploring the ruins of that ancient city of Akh-en-Aten . . .

At that time I think perhaps I was the most fortunate member [of the team], for within the next few days I had to leave the expedition. By a mutual arrangement, I had been seconded to W. M. Flinders Petrie, under whom I was to work on behalf of Lord Amherst of Hackney, who had taken over part of Petrie's concession at El-Amarna. A transformation from a draughtsman to excavator. Although I had always a longing to excavate, it was in fact one of my daydreams in life, I must admit to misgivings regarding this sudden new departure. The vagueness of the project for which I had not any previous experience, moreover, my knowledge of Arabic was still embryonic. It was all rather perplexing. At the moment I felt like one of the order of insects called 'Lepidoptera', or rather what I imagined those insects must feel when going through life cycles. However, in spite of this fact, in the morning I arose earlier than usual and set myself, with some enthusiasm, to arrange my things and pack. In this way began another phase in my career.

After many farewells, I made my way across the desert, by camel. The sense of vast space and loneliness made me feel not a little homesick. Sheikh Sid, who accompanied me, babbling like a brook the whole way in his curious Arabic, of which I understood but little.

By noon I arrived at Flinders Petrie's domain at Haggi-Qaudîl. He had not yet returned from his work, but one of his men explained to me that he would come shortly for lunch.

So I paid off Sheikh Sid, who, after unloading my things, made me understand that he was an eternal friend and servant. He returned immediately to his Orbâu (people). While waiting I wandered about the precincts of Petrie's establishment, and among other things I noticed behind his own particular dwelling a large stack of sun-dried mud bricks and a mortar bed full of freshly prepared mud mortar mixed with a little straw; the meaning of which intrigued me.

A half-hour had hardly elapsed when Petrie came from his works. He greeted and received me very kindly, and suggested that we sat down immediately for lunch. For about an hour after lunch, he explained to me my various future duties, of which I only took in but a vague conception. I gleaned, however, that I was to spend a week watching him at work and then, with a number of workmen that he would hand over to me, I would start upon digging in the section of the ancient town he had portioned off for Lord Amherst.

One of the first questions he asked was whether I had any money with me. When I told him that I had received fifty pounds to start with, he said, 'Then wait until it is dark and bury them!'

We spent rather an uncommunicative first evening. Petrie hardly said a word unless addressed. Then, indeed, he would make the briefest reply and betook himself back into his thoughts in mind. He was absorbed, I imagine, in some abstract problem in connection with his investigations. 'Take my advice,' he said eventually, 'and get to bed as soon as you can, I shall be routing you out at day-break, so that you may build a room for yourself.' This ended my first night at Haggi-Qaudîl, and solved the problem of those bricks and mortar . . .

For a roof I was given a number of deal boards and a quantity of 'dhurra' straw by which to form a kind of thatch. For a door a native 'hasûra' (rush mat) was also supplied and to be suspended by nails from the wooden lintel. The inner surfaces of the walls were not to be plastered; thereby, the cavities between the bricks afforded perfect hiding places for beetles, spiders – big fat spiders, as time proved – and scorpions.

For chair and table, empty boxes and packing cases were provided. A small paraffin lamp for cooking. A number of cases containing each a complete month's stores – tinned foods etc. – were also handed over to me, all charged to my account with strict instructions to keep the empty tins and boxes for antiquities. Sheets, table clothes and napkins were disapproved and expelled, but the luxury of the substitute, old newspapers, was allowed. Another peculiarity that I discovered was that servants were tabooed. One had to make one's own bed, clean up the slops, prepare and cook one's meals, wash up; in fact no servant of any kind was permitted within the domain.

Petrie, without question, was a distinguished Egyptologist, a genius endowed with an extraordinary aptitude for interpreting past history from out of chaos, who taught us the ABC of archaeological research work and excavation in Egypt, for which and for whom, I had a deep reverence; nevertheless, I found him a pedant.

My cocoon thus completed without any silken lining! now for the metamorphosis – the sudden bursting into function of new organs – the histolysis and histogenesis – from draughtsman to an excavator. I was in haste to begin the reformation!

◨ ◉ ◧ ◉ ◧ ◉

In October 1893 Howard Carter accepted a new post as draughtsman with the Egypt Exploration Fund at El-Deir-el-Bahari, where the cliffside mortuary temple of Queen Hatshepsut was in the process of being cleared. His comments on the techniques of copying inscriptions and wall paintings which were then commonly used owe a lot to the thinking of the British Arts and Crafts Movement in the late nineteenth century, and in particular to the writings of John Ruskin. It was Ruskin who had written, 'The best art is that which proceeds from the heart, that which involves all the emotions – associates these with the head, yet as inferior to the heart; and the hand, yet as inferior to the heart and head; and thus brings out the *whole* person', and Carter continued to quote Ruskin, with approval, in Volume 2 of his book *The Discovery of the Tomb of Tutankhamen*. Carter's remarks about 'honest work, a free hand, a good pencil and suitable paper', with their emphasis on the value of solid craftsmanship, were embedded in the arts and crafts tradition in which he grew up.

My task was to copy, for the purpose of reproduction, all these important sculptures and historical inscriptions [in the mortuary temple] . . .

I have remarked upon the unsatisfactory methods generally employed when copying Egyptian art for archaeological purposes. And now I feel it incumbent upon me to devote a few paragraphs on this subject. A problem which is intensified by the fact that to obtain really satisfactory results, the skill of the Egyptian artists who made those beautiful reliefs is required. There is also another difficulty, as most of the Egyptian themes depend so largely upon their size, their relative dimensions, they, when reduced to a common scale, must lose some of their natural grandeur. Those ancient Egyptians understood more than most nations of antiquity the worth and the power of dimension. The very dignity of their monuments, the figures with which they adorned them, depended largely upon this factor. For instance, to use a simile, the most perfect replica of the great pyramid, let us say two inches high, would never convey to the mind the grandeur of that great but simple cairn. The impression conveyed by it would be not even a faint shadow of the reality. But in our case, as only a convenient scale can be considered in the problem of reproducing the works in book form, should we not employ our very best means to convey all the other subtleties of this art?

To my mind this question has but one answer. The same infinite pains and competency to meet the task should be employed as in the case of any other archaeological problem. The more so in this case, for Egyptian art depends so much upon its graceful and understanding line.

In connection with Egyptological work I could never quite understand the axiom, 'Mechanical exactitude of facsimile-copying is required rather than free hand or purely artistic work.' It has always struck me that in this case, when using the term 'mechanical exactitude', a very important point is forgotten: that mechanical exactitude when copying in art may not be necessarily wholly accurate. This by leaving out the intellectual part of the art. 'In true art,' says Ruskin, 'the head, the hand, and the heart of man go together.' The ambiguous expression 'purely artistic work' has also been a puzzle to me. Unless it means, as it seems to suggest, 'inaccuracy'! But why purely artistic work should be necessarily inaccurate I fail to fathom.

We must recollect that mechanical copying incorporates nothing of an art itself; no more than a child carefully tracing a map (about the making of which the child knows nothing) for a lesson in geography.

> Unknown to them the subtle skill
> With which the artist eye can trace
> In rock and tree, and lake and hill,
> The outlines of divinest grace.

I wish in no way to appear cynical, that is the last thing it would be proper for me to be, but as there exists an idea that tracing is an accurate method of obtaining a copy of a work of art, I would like to point out that it is a mistaken idea that the action of following an original line with a pencil point, and thus delineating a line upon tracing paper, is analogous to something being drawn over a surface and leaving a mark. The line thus made may be in many ways accurate, careful, or even an excellent pattern, but the line so made will lack meaning, it will lack the knowledge required if it is to be in conformity with truth. The traced line may be an accurate copy of detail, size and proportion, but in no way will it express the subtle rendering in the fact of the third dimension of form. To do this, the delineator must have the knowledge of the form – that which makes up the form – he is rendering, and thus put intelligent expression in his line, which appeals to all intellectual minds. In fact, any method of copying that limits the student from such expression to mere mechanical drawing is erroneous.

To illustrate my meaning, let the student trace, and with care, a good portrait (picture or photograph) of a person we know. When the tracing is completed, let us examine it and see what it is like. What we will find lacking in the tracing of the portrait, will be also missing in the tracing of an ancient art, only in the latter case the defects will not be quite so obvoius because we are familiar with that art.

When reproducing an ancient art, let us by all means be accurate, and employ every kind of mechanical aid to obtain that objective, but let that mechanical aid be our assistant, not our master!

Donatello said, 'I give you the whole art of sculpture when I tell you to draw.' Through archaeological research in Egypt we have learnt that those ancient Egyptians certainly knew how to draw. Egyptian sculptures and paintings give a clearer and more vivid idea of a subject than Egyptian literature. They not only give pleasure to the spectator but they are easier understood by the ordinary person than the hieroglyphs. By sculpture and painting the Egyptian represents nature, but he worked under conditions which bound him, and fine as his works are, like their literature, they are full of polite fiction, of which the oriental world has always been singularly tolerant. Their works, therefore, cannot be legitimately copied without a proper knowledge of drawing. And as Egyptian art pours its riches into our laps, should we not honour it with the best of our ability?

My excuse for this somewhat lengthy exercise is simply because I felt that if I attempted to copy the scenes sculptured upon the walls of Hat-Shep-Sut's mortuary temple by the prevailing system of tracing, the essential charm of those beautiful reliefs would have vanished in my copy . . . I tried many expedients, but they resolved in the simple solution. To first observe the fundamental laws of Egyptian art, how it eliminates the unessentials, to copy that art accurately and intelligently with honest work, a free hand, a good pencil, and suitable paper.

All my life I have looked back on Deir-el-Bahari as a place having a charm of its own, although I cannot say it was a perfect situation to live in except for the winter months. The surrounding cliffs which formed a sun trap made it impossible to live there during the warmer months. But artistically the site was a continual joy.

The temple setting at Deir-el-Bahari, with the delicate sculptured reliefs on its walls, was to be my workplace for the next 6 years. What natural talent as an artist [I had] now was to support me in my every day's work. After my time with Flinders Petrie and his magnificent knowledge and training, it was my great desire to be an excavator. To me that calling had an extraordinary attraction, and though my fingers itched to dig and discover, this would have to wait some time yet. To be a complete excavator one has to start by gaining knowledge of the ancient Egyptian way of life, the religious rites and rules.

Like a detective investigating a crime, every scrap of information must be learnt, every clue observed and analysed. The all-important method used by the Egyptian craftsman, the funerary protocol, together with the motives of these who chose the sacred burial places of their beloved kings, must be understood so that one knows where to excavate. So much time, energy and expense has been lost by those who failed to learn often the simplest message from the past.

However, for some time the pen and pencil were to be my tools rather than the spade, my gaze would be on to white paper rather than dark underground cavities, so much still waits to be found and wait it must till my knowledge grows. My pen served me well; although the next 6 years were hard work, I learnt much more of Egyptian art, its severe simplicity, than

in any other place or time.

◻ ◉ ◻ ◉ ◻ ◉

Howard Carter continued to spend his leisure hours birdwatching, and drawing, and – unusually for the period – mixing with the local villagers and workmen.

By this time I was able to converse with the people among whom I was residing with tolerable ease. So, to while away the darker nights, when the pestilential gnats and midges tired me out of all patience, I occasionally indulged in the diversions of the 'guest house' of the headman or mayor of the villages. Here in the evenings the select men of the village – the sheikhs and the fathers of the people – are generally gathered, and contrasting with these, a fair representation of the commonalty.

I must admit, however, that this practice was liable to serious criticism: some colleagues in the government service frowned upon it as a bad habit. They thought it degrading. But whether that be a fact or not, what I found was so valuable in this practice, or study, if it can be called such, was that it thereby brought me into contact with people with whom I had to deal. It enabled me to study their manners and customs, and there can be no doubt that by it I acquired to a large extent their opinion and at least some of their confidence.

At this coffee hearth one could at times listen to reciters of romances, who, without book, commit their subject to memory, afford attractive entertainment, and are often highly amusing. Some of their recitations contain a deal of history and romance. Moreover, they are told in lively and dramatic manner, with moral teaching, and are extremely indecent. They therefore cannot be repeated.

On 1 January 1900 Carter took up an appointment as Inspector of Monuments of Upper Egypt, reporting to the French-administered Antiquities Service. His job was to organize a 'system for the protection of the tombs' (including the installation of iron gates and, in some cases in the Valley of the Kings, electric lighting), and to oversee the security of the monuments. This occasionally gave him the opportunity to behave – as he put it – 'like a detective investigating a crime', as well as an excavator who had learnt his trade in a 'hands-on' way.

At home the eye travels over crofts and pastures, the rounded forms of full-foliaged trees, a never-ending festival of nature. Here, serenity characterizes this eastern landscape, where a race once lived beneath the pure light of the sun.

Everyone who has been to an eastern country will agree that a few weeks' experience on the spot is far more helpful to realize the scene than descriptions, pictures and photographs. We may have read the most vivid and accurate accounts, we may have pored over maps and plans, yet reality will burst upon us like a revelation . . .

What happened was this. To stimulate local popular sympathy towards Amenophis II, I purposely gave as much publicity as possible of the fact that his mummy had been robbed in ancient times, and there was nothing of value left upon it. Perhaps that was where I made my mistake. For in spite of the fact, a modern tomb-robber, possibly in connivance with the guard, forced open the steel gate of the tomb and subjected Amenophis to another rifling.

According to the declaration made by the guard, late in the evening of 24 November 1901, they were surprised by a masked band of robbers who threatened to shoot them if they attempted to move or raise an alarm. They alleged that some of the robbers stood guard over them, while the remainder broke into the tomb of Amenophis, robbed it, and escaped with their plunder. The remaining robbers then went away by the mountain pass in the direction of Medinet-Habou. The guard also declared that they followed the robbers, but after being shot at three times they gave up the chase. The chief of the guard then repaired to the village, reported the raid to Monsûr Effendi, the local inspector. Monsûr Effendi advised the Ombdah (mayor) of the village, who, with some of the village gaffirs (guards), went to the Valley of the Kings. There they discovered that the royal mummy had been taken out of its sarcophagus and that its wrappings had been ripped off. The mummy on the boat in the antechamber had been broken and thrown on the floor, and the boat was missing. The Ombdah informed the police authorities at Luxor. The police, accompanied by the Parquet (the official concerned in the administration of law), made an investigation the following day.

The guard alleged that they were able to recognize three of the robbers. As these men were inhabitants of the village of Gurna, they were immediately arrested and also locked up by the guard provisionally.

At the time of these happenings, I was at Kom Ombo, eighty miles south of Luxor. When I arrived at Aswan I found a telegram from Monsûr Effendi requesting me to return to Luxor immediately. At Luxor station I was met by Monsûr Effendi, who informed me of what had taken place. I therefore went to the Parquet, an astute and pleasant colleague, who I found in the act of examining the guard. They certainly looked a sorry lot, and their statements were far from convincing.

On the following morning I inspected the tomb of Amenophis. A rapid examination showed that the wrappings of the king's mummy had been ripped open with a sharp knife, and that the work appeared to be that of an expert. The presence of objects within folds of linen after a period of several thousand years invariably leaves some impression or mark upon the linen. A careful examination proved there were none, and the natural conclusion was that nothing had been found on the mummy. The evidence suggesting that an expert hand had cut open the wrappings, coupled with the unconvincing statements of the guard, led me to realize that the datum suggested by inanimate objects would in this particular case be far more reliable than any evidence furnished by animate beings of that ilk. I therefore focused my energies upon a thorough examination of the tomb itself. The steel gate showed distinct marks, suggesting that a metal lever had been employed to wrench off the heavy padlock. On the ground beneath the gate I discovered some pieces of lead-paper (commonly known as silver-paper) and a small piece of gum cylindrical in shape. A patient search in the vicinity of the damaged

mummy in the antechamber and around the sarcophagus of Amenophis in the sepulchral chamber revealed impressions upon the dust of bare feet. Measurements and a careful scrutiny suggested that they were footprints of one man only. The footprints of the officials who previously examined the tomb were easily recognized, for they all wore boots.

The Parquet had already taken charge of the broken padlock. When I examined it, I found that its staple-like bolt showed marks of the lever by which it had been broken, and when I compared the cylindrical piece of gum, mentioned above, with the socket of the padlock it proved to fit exactly. There were also minute traces of gum and lead-paper in the socket. Clearly an attempt had been made to stick together the broken portions of the padlock, in order to make it appear intact. This fact did not tally with the guards' tale of the raid. Nevertheless, their account had to be investigated. Through inquiries made by the Parquet, it was found that the guard in charge of the temple of Deir-el-Bahari, on the opposite side of the cliff, distinctly heard the echoes of three gun reports about the time of the alleged raid. The ammunition of the guard of the Valley of the Kings was found to have three rounds missing. Their rifles showed traces of having been discharged recently.

Facts gradually came to light that proved the guards' account to be mere fabrication, made up either to cover their negligence or connivance.

Clearly the robbery had been perpetrated secretly, by one man only and the thief had patched up the lock to cloak his crime.

The main question now was, who committed

the crime? Here I was fortunate, in so far that a peculiar coincidence helped me to suspect the real culprit. It was a chance as may happen but once in a lifetime. Earlier that autumn a private tomb-chapel at Sheikh Abd El-Gurna, in which some private materials of an archaeologist had been stored, was burgled. The padlock that secured the gate had been broken open by a lever, and subsequently stuck together with gum(? from an acacia tree) and wedges made of lead-paper. At the time I had reasons to suspect that it was the work of a well-known robber – a member of the famous Abd E'-Rasool family unable to withstand temptation – whose home was not very far from the chapel. Luckily I had made photos of the footprints I found in the chapel. When I compared these records with the photographs I made of the footprints in the tomb of Amenophis, the dimensions and peculiarities were identical. As to the method, both these crimes in no way differed.

I obtained a warrant from the Parquet to have this man, Mohamed Abd E'-Rasool arrested . . . For some days he was missing. He was, however, arrested the moment he returned to the village of Sheikh Abd El-Gurna, and while in custody impressions were taken of his feet. Their resemblance to my records were so remarkable that it was looked upon by the Parquet as conclusive evidence as to the real culprit. This Mohamed Abd E'-Rasool was remanded, the other suspects released, the guards dismissed, and the local inspector's reign was short.

The trial was equally remarkable. The whole story was discussed at great length, but I failed completely to convince the court of the man's guilt. Although it was agreed that my (half-plate) photographs of the footprints in the two tombs tallied with the characteristics of the feet of the accused, they were not allowed as sufficient evidence. Indeed, from a remark that I overheard made by a member of the court they were considered too small. Afterwards I wished I had had those photographs enlarged to natural size. The whole proceedings reminded me very forcibly of the records of ancient tomb-robbery, and I was forced to the conclusion that in many ways the Egyptian of the present day differs little from his ancestors in the reign of Rameses IX.

The thief, disappointed at finding nothing upon the mummy of Amenophis II, stole the model boat from the antechamber of the tomb. For eighteen months I made every possible search throughout Egypt for the boat. I employed secret police, port and frontier officials were supplied with photographs and were advised to prevent, if possible, the boat being exported by dealers or collectors. I am, however, happy to say that eventually I did find the boat. But where? In a glass case in the Cairo Museum. It was purchased from an antiquity dealer out of the state funds by an authority in the Museum, but he never advised me of the fact. Subsequently, it was revealed that Mohamed Abd E'-Rasool sold it to a dealer at Ghiza.

One moral we can draw from the above episode and I commend it to the critics who call us vandals for taking objects from the tombs. By removing antiquities to museums in safely guarded centres we are assuring them security as far as within our powers. Left *in situ* they would, I fear, as the reader may easily guess, become the prey of thieves.

I have noticed from time to time letters written to the editors of the daily newspapers commenting upon the so-called 'profanation' on the part of archaeologists; some of these letters specially aimed at myself. Those who make such complaint seem unaware that the profanation they allude to is really applicable to the tomb-plunderers of the past and the present day. They seem to forget that what the archaeologist is doing in Egypt and elsewhere, for the sake of the history of man, is to endeavour to rescue these remains of the past from the destructive vandalism of the grave-robber.

◼ ◉ ◻ ◉ ◻ ◉

In the autumn of 1909 Howard Carter, who had resigned his post as Inspector in 1902 and since then had scraped a living as a freelance 'gentleman dealer' and water colourist, started working for Lord Carnarvon in the necropolis of Thebes. This extract from Carnarvon and Carter's *Five Years' Exploration at Thebes*, written by Lord Carnarvon, tells of some of the excavation work they did together.

The necropolis of Thebes – the great city which for so many centuries had been the capital of Egypt – lies on the western side of the Nile valley, on the margin of the desert opposite the modern village of Luxor. No ancient site has yielded a greater harvest of antiquities than this famous stretch of rocky land. From time immemorial it has been the profitable hunting-ground of the tomb-robber; for more than a century a flourishing trade in its antiquities has been carried on by the natives of the district, and for nearly a hundred years archaeologists have been busy here with spade and pencil. The information that has been gleaned from its temple walls and tombs has enabled scholars to trace, point by point, the history of the city from at least 2500 BC to Ptolemaic times. The necropolis itself extends for some five miles along the desert edge, and evidences of the explorer and robber present themselves at every turn. Open or half-filled mummy pits, heaps of rubbish, great mounds of rock débris, with, here and there, fragments of coffins and shreds of linen mummy-wrappings protruding from the sand, show how active have been the tomb-despoilers. Notwithstanding all the work that has been done here, very little can, in any sense, pretend to have been carried out in a systematic manner; and as few records of the various excavations have been kept, the work of the present-day explorer must necessarily be a heavy one. Often he will get no further in his excavations than the well-sorted-over dust of former explorers; and if he is fortunate enough to make a 'find', it is often only after clearing away a vast amount of rock débris and rubbish to the bed-rock below.

With a view to making systematic excavations in this famous necropolis, I began tentative digging among the Kurneh hills and desert margin in the spring of 1907. My workmen were all from the neighbouring villages and their number has varied from seventy-five to two hundred and seventy-five men and boys. I had three head reises – Mansûr Mohammed el Hashâsh, Mohammed Abd el Ghaffer, and Ali Hussên – who all worked well and satisfactorily. The labourers themselves were a willing and hard-working lot: but though they were no more dishonest than other Egyptian fellahin, inducements for them to steal were many, and we found it essential to proceed in our work with great care. I made it a rule that when a tomb was found, as few workmen as possible should be employed; and, in order that the opportunity for stealing should be reduced to a minimum, no clearing of a chamber or pit was carried on unless Mr Carter or I was present. That nothing should escape us, we also, in certain cases, had to sift over the rubbish from the tombs three times.

My preliminary excavations eventually resulted in my confining attention to three sites in that part of the necropolis which lies between the dromos leading to Dêr el Bahari and the great gorge giving entrance to the Valley of the Tombs of the Kings . . .

In the early spring of 1909 work was continued on the Birâbi site [which is near the desert edge and adjoins the entrance to the dromos of Hatshepsût's famous terrace temple]. The tomb discovered the previous season was finally cleared, but nothing further was found in it. Jutting out of one side of the hole caused by the excavation of the tomb, however, appeared the beginning of a well-built stone wall. About forty metres' length of this wall was cleared, and though unfinished, the masonry in general was good. A doorway, giving ingress from the north, eighteen metres along its length, showed that its northern side formed its exterior face. The facing of the stone blocks, not agreeing in direction of their chiselling, showed that they had been reused from some older building, and as the size of the blocks and their chiselling were similar to the masonry of the Mentuhotep temple at Dêr el Bahari, it was conjectured that the wall must be

of a date posterior to the XIth Dynasty. Regarding the purpose of the wall, we obtained no clue in 1909, nor could we then date it with any precision. In 1910, however, we found several blocks lying near the wall which bore hieratic inscriptions giving the name of Hatshepsût's master-builder, Pu-am-ra. Afterwards, similar inscriptions were found on the blocks built in the masonry. These, together with a single block bearing the name of the great queen's famous architect, Senmut, clearly proved that the wall which we had found must have belonged to some building of Hatshepsût's reign. Further clearance revealed that the building was of the nature of a terrace temple like that at Dêr el Bahari. So far as we can at present see, the axis of the building corresponds to the axis of the dromos leading to Hatshepsût's temple. This point, together with the fact that a foundation deposit with objects bearing the prenomen of the queen and the name of her temple was brought to light, apparently in the centre of our monument, shows that we are dealing with a building in some way connected with the temple at Dêr el Bahari. The probable interpretation is that this newly discovered 'Terrace Temple' is in reality a 'Valley'-Temple or 'Portal' to Hatshepsût's noble monument at Dêr el Bahari. It would, therefore, correspond to the so-called 'Valley'-Temples of Gizeh and Abusîr. Another interesting fact relating to Hatshepsût's Dêr el Bahari temple was the discovery of a foundation deposit at the north-west corner of the dromos where it joins the temple. This is the largest deposit that has hitherto been discovered, and exhibits two new features in connection with the custom of placing of such deposits, namely, the consecration of the building by unction and flesh and blood offerings. These offerings were kept separate from the usual model tools and implements which were found near by, and the vessels containing the unguents and wines were smashed, and their contents, as well as grains of corn, were poured over the clean sand that filled the cache. In 1911 search was made for the companion deposit in the south-west corner, this was soon found, and it differed only in the fact that the secondary group – i.e. the tools and implements – was missing.

Beneath the foundations of the 'Valley'-Temple we cut through a layer of rock débris averaging two metres in thickness, and discovered a series of pit and corridor tombs hewn in the rock-bed below. These had all been plundered, some indeed twice, and most of their contents had been scattered and some burnt. Several bore evidence of having been pilfered, in the first instance, shortly after the close of the Middle Kingdom, and then again during Hatshepsût's reign, probably by the workmen employed in building the 'Valley'-Temple. As evidence of the earlier plundering we may mention the fact that fragments of one stela were found in two separate tombs on opposite sides of the great wall. After this first plundering, the rock débris must have collected to a considerable depth above the tombs before the second spoliation took place, for rough retaining walls, built of stones and bricks found in the mounds, were made to support the sides of the shafts pierced through the earth by the later robbers.

The tombs are of two types: (1) pit tombs, comprising a vertical shaft with one or more chambers at the bottom, and (2) corridor tombs, with open court in front, vestibule and passage leading to chambers with vertical shafts, and sarcophagus chamber below. In all cases the original contents had been plundered and some of the tombs had been re-used towards the end of the Intermediate period. One of the pit tombs, however, contained an unopened coffin and objects scattered about the chambers, which all clearly belonged to the original burial . . .

Altogether about 11,000 square metres of débris were cleared from the Birâbi site and, of course, many miscellaneous antiquities were brought to light in the course of the excavation.

■ ◉ ■ ◉ ■ ◉

While he was working as Inspector of Monuments, Howard Carter had supervised some excavations directed by Theodore Davis, a retired lawyer from Newport, USA, and a sponsor of archaeologists. In 1906, when Carter was struggling to make ends meet in Luxor, the archaeologist Edward Ayrton, employed by Davis, had found a small blue ceramic cup bearing the name of 'Tutankhamun'. Then, in December 1907, Ayrton had discovered a small pit, about 5 feet deep, containing embalming materials and the remains of a funeral meal which had been used at the burial of the boy-pharaoh. Further finds – bits and pieces of gold foil, some of them again bearing the name of Tutankhamun – in January 1909 convinced Davis that this was no less than the discovery of the rifled tomb itself. This extract from his *The Finding of the Tombs of Harmhabi and Touatânkhamanou (1912)* explains why.

In the winter of 1906, while digging near the foot of a high hill in the Valley of the Tombs of the Kings, my attention was attracted to a large rock tilted to one side, and for some mysterious reason I felt interested in it, and on being carefully examined and dug about by my assistant, Mr Ayrton, with the hands, the beautiful blue cup ... was found. This bore the cartouche of Touatânkhamanou. The following year, in digging to the north of Harmhabi's tomb, we came upon signs of another, and my assistant, Mr E. Harold Jones, put his men to work, and at the depth of 25 feet we found a room filled almost to the top with dried mud, showing that water had entered it. And it was curious to see the decorative manner in which the mud had dried.

We found a broken box containing several pieces of gold leaf stamped with the names of Touatânkhamanou and his wife Ankhousnamanou – also the names Divine Father Aîya and his wife Tiyi, but without title or prenomen. We also found under the mud, lying on the floor in one corner, a beautiful alabaster statuette ... A few days after this we came upon a pit, some distance from the tomb, filled with large earthen pots containing what would seem to be the débris from a tomb such as dried wreaths of leaves and flowers, and small bags containing a powdered substance. The cover of one of these jars had been broken, and wrapped about it was a cloth on which was inscribed the name of Touatânkhamanou.

The finding of the blue cup with the cartouche of Touatânkhamanou, and not far from it the quite undecorated tomb containing the gold leaf inscribed with the names of Touatânkhamanou and Ankhousnamanou, in connection with the Divine Father Aîya and his wife Tîyi, and the pit containing the jars with the name of Touatânkhamanou, lead me to conclude that Touatânkhamanou was originally buried in the tomb described above, and that it was afterwards robbed, leaving the few things that I have mentioned.

I fear that the Valley of the Tombs is now exhausted.

◻ ◉ ◻ ◉ ◻ ◉

Percy White was, until the mid-1920s, Professor of English Literature at the Egyptian University, Cairo. He was a prolific novelist – the British Library catalogue lists nearly thirty titles – specializing in romantic stories set among the 'upper set' living in modern cities. He was also a close friend of Howard Carter: by the 1920s Carter was referring to him as 'an old acquaintance', and they holidayed together (in England), spent Christmas together (in Cairo), and commiserated with each other about the behaviour of the press in the Valley of the Kings in the overheated atmosphere of 1923–5. White helped Carter to write Volumes 1 and 2 of *The Discovery of the Tomb of Tutankhamen* (Volume 3 appears to have been a solo effort), and he remained the archaeologist's most loyal friend in Egypt – no mean feat, at times. This extract from *Cairo* (published 1914, reprinted 1919, a follow-up to the same author's *Mayfair*) provides an atmospheric account of life in the city the year before the outbreak of the First World War, a time when young Egyptian Nationalists were beginning to organize themselves.

The soft pink light stealing into the white-washed room through closed shutters was faintly colouring the curtains of the bed when Daniel Addington awoke and drowsily wondered why he did not feel the vibrations of the screw, and as he wondered, sounds from the street – shuffling feet, harsh cries, braying donkeys – brought him the message from the unseen city.

Dreamily excited, it dawned upon him how he had reached Cairo late last night, and how an energetic tout with a tremendous voice had, almost in spite of himself, carried him off to the nearest hotel. Scrambling out of the unaccustomed mosquito-netting, he crossed the cheap French carpet covering the stone floor and threw open the shutters.

It was a beautiful November morning, and the shabby street glowed in a flood of rosy light. Yet that first impression lacked something of anticipated wonder and beauty, because the edge of Eastern charm was blunted by Western commonness. In Cairo the ugly fringes jostle contemptuously without mingling. A man tricked by dreams, he expected too much.

In the unkempt back street, flanked by European houses, he saw blue-gowned, bare-footed, brown-visaged peasants trotting behind donkeys half hidden under immense loads of green fodder, and a string of camels, bearing blocks of white stone, swinging past a cluster of mean shops and squalid cafés, in front of which groups of men in ill-cut Western clothes sat at the rusty tables that obstructed the rubbish-strewn, unpaved footway. Then he glanced upwards and listened. The luminous air, resonant with the sounds of a big city, included the rattling of electric tramcars. High in the sky above the flat roofs graceful kites were wheeling, uttering at intervals thin musical cries. The colour, the strangeness, the impact of West on East, whilst it deeply interested him, left at the same time a faint impression of disappointment. Perspectives seemed awry. But for the camels, the bare brown feet and faces, flowing garments, and the bewitching quality of the morning light, Addington felt that he might be looking out on some dingy quarter of a city in Southern Italy. But having looked outward, he now looked within. What, he wondered, had really brought him to Egypt. One of the inducements, of course, was Abdul Sayed, a leader of the Young Egyptian party with whom he had been at Oxford. They had first met, years ago, at the Union, at a debate on 'The British Occupation', the memory of which suddenly flooded his memory, and in that pure morning light, in some mysterious way, Sayed's arguments seemed less crude. Egypt, he told them, had shaken off her conquerors in turn, 'even as the patient ox shakes off the flies that vex it'. But patience had ceased to be a political virtue. A new spirit now ruled the world, the democratic spirit, a spirit, he declared, 'innate in his countrymen'. Egypt, he further insisted, thus raising a laugh, was the only country where snobbery, political and social, was still non-existent, although a foreign yoke was beginning to undermine the ancient dignity of a race whose future was no question of cotton crops nor yet of education, the problem being to organize and guide the spirit of self-government which, in spite of

European detractors, was inborn in this patient and law-abiding people. The question was a spiritual, not a material question, but to this fact the English, like the Turks, were blind.

'Let us,' he said in conclusion, 'choose our leaders, and you will see the rebirth of a once great race. Turkey, in the fullness of her decrepitude, may "go under", but Egypt, where Islam is a living force and continuity the law of life, will remain indestructible, her future as great as her past is impressive.'

And as the dreamer looked from his window, he remembered how, from being an over-fervid speaker at the Union, Abdul Sayed, after succeeding to his father's wealth, had developed into a cautious agitator. With his fine presence, and occasional bursts of florid eloquence, he seemed a fitting leader for the variegated crowd Addington was watching in the street. He recalled, too, that semi-political dinner at the National Liberal Club in honour of Sayed Bey, then on a mission to his Radical and Socialist friends. 'As the generous friend of oppressed races,' Sayed had said, 'your place, my dear Addington, is in Egypt. Providence has given you the means to help us, a sense of justice has given you the will. Reject official views. If you find that you cannot sympathize with us, you can at least tell your countrymen the truth, in the journal you control.'

But in spite of the attraction that Sayed had for him, he nevertheless distrusted him as a complicated exotic, as the hybrid product of a Western culture on an unsound Eastern foundation. Was the man really sincere in his promise to work with him? It was useless to pretend, as he tried to pretend, that any nobler spirit than that of curiosity had brought him to Cairo. Like a child with a watch, he wanted 'to see the wheels go round'. A political dilettante, a Radical prepared for no serious sacrifices, he had come to the land of political and economical experiment, 'just to see things', and with no fixed purpose. To assume, as Sayed had assumed for him, that he was there on a self-imposed mission was an absurd attempt to flatter his sense of self-importance. Why not admit it at once? He (Addington) was seeking adventures in a land where his friends told him nothing was impossible under the surface of things.

Turning away from the window, Addington's eye fell on the little square service card informing him that it was necessary to ring thrice if he wanted the 'Arab'. Impressed by the servile sense of the word, he pressed the button. A tall, white-gowned, red-sashed Sudanese with heelless slippers on sockless feet promptly appeared.

Pleased to feel himself, as it were, a step nearer the Arabian Nights, Addington ordered a bath, and an hour later, dressed in a thin blue serge suit, went down to the dining-room, where a few commercial gentlemen of doubtful nationality, their napkins tucked under their collars, were drinking coffee and eating rolls.

A plump Swiss *maître d'hôtel*, suspecting a promising client, waved him obsequiously to a table, where he sat down and gazed about the lofty, garish room, boisterous with the graphic surprises that the Cairo decorator prepares for the trusting tourist. Hung with gaudy Oriental tapestries, adorned with crude paintings of monstrous shapes, the strident walls still smelt of size and the craftman's glue.

Reading the guest's face, the *maître d'hôtel*

ordered one of the *soffragis*, whose manoeuvres he controlled, to open the window. The room, he admitted, had just been redecorated. Naturally monsieur was interested in Egyptology? That figure – the one with the dog's head – was Anubis, that opposite – the lady feeding the child – Isis. Addington further learnt that the Italian responsible for these mural mythologies had started for Chicago to decorate the reception rooms of an American gentleman now at Luxor.

Having thus displayed his urbanity, the *maître d'hôtel* turned his attention and altered his language to confront the voluble complaints of a swarthy gentleman enraged by his bill.

Addington had just finished breakfast when Sayed Bey, gently smiling, strolled into the room, elegantly dressed in grey clothes and wearing the tarbouche.

'But how on earth did you know I was here?' Addington exclaimed as they shook hands.

'Because you were not at Shepheard's or the Continental, and this is the only other place open.'

As the Egyptian took his seat at the little square table, the life-sized painting of cow-headed Hathor on the wall above his dark, handsome face seemed less absurd as a decoration.

'You're bang in it now, my friend,' said Sayed Bey, half guessing the other's thought, and determined to be modern. '"Up against" my old Gods – what? But they are not meant only for the tourist's consumption. The English make a sort of flattering unction out of our mythology for themselves and us too! With such a past, with all those dog-faced Deities to

interest you, they seem to say, "What business have you to worry about the present, especially when we're here to arrange it for you?" Can't you imagine my swaddled country in an ugly perambulator and your Government pushing it along, Addington?'

'Not a bad cartoon for a Nationalist paper,' observed the other. 'John Bull is an ox-headed Deity.'

'Press jokes of that sort are not safe in Egypt, as the editor of *El Nur* will tell you. But you mustn't stay here. To see things as they are – to learn why the English are really loved – you must rub shoulders with the satellites of the governing class, not with Greek bagmen. You must take a room at the Semiramis or the Savoy – they open next week – if you are fully to appreciate the British attitude. Two races, mutually despising each other, as ours do, can't hope to collaborate very successfully. That is what you must make the Radicals understand. Our hope of justice is with them.'

'But,' the other interrupted, 'you admit we've done good work on the material side of things.'

'If you hadn't you couldn't have stayed. But, as a French friend pointed out the other day, you're failing on the spiritual side. Even the Egyptian fellah can't live on bread alone. You've given us police, dams, irrigation, drainage, and what you call justice. You repay yourself for what you've done by wiping your boots on us.'

'But then we are such miles apart!' Addington protested.

'The distance is part of your policy! Meek as we are, my friend, we've no taste for the "damned-nigger" treatment!'

'You're too bitter!' exclaimed Addington.

'Am I? Stay a month or two at one of the swagger hotels where British subalterns and their ladies display themselves. Hear what they say of us, then you'll understand how much the English really love us. That side of it – the "Imperial-race" side of it, they call it – you can study for yourself and show up in *The Oracle*, the Egyptian progressive side I will show you!'

'But your aims are too indefinite,' reasoned Addington, 'your strategy too wild.'

'When you gag the Press and suppress the right of public meeting there isn't much scope for constitutional agitation,' Sayed Bey replied, 'and that's the plight you've reduced us to.'

But Addington shook his smooth, neat head.

'Make it clear how we can help,' he said, 'and we'll try to help you at home. Radicalism that accepts no distinctions of race is a new force in politics. Our hope is – now you have our sympathy – that there will be no violence.'

'Quite so,' replied the Egyptian, who had suddenly become tired of the discussion.

The two men were silent for a moment. Outside the life of the street, vibrating with sunshine and colour, noisy with the cracking of whips, the rattling of brazen vessels, and the moaning of a string of camels, drew Addington to the window.

'I feel I want to see everything at once!' he said, as he turned to Sayed Bey.

'Come along then, and I'll hand you over to an honest guide.'

Rising from his chair to his great height, the stately Egyptian accompanied his confiding friend to the hotel entrance, where a superb blue-turbaned dragoman in a short dark braided jacket and Zouave trousers was dis-

cussing the prospects of the coming season with the Swiss hall-porter in German.

'This,' said, Sayed, introducing the obsequious guide, 'is Ahmed, who talks English almost as well as I do. He will take you to the bazaars and see that you are not bothered.'

Ahmed smiled, murmured swiftly in Arabic to Sayed Bey, then, turning to Addington, said: 'I understand, sir, that you are one of us.'

But the spark of discretion was kindling in Addington's caution. Remembering the history of 'Paget, MP,' his only reply to Ahmed's ingratiating yet half-satirical smile was the stony English stare.

But for that stare, although Addington did not know it, the dragoman would have sat beside him in the *araba* waiting to take them to Mousky. As it was, at a word from Sayed Bey, he mounted the box by the driver, whose feet were cushioned on a pile of moist fodder.

Sayed Bey waved his hand in salute as the light two-horsed cab dashed into the variegated traffic of the street, where tram-cars clanged past strings of donkeys and camels, and motor-cars, bearing veiled and painted beauties, threatened horrid forms of death to careless crowds of imperturbable Orientals.

In the Ezbekieh Square the traffic was held up by a British regiment. As the long, sturdy khaki line swung on between the Opera House and Mohammet Ali's statue the fifes and drums struck up a heady march, and Ahmed, the dragoman, turning sparkling eyes on Addington, looked down from his seat and exclaimed: 'English soldiers! Yes. All dusty from desert, but nice. Go home down Mohammet Ali Street to Citadel. Good music, pretty music. Oh yes!'

And whilst the guide nodded his head in time to the lilt of the music, Addington recognized another force. He had already felt the ragged fringes where West jostles East. He had been conscious, too, of the weight of Islam dreaming behind the confusion but now he was aware of that third element modifying both.

The drums rolled, the fifes shrilled, a crowd of little white- and blue-gowned boys strutted in the regiment's wake as it passed from the sun-lit square into the long dark street beyond.

'Wonderful Things . . .'

Howard Carter was convinced that Theodore Davis *hadn't*, in fact, discovered the tomb of Tutankhamun but rather that the fragments of material from the boy-pharaoh's funeral suggested the tomb proper might be nearby. With this in mind, in 1917 he started, on behalf of Lord Carnarvon, a 'systematic' approach to clearing the area of the Valley of the Kings, where 'we hoped the tomb of Tutankhamen might be situated'. This elaborate campaign 'was rather a desperate undertaking', he later wrote, 'the site being piled high with enormous heaps of thrown-out rubbish, but I had reason to believe that the ground beneath had never been touched, and a strong conviction that we should find a tomb there'. But several years of hard and expensive labour produced 'extremely scanty results, and it became a much debated question whether we should continue the work, or try for a more profitable site elsewhere. After these barren years were we justified in going on with it?' In the summer of 1922, Lord Carnarvon was tempted to pull out, but in the end they decided to give it one last try.

The following account of the discovery of the tomb of Tutankhamun has been extracted from Howard Carter's three-volume book on the subject (published 1923, 1927 and 1933) and from comments by other members of the team (a team which he assembled between 7 and 18 December 1922). In their own words, they evoke the excitement of, and the sheer hard work involved in, the greatest archaeological discovery of modern times.

The Valley of the Tombs of the Kings – the very name is full of romance, and of all Egypt's wonders there is none, I suppose, that makes a more instant appeal to the imagination. Here, in this lonely valley-head, remote from every sound of life, with the 'Horn', the highest peak in the Theban hills, standing sentinel like a natural pyramid above them, lay thirty or more kings, among them the greatest Egypt ever knew. Thirty were buried here. Now, probably, but two remain – Amen·hetep II – whose mummy may be seen by the curious lying in his sarcophagus – and Tut-ankh-Amen, who still remains intact beneath his golden shrine. There, when the claims of science have been satisfied, we hope to leave him lying . . .

The history of The Valley . . . has never lacked the dramatic element, and in this, the latest episode, it has held to its traditions. For consider the circumstances. This was to be our final season in The Valley. Six full seasons we had excavated there, and season after season had drawn a blank; we had worked for months at a stretch and found nothing, and only an excavator knows how desperately depressing that can be; we had almost made up our minds that we were beaten, and were preparing to leave The Valley and try our luck elsewhere; and then – hardly had we set hoe to ground in our last despairing effort than we made a discovery that far exceeded our wildest dreams. Surely, never before in the whole history of excavation has a full digging season been compressed within the space of five days.

Let me try and tell the story of it all. It will not be easy, for the dramatic suddenness of the initial discovery left me in a dazed condition, and the months that have followed have been so crowded with incident that I have hardly had time to think. Setting it down on paper will perhaps give me a chance to realize what has happened and all that it means.

I arrived in Luxor on October 28th [1922], and by November 1st I had enrolled my workmen and was ready to begin. Our former excavations had stopped short at the north-east corner of the tomb of Rameses VI, and from this point I started trenching southwards ... In this area there were a number of roughly constructed workmen's huts, used probably by the labourers in the tomb of Rameses. These huts, built about three feet above bed-rock, covered the whole area in front of the Ramesside tomb, and continued in a southerly direction to join up with a similar group of huts on the opposite side of The Valley, discovered by Davis ... By the evening of November 3rd we had laid bare a sufficient number of these huts for experimental purposes, so, after we had planned and noted them, they were removed, and we were ready to clear away the three feet of soil that lay beneath them.

Hardly had I arrived on the work next morning (November 4th) than the unusual silence, due to the stoppage of the work, made me realize that something out of the ordinary had happened, and I was greeted by the announcement that a step cut in the rock had been discovered underneath the very first hut to be attacked. This seemed too good to be true, but a short amount of extra clearing revealed the fact that we were actually in the entrance of a steep cut in the rock, some thirteen feet below the entrance to the tomb of Rameses VI, and a similar depth from the present bed level of The Valley. The manner of cutting was that of the

sunken stairway entrance so common in The Valley, and I almost dared to hope that we had found our tomb at last. Work continued feverishly throughout the whole of that day and the morning of the next, but it was not until the afternoon of November 5th that we succeeded in clearing away the masses of rubbish that overlay the cut, and were able to demarcate the upper edges of the stairway on all its four sides.

It was clear by now beyond any question that we actually had before us the entrance to a tomb, but doubts, born of previous disappointments, persisted in creeping in. There was always the horrible possibility that the tomb was an unfinished one, never completed and never used: if it had been finished there was the depressing probability that it had been completely plundered in ancient times. On the other hand, there was just the chance of an untouched or only partially plundered tomb, and it was with ill-suppressed excitement that I watched the descending steps of the staircase, as one by one they came to light. The cutting was excavated in the side of a small hillock, and, as the work progressed, its western edge receded under the slope of the rock until it was, first partially, and then completely, roofed in, and became a passage, ten feet high by six feet wide. Work progressed more rapidly now; step succeeded step, and at the level of the twelfth, towards sunset, there was disclosed the upper part of a doorway, blocked, plastered, and sealed.

A sealed doorway – it was actually true, then! Our years of patient labour were to be rewarded after all, and I think my first feeling was one of congratulation that my faith in The

Valley had not been unjustified. With excitement growing to fever heat I searched the seal impressions of the door for evidence of the identity of the owner, but could find no name: the only decipherable ones were those of the well-known royal necropolis seal, the jackal and nine captives. Two facts, however, were clear: first, the employment of this royal seal was certain evidence that the tomb had been constructed for a person of very high standing; and second, that the sealed door was entirely screened from above by workmen's huts of the Twentieth Dynasty was sufficiently clear proof that at least from that date it had never been entered. With that for the moment I had to be content.

While examining the seals I noticed, at the top of the doorway, where some of the plaster had fallen away, a heavy wooden lintel. Under this, to assure myself of the method by which the doorway had been blocked, I made a small peephole, just large enough to insert an electric torch, and discovered that the passage beyond the door was filled completely from floor to ceiling with stones and rubble – additional proof this of the care with which the tomb had been protected.

It was a thrilling moment for an excavator. Alone, save for my native workmen, I found myself, after years of comparatively unproductive labour, on the threshold of what might prove to be a magnificent discovery. Anything, literally anything, might lie beyond that passage, and it needed all my self-control to keep from breaking down the doorway, and investigating then and there.

One thing puzzled me, and that was the smallness of the opening in comparison with the ordinary Valley tombs. The design was certainly of the Eighteenth Dynasty. Could it be the tomb of a noble buried here by royal consent? Was it a royal cache, a hiding-place to which a mummy and its equipment had been removed for safety? Or was it actually the tomb of the king for whom I had spent so many years in search?

Once more I examined the seal impressions for a clue, but on the part of the door so far laid bare only those of the royal necropolis seal already mentioned were clear enough to read. Had I but known that a few inches lower down there was a perfectly clear and distinct impression of the seal of Tut-ankh-Amen, the king I most desired to find, I would have cleared on, had a much better night's rest in consequence, and saved myself nearly three weeks of uncertainty. It was late, however, and darkness was already upon us. With some reluctance I reclosed the small hole that I had made, filled in our excavation for protection during the night, selected the most trustworthy of my workmen – themselves almost as excited as I was – to watch all night above the tomb, and so home by moonlight, riding down The Valley.

Naturally my wish was to go straight ahead with our clearing to find out the full extent of the discovery, but Lord Carnarvon was in England, and in fairness to him I had to delay matters until he could come. Accordingly, on the morning of November 6th I sent him the following cable: 'At last have made wonderful discovery in Valley; a magnificent tomb with seals intact; re-covered same for your arrival; congratulations.'

My next task was to secure the doorway against interference until such time as it could finally be re-opened. This we did by filling our excavation up again to surface level, and rolling on top of it the large flint boulders of which the workmen's huts had been composed. By the evening of the same day, exactly forty-eight hours after we had discovered the first step of the staircase, this was accomplished. The tomb had vanished. So far as the appearance of the ground was concerned there never had been any tomb, and I found it hard to persuade myself at times that the whole episode had not been a dream.

I was soon to be reassured on this point. News travels fast in Egypt, and within two days of the discovery congratulations, inquiries, and offers of help descended upon me in a steady stream from all directions. It became clear, even at this early stage, that I was in for a job that could not be tackled single-handed, so I wired to Callender, who had helped me on various previous occasions, asking him if possible to join me without delay, and to my relief he arrived on the very next day. On the 8th I had received two messages from Lord Carnarvon in answer to my cable, the first of which read, 'Possibly come soon', and the second, received a little later, 'Propose arrive Alexandria 20th.'

We had thus nearly a fortnight's grace, and we devoted it to making preparations of various kinds, so that when the time of re-opening came, we should be able, with the least possible delay, to handle any situation that might arise. On the night of the 18th I went to Cairo for three days, to meet Lord Carnarvon and make a number of necessary purchases, returning to Luxor on the 21st. On the 23rd Lord Carnarvon arrived in Luxor with his

daughter, Lady Evelyn Herbert, his devoted companion in all his Egyptian work, and everything was in hand for the beginning of the second chapter of the discovery of the tomb. Callender had been busy all day clearing away the upper layer of rubbish, so that by morning we should be able to get into the staircase without any delay.

By the afternoon of the 24th the whole staircase was clear, sixteen steps in all, and we were able to make a proper examination of the sealed doorway. On the lower part the seal impressions were much clearer, and we were able without any difficulty to make out on several of them the name of Tut-ankh-Amen. This added enormously to the interest of the discovery. If we had found, as seemed almost certain, the tomb of that shadowy monarch, whose tenure of the throne coincided with one of the most interesting periods in the whole of Egyptian history, we should indeed have reason to congratulate ourselves.

With heightened interest, if that was possible, we renewed our investigation of the doorway. Here for the first time a disquieting element made its appearance. Now that the whole door was exposed to light it was possible to discern a fact that had hitherto escaped notice – that there had been two successive openings and re-closings of a part of its surface: furthermore, that the sealing originally discovered, the jackal and nine captives, had been applied to the re-closed portions, whereas the sealings of Tut-ankh-Amen covered the untouched part of the doorway, and were therefore those with which the tomb had been originally secured. The tomb then was not absolutely intact, as we had hoped. Plunderers

had entered it, and entered it more than once –
from the evidence of the huts above, plunderers
of a date not later than the reign of Rameses VI
– but that they had not rifled it completely was
evident from the fact that it had been re-sealed.

Then came another puzzle. In the lower
strata of rubbish that filled the staircase we
found masses of broken potsherds and boxes,
the latter bearing the names of Akh-en-Aten,
Smenkh·ka·Re and Tut·ankh·Amen, and, what
was much more upsetting, a scarab of Thothmes III and a fragment with the name of Amen-
·hetep II. Why this mixture of names? The
balance of evidence so far would seem to
indicate a cache rather than a tomb, and at this
stage in the proceedings we inclined more and
more to the opinion that we were about to find
a miscellaneous collection of objects of the
Eighteenth Dynasty kings, brought from Tell el
Amarna by Tut-ankh-Amen and deposited here
for safety.

So matters stood on the evening of the 24th.
On the following day the sealed doorway was
to be removed, so Callender set carpenters to
work making a heavy wooden grille to be set
up in its place. Mr Engelbach, Chief Inspector
of the Antiquities Department, paid us a visit
during the afternoon, and witnessed part of the
final clearing of rubbish from the doorway.

On the morning of the 25th the seal impressions on the doorway were carefully noted and
photographed, and then we removed the actual
blocking of the door, consisting of rough
stones carefully built from floor to lintel, and
heavily plastered on their outer faces to take
the seal impressions.

This disclosed the beginning of a descending
passage (not a staircase), the same width as the
entrance stairway, and nearly seven feet high.
As I had already discovered from my hole in
the doorway, it was filled completely with
stone and rubble, probably the chip from its
own excavation. This filling, like the doorway,
showed distinct signs of more than one opening
and re-closing of the tomb, the untouched part
consisting of clean white chip, mingled with
dust, whereas the disturbed part was composed
mainly of dark flint. It was clear that an
irregular tunnel had been cut through the
original filling at the upper corner on the left
side, a tunnel corresponding in position with
that of the hole in the doorway.

As we cleared the passage we found, mixed
with the rubble of the lower levels, broken
potsherds, jar sealings, alabaster jars, whole
and broken, vases of painted pottery, numerous fragments of smaller articles, and water
skins, these last having obviously been used to
bring up the water needed for the plastering of
the doorways. These were clear evidence of
plundering, and we eyed them askance. By
night we had cleared a considerable distance
down the passage, but as yet saw no sign of
second doorway or of chamber.

The day following (November 26th) was the
day of days, the most wonderful that I have
ever lived through, and certainly one whose
like I can never hope to see again. Throughout
the morning the work of clearing continued,
slowly perforce, on account of the delicate
objects that were mixed with the filling. Then,
in the middle of the afternoon, thirty feet down
from the outer door, we came upon a second
sealed doorway, almost an exact replica of the
first. The seal impressions in this case were less
distinct, but still recognizable as those of

Tut-ankh-Amen and of the royal necropolis. Here again the signs of opening and re-closing were clearly marked upon the plaster. We were firmly convinced by this time that it was a cache that we were about to open, and not a tomb . . . We were soon to know. There lay the sealed doorway, and behind it was the answer to the question.

Slowly, desperately slowly it seemed to us as we watched, the remains of passage debris that encumbered the lower part of the doorway were removed, until at last we had the whole door clear before us. The decisive moment had arrived. With trembling hands I made a tiny breach in the upper left-hand corner. Darkness and blank space, as far as an iron testing-rod could reach showed that whatever lay beyond was empty, and not filled like the passage we had just cleared. Candle tests were applied as a precaution against possible foul gases, and then, widening the hole a little, I inserted the candle and peered in, Lord Carnarvon, Lady Evelyn and Callender standing anxiously beside me to hear the verdict. At first I could see nothing, the hot air escaping from the chamber causing the candle flame to flicker, but presently, as my eyes grew accustomed to the light, details of the room within emerged slowly from the mist, strange animals, statues, and gold – everywhere the glint of gold. For the moment – an eternity it must have seemed to the others standing by – I was struck dumb with amazement, and when Lord Carnarvon, unable to stand the suspense any longer, inquired anxiously, 'Can you see anything?' it was all I could do to get out the words, 'Yes, wonderful things.' Then widening the hole a little further, so that we both could see, we inserted an electric torch.

I suppose most excavators would confess to a feeling of awe – embarrassment almost – when they break into a chamber closed and sealed by pious hands so many centuries ago. For the moment, time as a factor in human life has lost its meaning. Three thousand, four thousand years maybe, have passed and gone since human feet last trod the floor on which you stand, and yet, as you note the signs of recent life around you – the half-filled bowl of mortar for the door, the blackened lamp, the finger-mark upon the freshly painted surface, the farewell garland dropped upon the threshold – you feel it might have been but yesterday. The very air you breathe, unchanged throughout the centuries, you share with those who laid the mummy to its rest. Time is annihilated by little intimate details such as these, and you feel an intruder.

That is perhaps the first dominant sensation, but others follow thick and fast – the exhilaration of discovery, the fever of suspense, the almost overmastering impulse, born of curiosity, to break down seals and lift the lids of boxes, the thought – pure joy to the investigator – that you are about to add a page to history, or solve some problem of research, the strained expectancy – why not confess it? – of the treasure-seeker. Did these thoughts actually pass through our minds at the time, or have I imagined them since? I cannot tell. It was the discovery that my memory was blank, and not the mere desire for dramatic chapter-ending, that occasioned this digression.

Surely never before in the whole history of excavation had such an amazing sight been seen as the light of our torch revealed to us. The reader can get some idea of it by reference to the photographs, but these were taken afterwards when the tomb had been opened and electric light installed. Let him imagine how they appeared to us as we looked down upon them from our spy-hole in the blocked doorway, casting the beam of light from our torch – the first light that had pierced the darkness of the chamber for three thousand years – from one group of objects to another, in a vain attempt to interpret the treasure that lay before us. The effect was bewildering, overwhelming. I suppose we had never formulated exactly in our minds just what we had expected or hoped to see, but certainly we had never dreamed of anything like this, a roomful – a whole museumful it seemed – of objects, some familiar, but some the like of which we had never seen, piled one upon another in seemingly endless profusion.

Gradually the scene grew clearer, and we could pick out individual objects. First, right opposite to us – we had been conscious of them all the while, but refused to believe in them – were three great gilt couches, their sides carved in the form of monstrous animals, curiously attenuated in body, as they had to be to serve their purpose, but with heads of startling realism. Uncanny beasts enough to look upon at any time: seen as we saw them, their brilliant gilded surfaces picked out of the darkness by our electric torch, as though by limelight, their heads throwing grotesque distorted shadows on the wall behind them, they were almost terrifying. Next, on the right, two statues caught and held our attention; two life-sized figures of a king in black, facing each other like sentinels, gold kilted, gold sandalled, armed with mace and staff, the protective

sacred cobra upon their foreheads.

These were the dominant objects that caught the eye at first. Between them, around them, piled on top of them, there were countless others – exquisitely painted and inlaid caskets; alabaster vases, some beautifully carved in openwork designs; strange black shrines, from the open door of one a great gilt snake peeping out; bouquets of flowers or leaves; beds; chairs beautifully carved; a golden inlaid throne; a heap of curious white oviform boxes; staves of all shapes and designs; beneath our eyes, on the very threshold of the chamber, a beautiful lotiform cup of translucent alabaster; on the left a confused pile of overturned chariots, glistening with gold and inlay; and peeping from behind them another portrait of a king.

Such were some of the objects that lay before us. Whether we noted them all at the time I cannot say for certain, as our minds were in much too excited and confused a state to register accurately. Presently it dawned upon our bewildered brains that in all this medley of objects before us there was no coffin or trace of mummy, and the much-debated question of tomb or cache began to intrigue us afresh. With this question in view we re-examined the scene before us, and noticed for the first time that between the two black sentinel statues on the right there was another sealed doorway. The explanation gradually dawned upon us. We were but on the threshold of our discovery. What we saw was merely an antechamber. Behind the guarded door there were to be other chambers, possibly a succession of them, and in one of them, beyond any shadow of doubt, in all his magnificent panoply of death, we should find the Pharaoh lying.

We had seen enough, and our brains began to reel at the thought of the task in front of us. We re-closed the hole, locked the wooden grille that had been placed upon the first doorway, left our native staff on guard, mounted our donkeys and rode home down The Valley, strangely silent and subdued . . .

Our natural impulse was to break down the door, and get to the bottom of the matter at once, but to do so would have entailed serious risk of damage to many of the objects in the Antechamber, a risk which we were by no means prepared to face. Nor could we move the objects in question out of the way, for it was imperative that a plan and complete photographic record should be made before anything was touched, and this was a task involving a considerable amount of time, even if we had had sufficient plant available – which we had not – to carry it through immediately. Reluctantly we decided to abandon the opening of this inner sealed door until we had cleared the Antechamber of all its contents.

■ ◉ ▣ ◉ ▢ ◉

Actually, Howard Carter did *not* 'decide to abandon the opening of this sealed inner door'. He would have been exercising almost super-human self-control if he had. At some stage – possibly that same night – the group decided to go back to the tomb and find out for themselves exactly what secrets lay beyond the ante-chamber. This unusual behaviour – quite understandable in the circumstances – remained a closely guarded secret until Alfred Lucas, the Manchester-born chemist who joined the team in order to analyse and conserve the materials found inside the tomb, pub-

lished two short notes in the *Annales du Service des Antiquités de l'Egypte* (1942 and 1947). As another surviving member of the group put it, the cat was out of the bag. Apparently, Carter, Carnarvon and Lady Evelyn had re-opened a small hole originally made by the tomb-robbers in order to gain access to the burial chamber.

[1942]
Of the door leading into the burial chamber, it is stated [in Howard Carter's book] that 'close examination revealed the fact that a small breach had been made near the bottom . . . and that the hole made had subsequently been filled up and re-sealed'. A considerable amount of mystery was made about this robbers's hole. When I first saw the tomb about December 20th, the hole was hidden by the basketwork tray, or lid, and some rushes taken from the floor that Mr Carter had placed before it. [The photographs] show the hole closed, but Lord

Carnarvon, his daughter and Mr Carter certainly entered the burial chamber and also entered the store chamber, which latter had no door, before the formal opening. Whether Mr Callender, who was present at the time, also entered the burial chamber, I am not sure, but he was a very big man and I once heard a remark that made me think that the hole was too small to admit him.

The question of the hole and its condition when found, whether open or closed, is a small matter of no archaeological importance and, by itself, is hardly worth mentioning . . .

The hiding of the hole while the antechamber was being emptied, was most reasonable, otherwise Mr Carter would have been pestered constantly by people wanting to go in. An analogous problem presented itself with respect to the robbers's hole leading into the annexe, but this difficulty solved itself, since, when the antechamber was cleared and the wall dividing it from the burial chamber was taken down, the south end of the antechamber was used as a temporary store room for parts of the large shrines from round the sacrophagus, and these blocked the access to the annexe.

[1947]

With reference to the robbers' hole in the door of the burial chamber I stated that 'Lord Carnarvon, his daughter and Mr Carter certainly entered the burial chamber', and that '[The photographs] show the hole closed.' This leaves to the imagination the identity of the person who closed the door and the date when it was closed, and to that extent is ambiguous, an ambiguity that I now wish to remove. Mr Carter states that 'close examination revealed the fact that a small breach had been made near

the bottom . . . and that the hole made had subsequently been filled up and re-sealed'. This is misleading, since the hole, unlike that in the outermost doorway, had not been closed and re-sealed by the cemetery officials, but by Mr Carter. Soon after I commenced work with Mr Carter he pointed out to me the closing and re-sealing, and when I said that it did not look like old work he admitted that it was not and that he had done it.

◨ ◉ ◩ ◉ ◨ ◉

Another member of the team, Professor James Henry Breasted of the Oriental Institute, University of Chicago, an eminent historian of ancient Egypt, was voyaging down the Nile when news of the great discovery first reached him. His 'Some Experiences in the Tomb of Tutenkhamon' were recalled soon afterwards, in the January–February 1924 issue of the periodical *Art and Archaeology – The arts throughout the ages.*

We were drinking tea on the deck of the dahabiyah *Cheops* as we drifted past the now somber and palmless Island of Philae to a mooring place at Shellâl at the head of the First Cataract. It was the sixth of December; and, aided by a tug, we had run from the cataract to the wonderful temple of Abu Simbel and back in five days. Abu Simbel is three hundred miles above Luxor, and we were congratulating ourselves that we had done all this within a week and a day after leaving Luxor. The next morning brought a bag of letters from the Aswan post-office. Among them was a kind note from Lord Carnarvon in which he said: 'Two days after opening the cache or tomb I learned you had been through Luxor. I wish I had known, for I might then have persuaded you to stop a day and see a marvellous sight. Still there is another sealed door to be opened and I hope I shall then have the pleasure of seeing you there.' He did not say what it was. He knew we would understand that the lost tomb of Tutankhamon had been found.

A few days later the *Cheops* tied up at Luxor. Lord Carnarvon had returned to England to complete arrangements for the proper care of the great discovery. I found Carter just returned from Cairo, bringing with him a heavy iron door for closing the tomb. From his Cairo train he came over to see us and sat for an hour resting and telling of the great find. He was weary of telegrams and sick to death of reporters, and he had on his shoulders a very heavy responsibility. In order to make all safe, he had filled in the outer entrance of the tomb with a great many tons of limestone chips, which it would take several days to remove. Then he must install the iron door and run down a wire from the neighbouring small electric-light plant used to light the other royal tombs for the tourists, for it would of course be very unsafe to work with candles in such a place. When all was in readiness he would send me word to come and have a first view. Meantime nothing would be moved and the chamber would be left exactly as when first opened.

Before the war, Luxor had become a fashionable winter resort. It has not yet recovered its former popularity, but there was no lack of winter guests. When Carter's native runner finally brought his note on board, it contained a warning against being followed. In order to mislead the prying and the curious, and especially to avoid being followed by gentlemen of the press, we unconcernedly crossed the river in our felucca and ostentatiously engaged our donkeys to take us only to the foot of the western cliffs and not around through the entrance to the Valley of the Kings' Tombs, where Carter had his house. Having crossed the broad Theban plain, a ride of three quarters of an hour, we left our donkeys and, climbing the steep cliffs in the blazing Egyptian sunshine, we dropped down into the royal cemetery valley on the other side without having been followed by any one. As we came down, we could see just above the tomb of Rameses VI the huts of the government watchmen who guard the place at the present day. Immediately below this tomb Carter's clearance had exposed a flight of steps hewn into the limestone of the mountain. This had led to the discovery of the new tomb.

At the foot of these steps we saw a stout wooden grating fastened by many padlocks, which Carter's people at once began unlocking. When this was removed, it revealed a spacious gallery some twenty-five feet long, likewise hewn in limestone, descending at a sharp incline and terminating below in Carter's heavy iron door. These two doors, the first of wood, the second of iron, replaced two ancient closures of masonry which Carter had found filling the two doorways. The plastered face of the closing masonry, when found by Carter, still bore many royal seal impressions which he broke away in forcing an opening. As we descended the gallery we found the iron door covered with a white sheet to moderate the drafts. Suddenly electric bulbs of three thousand candle power hanging behind the sheet were turned on, and there was a blaze of light seen through the white fabric. The door was a heavy open grill; and as Carter pulled down the sheet, I saw through the open work of the door a sight I had never dreamed of seeing. Under this blaze of light I beheld the ante-chamber of a pharaoh's tomb still filled with the magnificent equipment which only the wealth and splendor of the Imperial Age in Egypt in the fourteenth century before Christ could have wrought or conceived – and, as it at first seemed, with everything still standing as it was placed there when the tomb was closed three thousand two hundred and fifty years ago.

The gorgeousness of the sight, the sumptuous splendor of it all, made it appear more like the confused magnificence of those counterfeit splendors which are heaped together in the property-room of some modern grand opera than any possible reality surviving from antiquity. Never was anything so dramatic in the whole range of archaeological discovery as this first view vouchsafed us here when the white curtain was pulled down. Carter was busy at the padlocks (American Yale locks!) and steel chains, and then the door swung open. Stepping in at last, I was utterly dazed by the overwhelming spectacle. The chamber was, I should guess, about fourteen by somewhat more than twenty feet in size. Against the rear wall, and occupying almost its entire length of over twenty feet, were placed head to foot three magnificent couches all over-wrought with gold. As we faced them they were breast high and evidently required a flight of portable steps when majesty mounted to bed. The one at the right was made in the form of a standing panther, the creature's head rising as the bedpost at

the head of the couch where his forelegs furnished also the supporting legs of the couch, his hind legs serving the same function at the foot. In the same way the middle couch had the form of a mottled cow with tall horns, and the third at the left was a grotesque Typhon-like hippo with mouth open showing the grinning teeth. Under the couches were chairs and caskets, chests and boxes. The chairs were sumptuous and magnificent beyond description. One of them, indeed, and by far the finest, which was mentioned in the dispatches as a throne (though this is not correct), displays in the inside of the back representations of the king and queen standing together, the work done in gold and silver with incrustation and inlay of semi-precious stones in bright colors. In art and craftsmanship it is one of the finest pieces of work now in existence from any age of the world, and far surpasses the best work of the craftsman now surviving from any other early time or people.

Literally stunned with surprise and admiration, I could only utter one ejaculation of amazement after another, and then turn and shake Carter's hand. Emotion struggled with the habit of years to observe and to understand. The critical faculties were getting much the worst of it in the struggle. There was reason enough, for all about us lay a completely new revelation of ancient life, quite transcending anything of which we had ever known before. In a corner at the right I knelt before a lovely casket containing part of the royal raiment. The outside of the casket was all painted with scenes in miniature representing the pharaoh and the royal suite engaged in hunting and in war. Description can but feebly suggest the exquisite character of this painted decoration, and the power of the unknown master who did it. The dying lion clutches with his mighty paw at the arrow which has entered his open mouth and hangs broken at his gnashing teeth. His wounded comrades of the jungle lie all about him in postures of pathetic suffering; and all this is done with such marvellous refinement of detail, especially in depicting the hairy manes, that one is reminded of similar work by Albrecht Dürer. Indeed the whole suggests the art of the Japanese painters of a century or two ago.

In the left corner of the front wall lay the dismounted wheels and other parts of a number of royal chariots. They were adorned with sumptuous designs in gold and incrustation of semi-precious stones like the back of the royal chair, and were fully equal to it in art and craftsmanship. The wheels bore evident traces of having been driven over rough Theban streets three thousand two hundred and fifty years ago. They were therefore not show pieces especially prepared for the king's tomb, but were vehicles intended for actual use. And nevertheless adorned like this! Not vulgar and ostentatious magnificence, but the tempered richness of refined art, formed the daily environment of these great emperors of the East in the fourteenth century before Christ along the Nile. The splendor of Nineveh and Babylon now begins to seem but a rough foil, setting off the refined culture of a higher civilization at Egyptian Thebes which could boast such craftsmen as this royal furniture was revealing for the first time – men quite worthy to stand beside Lorenzo Ghiberti and Benvenuto Cellini. As I stood in that rock-hewn chamber, I felt the culture values of the ancient world shifting so rapidly that it made one fairly dizzy.

I wandered up and down before the couches, aimlessly fingering note-book and pencil. Of what use were notes made in such a state of mind, with a whirling myriad of thoughts and details crowding for record all at once? There between two of the couches were four alabaster vases carved with open-work flowers growing on each side and forming the handles. No one had ever seen such vases before. Yonder was a casket of jewelry, and under one of the couches lay a magnificent courtier's baton with a superb handle of gleaming gold, the designs being done in filigree and lovely chevrons made up of tiny spheres of gold, laid scores of them to the inch, on the background of sheet gold. Just behind it was a door in the back wall of the chamber, opposite the chariots and accessible only by crawling under the left-hand couch. Carter handed me a portable electric bulb and I crawled under the tall couch to peep through the door. It had been masoned up, but this masonry had been broken through at the bottom. Through this breach, as I thrust in the bulb, I could see a second room, the 'annex chamber', so filled with royal furniture that it was impossible to enter the place without injury to its contents.

At the opposite end of the antechamber (the right end as one entered) there were further indications of additional chambers of the tomb. There, facing each other on either side of a sealed and still unopened doorway in the end wall of the chamber, stood two life-sized statues of the king like silent sentries guarding the sealed inner chamber at whose door they stood. The statues were of oiled wood, blackened with age, which, in spite of their sumptuous gilding, had invested the royal figures with something of the 'somber livery of the burnished sun' under which the king had lived. The figures stood on two reed mats, which were still in position under them.

A second glance had quickly dispelled the first impression that the royal tomb equipment was undisturbed. Evidences of disturbance and robbery were unmistakable. Sumptuous openwork designs in heavy sheet gold which filled the spaces between the legs of the finer chairs had been wrenched out and carried away. The chariots had suffered in the same way, and when the robbers finished with them they threw the parts down in confusion. They left the inner or annex chamber in great disorder. Of two shrines under the right-hand couch, one had been broken open and when the golden serpent-goddess within was found not to be of massive gold, it was left with the door open; while its companion shrine of identical design and of the same size, was left with the clay seal still unbroken protecting its tiny double doors. As the robbers left, they found in their way a common couch for ordinary household use. They tossed it hastily aside as they escaped from the tomb, where they were perhaps interrupted at their work, and it still lies high on the top of the Hathor couch, with one of the cow's horns sticking through the plaited thongs tightly stretched across the couch frame. Of course, the marauders must have taken with them many golden vessels and other objects made entirely of gold.

Besides being a Sherlock Holmes task of unusual interest, it was at that juncture a matter of importance to determine who these early tomb-robbers were, or at least to gain some rough approximation of the date when they forced their entrance. Carter had found the two outside doorways, at the two ends of the descending gallery, still displaying clear evidences of having been broken through and then sealed up again. The forced holes had not been large. They were made in the rubble masonry with which the doorways were closed. The roughly plastered face of this closing masonry, still bearing the precious seal impressions, had of course been carefully preserved by Carter. It did not seem to me possible that the post-Empire storm of destruction which swept over this royal cemetery could have included this tomb among its victims and still have left the contents of the place so largely intact. Having ventured to doubt the current report that this tomb, like all the other tombs in the valley, had been looted by post-Empire robbers, I raised the question in conversation with Carter. His reply was an urgent request to come over the next day and study the door sealings carefully, for he said that his many duties and responsibilities had not given him any opportunity to examine them with any care.

The rough masses and lumps of plaster bearing the seals were stored in a neighboring tomb which Carter was using as a workshop and laboratory. The next day found us busily poring over these fragments. Unfortunately, the ancient officials who had made the seal impressions had neglected to use enough dust on the seal. The plaster had consequently stuck to the seal and when it was pulled away the plaster under it came away with it, leaving the impression almost or totally illegible. However, the same seal was used many times and by putting together all the impressions of each one it was possible to read four different seals on the two doors. Three of them contained the name of Tutenkhamon, and the fourth was that of the cemetery administration and not necessarily post-Empire. The resealing after the robbery was not marked by the name of any post-Empire king. These facts were in themselves evidence that we were dealing with the *tomb* of Tutenkhamon, and not with a cache merely containing his mortuary furniture. They likewise made it highly probable that there had been no post-Empire robbery.

In a cemetery where the post-Empire catastrophe had been so complete, was it conceivable that any royal tomb should escape destruction? What could have saved this royal burial from the greedy hands of the post-Empire robbers? In considering this question it is important to recall that the tomb of Rameses VI is almost directly over that of Tutenkhamon. The many tourists who have for years visited the beautiful tomb of the former king have little dreamed that below their feet lay the magnificent burial of Tutenkhamon. When Rameses VI's workmen were excavating his tomb, the Egyptian Empire had just fallen (about 1150 BC). The robberies which were to wreck the burials of the great pharaohs were just beginning. Immediately below these workmen, the tomb of Tutenkhamon was over two hundred years old. As they proceeded with the excavation of Rameses VI's tomb, they carried out their baskets of limestone chips and other rubbish and threw them down the slope right over the mouth of Tutenkhamon's tomb. It is not likely that they knew it was there, for they

built directly across the entrance of Tutenkhamon's tomb a line of stone huts, in which they slept at night. Covered still deeper by the workmen's huts, the tomb of Tutenkhamon was never discovered by the post-Empire tomb robbers, and it thus became the only royal tomb which escaped their depredations. This is clear enough to me now as I write, but it was not by any means demonstrated at the end of our first day's examination of the door seals from the two upper doors. There was still the inner, unopened doorway, guarded by the king's statues! So Carter urged me to come over for a third visit the next day, especially to examine this unopened doorway, which likewise bore royal seals.

As I rode across the Theban plain the next morning, my mind was absorbed with the problem on which we were engaged. If Tutenkhamon's tomb had really escaped the post-Empire robbers, as seemed highly probable, who could have robbed it under the power and wealth and efficiency of the great pharaohs of the Empire – rulers quite capable of protecting the tombs of their ancestors? There was only one bit of evidence which might throw light on this question. If you enter the tomb of Thutmose IV at the present day, you will find on the wall, written in ink by an excellent scribal penman, a neat memorandum to the effect that the royal burial in this tomb was restored by order of King Harmhab. Now Harmhab was the almost immediate successor of Tutenkhamon. That means that a royal burial had suffered robbery soon after the death of Tutenkhamon. His tomb may likewise have been entered by the same robbers. The thought of this bit of evidence made my ride across the beautiful Theban plain that morning quite different from any ride I had ever taken there before. Behind the majestic, sun-bathed cliffs of the western plateau rising before me slept still undisturbed in imperial magnificence one of the great sovereigns of the ancient East, just as he had been laid away three thousand two hundred and fifty years ago. Behind the still unopened sealed doorway must be the chamber where he lay, and there we should gain an even more splendid vision of ancient life from the marvelous works of art with which the lords of the Egyptian Empire had furnished the burial of their imperial sovereign in the fourteenth century before Christ. Would post-Empire seals on the inner doorway dispel this pipe-dream?

I found Carter with a sheaf of telegrams and letters from all sorts of people who were trying to gain a glimpse of the wonderful tomb. When he had disposed of these, we rode up through the mouth of the wild and impressive valley, just outside of which Carter has for many years had his house. Under the burning Egyptian sun the valley was glowing with tremulous light which touched the rocks with splendor – a fitting place for the sepulchers of Egypt's greatest dead, the 'sons of the sun', as the pharaohs called themselves. Over our heads rose a mountain of sunlit limestone above the chamber to which we descended. The silence of forgotten ages seemed to brood over the place as the echoes of our footfalls faded and we stood quietly in the great king's tomb.

Before us was the still unopened door. The floor before it was encumbered with small objects, which it was unwise to move before the preliminary records of the conditions in the

tomb were made. To our regret also, we were obliged to stand on the ancient reed matting on which the king's statues had so long ago been placed. Otherwise we could not bring our eyes near enough to the seal-impressed mortar. Then began the detailed examination of one broken, imperfect and mostly illegible seal impression after another. As the work absorbed us, there seemed to be voices haunting the silence. Certainly there were quite audible noises. From strange rustling sounds they increased now and then to a sharp snapping report. These were the evidences of melancholy changes which were already taking place around us. For some three thousand two hundred and fifty years before Carter first entered it, the air in this chamber had been unchanged. In all likelihood the temperature too had changed but slightly if at all in all that time. Now the incoming draughts were changing the temperature and altering the air. Chemical changes were going on, and the wood in the furniture was adjusting itself to new strains with resulting snapping and fracturing which we could plainly hear. It meant that the life of these beautiful things around us was limited. A few generations more and the objects not of pottery, stone or metal will be gone.

At either shoulder, as I worked, looked down upon me the benign face of a ruler who had dominated the ancient world in the days when the Hebrews were captives in Egypt and long before Moses their leader and liberator was born. It was a noble portrait gazing down upon me in quiet serenity, as I puzzled over the seals impressed there when the king had not been long dead. Only the soft rays of the electric light suggested the modern world into which these amazing survivals from a past so remote had been so unexpectedly projected. [As I sat copying the 150 or so seals, a curious incident occurred. I happened to glance up at the face of one of the statues of the King – and as I did so, he clearly and unmistakably *winked* at me! For a moment this was strangely disturbing, but I quickly found the explanation. Attached to a virtually invisible filament hanging from the King's eyebrow in front of his eyes, was a tiny piece of dark pigment which had been used in coloring the statues and was now dropping off in small iridescent, shiny, mica-like flakes. In the faint movement of the air from the doorway, the suspended flake had caught and reflected the light in a manner exactly resembling a wink!]* Thus in the silence of the tomb, always conscious of the royal face contemplating me at either elbow, I continued the examination of the seals, till I had inspected every impression from the top of the doorway to a point near the bottom, where the small objects and the reed matting interfered with the examination. It was evident that this mysterious unopened inner doorway contained the same seals which I had found on the other two. A new one also, of which there were fifteen impressions, contained the name of Tutenkhamon himself. There was no Ramses, no post-Empire seal or resealing, and consequently there had been no post-Empire robbery!

What I had dreamed of, in crossing the Theban plain that morning, was an undoubted reality. As I stood in the silent chamber between the two statues of the pharaoh still imperturbably guarding the sealed doorway before me, it was evident that behind it lay the body of the only pharaoh of the Empire which had escaped the destruction wrought by post-Empire disorder and lawlessness. There he was unquestionably awaiting us, lying in undisturbed magnificence. For the hole at the bottom of this doorway was evidently much too small to have permitted the removal of anything but quite small objects.

▣ ◉ ▣ ◉ ▣ ◉

Howard Carter takes up the story:

Clearing the objects from the Antechamber was like playing a gigantic game of spillikins. So crowded were they that it was a matter of extreme difficulty to move one without running serious risk of damaging others, and in some cases they were so inextricably tangled that an elaborate system of props and supports had to be devised to hold one object or group of objects in place while another was being removed. At such times life was a nightmare. One was afraid to move lest one should kick against a prop and bring the whole thing crashing down. Nor, in many cases, could one tell without experiment whether a particular object was strong enough to bear its own weight. Certain of the things were in beautiful condition, as strong as when they first were made, but others were in a most precarious state, and the problem constantly arose whether it would be better to apply preservative treatment to an object *in situ*, or to wait until it could be dealt with in more convenient surroundings in the laboratory. The latter course was adopted

*This reminiscence was later added to Breasted's account by his son.

whenever possible, but there were cases in which the removal of an object without treatment would have meant almost certain destruction.

There were sandals, for instance, of patterned bead-work, of which the threading had entirely rotted away. As they lay on the floor of the chamber they looked in perfectly sound condition, but, try to pick one up, and it crumbled at the touch, and all you had for your pains was a handful of loose, meaningless beads. This was a clear case for treatment on the spot – a spirit stove, some paraffin wax, an hour or two to harden, and the sandal could be removed intact, and handled with the utmost freedom. The funerary bouquets again: without treatment as they stood they would have ceased to exist; subjected to three or four sprayings of celluloid solution they bore removal well, and were subsequently packed

with scarcely any injury. Occasionally, particularly with the larger objects, it was found better to apply local treatment in the tomb, just sufficient to ensure a safe removal to the laboratory, where more drastic measures were possible. Each object presented a separate problem, and there were cases in which only experiment could show the proper treatment.

It was slow work, painfully slow, and nerve-racking at that, for one felt all the time a heavy weight of responsibility. Every excavator must, if he have any archaeological conscience at all. The things he finds are not his own property, to treat as he pleases, or neglect as he chooses. They are a direct legacy from the past to the present age, he but the privileged intermediary through whose hands they come; and if, by carelessness, slackness, or ignorance, he lessens the sum of knowledge that might have been obtained from them, he knows himself to be

The antechamber: note the basketwork tray and reeds covering up the hole in the lower far wall, made by Howard Carter when he secretly entered the further chambers of the tomb.

guilty of an archaeological crime of the first magnitude. Destruction of evidence is so painfully easy, and yet so hopelessly irreparable. Tired or pressed for time, you shirk a tedious piece of cleaning, or do it in a half-hearted, perfunctory sort of way, and you will perhaps have thrown away the one chance that will ever occur of gaining some important piece of knowledge.

Too many people – unfortunately there are so-called archaelogists among them – are apparently under the impression that the object bought from a dealer's shop is just as valuable as one which has been found in actual excavation, and that until the object in question has been cleaned, entered in the books, marked with an accession number, and placed in a tidy museum case, it is not a proper subject for study at all. There was never a greater mistake. Field-work is all-important, and it is a sure and certain fact that if every excavation had been properly, systematically, and conscientiously carried out, our knowledge of Egyptian archaeology would be at least 50 per cent greater than it is. There are numberless derelict objects in the storerooms of our museums which would give us valuable information could they but tell us whence they came, and box after box full of fragments which a few notes at the time of finding would have rendered capable of reconstruction.

Granting, then, that a heavy weight of responsibility must at all times rest upon the excavator, our own feelings on this occasion will easily be realized. It had been our privilege to find the most important collection of Egyptian antiquities that had ever seen the light, and it was for us to show that we were worthy of the trust. So many things there were that might go wrong. Danger of theft, for instance, was an ever-present anxiety. The whole countryside was agog with excitement about the tomb; all sorts of extravagant tales were current about the gold and jewels it contained; and, as past experience had shown, it was only too possible that there might be a serious attempt to raid the tomb by night. This possibility of robbery on a large scale was negatived, so far as was humanly possible, by a complicated system of guarding, there being present in The Valley, day and night, three independent groups of watchmen, each answerable to a different authority – the Government Antiquities Guards, a squad of soldiers supplied by the Mudir of Kena, and a selected group of the most trustworthy of our own staff. In addition, we had a heavy wooden grille at the entrance to the passage, and a massive steel gate at the inner doorway, each secured by four padlocked chains; and, that there might never be any mistake about these latter, the keys were in the permanent charge of one particular member of the European staff, who never parted with them for a moment, even to lend them to a colleague. Petty or casual theft we guarded against by doing all the handling of the objects ourselves.

Another and perhaps an even greater cause for anxiety was the condition of many of the objects. It was manifest with some of them that their very existence depended on careful manipulation and correct preservative treatment, and there were moments when our hearts were in our mouths. There were other worries, too – visitors, for instance . . . and I fear that by the time the Antechamber was finished our nerves, to say nothing of our tempers, were in an extremely ragged state. But here am I talking about finishing before we have even begun. We must make a fresh start. It is not time to lose our tempers yet.

Obviously, our first and greatest need was photography.

▣ ◉ ▣ ◉ ▣ ◉

Harry Burton, the Lincolnshire-born archaeologist and photographer who was working for the Metropolitan Museum in New York when he was invited to join the team, was responsible for producing a complete photographic record of the discovery. Carter had wired the curator of the Metropolitan's Egyptian Department (who happened to be staying at the Burlington Hotel, Pall Mall), on 3 December, to ask whether he could 'consider loan of Burton in recording in time being'. Four days later, the reply came: 'Please call upon Burton and any other members of our staff. Am cabling Burton to this effect.' The resulting photographs, today kept in the Griffith Institute, Oxford, and the Metropolitan Museum, are classics in the history of archaeological photography. The following article by Harry Burton was published in the *New York Times* on 15 February and *The Times* on 16 February 1923.

In view of the great interest that has been aroused by the discovery of the tomb of Tutankhamen by Lord Carnarvon and Mr Howard Carter, a few notes on the photographic work in connexion with the clearing may be of interest.

Few people realize the importance of photography in archaeological research, but if it were not for the camera much evidence would be entirely lost, and certain details would never be noticed. Before excavations are commenced, several general views of the site are taken, and it is from these that very useful information is obtained as to ground plans, which are frequently invisible to the naked eye, yet are very distinct in a photograph.

The work above ground is comparatively simple, as it is chiefly a question of choosing the right moment – *i.e.*, when the light will give the best results of the site or the objects to be photographed. Not so, however, in the work of photographing the interior of tombs, where the light is, more often than not, practically nil, and the question is how to get it into the tomb to enable one to make an exposure. Until comparatively recently such photographs were taken with flashlight, but these were rarely satisfactory, and, moreover, after one photograph had been taken it was necessary to wait a considerable time for the smoke to disperse before another could be taken. I have had considerable experience in photographing the paintings and reliefs in the tombs of Thebes, and I have invariably succeeded, with a little management, in throwing sunlight into underground chambers – sometimes over 100ft below the surface – that have never before seen the light of day.

This is done with the aid of large mirrors. One mirror is placed outside the tomb entrance in the sunshine, and the shaft of sunlight sent from this into the chamber is caught by a silver-papered reflector, and thence thrown on the part of the wall that is to be photographed, being kept constantly in motion to ensure equal lighting.

When an intact tomb is found – unfortunately a very rare occurrence – one usually finds the entrance bricked up and, in some cases, the entire surface of the plaster covered with seals. In such a case the first thing to be done is to photograph this sealed entrance, and nothing further must be done until the picture is developed and pronounced satisfactory. Duplicate negatives are invariably taken, as once the seals and bricks are removed, the photograph is the only evidence that remains. The entrance is then cleared, other general views are taken of the interior, and nothing is touched until satisfactory results have been obtained, as it is most important to have photographic records of how the objects were placed.

These general views taken, the work of clearing begins, and, as it progresses, detail photographs are taken of any new piece of evidence that turns up, or of any object or group of objects which the general views have failed to disclose. It may even, in some cases, be necessary to take a series of a dozen or more views of a single object, in order to illustrate the various stages in its clearing or unwrapping. It sometimes happens that the photographs taken in the tomb are the only ones that it is possible to get, as frequently the objects collapse when touched. I remember, when we were clearing a series of XVIIth Dynasty tombs, which had been infested with white ants, the preliminary photographs were literally the only record of most of the wooden objects found. The coffins appeared to be in perfect condition, but when touched they collapsed into dust.

There was one very attractive small wooden statuette of a girl in one of these tombs, which appeared to be quite sound. It was standing quite alone, and after the general view of the chamber had been taken, the camera was turned on to it. I intended to expose a plate for two minutes, but after it had been exposed for one and three-quarter minutes the figure suddenly collapsed, and nothing remained but a small heap of dust. I immediately switched off the beam of light, put a cap on the camera, and went off to develop the plate. Fortunately the negative turned out to be quite good, and, although the statuette no longer existed, we had a complete record of it. This is only one of many similar cases.

When Lord Carnarvon and Mr Carter told me they were going to ask the Metropolitan Museum for the loan of my services to assist in the recording of the tomb of Tutankhamen, the first idea that came to me was the question of lighting, and I was greatly relieved to learn that electric light was to be used, and that we should be able to work independently of the sun. The Tombs of the Kings are lighted by electricity, so that it was only a question of extra wire and more powerful lamps.

Another point that is very important in tomb-photography is colour-rendering. In the first chamber of the tomb in question the predominant colour is gold, and the two statues of the King guarding the sealed entrance are black and gold. Gold on an ordinary plate comes out black, and even on an orthochromatic plate the difference between black and gold is not very marked. Therefore the only way to get a correct colour-rendering is to use panchromatic plates.

These have to be manipulated in total darkness, which is not at all a difficult business in a well-appointed dark-room; but it is not so easy in the desert, in a tomb. My dark-room is the so-called *cache* of Akhenaten, the father-in-law of Tutankhamen, discovered by Mr Theodore Davis and Mr Ayrton in 1909, within a stone's throw of Tutankhamen's tomb.

In the tomb itself I have two electric lamps – one stationary 2,000 c.p. half-watt, and one portable 1,000 c.p. half-watt. The latter I use for breaking up the shadows by keeping it constantly in motion. I began by taking general views of the chamber from the entrance, with a good over-lap to ensure the record of all the objects. Since then, I have been photographing them in groups, and, when each group has been done, it is removed to the tomb of Seti II, in which the objects are being cleaned and restored. The final photographs will be taken when these processes are completed.

■ ◉ ▣ ◉ ▣ ◉

Howard Carter continues:

By the middle of February [1923] our work in the Antechamber was finished. With the exception of the two sentinel statues ... all its contents had been removed to the laboratory, every inch of its floor had been swept and sifted for the last bead or fallen piece of inlay, and it now stood bare and empty. We were ready at last to penetrate the mystery of the sealed door.

Friday, the 17th, was the day appointed, and at two o'clock those who were to be privileged to witness the ceremony met by appointment above the tomb ...

In the Antechamber everything was prepared and ready, and to those who had not visited it since the original opening of the tomb it must have presented a strange sight. We had screened the statues with boarding to protect them from possible damage, and between them we had erected a small platform, just high enough to enable us to reach the upper part of the doorway, having determined, as the safest plan, to work from the top downwards. A short distance back from the platform there was a barrier, and beyond, knowing that there might be hours of work ahead of us, we had provided chairs for the visitors. On either side standards had been set up for our lamps, their light shining full upon the doorway. Looking back, we realize what a strange, incongruous picture the chamber must have presented, but at the time I question whether such an idea even crossed our minds. One thought and one only was possible. There before us lay the sealed door, and with its opening we were to blot out the centuries and stand in the presence of a king who reigned three thousand years ago. My own feelings as I mounted the platform were a strange mixture, and it was with a trembling hand that I struck the first blow.

My first care was to locate the wooden lintel above the door: then very carefully I chipped away the plaster and picked out the small stones which formed the uppermost layer of the filling. The temptation to stop and peer inside at every moment was irresistible, and when, after about ten minutes' work, I had made a hole large enough to enable me to do so, I inserted an electric torch. An astonishing sight its light revealed, for there, within a yard of the doorway, stretching as far as one could

impressions upon the thick mortar of the outer face, and this added considerably to the difficulty of handling the stones. Mace and Callender were helping me by this time, and each stone was cleared on a regular system. With a crowbar I gently eased it up, Mace holding it to prevent it falling forwards; then he and I lifted it out and passed it back to Callender, who transferred it on to one of the foremen, and so, by a chain of workmen, up the passage and out of the tomb altogether.

With the removal of a very few stones the mystery of the golden wall was solved. We were at the entrance of the actual burial-chamber of the king, and that which barred our way was the side of an immense gilt shrine built to cover and protect the sarcophagus. It was visible now from the Antechamber by the light of the standard lamps, and as stone after stone was removed, and its gilded surface came gradually into view, we could, as though by electric current, feel the tingle of excitement which thrilled the spectators behind the barrier ... We who were doing the work were probably less excited, for our whole energies were taken up with the task in hand — that of removing the blocking without an accident. The fall of a single stone might have done irreparable damage to the delicate surface of the shrine, so, directly the hole was large enough, we made an additional protection for it by inserting a mattress on the inner side of the door-blocking, suspending it from the wooden lintel of the doorway. Two hours of hard work it took us to clear away the blocking, or at least as much of it as was necessary for the moment; and at one point, when near the bottom, we had to delay operations for a

see and blocking the entrance to the chamber, stood what to all appearance was a solid wall of gold. For the moment there was no clue as to its meaning, so as quickly as I dared I set to work to widen the hole. This had now become an operation of considerable difficulty, for the stones of the masonry were not accurately squared blocks built regularly upon one another, but rough slabs of varying size, some so heavy that it took all one's strength to lift them: many of them, too, as the weight above was removed, were left so precariously balanced that the least false movement would have sent them sliding inwards to crash upon the contents of the chamber below. We were also endeavouring to preserve the seal-

space while we collected the scattered beads from a necklace brought by the plunderers from the chamber within and dropped upon the threshold. This last was a terrible trial to our patience, for it was a slow business, and we were all of us excited to see what might be within; but finally it was done, the last stones were removed, and the way to the innermost chamber lay open before us . . .

Lord Carnarvon and M. Lacau [Director-General of the Service of Antiquities] now joined me, and, picking our way along the narrow passage between shrine and wall, paying out the wire of our light behind us, we investigated further.

It was, beyond any question, the sepulchral chamber in which we stood, for there, towering above us, was one of the great gilt shrines beneath which kings were laid. So enormous was this structure (seventeen feet by eleven feet, and nine feet high, we found afterwards) that it filled within a little the entire area of the chamber, a space of some two feet only separating it from the walls on all four sides, while its roof, with cornice top and torus moulding, reached almost to the ceiling. From top to bottom it was overlaid with gold, and upon its sides there were inlaid panels of brilliant blue faience, in which were represented, repeated over and over, the magic symbols which would ensure its strength and safety. Around the shrine, resting upon the ground, there were a number of funerary emblems, and, at the north end, the seven magic oars the king would need to ferry himself across the waters of the underworld. The walls of the chamber, unlike those of the Antechamber, were decorated with brightly painted scenes and inscriptions, brilliant in

their colours, but evidently somewhat hastily executed.

These last details we must have noticed subsequently, for at the time our one thought was of the shrine and of its safety. Had the thieves penetrated within it and disturbed the royal burial? Here, on the eastern end, were the great folding doors, closed and bolted, but not sealed, that would answer the question for us. Eagerly we drew the bolts, swung back the doors, and there within was a second shrine with similar bolted doors, and upon the bolts a seal, intact. This seal we determined not to break, for our doubts were resolved, and we could not penetrate further without risk of serious damage to the monument. I think at the moment we did not even want to break the seal, for a feeling of intrusion had descended heavily upon us with the opening of the doors, heightened, probably, by the almost painful impressiveness of a linen pall, decorated with golden rosettes, which drooped above the inner shrine. We felt that we were in the presence of the dead King and must do him reverence, and in imagination could see the doors of the successive shrines open one after the other till the innermost disclosed the King himself. Carefully, and as silently as possible, we re-closed the great swing doors, and passed on to the farther end of the chamber.

Here a surprise awaited us, for a low door, eastwards from the sepulchral chamber, gave entrance to yet another chamber, smaller than the outer ones and not so lofty. This doorway, unlike the others, had not been closed and sealed. We were able, from where we stood, to get a clear view of the whole of the contents, and a single glance sufficed to tell us that here, within this little chamber, lay the greatest treasures of the tomb. Facing the doorway, on the farther side, stood the most beautiful monument that I have ever seen – so lovely that it made one gasp with wonder and admiration. The central portion of it consisted of a large shrine-shaped chest, completely overlaid with gold, and surmounted by a cornice of sacred cobras. Surrounding this, free-standing, were statues of the four tutelary goddesses of the dead – gracious figures with outstretched protective arms, so natural and lifelike in their pose, so pitiful and compassionate the expression upon their faces, that one felt it almost sacrilege to look at them. One guarded the shrine on each of its four sides, but whereas the figures at front and back kept their gaze firmly fixed upon their charge, an additional note of touching realism was imparted by the other two, for their heads were turned sideways, looking over their shoulders towards the entrance, as though to watch against surprise. There is a simple grandeur about this monument that made an irresistible appeal to the imagination, and I am not ashamed to confess that it brought a lump to my throat.

▣ ◉ ▣ ◉ ▣ ◉

Arthur Mace, Tasmanian-born (but London and Herefordshire raised), an associate curator of the Metropolitan Museum's Egyptian Department, joined the team as conservator and record-keeper, mainly working in the 'laboratory tomb' (Seti II). He also co-wrote the first volume of *The Discovery of the Tomb of Tutankhamen* with Howard Carter. His account of the initial season's work in the tomb was published in a supplement to the Metro-

politan Museum's *Bulletin*, December 1923, just as the second season was beginning to get under way. Mace's modesty about his considerable talents as a record-keeper, which were noted by all concerned, is apparent throughout the piece.

Lord Carvarvon's and Howard Carter's discovery of the tomb of Tutenkhamon has aroused an interest, not merely in this particular find, but in archaeology generally, that to the excavator is almost embarrassing. Ordinarily he spends his time quietly and unobtrusively enough, half the year burrowing mole-like in the ground, and the other half writing dull papers for scientific journals, and now suddenly he finds himself in the full glare of the limelight, with newspaper reporters lying in wait for him at every corner, and snapshotters recording his every movement. He can not even hammer in a nail without five continents knowing all about it by breakfast time next morning. It is, as I said, embarrassing and a little bewildering, and the excavator feels sometimes that he would like to know why the ordinary details of his daily work should suddenly have become of intense and absorbing interest to the world at large. Why is it? Whence has the ordinary every-day citizen derived this sudden enthusiasm for the funeral furniture of a long-dead Pharaoh?

The explanation is, I suppose, simple enough really. It lies in the fact that we are all, even the most prosaic of us, children under our skins, and thrill deliciously at the very idea of buried treasure. Sealed doorways, jewelled robes, inlay of precious stones, kings' regalia – the phrases grip, and we can now, under cover of scientific interest, openly and unashamedly indulge an intellectual appetite that has hitherto been nourished surreptitiously on detective stories and murder cases in the press. Now at last we can claim open fellowship with John Silver's parrot, and gabble over 'pieces of eight, pieces of eight' without shame. How Stevenson, by the way, would have loved excavating.

In view of this widespread interest and the general familiarity with Tutenkhamon's name, it comes as almost a shock to find how little we really know about this monarch. Before the finding of the tomb he was little more than a name, and even now, though we know with almost embarrassing detail the extent of his possessions, we are still almost entirely in the dark as to his origin, his life, and his personal character.

He became king (about 1360 BC) by virtue of his marriage with Enkhosnepaaton, third daughter of the so-called heretic king, Ikhnaton, but we have at present no means of telling whether the marriage took place during Ikhnaton's lifetime, or was contracted hastily after his death to give Tutenkhamon a pretext for seizing the throne. It was not, one would have thought, a particularly enviable or safe position to aspire to at this juncture, for the country was in a state of chaos, and the people were seething with discontent. In his short reign Ikhnaton 'The Dreamer' had thrown away an empire, and alienated nine-tenths of his own subjects, and now at his death there was no obvious person to succeed him. Sons he had none, and our interest centers upon a group of little girls, his daughters. The eldest of

these, Meritaton, had been married a year or two before her father's death to a certain Sakere, a vague person of whom we know nothing but the facts that he acted as co-regent with Ikhnaton during the last year or two of his reign, and that he disappears from the scene immediately after Ikhnaton's death. This latter circumstance is suspicious, to say the least of it. In oriental countries coincidences of this nature are generally very carefully arranged beforehand, and it is more than likely that Sakere was quietly and effectively – what shall we say? – abolished.

The second daughter died in Ikhnaton's lifetime, and the third, a girl of ten or thereabouts, was the Enkhosnepaaton who was married to our king.

It must have been immediately obvious to Tutenkhamon or to his advisers that a complete surrender must be made of all Ikhnaton's ideas and principles, an unconditional return to the old order and the old gods, if the country was to recover from the chaos into which it had lapsed. In pursuance of this policy Tell el Amarna, the heretic capital, was abandoned, the Court was transferred back again to Thebes, the new king changed his name from Tutenkhaton to Tutenkhamon, and the favor of the powerful priests was courted by putting in hand restorations and additions to the Amon temples. How far these concessions to popular opinion were effectual we do not know, but that they must have gone some way towards stabilizing the government of the country is evident from the scenes in the tomb of one of the king's viceroys, Huy by name, wherein both Syrians and Nubians are represented as bringing tribute to Tutenkhamon's Court.

That exhausts the facts of Tutenkhamon's life as we know them from the monuments. The rest is pure conjecture. We do not even know the length of his reign – in fact, the one dated object we possess, a piece of inscribed cloth of the sixth year, is in our own Metropolitan Museum collection. We have reason to believe that he was little more than a boy when he died, and that it was his successor, Eye, who supported his candidature to the throne and acted as his adviser during his brief reign. It was Eye, moreover, who arranged his funeral ceremonies, and it may even be that he arranged his death, judging that the time was now ripe for him to assume the reins of government himself . . .

The story of the actual discovery and of the general details of the work of clearing is well enough known from other sources, and there is no need for us to dwell upon it here. I should like, however, to devote some space to the share in the work taken by the members of our own Expedition.

Photography was the first and most pressing need at the outset, for it was absolutely essential that a complete photographic record of the objects in the tomb should be made before anything was touched. This part of the work was undertaken by Burton, and the wonderful results he achieved are known to every one, his photographs having appeared in most of the illustrated papers throughout the world. They were all taken by electric light, wires having been laid to connect the tomb with the main lighting system of the Valley, and for a dark-room, appropriately enough, he had the unfinished tomb which Tutenkhamon had used as cache for the funerary remains of the Tell el Amarna royalties.

Hall and Hauser were responsible for the plan of the tomb. Each individual object was drawn to scale in the exact position in which it lay, and a reference to the photographs of the interior, which illustrate the confused and haphazard manner in which these objects were piled one upon another, will give some idea of the difficulties that confronted them.

My own share of the work was largely confined to the laboratory, which was established, with the consent of the Department of Antiquities, in the tomb of Seti II, conveniently situated in a secluded spot at the extreme end of the Valley. Here, working in collaboration with Mr Lucas, Director of the Government Chemical Laboratories, who most generously sacrificed three months' leave to come and help us, and whose chemical knowledge was invaluable, I spent the greater part of the winter, receiving the objects as one by one they were brought up out of the tomb, noting and cataloguing them, and carrying out such repairs and restorations as were necessary.

Obviously, in dealing with this enormous mass of material, it was impossible to attempt anything in the shape of final restorations or notes. We had neither the time nor the space, even had the necessary plant been available, and all we could hope to do was to make a preliminary series of notes, and render such first-aid treatment as was required to make the objects fit to travel. Years of work lie ahead of us, and it will need all our patience and the cooperation of a number of skilled workmen if the fullest use is to be made of the wonderful opportunity that has been presented to us. Restoration work of the most drastic character will be necessary owing to the condition to which some of the objects have been reduced. Take the chariots, for example. The woodwork is in good condition, and will need little in the way of repairs except for the fixing of the gesso and gold foil to the surface, and the restoration of a few fallen pieces of inlay. With the horse-trappings it is quite another story, for the leather parts have almost entirely perished, leaving nothing but the gold ornamentation with which they were covered. Here new harness will have to be made to which the original gold can be affixed.

The elaborately decorated robes are another case in point. In many of them the linen body of the garment has been reduced almost to powder, but, by careful noting before anything was touched, it was possible in many cases to work out the complete scheme of decoration – beadwork, gold sequins, etc. – with which they were covered, and the approximate size of the garment itself. In this case garments of fresh cloth will have to be made and the old decoration applied to them, an appalling task to contemplate, for on one of the robes in question I calculated that there were close on fifty thousand beads. Or take the sandals, whose entire surface was covered with gold decoration. Here, again, the leather had perished, but we have exact notes of the scheme of decoration, and shall have made new sandals to which the original gold may be applied.

These restorations are not only legitimate but absolutely essential to a proper appreciation and study of the material. By their means you acquire complete objects, things of beauty in themselves, and of enormous archaeological value; without restorations you would have gained nothing but a large boxful of beads, a few pieces of ill-preserved cloth, and a number of meaningless shells of gold decoration, things of but small archaeological value, and from an artistic point of view of no value at all.

The most exciting of the laboratory tasks was the unpacking of the boxes and caskets, for, owing to the confused nature of their contents, you could never be certain of anything, and at any moment, tucked away in a corner, or concealed in the fold of a garment, you might come across a magnificent scarab or piece of jewelry, or a wonderful statuette. The jumble was amazing, the most incongruous things being packed together, and for some time we were completely in the dark as to its meaning. The explanation, as we worked it out later, is as follows.

Some ten or fifteen years after the burial of the king, plunderers had contrived to tunnel their way into the tomb and had made a hurried and ruthless search for treasure that was portable, ransacking the boxes and throwing their contents all over the floor. Then, probably while the plunderers were still at work, the officials responsible for the safe-keeping of the royal necropolis got wind of the affair, and came post-haste to investigate. Some of the thieves made good their escape – the faience cup beneath the rock which we referred to above was probably hidden by one of them – but others were evidently either caught on the spot, or apprehended later with the loot still in their possession. Then came the question of making good the damage, and a hurried and perfunctory job the officials seem to have made of it. No attempt was made to re-sort the material or pack the objects back into the boxes that were originally intended for them.

Instead, they were gathered up in handfuls and bundles and hastily crammed into the nearest box. As a result we get the most incongruous mixtures, walking-sticks and underlinen, jewelry and faience vases, headrests and robes of state.

From the point of view of our laboratory work it would have been far better if the contents of the boxes had been left lying as the thieves had scattered them. As repacked they were extraordinarily difficult to handle, and one had to exercise constant care lest, in removing an object from an upper layer, one did some damage to a still more valuable object which lay beneath. Nor was it always possible to remove one single piece at a time, for in the sweeping-up process a number of the objects inevitably became tangled and interfolded, with the result that in some cases three or four garments were so hopelessly involved that they had to be treated as one. What this meant in dealing with heavily decorated robes, of which the actual cloth was in such bad condition that it could not even be touched, and when the only chance of working out the size and shape was by noting the exact scheme of decoration, will more readily be comprehended when I explain that it took three weeks of hard work to clear a single box.

Slow and exacting the work was, but intensely interesting, and worth every minute of the time that was spent upon it. No trouble could be too great, for we have been given an opportunity such as archaeology has never known before, and in all probability will never see again. Now for the first time we have what every excavator has dreamt of, but never hoped to see, a royal tomb with all its furniture intact.

The increase to our sum of archaeological knowledge should be enormous, and we, as a Museum, should count it as a privilege to have been able to take such a prominent part in the work.

Some idea of the extent of the discovery may be gleaned from the fact that the objects so far removed represent but a quarter of the contents of the tomb, and that, probably, the least valuable quarter. We have cleared the Antechamber. There remain the Sepulchral Chamber, the inner Store Chamber, and the Annex, and, to all appearance, each contains far finer objects than any we have handled yet. It is the first of these chambers that will occupy us in the opening months of the coming season. There, beneath the sepulchral shrines, three thousand years ago the king was laid to rest, and there, or ever these words appear in print, we hope to find him lying.

◼ ◉ ◼ ◉ ◼ ◉

The second volume of Howard Carter's *The Discovery of the Tomb of Tutankhamen* continues where Mace left off.

The second season's work actually began in the laboratory, under Mr Mace, who dealt with the magnificent chariots and the ceremonial couches that were left over from the first season. While he was carrying out this work of preservation and packing, with the aid of Mr Callender, I began by removing the two guardian statues that stood before the doorway of the Burial Chamber, and then, as it was necessary, demolished the partition wall dividing it from the Antechamber.

touched, tended to crush and fall away. Thus our problem was how to deal in that very limited space with those sections of the shrines, weighing from a quarter to three-quarters of a ton, when taking them apart and removing them, without causing them undue damage.

Without first demolishing that partition wall, it would have been impossible to have dealt with the great shrines within the Burial Chamber, or to remove many of the funereal paraphernalia therein. Even then our great difficulty was due to the confined space in which we had to carry out the most difficult task of dismantling those shrines, which proved to be four in number, nested one within the other.

Beyond the very limited space and high temperature which prevailed, our difficulties were further increased by the great weight of the various sections and panels of which those complex shrines were constructed. These were made of 2¼-inch oak planking, and overlaid with superbly delicate gold-work upon gesso. The wood-planking, though perfectly sound, had shrunk in the course of three thousand three hundred years in that very dry atmosphere, the gold-work upon the gesso had, if at all, slightly expanded; the result in any case was a space between the basic wood-planking and the ornamented gold surface which, when

Other complications arose during this undertaking, and one of them was due to the fact that those sections were held together by means of secret wooden tongues let into the thickness of the wood-planking of the panels, roof sections, cornice pieces and 'styles'. It was only by slightly forcing open the cracks between those different sections, and by that means discovering the positions of the tongues that held them together, inserting a fine saw and severing them, that we were able to free them and take them apart. No sooner had we discovered the method of overcoming this complication, had dealt with the various sections of the great outermost shrine, and become proud of ourselves, anticipating that we had learnt how to treat the next shrine or shrines, than we found that, in the very next shrine, although held together in a similar manner, many of the hidden tongues were of solid bronze, inscribed with the names of Tut-ankh-Amen. These could not of course be sewn through as in the first case. We had therefore to find other methods. In fact, contrary to our expectations, the farther we proceeded, although the space in which we could work had been increased, new and unforeseen obstacles continually occurred.

For instance, after our scaffolding and hoisting tackle had been introduced it occupied practically all the available space, leaving little for ourselves in which to work. When some of the parts were freed, there was insufficient room to remove them from the chamber. We bumped our heads, nipped our fingers, we had to squeeze in and out like weasels, and work in all kinds of embarrassing positions. I think I remember that one of the eminent chemists assisting us in the preservation work, when taking records of various phenomena in the tomb, found that he had also recorded a certain percentage of profanity! Nevertheless, I am glad to say that in the conflict we did more harm to ourselves than to the shrines.

Such was our task during the second season's work in the Burial Chamber . . .

At this point of our undertaking we realized that it would now be possible, by opening those further doors, to solve the secret the shrines had so jealously guarded throughout the centuries. I therefore decided before any other procedure to make the experiment. It was

an exciting moment in our arduous task that cannot easily be forgotten. We were to witness a spectacle such as no other man in our times has been privileged to see. With suppressed excitement I carefully cut the cord, removed that precious seal, drew back the bolts, and opened the doors, when a fourth shrine was revealed, similar in design and even more brilliant in workmanship than the last. The decisive moment was at hand! An indescribable moment for an archaeologist! What was beneath and what did that fourth shrine contain? With intense excitement I drew back the bolts of the last and unsealed doors; they slowly swung open, and there, filling the entire area within, effectually barring any further

progress, stood an immense yellow quartzite sarcophagus, intact, with the lid still firmly fixed in its place, just as the pious hands had left it. It was certainly a thrilling moment, as we gazed upon the spectacle enhanced by the striking contrast – the glitter of metal – of the golden shrines shielding it. Especially striking were the outstretched hand and wing of a goddess sculptured on the end of the sarcophagus, as if to ward off an intruder. It symbolized an idea beautiful in conception, and, indeed, seemed an eloquent illustration of the perfect faith and tender solicitude for the well-being of their loved one, that animated the people who dwelt in that land over thirty centuries ago.

We were now able to profit by the experience we had acquired and had a much clearer conception of the operation immediately before us: the three remaining shrines would have to be taken to pieces and removed before the problem of the sarcophagus could be contemplated . . .

Many strange scenes must have happened in the Valley of the Tombs of the Kings since it became the royal burial ground of the Theban New Empire, but one may be pardoned for thinking that the present scene [the official opening of the sarcophagus] was not the least interesting or dramatic. For ourselves it was the one supreme and culminating moment – a moment looked forward to ever since it became evident that the chambers discovered, in November, 1922, must be the tomb of Tutankh-Amen, and not a cache of his furniture as had been claimed. None of us but felt the solemnity of the occasion, none of us but was affected by the prospect of what we were about to see – the burial custom of a king of ancient

Egypt of thirty-three centuries ago. How would the king be found? Such were the anticipatory speculations running in our minds during the silence maintained.

The tackle for raising the lid was in position. I gave the word. Amid intense silence the huge slab, broken in two, weighing over a ton and a quarter, rose from its bed. The light shone into the sarcophagus. A sight met our eyes that at first puzzled us. It was a little disappointing. The contents were completely covered by fine linen shrouds. The lid being suspended in mid-air, we rolled back those covering shrouds, one by one, and as the last was removed a gasp of wonderment escaped our lips, so gorgeous was the sight that met our eyes: a golden effigy of the young boy king, of most magnificent workmanship, filled the whole of the interior of the sarcophagus. This was the lid of a wonderful anthropoid coffin some seven feet in length, resting upon a low bier in the form of a lion, and no doubt the outermost coffin of a series of coffins, nested one within the other, enclosing the mortal remains of the king. Enclasping the body of this magnificent monument are two winged goddesses, Isis and Neith, wrought in rich gold-work upon gesso, as brilliant as the day the coffin was made. To it an additional charm was added, by the fact that, while this decoration was rendered in fine low bas-relief, the head and hands of the king were in the round, in massive gold of the finest sculpture, surpassing anything we could have imagined. The hands, crossed over the breast, held the royal emblems – the Crook and the Flail – encrusted with deep blue faience. The face and features were wonderfully wrought in sheet-gold. The eyes were of aragonite and obsidian, the eyebrows and eyelids inlaid with lapis lazuli glass. There was a touch of realism, for while the rest of this anthropoid coffin, covered with feathered ornament, was a brilliant gold, that of the bare face and hands seemed different, the gold of the flesh being of different alloy, thus conveying an impression of the greyness of death. Upon the forehead of this recumbent figure of the young boy king were two emblems delicately worked in brilliant inlay – the Cobra and the Vulture – symbols of Upper and Lower Egypt, but perhaps the most touching by its human simplicity was the tiny wreath of flowers around these symbols, as it pleased us to think, the last farewell offering of the widowed girl queen to her husband, the youthful representative of the 'Two Kingdoms'.

Among all that regal splendour, that royal magnificence – everywhere the glint of gold – there was nothing so beautiful as those few withered flowers, still retaining their tinge of colour. They told us what a short period three thousand three hundred years really was – but Yesterday and the Morrow. In fact, that little touch of nature made that ancient and our modern civilization kin . . .

The lid was fastened to the shell by means of eight gold tenons (four on each side), which were held in their corresponding sockets by nails. Thus, if the nails could be extracted the lid could be raised. In the narrow space between the two coffins ordinary implements for extracting metal pins were useless, and others had to be devised. With long screwdrivers converted to meet the conditions, the nails or pins of solid gold, that unfortunately had to be sacrificed, were removed piecemeal.

The lid was raised by its golden handles and the mummy of the king disclosed.

At such moments the emotions evade verbal expression, complex and stirring as they are. Three thousand years and more had elapsed since men's eyes had gazed into that golden coffin. Time, measured by the brevity of human life, seemed to lose its common perspectives before a spectacle so vividly recalling the solemn religious rites of a vanished civilization. But it is useless to dwell on such sentiments, based as they are on feelings of awe and human pity. The emotional side is no part of archaeological research. Here at last lay all that was left of the youthful Pharaoh, hitherto little more to us than the shadow of a name.

Before us, occupying the whole of the interior of the golden coffin, was an impressive, neat and carefully made mummy, over which had been poured anointing unguents as in the case of the outside of its coffin – again in great quantity – consolidated and blackened by age. In contradistinction to the general dark and sombre effect, due to these unguents, was a brilliant, one might say magnificent, burnished gold mask or similitude of the king, covering his head and shoulders, which, like the feet, had been intentionally avoided when using the unguents. The mummy was fashioned to symbolize Osiris. The beaten gold mask, a beautiful and unique specimen of ancient portraiture, bears a sad but calm expression suggestive of youth overtaken prematurely by death. Upon its forehead wrought in massive gold were the royal insignia – the Nekhebet vulture and Buto serpent – emblems of the Two Kingdoms over which he had reigned. To the chin was attached the conventional Osiride beard, wrought in gold and lapis-lazuli-coloured glass; around the throat was a triple necklace of yellow and red gold and blue faience disk-shaped beads; pendent from the neck by flexible gold inlaid straps was a large black resin scarab that rested between the hands and bore the *Bennu* ritual. The burnished gold hands, crossed over the breast, separate from the mask, were sewn to the material of the linen wrappings, and grasped the Flagellum and Crozier – the emblems of Osiris . . .

But, alas! both the mask and the mummy were stuck fast to the bottom of the coffin by the consolidated residue of the unguents, and no amount of legitimate force could move them. What was to be done?

Since it was known that this adhesive material could be softened by heat, it was hoped that an exposure to the midday sun would melt it sufficiently to allow the mummy to be raised. A trial therefore was made for several hours in sun temperature reaching as high as 149° Fahrenheit (65° C) without any success and, as other means were not practicable, it became evident that we should have to make all further examination of the king's remains as they lay within the two coffins.

As a matter of fact, after the scientific examination of the king's mummy *in situ*, and its final removal from the gold coffin, that very difficult question of removing the gold mask and extricating the gold coffin from the shell of the second coffin had to be solved.

Originally something like two bucketsful of the liquid unguents had been poured over the golden coffin, and a similar amount over the body inside. As heat was the only practical means of melting this material and rendering it amenable, in order to apply a temperature sufficiently high for the purpose, without causing damage to those wonderful specimens of ancient Egyptian arts and crafts, the interior of the golden coffin had to be completely lined with thick plates of zinc, which would not melt under a temperature of 968° Fahrenheit (520° C). The coffins were then reversed upon trestles, the outside one being protected against undue heat and fire by several blankets saturated and kept wet with water. Our next procedure was to place under the hollow of the gold coffin several Primus paraffin lamps burning at full blast. The heat from the lamps had to be regulated so as to keep the temperature well within the melting-point of zinc. It should be noted here that the coating of wax upon the surface of the second coffin acted as a pyrometer – while it remained unmelted under the wet blanketing there was manifestly no fear of injury.

Although the temperature arrived at was some 932° Fahrenheit (500° C), it took several hours before any real effect was noticeable. The moment signs of movement became apparent, the lamps were turned out, and the coffins left suspended upon the trestles, when, after an hour, they began to fall apart. The movement at first was almost imperceptible owning to the tenacity of the material, but we were able to separate them by lifting up the wooden shell of the second coffin, thus leaving the shell of the gold coffin resting upon the trestles. Its very nature was hardly recognizable, and all we could see was a dripping mass of viscous pitch-like material which proved very difficult to remove, even with quantities of various solvents – the principal of which was acetone.

In the same manner that the outside of the golden coffin was covered with a viscid mass, so was the interior, to which still adhered the gold mask. This mask had also been protected by being bound with a folded wet blanket continually fed with water, its face padded with wet wadding. As it had necessarily been subjected to the full power of the heat collected in the interior of the coffin, it was freed and lifted away with comparative ease, though to its back, as in the case of the coffin, there adhered a great mass of viscous unguents, which had eventually to be removed with the aid of a blast lamp and cleaning solvents . . .

The more one considers it the more deeply one is impressed by the extreme care and enormous costliness lavished by this ancient people on the enshrinement of their dead. Barrier after barrier was raised to guard their remains from the predatory hands against which, in death, these great kings too ineffectually sought protection. The process was as elaborate as it was costly.

First we have the golden shrines profusely decorated and of magnificent workmanship. They were sealed and nested one in the other over an immense and superbly sculptured monolithic quartzite sarcophagus. The sarcophagus, in its turn, contained three great anthropoid coffins of wood and gold which bear the likeness of the king with repeated *Rishi* and Osiride symbolism.

Everywhere there was evidence of the accomplished artist and skilful craftsman, intent on the mysteries of a vanished religion, and the problems of death. Finally we reach the monarch himself, profusely anointed with sacred unguents and covered with numberless amulets and emblems for his betterment, as well as personal ornaments for his glory.

The modern observer indeed is astounded at the enormous labour and expense bestowed on these royal burials, even when the titanic excavations of their rock-cut tombs is disregarded. Consider the carving and gilding of the elaborate shrines; the hewing and transport of that quartzite sarcophagus; the moulding, carving, inlaying of the magnificent coffins, the costly and intricate goldsmith's work expended upon them, the crowd of craftsmen employed, the precious metal and material so generously devoted to the princely dead . . .

Around the forehead [of the mummy itself] underneath a few more layers of linen, was a broad temple-band of burnished gold terminating behind and above the ears. At its extremities are slots through which linen tapes were passed and tied in a bow at the back of the head. This band held in place, over the brow and temples, a fine cambric-like linen *Khat* head-dress, unfortunately reduced by decay to such an irreparable condition that it was only recognizable from a portion of the kind of pigtail at the back common to this head-dress. Sewn to this *Khat* head-dress were the royal insignia, being a second set found upon the king. The uraeus, with body and tail in flexible sections of gold-work threaded together, and bordered with minute beads, was passed over the axis of the crown of the head as far back as the *lambda*, whilst the Nekhebet vulture (in this case with open wings, and with characteristics identical with those already described) covered the top of the head-dress, its body being parallel with the uraeus. In order that the soft linen of this head-dress should take its conventional shape, pads of linen had been placed under it and above the temples.

Beneath the *Khat* head-dress were further layers of bandaging that covered a skull-cap of the fine linen fabric, fitting tightly over the shaven head of the king, and embroidered with an elaborate device of uraei in minute gold and faience beads. The cap was kept in place by a gold temple-band similar to that just described. Each uraeus of the device bears in its centre the *Aten* cartouche of the Sun. The fabric of the cap was unfortunately much carbonized and decayed, but the bead-work had suffered far less, the device being practically perfect, since it adhered to the head of the king. To have attempted to remove this exquisite piece of work would have been disastrous, so it was treated with a thin coating of wax and left as it was found.

The removal of the final wrappings that protected the face of the king needed the utmost care, as owing to the carbonized state of the head there was always the risk of injury to the very fragile features. We realized the peculiar importance and responsibility attached to our task. At the touch of a sable brush the last few fragments of decayed fabric fell away, revealing a serene and placid countenance, that of a young man . . .

Before I bring this narrative to a close I should mention that the charred remains of the mummy itself show no traces of the cause or causes of the young king's death, but the masses of swathings, ornaments and amulets, at least conveyed to us the care that was taken with his mortal remains and for his future life. A feeling, a sense and a care, that cannot be better expressed than in the words of Sir Gardener Wilkinson, who did so much wonderful research work in Egypt during the early half of the last century.

'Love and respect were not merely shown to the sovereign during his lifetime, but were continued to his memory after his death; and the manner in which his funeral obsequies were celebrated tended to show, that, though their benefactor was no more, they retained a grateful sense of his goodness, and admiration for his virtues. And what, says the historian [meaning Diodorus], can convey a greater testimony of sincerity free from all colour of dissimulation, when the person who conferred it no longer lives to witness the honour done to his memory?'

◨ ◉ ◨ ◉ ◨ ◉

Howard Carter concludes the story of the clearing of the tomb in the third volume of his book, with yet another admission that he could not find the words to describe the 'awe and wonder' he experienced.

The time came in the sequence of our work to direct our energies towards the Storeroom beyond the Burial Chamber, perhaps in this case better named 'The Innermost Treasury' . . .

Small and simple, as it is, the impressive memories of the past haunt it none the less. When, for the first time, one enters a room such as this, the sanctity of which has been inviolate for more than thirty centuries, a sense of reverence, if not of fear, is felt on the part of the intruder. It seems almost desecration to trouble that long peace and to break that eternal silence. Even the most insensitive person, passing this inviolate threshold, must surely feel awe and wonder distilled from the secrets and shadows of that Tremendous Past. The very stillness of its atmosphere, intensified by the many inanimate things that fill it, standing for centuries and centuries as pious hands had placed them, creates the sense of sacred obligation which is indescribable and which causes one to ponder before daring to enter, much less to touch anything. Emotions thus aroused, of which the sense of awe is the root, are difficult to convey in words; the spirit of curiosity is checked; the very tread of one's foot, the slightest noise, tends to increase a fear and magnify an unconscious reverence – the intruder becomes mute.

That appeal of the past made one hesitate before venturing to enter and explore, until one remembered that, however much one may respect it, an archaeologist's duty is to the present, and it is for him to interpret what is hidden and note whatever steps may lead him to his goal.

◻ ◉ ◻ ◉ ◻ ◉

The American members of the team lived, for the duration, in the 'American House' near El-Deir-el Bahari, on the edge of the Valley of Kings. It was a mud-brick residence built ten years before, in the Coptic style, for archaeologists and their families working on the American concession there. The costs for this construction had been underwritten by J. P. Morgan. According to Winifred Mace (wife of Arthur), the residence was 'most charming, with the furniture suitable for it and lovely cushions of Bochara work, beautiful hanging lamps, old woodwork dividing hall and dining room'. By Christmas 1922 it housed, among

others, the architectural draughtsmen Walter Hauser and Lindsley Foote Hall, Arthur and Winifred Mace with their daughter Margaret, Herbert Winlock (of the Metropolitan Museum), his wife and daughter Frances, and a little later, Albert Lythgoe (also of the Metropolitan Museum) and his wife. Then there were Harry and Minnie Burton.

The story of the discovery is usually told entirely from the points of view of the specialist members of the team (who were all male). But the recent rediscovery of the diary of Minnie Burton provides a different perspective – that of the families of the archaeologists, who found themselves living near the site, during the November–April season, sometimes for several years. Minnie Burton describes the daily round of breakfast, lunch, tea (especially tea) and dinner, and carefully lists all the members of the American and European communities who were present at these meals. Her account of life in the American residence is also full of references to the sweltering heat, illnesses (she spent a fair amount of her time nursing the casualties), domestic duties (such as sewing Howard Carter's curtain for him), shopping trips to Luxor, careful conversations with journalists, evening walks around El-Deir-el-Bahari and the Ramesseum, and of course, private views of the contents of the tomb of Tutankhamun – either *in situ* or in the laboratory tomb of Seti II. On one occasion she writes that she is shown the 'King's Cup' in Howard Carter's nearby house, known informally as Castle Carter. She was definitely proud of the fact that she was the second woman to enter the tomb, after Lady Evelyn Herbert.

We know from other sources that there were

children's parties at the American residence, and games called 'setting up tombs', involving Frances Winlock, Margaret Mace and assorted chairs covered with sheets, but Minnie Burton doesn't mention them. We also know that Minnie was not the most popular of residents – Winifred Mace refers to her short temper, which was apparently 'like a volcano', and opines that she 'would have liked to have been the Queen Bee'. So it comes as no surprise to discover (from entries for 8 and 21 February and 23 November) that she did not seem to get on with Howard Carter, who had a similar temperament. In general, traces of her emotions are absent from the down-to-earth entries in the diary – except for when she mentions the death of Lord Carnarvon (5–10 April), which reminds her of her own father's final illness.

The following extracts from Minnie Burton's unpublished diary are printed for the first time by kind permission of Rosalind Berwald. The only surviving volume of the diary begins on 4 May 1922 and ends on 20 October 1926. Although there are entries for every single day in between, I have selected the most interesting ones from the first season (especially those which refer to the discovery itself, or to members of the archaeological team), and abridged some of her long guest-lists for tea and supper.

The diary provides a unique insight into how one of 'the wives' – who, it appears, didn't have much of an interest in Egyptology – passed her time while her husband was busy photographing those 'wonderful things' just over the hill, and how, very occasionally, she 'helped H.' with the resulting prints. We join the couple (who were married in 1914, and who first went to Egypt together a year later) in Cairo, where Harry Burton had been seconded to the Cairo Museum.

1922
Continental Hotel, Cairo

5 Dec H.'s birthday. Morning in bed (with bad cold), but better. Then to umbrella man . . . Talk with Lord Carnarvon about wonderful find. He arrived from Luxor this morning. Walk with H. after tea.

7 Dec . . . H. & I to tea with Murray Grahams. Mr. Hall & Mr. Hauser left for Luxor.

8 Dec Mr. Carter lunched at our table . . .

11 Dec To dentist, Mr. Brett Day, in morning. Also bank. Packing. After dinner with the Bernards as usual, also Mr. Carter, Mr. Fitzgerald, Mr. Percy White. All of us ill with bad colds.

12 Dec . . . Packing. Tired and feeling very ill. In aft to say goodbye to Contessa, Lady Bernard . . . The Wilsons in hall and Balchin. He came to the station to see us off by the 8 p.m. train for Luxor. Dinner on board. Very seedy.

13 Dec Had an awful night of incessant coughing. No sleep. Arrived 9.50. To Winter Palace and saw the doctor, Dr. Deacon, who stethoscoped me. H. went to see the Breasteds on their dahabyah. They invited us to breakfast but I too seedy. Talking to Mrs. Chapman's nurse, Miss Fitzgibbon, got down to Gurneh in time for lunch. Cold windy day. Mr. Hauser and Mr. Hall to receive us . . . to bed as soon as boxes came.

American House, near El-Deir-el-Bahari

14 Dec Got up for lunch – rather better . . .

H. came to see Mr. Carter after tea . . .

15 Dec Very bad night coughing. Up for lunch. Mr. Hauser and Mr. Hall left for Assuan at 8 a.m. After lunch washed wardrobe. After tea helped Harry catalogue prints. Cold. H. over to Tombs of Kings in morning to meet Mr. Carter. H. & I alone all day. Carpenter in morning.

16 Dec Still coughing a lot. Sprained my foot after lunch. Great pain. Aft lying down, but to dinner. H. and I alone . . . Dusted books in drawing room in morning. Had my room washed and wardrobe moved in.

17 Dec The Winlocks arrived in time for lunch, bringing Dr. Breasted and Jamie with them for lunch and tea. After tea H. and I to Mr. Carter's and saw the King's Cup. Mr. Callender there. After dinner Mr. Carter came here.

18 Dec Mr. C. sent over curtain for me to sew . . . The Winlocks went over to see Tutankhaton. I for a walk to Der El Bahari.

19 Dec Painting my furniture in morning and afternoon. Mr. Carter sent over for me his donkey to ride over to see 'the' tomb Tutankhamen. *Wonderful.* Mr. Callender there and later Dr. and Mrs. Breasted and the little girl. Went over the hill both ways. Mr. Hauser and Mr. Hall came back from Assuan . . .

21 Dec Painting Harry's chest of drawers. Before tea to top of cliff and met H. and walked back with him. Mr. Carter for dinner.

25 Dec Xmas Gave Frances a Florentine leather bag. H. gave her a hat. I walked twice round by Der El Bahari. Mrs. W[inlock] in bed all day [with colitis]. To dinner the Davies', Mr. Wilkinson, Mr. Carter and Mr. Lucas. Mr. Mace arrived in the morning. H. not over to tombs.

28 Dec Walked over to the Tombs of the Kings before tea and back with Harry. Talking to Mr. Lucas. With Mrs. Winlock after tea. Her temp 100°. Mrs Davies in.

29 Dec No lunch . . . For a walk after by moonlight to Ramesseum with Mr. Hall. Very hot day. 72° in my room.

31 Dec My birthday. The Engelbachs to lunch . . .

1923

1 Jan Sewing all day for Mrs. Mace's room. After tea with Harry and Mr. Hall for walk on cliffs by moonlight.

2 Jan Mr. Hall, H. and I over to Luxor. Pottering about the shops . . . Mr. Carter and Mrs. Lucas with Mrs. Merton. After lunch our party w. Mr. Percy White went to the derelict gardens of the Grand Hotel – to see Moussa catch snakes. He caught 2 cobras and a small viper. Tea with . . . Mrs. W. and Mr. H. and back by moonlight. Frances laid up too.

3 Jan . . . Headache all day. Mrs. W. to tea and dinner. F. ill. Mr. Mace dined at the Davies, to meet Alan Gardiner . . .

5 Jan Mr. and Mrs. Macy and their son and daughter to lunch. Dr. Gardiner to tea. Walked round Der el Bahari.

6 Jan Writing all morning. After lunch to Tombs of Kings and Mr. Carter showed me the things in [the tomb of] Seti II. Walked back with Mr. Mace and Harry. Walk after tea with Mr. Hall round by cultivation . . .

7 Jan Mr. Carter and Mr. Lucas to tea. They came over in the car, bringing Harry and Mr. Mace. Walk after tea with H. round cultivation. Washed my hair. Dr. Gardiner dined here.

9 Jan H. & I rode Mr. Carter's donkeys to his

house, and then with him in the new Ford car to the river bank. To Winter Palace for a moment then shopping and to lunch with Mrs. Wright, or rather at her table. Mr. C. with the Contessa. We all had tea with the Contessa, also Mrs. Merton, wife of the 'Times' correspondent. Mr. C. brought us back in the Ford to the door. Mr. Hauser and Mr. Wilkinson also at the Luxor Hotel for lunch . . .

23 Jan   The car for us at 11 and to pick up Mr. Carter and Mr. Lucas to Luxor, lunched with Allans on their dahabyah the Truisah. Then for the Contessa and to tea with her at the Winter Palace. Also at tea the Allans, the Winlocks, Mrs. Wright and Mr. Carter. Talking to Mr. Weigall, Mr. Engelbach, the Brett Youngs, Wilsons etc. Very warm heavy day. Car back to Mr. Carter's and walked home.

24 Jan   Went over to the Tombs of the Kings in morning to see the couch being brought out. Harry with 'movie', and I took some snapshots. Crowds of people. Back in the car with Mr. Hauser and Mr. Hall. Very hot . . . Mr. Carter to dinner. In [tomb] number 15 in morning and saw the glove and the reconstructed sandals.

29 Jan   Cooler. Blouses arrived from Harrod's. Walk to top of cliffs before tea. Mending sheet most of day.

30 Jan   H. & I started to go over to Luxor this morning and going down the hill by the hamlet Harry's stirrup broke. He was thrown forward on the donkey's neck and his leg tripped the donkey, who fell and Harry was flung on his face. He skinned it badly. We came back here to Dr. Derry, who had just come up from Cairo to stay here for a few days, helped to clean him up. Looks very nasty, and very sore and painful. Mrs. Austin in after lunch. Helping H. with prints all the afternoon. H. & I for walk after tea round the cultivation. Met Mr. Carter and Mr. Lucas.

8 Feb   To the Valley with Mr. Lythgoe in morning, over the hill. Very hot. To Seti II and saw everything splendidly. Mr. Carter asked me to stay to lunch, but didn't want to, so came back alone. Mrs. Lythgoe up. Der El Bahari after tea.

10 Feb   . . . Mr. Carter and Lord Carnarvon for tea. Walk after and to Mrs. Davies with Mrs. Lythgoe and Mrs. Winlock.

13 Feb   H. & I to Luxor at 11.15 . . . Lunched at Winter Palace Hotel with Mrs. Scott. Mrs. Topliffe and Mr. Morton (Daily Express). Talking to Lord C., Sir John Maxwell, Mr. Weigall, Dr. Deacon, etc. Mr. Lucas, Lady Evelyn Herbert. Shopping afterwards and to tea at the Luxor Hotel with the Contessa.

15 Feb   Mr. Breasted and Mr. Bull arrived to stay. They, with Dr. Gardiner, went over to the Tombs of the Kings, and only Mr. Bull back for lunch . . . Lord C. with invitations to the opening of the sealed door on Sunday. Walk after tea to Der El Bahari.

16 Feb   With Mr. Bull to the Ramesseum in morning. Two ladies to tea (the author of 'Rain'). Didn't see them. After tea by Der El Bahari. The sealed door was opened today. Mr. Lythgoe and Mr. Winlock and Mr. Breasted went over and Harry and Mr. Macy there. 15(?) people present. Great excitement! Mr. Carter dined here and Mr. Gardiner in before. Very interesting talk.

17 Feb   I walked over the hill and Mrs. W. rode and the Lythgoes drove, and we three had a private view of the inner chambers. Enormous gold and blue faience catafalque inside the door. Difficult to get in. Small 4th chamber full of caskets and boxes. Very thrilling. Lovely things. Lord C. and Mr. Maudesley. I walked back in time for lunch. Monsieur Capart here after.

18 Feb Lunch at 11.30. The Macys here. Afterwards I walked to the Valley for the official opening with Mr. Hauser, Mr. Hall and Mr. Bull. Very hot in the fresh breeze. Long wait for the Allenbys and the Queen of the Belgians and Prince Leopold. The Macys went after the Allenbys. Cold buffet up near Seti II. Lady Evelyn Herbert received. The Maudesley's, Thomases, Miss Putnam, Thompsons, Hetheringtons, Drs. Breasted, Carpart, Allan Gardiner, the Davieses, Mertons, etc. etc. Drove home with the Macys. Everybody dead tired. 1 year since To-To died.

21 Feb Met the Contessa at the Ramesseum and drove with her to the Valley. Took her to Seti II and then Mr. Carter took her down to the tomb. The Wiggins there, Mrs. Merton, etc. Had a row with Mr. Carter! He was very rude. Drove back with the Contessa. Very hot and dusty. Got back in time to change for lunch. The Q. of the Belgians, Prince Leopold ... Dr. Capart and Colonel Watson lunched here. Afterwards the Queen ... lay down for an hour and then they all went off to the Valley ... Very hot day. After tea with H. up to a tomb where he took a flash-light photograph.

26 Feb The tomb was closed today. Harry here. To hill tomb with H. to photograph.

3 Mar Mr. Hall laid up and nursing him all day. Walk with Mrs. L. ...

4 Mar Dr. McClanaghan for Mr. Hall and he lunched here ...

5 Mar Nursing Mr. Hall ...

6 Mar H. and I to Luxor and lunched with Colonel and Mrs. Burges. Tea with Mrs. Scott.

7 Mar ... Harry and Mr. Mace over at the Valley again. Still nursing Mr. Hall.

8 Mar Sir John Maxwell to lunch. McClanaghan and Miss Hedges after, and they decided that Mr. Hall had better go into hospital at Cairo and Miss H. would take him down tonight. Sent for Lord C.'s motor and Mr. Hall was packed off soon after 4 ... Bed early.

14 Mar The Lythgoes left in morning ... Mr. Winlock lunched at the Valley. Ld. Carnarvon and Mr. Bethell here to say goodbye ... Very hot.

19 Mar ... Walk with H. after tea. Mr. Carter had wire from Lady Evelyn saying Ld. C. was very ill.

20 Mar Harry had a day off, and rested all the afternoon. Walk with me after tea. Mr. Carter went to Cairo.

23 Mar ... H. working here every day since Tuesday. Ld. C. better.

24 Mar H. to Valley again ...

27 Mar H. & I started at 10.15 for Luxor, H. with the movie. He took water wheel near Ramesseum, while I rode back for some money he had forgotten. Got to bank long before time and crossed with Winlocks and Mr. Mace, Mr. Callender and Mr. Lucas. H. arrived at 1 ... Back by moonlight. Splitting headache. Very hot. Crowd of American tourists at Hotel. Last party for the season.

29 Mar Mr. Engelbach here in morning. Mr. Mace had a wire from Mr. C. to say that Lord Carnarvon was worse. Walk after tea with Mrs. Winlock and Frances by the cultivation. Hot day.

5 April   H. at home. Wire from Mr. C. to say Ld. Carnarvon died last night, the 4th. A year since Paña told me Papa could not live.

6 April   Hot day. Windstorm at night (spent all day running about trying to find a place for Papa, this day last year).

10 April   Papa died a year ago. Stayed in bed in morning. Seedy. Walk after tea with H. as far as Ramasseum. He did not go the Valley. Mr. Mace went.

16 April   Mr. Carter came back. Mr. Engelbach to lunch and tea. Mr. Carter sent me (given by someone, who?) a group of J.H.Q. taken in Cairo 1907 with Papa in it and General Bullock. Walk with H. to see tomb of Kheti.

17 April   Mr. Engelbach to lunch and tea. Mr. Wilkinson left for Cairo. Harry here all day. Mr. Mace teaed and dined with Mr. Carter. Walk alone after tea by Der El Bahari.

19 April   . . . Walked alone after tea.

20 April   . . . Walked alone after tea. Packing.

21 April   . . . Mr. Hauser left at 4. Walk alone. Mr. Carter, Mr. Lucas and Mr. Callender to dinner.

22 April   The Winlocks left after tea for Luxor. H. and I on to hill and then round Der El Bahari. We and Mr. Mace alone at dinner.

23 April   H. back for lunch. My baggage left at 10 a.m. We left at 3.30. Tea at Luxor Hotel. Mrs. Scott and Mrs. Topliffe, Mrs. Winlock and Frances and H. and I to station soon after 5, and Harry went back to Qurna before our train left at 6. Mrs. W. F. and I dined together. Mr. Winlock got on at Bahira at 9. He had been spending the day at Abydos with Mr. Wainwright. Musa and Mons. Baraige and a lot of the servants to see us off.

Cairo

24 April   Arrived about 7 . . .

Luxor

8 Nov   Couldn't sleep for the heat. 89°. Busy all morning putting things away. Mr. Callender to tea. Not out all day . . . After tea (on Wed. 7th) we all went out on the new motor presented to the expedition by Mr. Blumenthal – a sort of omnibus, which carries 10 people. Up the Valley of the Kings. 90°.

23 Nov   Scirocco and had splitting headache. Invitation to dinner from Mr. Carter and Harry furious because I declined. Walked alone . . .

◼ ◎ ◻ ◎ ◼ ◎

Another little-known member of the group was Acting-Sergeant Richard Adamson, who in later life recalled that he had served as a guard

On guard outside the tomb.

outside the tomb – for no less than seven seasons – at Lord Carnarvon's request. Although severely disabled, he revisited the Valley of the Kings over fifty years after the discovery. His main recollection at that time was about the kit he required for the long nights spent sleeping in the tomb: this included: 'A decent gramophone; records: musical, light opera, operetta, especially *Chu Chin Chow*; uniform from my barracks in Cairo; my medal ribbons; books: Edgar Wallace and crime; extra tropical kit; toilet requisites and confectionery.'

Adamson does not appear in any of the contemporary photographs taken at the site, or in any of the participants' recollections, and it has to be said there is some doubt about the accuracy of his own memories. But in August 1980 he was interviewed about them by the *Daily Mail*.

Old soldier Richard Adamson laughs at the 'Curse of Tutankhamun'. He should know. He was there when the story was invented to keep unwelcome visitors away from the newly discovered tomb. For seven years he actually slept in the chilly chamber, 60 feet below the shifting desert sands, his head within inches of the mummified remains of the boy king in his solid-gold coffin, his feet pointing in the general direction of the two Ka statues, guards over the tomb for more than 3,300 years.

His main defence against the ghosts and light-fingered tribesmen – an old, wind-up gramophone.

Not once was his rest disturbed. The sound of the triumphal march from *Aida* – one of his

three chipped 78 r.p.m. records – wafting eerily into the desolate wastes of the Valley of the Kings was enough to deter any bird-headed demon or flesh-and-bone tribesman loitering with intent. Sergeant Adamson had been sent to Egypt in 1921 as a military policeman, part of a detachment literally forming a human barrier between the British Army of occupation and the restless Egyptian people.

In November 1922 he was ordered to assist Lord Carnarvon's archaeological expedition to leave the Valley of the Kings. The Egyptian concession to search for the tomb of King Tut was running out and sixteen years had been spent on the apparently fruitless 'dig'.

By chance, on 4 November 1922, as the expedition's equipment was being moved out, the four remaining Egyptian workmen were poking about some boulders around the already opened tomb of Rameses VI when they discovered some stone steps leading down into the sand.

A week later, at the bottom of the steps, the chief excavator, Howard Carter found another tomb and an inscription confirming it as Tutankhamun's: 'Lo, I am here.' Those few words unleashed an avalanche of press and public interest. Adamson recalls the scene as though it were yesterday. 'By that time I had been put in charge of security and when Carter and I saw the armies of curious people arriving we realized we needed something to keep them away.

'Not only were the crowds hampering the digging work but there was a real danger that thieves would come at night and plunder the tomb before we had excavated it. Many items down there would have crumbled in the hands of people trying to carry them off.

'Quite suddenly, we thought about a curse. Inscriptions laying curses on intruders had been found on the walls of tombs nearer Cairo and it so happened that a reporter had been hanging around asking about curses there.

'We saw no such inscriptions laying curses in Tut's tomb but, let's say, we didn't discourage him from thinking there was.

'With a wink and a nod from us he was quite happy to make up the tale of a curse over King Tut's tomb.'

Adamson chuckled to himself with the sort of relish that suggested he was still at the scene of the historic discovery and participating in the hoax that fooled the world, rather than being confined to a home for disabled servicemen in Surrey nearly sixty years later.

Adamson, eighty-one-years-old, both legs amputated, says surprisingly: 'I am happy with my life. I was once asked by Prince Charles, whom I lectured about Tutankhamun when he was at Cambridge, if I thought the loss of my legs was the effect of the curse.

'I told him they were the late results of injuries in the First World War – a war is a curse, nothing to do with King Tut.'

Since leaving the Middlesex Regiment in 1932 and being invalided out of the Civil Service in 1964, Adamson has spent a good deal of his time – often vainly – trying to separate fact from fiction about King Tut's tomb.

As the last survivor of the expedition he feels a great responsibility to get the facts straight . . .

Despite his own misfortunes and those of others associated with the tomb – twenty-one are supposed to have died under mysterious circumstances – Adamson has always steadfastly refuted the curse idea in the lectures he still gives around the country.

Adamson says: 'Lord Carnarvon did die in Egypt but he was bitten by a mosquito and the bite turned septic. Unfortunate, but it could have happened to anyone . . .'

Nowadays the old soldier is preoccupied with the history of Tutankhamun.

As we wandered through the marble corridors of the Royal Star and Garter Home, Adamson, driving himself in his electric wheelchair, said he dearly wished King Tut could be remembered for his achievements rather than his supposed curse. I agreed: until a car nearly backed into me on the way home.

■ ◉ ■ ◉ ■ ◉

The Pharaoh Awakes

ystery writers had been producing stories of strange happenings in and around the world of Egyptology and archaeological excavation for nearly a century, and public expectations surrounding the discovery of the tomb of Tutankhamun were undoubtedly stimulated by the best-known examples. The very first mummy story was probably Jane Webb's triple-decker novel *The Mummy* (1827), and bibliographies of the Gothic abound in choice titles such as *Oriental Wanderings, or the Fortunes of Felix: an Egyptian Romance by R.C.* (three volumes, 1824). But the genre really got into its jerky stride in 1840 with Théophile Gautier's romantic short story *Le Pied de Momie* (known in English as *The Mummy's Foot* or *Princess Hermonthis*), which, incidentally, provided the idea for one of the earliest mummy movies, the magician Walter Booth's trick-film *The Haunted Curiosity Shop* (1902). I have preceded *The Mummy's Foot* with an extract from the prologue to Gautier's later and better-known *Le Roman de la Momie* (*The Romance of the Mummy*), published in 1857. This prologue is so uncannily like the real-life discovery of Tutankhamun's tomb sixty-five years later (allowing for a considerable amount of poetic licence and the attitudes of Gautier's time) that it goes some way towards explaining why Carter's finds were treated by the public as an exotic mix of fact and fantasy.

THÉOPHILE GAUTIER
The Romance of the Mummy
(1857)

Prologue

'I have an idea that we shall find in the Valley of Biban-el-Molouk a tomb that has never been tampered with,' said to a distinguished young Englishman a certain man of science, much famed for his knowledge of Egypt.

'May Osiris hear you,' replied the young English lord; 'that is an invocation one should use in front of ancient Diospolis Magna ... Many times we have been deceived. The treasure-hunters are always in advance of us.'

But his companion continued –

'A tomb that shall not have been ransacked by Egyptians, Greeks, Romans or Arabs, but that shall deliver up to us, untouched, all the riches of its virgin mystery.'

'And upon which you will publish an erudite work which will give you a place with Champollion, Rossellini, Wilkinson, Lepsius and Belzoni?'

'I will dedicate it to you, my lord, for without your royal munificence I should not have been able to test my system by seeing the monuments, and I should have died in my little German town without having contemplated the marvels of this ancient land.'

So replied the German doctor who was the young lord's companion. This conversation had taken place near the Nile, at the entry to the Valley of Biban-el-Molouk, between Lord Evandale, mounted on an Arab blood mare, and Doctor Rumphius, mounted on an ass.

The vessel that had brought them up the Nile, and was their temporary home, was moored the other side of the Nile, before Luxor, with furled sails. After having given several days to visiting and studying the astounding ruins of Thebes – gigantic fragments of a city of splendour – they had crossed the river and directed their steps to the arid belt of land that held within its breast the tombs of the ancient inhabitants of the palaces that once stood on the other side of the water. Some attendants followed his lordship and the doctor, and others calmly smoked upon the vessel in the cabin's shade.

Lord Evandale was one of those young Englishmen who appear to be beyond reproach in every way; a fine example of British high life. He had, too, the disdainful attitude that comes of the possession of a large inherited fortune and an historic name fully described in the *Peerage and Baronetage*, the second Bible of the English. In appearance he was almost too handsome for a man ... However, the firm gaze of his steely-blue eyes and a kind of sneer upon the lips corrected any impression people formed as to his rather effeminate appearance. A member of the Yacht Club, the young lord from time to time, by caprice, took a trip upon his light craft *Puck*. It was furnished like a boudoir, and managed by a few chosen sailors. This year he had chosen Egypt, and his yacht awaited him at Alexandria. He had brought with him a man of science, a doctor, a naturalist, a draughtsman and photographer, so that his tour could be turned to a good account. He himself was a well-informed man, and his social success had not made him forget his honours at Cambridge. He was dressed with the right note of style and

scrupulous care that is one of the distinguishing marks of the Englishman. They are as careful of their attire upon the sands of the desert as upon the sands and promenades of the seaside or the storied stones of the West End.

He was at this time principally in white clothing, because of the heat of the sun. Upon his head there was a very finely-made Panama, with a green gauze pugree. Rumphius, the Egyptologist, still wore the usual black costume of the man of science in spite of the heat, and one could see that he cleaned his pen upon his right trouser leg. His cravat was knotted carelessly around the prominent 'apple' in his throat. He was dressed with true scientific negligence, and he was most certainly not a handsome man. Some reddish hair streaked with grey stuck out behind his prominent ears. He was bald, and had a long nose. He brought to one's mind the figure of an ibis, perhaps a suitable simile for one who deciphered Egyptian cartouches.

The lord and the doctor made for the rocks of the funeral Valley of Biban-el-Molouk, necropolis used for the royalties of ancient Thebes, conversing in the style of the phrases we have quoted, when coming out like a cave-dweller from the black mouth of a sepulchre (often the homes of fellahs) they saw a personage who was strange to them, and who saluted. He was a Greek dealer in and maker of antique things, selling the new when he could not get the old. Nothing about him reminded one of the commonplace type that tricks the traveller. He wore a red cap, and was freshly barbered. His olive skin, black brows, nose and predatory eyes, his big moustaches and deeply-dented chin, would all have made up a brigand's aspect, if it had not been tempered by a servile smile. This Greek had closely observed the yacht, and had decided that the owner could be 'exploited'. He therefore waited his time to pounce, regarding all the funeral domain as his property, turning all away who would dispute that with him. With the skill peculiar to the mercantile Greek, from the first sight of Lord Evandale he had calculated, or tried to, the amount of his wealth.

He renounced the idea of showing the noble Englishman round the tombs; that had been 'done' hundreds of times. In this case, he thought, it was of no use to turn over places where nothing was to be found – places he had long ago denuded himself and profited by in the highest market overt. Argyropoulos (that was the Greek's name) in exploring the valley had found the entry to a place that had escaped the usual explorer. For two years he guarded his secret from other tomb-robbers. Now he approached Lord Evandale.

'His your lordship any intention of enterprising some researches?' Argyropoulos spoke in a sort of cosmopolitan dialect. 'If so I can find you a hundred fellahs who with their bare nails could scrape away the earth to its centre! We would lay bare a sphinx, an altar, a tomb.'

Seeing that the great lord remained calm and cool as he heard the foregoing phrases, and that the smile of the sceptic wavered upon the lips of the savant with him, Argyropoulos at once understood that he was not trading with fools, and he became convinced that the best thing he could next do would be to sell to these people, in this splendid market, his great discovery. Upon this find of his he really placed a high price, in his thoughts about it; he wanted to get enough from the idea for an income and

a marriage portion for his daughter.

'I can see that you are savants and not merely travellers, and that common curiosity does not call you here or detain you,' continued he, talking a mixture of Greek, Arabic, Italian and English. 'I can reveal to you the place where there is a tomb that has escaped the search of all. No one knows of it but my sole self, for it is a treasure that I have most closely guarded until the day came when some one worthy should be told the precious secret.'

'Some one who would pay you a worthy price?' said and smiled the lord.

'My love of truth forbids that I should contradict your lordship. I live in great hope of making a good price as payment for my discovery. Each lives in this land by his own little industry: I live by digging up the Pharaohs and selling them to strangers. They are becoming very rare; there are certainly not enough for all the world of seekers. It is an article in great demand that they have not been making for some time!'

'That is a fact,' said the doctor; 'it is centuries since the embalmers shut up shop, and the tranquil quarters of the dead have been deserted by the living of this land.'

The Greek sent a keen glance at the speaker, but continued talking to his lordship.

'For a tomb of great age that no human being had touched since the priests left the dead is a thousand pounds too much money? It is nothing to pay for such a thing. Perhaps the tomb has masses of gold, necklaces of diamonds and pearls, earrings of sapphires and rubies, and ancient gods moulded of precious metals.'

'Trickster!' said Rumphius. 'You reel off a string of treasures that you know full well one does not now find in Egyptian tombs.'

Argyropoulos, seeing clearly that his clever nonsense left them quite cold and unimpressed, dropped it at once, and turning to Evandale said plainly and very pointedly –

'Very good, my lord. Is it to be a bargain at my price as I have stated?'

'Go on, then,' said the young lord. 'A thousand pounds if the tomb has never been opened (as you represent to us), and . . . nothing at all if a single stone has been touched by the tools of any one.'

'Also upon this condition,' added the prudent Rumphius: 'that we can take away if we wish all that we shall find in the tomb.'

'I accept,' said the Greek, with an assured air. 'You can advance your gold and banknotes.'

'My good Rumphius,' said Lord Evandale to his friend, 'your dreams are to become true. This droll creature seems most positive about this find of his.'

'Heaven grant us that he is in earnest, and that we shall have success,' said the savant. 'The Greeks are such terrible liars; it has passed into a proverb.'

'This man is a Greek – past a doubt,' replied the lord. 'But I think, however, that this time, though it may be for this time only, he is indeed speaking the truth.'

The Director of the Ruins went before the savant and the lord with the air of a master of the ceremonies. They soon arrived at the narrow defile that gave one the entrance to the Valley of Biban-el-Molouk. It looked more like a cutting made by the hand of man through the thick wall of the mountain than a natural opening.

The genius of solitude seemed to have wished to keep unseen from men's eyes this dwelling-place of the dead. Pieces of broken sculpture could be seen about, until at last the valley, becoming a little larger, presented a spectacle of dull desolation.

On each side were rocks scarred, calcined, by the pitiless sun. In the flanks of the rocks opened here and there great black gaps or mouths, surrounded by blocks of stone, broken and in disorder. They were square holes flanked by columns storied with signs and cartouches (or names of the kings), and of the gods and goddesses. They were the tombs of the old-time kings of Thebes. At last it would seem their goal drew near, for Argyropoulos pointed out an enormous stone, and said with an air of triumphal satisfaction –

'It is there!'

He clapped his hands, and from all around them fellahs appeared with picks, hammers and all necessary tools. The Greek made a sign to some of the most robust, who put levers under the big mass of rock. It was moved, and two others as well. Then the entrance to a tomb appeared, a sort of square doorway hollowed in the rock. At the sides were pillars. The doorway was ornamented with hieroglyphics. Behind a wall of stone and brick they soon found a sort of flagstone that formed the door leading to the subterranean place of sepulchre. The German savant found the seal of the tomb intact.

'I really believe,' he said, 'that we have succeeded,' he cried.

'Do not let us rejoice too soon,' said Lord

Evandale. 'Belzoni made a great mistake once. *His* great find in the way of an "unopened" tomb had been opened at another side.'

'But here,' said Rumphius, 'the mountain chain is too great for any such opening to have been made by these men and these means.'

The men now attacked the great stone that masked any further door or passage, unearthing many tiny little images as they did so: images laid there by friends as we to-day lay flowers near the dead.

The door opened . . . it was the first time it had done so for thirty-five centuries, and the mountain, through this opened mouth, seemed to sigh with an air of relief. More hieroglyphics were the first things they saw with what little light there was. Torches were now lit, and they all pressed forward.

At the end of the passage was another sealed door of stone. The heat was intense. Argyropoulos sent for sponges full of fresh water, and these they breathed through. The second door was now down, and a stairway showed a sharp descent.

'Ouf!' gasped the doctor at the bottom of the stair. 'The heat increases as we go on. We cannot be very far now from the abode of the damned' . . .

'This labyrinth,' said the doctor, 'was not made for sheer amusement. There *must* be another passage that leads to . . . something. Without doubt the dead man or woman had a fear of being disturbed, and was securely sealed up somewhere. Where? With sufficient insistence one can get anywhere, and I think yet that we shall make discoveries. Probably a flagstone masked in some way covers the true descent to the funeral chamber.'

'You are right, I believe, dear doctor,' said Evandale. 'Let us search again and again.'

They struck every corner, every stone. At last, near a pillar, it sounded hollow, and when the dust of centuries had been cleared away an oblong flagstone was seen clearly marked out.

'I am half ashamed to take so many steps to trouble the last sleep of the poor body that is here somewhere,' now said Lord Evandale.

The stone was raised, and a staircase discovered that led to a chamber with little crypts containing figures made of enamel, bronze and sycamore. As they pressed forward into the chamber Lord Evandale had a strange sensation assail him. Modern life and all that it stood for to him seemed to pass away, out of sight and touch, out of thought. He forgot Great Britain, and the great fact that his name was upon the roll of its nobility, that he was one of its 'titled and landed' class. Forgot, too, his home in Lincolnshire, his town house in London's West End, his yacht, and all that made or aided his English life. An unseen hand put back the clock of time, had turned again the hour-glass of the ages. Sand by sand the centuries fell silently, sadly, as hours pass in the silence and solitude of the night. History was there, in the past, not here and now, viewed with the eyes of to-day. Moses lived, Pharaoh reigned, and he, the Lord Evandale, felt it strange that he was not coiffured and dressed as an Egyptian noble would be when in the presence of the royalty of Egypt. Then, too, a touch of religious horror came to him, for had he not violated this palace of the half-divine, royal dead – defended though it had been with such care against the hand of the profaner?

The attempt, and its success so far, now

seemed to him impious and a sacrilege, and he said –

'If there is a Pharaoh here he might rise upon his couch and strike me with his sceptre!'

For an instant he wished to let fall again for ever the stone screens that had tried to hide the corpse of this ancient dead civilization. But the doctor had other ideas. Dominated by his scientific enthusiasm, he cried in a loud voice –

'My lord, the sarcophagus is quite intact!'

This sentence recalled his lordship again to the things of real life. By a lightning leap of the mind he crossed again the centuries that his reveries had built up, and replied –

'In all truth, is it, my dear doctor, intact?'

'Unheard-of good fortune, marvellous chance, treasure-trove never to be equalled!' continued the doctor, with a deep and erudite joy.

Argyropoulos, seeing the enthusiasm of the doctor, had a feeling of remorse, the first he had ever had in his life. He now wished he had asked a great deal more. He told himself that he had been a simpleton, and that the young noble had got the best of the bargain. He made many resolutions to fare better in any similar affair in future days.

To increase the joy of sight in the find the fellahs had by now lit all their torches. The spectacle was strange and magnificent in the passages and chambers that led to the resting-place of the sarcophagus. Lord Evandale and Rumphius remained stupefied with admiration, although they were already familiar with the glories of funeral art in ancient Egypt.

Illuminated thus, the gilded salon showed, perhaps for the first time, the bright colours of its wall-paintings. Reds, blues, greens and whites shone with a virginal freshness from the golden varnish that served as a background to the figures and hieroglyphs.

In the midst there arose the massive sarcophagus, that had been hollowed in an enormous block of black basalt and closed with a rounded cover of the same material. The four sides of the monolith were covered with sculptures cut as carefully in intaglio as would be the gem in a ring.

At the angles of the sarcophagus were four alabaster vases with chased covers. These four vessels contained certain of the inner parts of the mummy, and at the head of the tomb an effigy of Osiris seemed to watch the ever-sleeping dead.

'Open the sarcophagus,' said his lordship, 'but with great care in the use of your levers, for I would like to take this tomb, perfect, for the British Museum.'

When the bier was at last opened, Rumphius, to his surprise, found the enswathed figure must be that of a woman, owing to the absence of the Osirian beard and also from the form of the wrapping. The Greek also expressed astonishment. It was a unique thing in his long experience, for the Valley of Biban-el-Molouk is the 'Saint Denis' of old-time Thebes and contained but the tombs of kings. The necropolis of the queens is situated further in another gorge of the mountain. Then, the tombs of the queens were very simple, and composed usually of one or two chambers. Women were regarded as inferior to men even in death. The greater number of such tombs, violated in far-off ages, have served as receptacles for mummies of the deformed and poorly embalmed.

'This disturbs,' said the doctor, 'all my thoughts and theories and overthrows the most firmly-seated system of Egyptian funeral rites followed exactly and closely for thousands of years! ... We are brought face to face with some obscure custom or happening of those days; a lost mystery of history. A woman was seated upon the throne of the Pharaohs and governed Egypt ...'

The doctor removed the wrappings of the body, and the last obstacle removed, the young woman was seen in all the chaste nudity of her beautiful form, guarding, in spite of the centuries, all the roundness of her former contours and the supple grace of her pure lines of breed. Her pose, rare among mummies, was that of the Venus of Milo, as though the Master of the Embalmers had wished with this sweet form to take away the sad, straight attitude and rigidity of the dead.

A cry of admiration came from the two beholders. Never did Greek or Roman statue offer a more elegant figure for the delight of the eye. The particular character of the ideal Egyptian gave to the beautiful body, so superbly preserved, a lightness of line that antique marbles rarely have. The fine hands and feet, with nails of polished agate; the cup of the breast, small and pointed; the swelling of the hip and thigh; the long leg, that recalled grace of dead players and dancers – all was of a type of grace that was very youthful and yet had the perfection, the completeness of the woman. As a rule mummies saturated with bitumen and natrum resemble ebony figures. Dissolution cannot take them, but all appearances of life depart. They do not return to the dust, but become, as it were, pertrified into a hideous form that one can only behold with fright or disgust. But here, the body prepared with great care and huge cost had preserved more nearly the look of flesh and of life. The warm and amber tone of flesh that one admires so much in the pictures of Titian or Giorgione must have been the lovely young Egyptian's tint in life. The head seemed sleeping, but it was a sleep of thirty centuries. Her body was almost covered with exquisite gold, gems and jewels.

Strange sensation, indeed, to be face to face with a glorious human being who lived when History and her records were vague and misty. A beautiful creature who was certainly contemporary with Moses, and still owned much of the glory of youth. Imagine touching a little hand that had probably been kissed by a Pharaoh, or that hair, more lasting than empires, more enduring than monuments of granite!

At the sight of the denuded form of the lovely lady, who must have queened it ages before, the young lord experienced that retrospective desire that a fine picture or statue can cause if it represents one who was famous for her charms: he thought that he would have loved her could he have lived in those ancient centuries, and his thought, a spiritual one, went forth, as it were, into the void to tell her soul.

Rumphius, less poetic, took an inventory of all the gems and jewels. Evandale did not desire them removed; to take the jewels from a dead woman is to kill her a second time!

All at once a roll of papyrus, hidden beneath the arm of the dead woman, caught the doctor's eye.

'My lord,' said he with deep intentness, 'we have the best of the man Argyropoulos, after all. This is the first time men have found an

Egyptian manuscript containing any other than mere hieratic formulas. I will decipher it and learn your secret, oh, you lovely dead thing! Moreover, I will by so doing cover myself with glory and be equal to Champollion. As for Lepsius, he shall die of jealousy!'

*

They returned to Europe, and the mummy was placed in the park of Lord Evandale in Lincolnshire. Often his lordship gazed at the coffin, dreamt and . . . longed.

THÉOPHILE GAUTIER
The Mummy's Foot
(1840)

I had entered, in an idle mood, the shop of one of those curiosity-venders, who are called *marchands de bric-à-brac* in that Parisian *argot* which is so perfectly unintelligible elsewhere in France.

You have doubtless glanced occasionally through the windows of some of these shops, which have become so numerous now that it is fashionable to buy antiquated furniture, and that every petty stockbroker thinks he must have his *chambre au moyen âge*.

There is one thing there which clings alike to the shop of the dealer in old iron, the ware-room of the tapestry-maker, the laboratory of the chemist, and the studio of the painter: – in all those gloomy dens where a furtive daylight filters in through the window-shutters, the most manifestly ancient thing is dust; – the cobwebs are more authentic than the guimp laces; and the old pear-tree furniture on exhibition is actually younger than the mahogany

which arrived but yesterday from America.

The warehouse of my *bric-à-brac* dealer was a veritable Capharnaum; all ages and all nations seemed to have made their rendezvous there; an Etruscan lamp of red clay stood upon a Boule cabinet, with ebony panels, brightly striped by lines of inlaid brass; a duchess of the court of Louis XV nonchalantly extended her fawn-like feet under a massive table of the time of Louis XIII with heavy spiral supports of oak, and carven designs of chimeras and foliage intermingled.

Upon the denticulated shelves of several sideboards glittered immense Japanese dishes with red and blue designs relieved by gilded hatching; side by side with enameled works by Bernard Palissy, representing serpents, frogs, and lizards in relief.

From disemboweled cabinets escaped cascades of silver-lustrous Chinese silks and waves of tinsel, which an oblique sunbeam shot through with luminous beads; while portraits of every era, in frames more or less tarnished, smiled through their yellow varnish.

The striped breastplate of a damascened suit of Milanese armor glittered in one corner; Loves and Nymphs of porcelain; Chinese Grotesques, vases of *céladon* and crackle-ware; Saxon and old Sèvres cups encumbered the shelves and nooks of the apartment.

The dealer followed me closely through the tortuous way contrived between the piles of furniture; warding off with his hand the hazardous sweep of my coat-skirts; watching my elbows with the uneasy attention of an antiquarian and a usurer.

It was a singular face, that of the merchant: – an immense skull, polished like a knee, and surrounded by a thin aureole of white hair, which brought out the clear salmon tint of his complexion all the more strikingly, lent him a false aspect of patriarchal *bonhomie*, counter-acted, however, by the scintillation of two little yellow eyes which trembled in their orbits like two louis-d'or upon quicksilver. The curve of his nose presented an aquiline silhouette, which suggested the Oriental or Jewish type. His hands – thin, slender, full of nerves which pro-jected like strings upon the finger-board of a violin, and armed with claws like those on the terminations of bats' wings – shook with senile trembling; but those convulsively agitated hands became firmer than steel pincers or lob-sters' claws when they lifted any precious article – an onyx cup, a Venetian glass, or a dish of Bohemian crystal. This strange old man had an aspect so thoroughly rabbinical and cabalistic that he would have been burnt on the mere testimony of his face three centuries ago.

'Will you not buy something from me to-day, sir? Here is a Malay kreese with a blade undulating like flame: look at those grooves contrived for the blood to run along, those teeth set backwards so as to tear out the entrails in withdrawing the weapon – it is a fine character of ferocious arm, and will look well in your collection: this two-handed sword is very beautiful – it is the work of Josepe de la Hera; and this *colichemarde*, with its fenes-trated guard – what a superb specimen of handicraft!'

'No; I have quite enough weapons and instruments of carnage; – I want a small figure, something which will suit me as a paper-weight; for I cannot endure those trumpery bronzes which the stationers sell, and which

may be found on everybody's desk.'

The old gnome foraged among his ancient wares, and finally arranged before me some antique bronzes – so called, at least; fragments of malachite; little Hindoo or Chinese idols – a kind of poussah toys in jade-stone, repre-senting the incarnations of Brahma or Vishnoo, and wonderfully appropriate to the very undivine office of holding papers and letters in place.

I was hesitating between a porcelain dragon, all constellated with warts – its mouth formid-able with bristling tusks and ranges of teeth – and an abominable little Mexican fetish, representing the god Zitziliputzili *au naturel*, when I caught sight of a charming foot, which I at first took for a fragment of some antique Venus.

It had those beautiful ruddy and tawny tints that lend to Florentine bronze that warm living look so much preferable to the grey-green aspect of common bronzes, which might easily be mistaken for statues in a state of putrefac-tion: satiny gleams played over its rounded forms, doubtless polished by the amorous kisses of twenty centuries; for it seemed a Corinthian bronze, a work of the best era of art – perhaps molded by Lysippus himself.

'That foot will be my choice,' I said to the merchant, who regarded me with an ironical and saturnine air, and held out the object desired that I might examine it more fully.

I was surprised at its lightness; it was not a foot of metal, but in sooth a foot of flesh – an embalmed foot – a mummy's foot: on examining it still more closely the very grain of the skin, and the almost imperceptible lines impressed upon it by the texture of the bandages, became perceptible. The toes were slender and delicate, and terminated by perfectly formed nails, pure and transparent as agates; the great toe, slightly separated from the rest, afforded a happy contrast, in the antique style, to the position of the other toes, and lent it an aerial lightness – the grace of a bird's foot; – the sole, scarcely streaked by a few almost imperceptible cross lines, afforded evidence that it had never touched the bare ground, and had only come in contact with the finest matting of Nile rushes, and the softest carpets of panther skin.

'Ha, ha! – you want the foot of the Princess Hermonthis,' – exclaimed the merchant, with a strange giggle, fixing his owlish eyes upon me – 'ha, ha, ha! – for a paper-weight! – an original idea! – artistic idea! Old Pharaoh would certainly have been surprised had some one told him that the foot of his adored daughter would be used for a paper-weight after he had had a mountain of granite hollowed out as a receptacle for the triple coffin, painted and gilded – covered with hieroglyphics and beautiful paintings of the Judgment of Souls,' – continued the queer little merchant, half audibly, as though talking to himself!

'How much will you charge me for this mummy fragment?'

'Ah, the highest price I can get; for it is a superb piece: if I had the match of it you could not have it for less than five hundred francs; – the daughter of a Pharaoh! nothing is more rare.'

'Assuredly that is not a common article; but, still, how much do you want? In the first place let me warn you that all my wealth consists of just five louis: I can buy anything that costs five louis, but nothing dearer; – you might search my vest pockets and most secret drawers without even finding one poor five-franc piece more.'

'Five louis for the foot of the Princess Hermonthis! that is very little, very little indeed; 'tis an authentic foot,' muttered the merchant, shaking his head, and imparting a peculiar rotary motion to his eyes. 'Well, take it, and I will give you the bandages into the bargain,' he added, wrapping the foot in an ancient damask rag – 'very fine! real damask – Indian damask which has never been redyed; it is strong, and yet it is soft,' he mumbled, stroking the frayed tissue with his fingers, through the trade-acquired habit which moved him to praise even an object of so little value that he himself deemed it only worth the giving away.

He poured the gold coins into a sort of mediaeval alms-purse hanging at his belt, repeating:

'The foot of the Princess Hermonthis, to be used for a paper-weight!'

Then turning his phosphorescent eyes upon me, he exclaimed in a voice strident as the crying of a cat which has swallowed a fishbone:

'Old Pharaoh will not be well pleased; he loved his daughter – the dear man!'

'You speak as if you were a contemporary of his: you are old enough, goodness knows! but you do not date back to the Pyramids of Egypt,' I answered, laughingly, from the threshold.

I went home, delighted with my acquisition.

With the idea of putting it to profitable use as soon as possible. I placed the foot of the divine Princess Hermonthis upon a heap of papers scribbled over with verses, in themselves an undecipherable mosaic work of erasures; articles freshly begun; letters forgotten, and posted in the table drawer instead of the letter-box – an error to which absent-minded people are peculiarly liable. The effect was charming, *bizarre*, and romantic.

Well satisfied with this embellishment, I went out with the gravity and pride becoming one who feels that he has the ineffable advantage over all the passers-by whom he elbows, of possessing a piece of the Princess Hermonthis, daughter of Pharaoh.

I looked upon all who did not possess, like myself, a paper-weight so authentically Egyptian, as very ridiculous people; and it seemed to me that the proper occupation of every sensible man should consist in the mere fact of having a mummy's foot upon his desk.

Happily I met some friends, whose presence distracted me in my infatuation with this new acquisition: I went to dinner with them; for I could not very well have dined with myself.

When I came back that evening, with my brain slightly confused by a few glasses of wine, a vague whiff of Oriental perfume delicately titillated my olfactory nerves: the heat of the room had warmed the natron, bitumen, and myrrh in which the *paraschistes*, who cut open the bodies of the dead, had bathed the corpse of the princess; – it was a perfume at once sweet and penetrating – a perfume that four thousand years had not been able to dissipate.

The Dream of Egypt was Eternity: her odors have the solidity of granite, and endure as long.

I soon drank deeply from the black cup of sleep: for a few hours all remained opaque to me; Oblivion and Nothingness inundated me with their somber waves.

Yet light gradually dawned upon the darkness of my mind; dreams commenced to touch me softly in their silent flight.

The eyes of my soul were opened; and I beheld my chamber as it actually was; I might have believed myself awake, but for a vague consciousness which assured me that I slept, and that something fantastic was about to take place.

The odor of the myrrh had augmented in intensity: and I felt a slight headache, which I very naturally attributed to several glasses of champagne that we had drunk to the unknown gods and our future fortunes.

I peered through my room with a feeling of expectation which I saw nothing to justify: every article of furniture was in its proper place; the lamp, softly shaded by its globe of ground crystal, burned upon its bracket; the water-color sketches shone under their Bohemian glass; the curtains hung down languidly; everything wore an aspect of tranquil slumber.

After a few moments, however, all this calm interior appeared to become disturbed; the woodwork cracked stealthily; the ash-covered log suddenly emitted a jet of blue flame; and the disks of the pateras seemed like great metallic eyes, watching, like myself, for the things which were about to happen.

My eyes accidentally fell upon the desk where I had placed the foot of the Princess Hermonthis.

Instead of remaining quiet – as behooved a foot which had been embalmed for four thousand years – it commenced to act in a nervous manner; contracted itself, and leaped over the papers like a startled frog; – one would have imagined that it had suddenly been brought into contact with a galvanic battery: I could distinctly hear the dry sound made by its little heel, hard as the hoof of a gazelle.

I became rather discontented with my acquisition, inasmuch as I wished my paper-weights to be of a sedentary disposition, and thought it very unnatural that feet should walk about without legs; and I commenced to experience a feeling closely akin to fear.

Suddenly I saw the folds of my bed-curtain stir; and heard a bumping sound, like that caused by some person hopping on one foot across the floor. I must confess I became alternately hot and cold; that I felt a strange wind chill my back; and that my suddenly rising hair caused my nightcap to execute a leap of several yards.

The bed-curtains opened and I beheld the strangest figure imaginable before me.

It was a young girl of a very deep coffee-brown complexion, like the bayadere Amani, and possessing the purest Egyptian type of perfect beauty: her eyes were almond-shaped and oblique, with eyebrows so black that they seemed blue; her nose was exquisitely chiseled, almost Greek in its delicacy of outline; and she might indeed have been taken for a Corinthian statue of bronze, but for the prominence of her cheekbones and the slightly African fulness of her lips, which compelled one to recognize her as belonging beyond all doubt to the hieroglyphic race which dwelt upon the banks of the Nile.

Her arms, slender and spindle-shaped, like those of very young girls, were encircled by a peculiar kind of metal bands and bracelets of glass beads; her hair was all twisted into little

cords; and she wore upon her bosom a little idol-figure of green paste, bearing a whip with seven lashes, which proved it to be an image of Isis: her brow was adorned with a shining plate of gold; and a few traces of paint relieved the coppery tint of her cheeks.

As for her costume, it, was very odd indeed.

Fancy a *pagne* or skirt all formed of little strips of material bedizened with red and black hieroglyphics, stiffened with bitumen, and apparently belonging to a freshly unbandaged mummy.

In one of those sudden flights of thought so common in dreams I heard the hoarse falsetto of the *bric-à-brac* dealer, repeating like a monotonous refrain the phrase he had uttered in his shop with so enigmatical an intonation:

'Old Pharaoh will not be well pleased: he loved his daughter, the dear man!'

One strange circumstance, which was not at all calculated to restore my equanimity, was that the apparition had but one foot; the other was broken off at the ankle!

She approached the table where the foot was starting and fidgeting about more than ever, and there supported herself upon the edge of the desk. I saw her eyes fill with pearly-gleaming tears.

Although she had not as yet spoken, I fully comprehended the thoughts which agitated her: she looked at her foot – for it was indeed her own – with an exquisitely graceful expression of coquettish sadness; but the foot leaped and ran hither and thither, as though impelled on steel springs.

Twice or thrice she extended her hand to seize it, but could not succeed.

Then commenced between the Princess

Hermonthis and her foot – which appeared to be endowed with a special life of its own – a very fantastic dialogue in a most ancient Coptic tongue, such as might have been spoken thirty centuries ago in the syrinxes of the land of Ser: luckily, I understood Coptic perfectly well that night.

The Princess Hermonthis cried, in a voice sweet and vibrant as the tones of a crystal bell:

'Well, my dear little foot, you always flee from me; yet I always took good care of you. I bathed you with perfumed water in a bowl of alabaster; I smoothed your heel with pumice-stone mixed with palm oil; your nails were cut with golden scissors and polished with a hippopotamus tooth; I was careful to select *tatbebs* for you, painted and embroidered and turned up at the toes, which were the envy of all the young girls in Egypt: you wore on your great toe rings bearing the device of the sacred Scarabaeus; and you supported one of the lightest bodies that a lazy foot could sustain.'

The foot replied, in a pouting and chagrined tone:

'You know well that I do not belong to myself any longer; – I have been bought and paid for; the old merchant knew what he was about; he bore you a grudge for having refused to espouse him; – this is an ill turn which he has done you. The Arab who violated your royal coffin in the subterranean pits of the necropolis of Thebes was sent thither by him: he desired to prevent you from being present at the reunion of the shadowy nations in the cities below. Have you five pieces of gold for my ransom?'

'Alas, no! – my jewels, my rings, my purses of gold and silver, they were all stolen from me,' answered the Princess Hermonthis, with a sob.

'Princess,' I then exclaimed, 'I never retained anybody's foot unjustly; – even though you have not got the five louis which it cost me, I present it to you gladly: I should feel unutterably wretched to think that I were the cause of so amiable a person as the Princess Hermonthis being lame.'

I delivered this discourse in a royally gallant, troubadour tone, which must have astonished the beautiful Egyptian girl.

She turned a look of deepest gratitude upon me; and her eyes shone with bluish gleams of light.

She took her foot – which surrendered itself willingly this time – like a woman about to put on her little shoe, and adjusted it to her leg with much skill.

This operation over, she took a few steps about the room, as though to assure herself that she was really no longer lame.

'Ah, how pleased my father will be! – he who was so unhappy because of my mutilation, and who from the moment of my birth set a whole nation at work to hollow me out a tomb so deep that he might preserve me intact until that last day, when souls must be weighed in the balance of Amenthi! Come with me to my father; – he will receive you kindly; for you have given me back my foot.'

I thought this proposition natural enough. I arrayed myself in a dressing-gown of large-flowered pattern, which lent me a very Pharaonic aspect; hurriedly put on a pair of Turkish slippers, and informed the Princess Hermonthis that I was ready to follow her.

Before starting, Hermonthis took from her

neck the little idol of green paste, and laid it on the scattered sheets of paper which covered the table.

'It is only fair,' she observed smilingly, 'that I should replace your paper-weight.'

She gave me her hand, which felt soft and cold, like the skin of a serpent; and we departed.

We passed for some time with the velocity of an arrow through a fluid and grayish expanse, in which half-formed silhouettes flitted swiftly by us, to right and left.

For an instant we saw only sky and sea.

A few moments later obelisks commenced to tower in the distance: pylons and vast flights of steps guarded by sphinxes became clearly outlined against the horizon.

We had reached our destination.

The princess conducted me to the mountain of rose-colored granite, in the face of which appeared an opening so narrow and low that it would have been difficult to distinguish it from the fissures in the rock, had not its location been marked by two stelae wrought with sculptures.

Hermonthis kindled a torch, and led the way before me.

We traversed corridors hewn through the living rock: their walls, covered with hieroglyphics and paintings of allegorical processions, might well have occupied thousands of arms for thousands of years in their formation; – these corridors, of interminable length, opened into square chambers, in the midst of which pits had been contrived, through which we descended by cramp-irons or spiral stairways; these pits again conducted us into other chambers, opening into other corridors,

likewise decorated with painted sparrow-hawks, serpents coiled in circles, the symbols of the *tau* and *pedum* – prodigious works of art which no living eye can ever examine – interminable legends of granite which only the dead have time to read through all eternity.

At last we found ourselves in a hall so vast, so enormous, so immeasurable, that the eye could not reach its limits; files of monstrous columns stretched far out of sight on every side, between which twinkled livid stars of yellowish flame; – points of light which revealed further depths incalcuable in the darkness beyond.

The Princess Hermonthis still held my hand, and graciously saluted the mummies of her acquaintance.

My eyes became accustomed to the dim twilight, and objects became discernible.

I beheld the kings of the subterranean races seated upon thrones – grand old men, though dry, withered, wrinkled like parchment, and blackened with naphtha and bitumen – all wearing *pshents* of gold, and breastplates and gorgets glittering with precious stones; their eyes immovably fixed like the eyes of sphinxes, and their long beards whitened by the snow of centuries. Behind them stood their peoples, in the stiff and constrained posture enjoined by Egyptian art, all eternally preserving the attitude prescribed by the hieratic code. Behind these nations, the cats, ibises, and crocodiles contemporary with them – rendered monstrous of aspect by their swathing bands – mewed, flapped their wings, or extended their jaws in a saurian giggle.

All the Pharaohs were there – Cheops, Chephrenes, Psammetichus, Sesostris, Amenotaph

– all the dark rulers of the pyramids and syrinxes: – on yet higher thrones sat Chronos and Xixouthros – who was contemporary with the deluge; and Tubal Cain, who reigned before it.

The beard of King Xixouthros had grown seven times around the granite table, upon which he leaned, lost in deep reverie – and buried in dreams.

Further back, through a dusty cloud, I beheld dimly the seventy-two pre-Adamite Kings, with their seventy-two peoples – forever passed away.

After permitting me to gaze upon this bewildering spectacle a few moments, the Princess Hermonthis presented me to her father Pharaoh, who favored me with a most gracious nod.

'I have found my foot again! – I have found my foot!' cried the Princess, clapping her little hands together with every sign of frantic joy: 'it was this gentleman who restored it to me.'

The races of Kemi, the races of Nahasi – all the black, bronzed, and copper-coloured nations repeated in chorus:

'The Princess Hermonthis has found her foot again!'

Even Xixouthros himself was visibly affected.

He raised his heavy eyelids, stroked his mustache with his fingers, and turned upon me a glance weighty with centuries.

'By Oms, the dog of Hell, and Tmei, daughter of the Sun and of Truth! this is a brave and worthy lad!' exclaimed Pharaoh, pointing to me with his scepter, which was terminated with a lotus-flower.

'What recompense do you desire?'

Filled with that daring inspired by dreams in which nothing seems impossible, I asked him for the hand of the Princess Hermonthis; – the hand seemed to me a very proper antithetic recompense for the foot.

Pharaoh opened wide his great eyes of glass in astonishment at my witty request.

'What country do you come from? and what is your age?'

'I am a Frenchman; and I am twenty-seven years old, venerable Pharaoh.'

'– Twenty-seven years old! and he wishes to espouse the Princess Hermonthis, who is thirty centuries old!' cried out at once all the Thrones and all the Circles of Nations.

Only Hermonthis herself did not seem to think my request unreasonable.

'If you were even only two thousand years old,' replied the ancient King, 'I would willingly give you the Princess; but the disproportion is too great; and, besides, we must give our daughters husbands who will last well: you do not know how to preserve yourselves any longer; even those who died only fifteen centuries ago are already no more than a handful of dust; – behold! my flesh is solid as basalt; my bones are bars of steel!

'I shall be present on the last day of the world, with the same body and the same features which I had during my lifetime: my daughter Hermonthis will last longer than a statue of bronze.

'Then the last particles of your dust will have been scattered abroad by the winds; and even Isis herself, who was able to find the atoms of Osiris, would scarce be able to recompose your being.

'See how vigorous I yet remain, and how mighty is my grasp,' he added, shaking my hand in the English fashion with a strength that buried my rings in the flesh of my fingers.

He squeezed me so hard that I awoke, and found my friend Alfred shaking me by the arm to make me get up.

'O you everlasting sleeper! – must I have you carried out into the middle of the street, and fireworks exploded in your ears? It is after noon; don't you recollect your promise to take me with you to see M. Aguado's Spanish pictures?'

'God! I forgot all, all about it,' I answered, dressing myself hurriedly; 'we will go there at once; I have the permit lying on my desk.'

I started to find it; – but fancy my astonishment when I beheld instead of the mummy's foot I had purchased the evening before, the little green paste idol left in its place by the Princess Hermonthis!

▣ ◉ ▣ ◉ ▣ ◉

Edgar Allan Poe's *Some Words with a Mummy* was first published in the *Broadway Journal* of 1 November 1845, or five years after Gautier's *The Mummy's Foot*. It fuses an experiment with galvanism (*Frankenstein*-style) with a critique of modern civilization from an ancient mummy's point of view. The moral seems to be that the history which has happened since the mummy's era is 'allamistakeo'.

EDGAR ALLAN POE
Some Words with a Mummy
(1845)

The symposium of the preceding evening had been a little too much for my nerves. I had a wretched head-ache, and was desperately drowsy. Instead of going out, therefore, to spend the evening as I had proposed, it occurred to me that I could not do a wiser thing than just eat a mouthful of supper and go immediately to bed.

A *light* supper of course. I am exceedingly fond of Welsh rabbit. More than a pound at once, however, may not at all times be advisable. Still, there can be no material objection to two. And really between two and three, there is merely a single unit of difference. I ventured, perhaps, upon four. My wife will have it five; – but, clearly, she has confounded two very distinct affairs. The abstract number, five, I am willing to admit; but, concretely, it has reference to bottles of Brown Stout, without which, in the way of condiment, Welsh rabbit is to be eschewed.

Having thus concluded a frugal meal, and donned my night-cap, with the serene hope of enjoying it till noon the next day, I placed my head upon the pillow, and through the aid of a capital conscience, fell into a profound slumber forthwith.

But when were the hopes of humanity fulfilled? I could not have completed my third snore when there came a furious ringing at the street-door bell, and then an impatient thumping at the knocker, which awakened me at once. In a minute afterward and while I was still rubbing my eyes, my wife thrust in my face a note from my old friend, Doctor Ponnonner. It ran thus:

Come to me by all means, my dear good friend, as soon as you receive this. Come and help us to rejoice. At last, by long perservering diplomacy, I have gained the assent of the Directors of the City Museum, to my examination of the Mummy – you know the one I mean. I have permission to unswathe it and open it, if desirable. A few friends only will be present – you, of course. The Mummy is now at my house, and we shall begin to unroll it at eleven to-night.

Yours ever

PONNONNER

By the time I had reached the 'Ponnonner', it struck me that I was as wide awake as a man need be. I leaped out of bed in an ecstacy, overthrowing all in my way; dressed myself with a rapidity truly marvellous; and set off, at the top of my speed, for the Doctor's.

There I found a very eager company assembled. They had been awaiting me with much impatience; the Mummy was extended upon the dining table; and the moment I entered, its examination was commenced.

It was one of a pair brought, several years previously, by Captain Arthur Sabretash, a cousin of Ponnonner's, from a tomb near Eleithias, in the Lybian Mountains, a considerable distance above Thebes on the Nile. The grottoes at this point, although less magnificent than the Theban sepulchres, are of higher interest, on account of affording more numerous illustra-tions of the private life of the Egyptians. The chamber from which our specimen was taken, was said to be very rich in such illustrations; the walls being completely covered with fresco paintings and bas-reliefs, while statues, vases, and Mosaic work of rich patterns, indicated the vast wealth of the deceased.

The treasure had been deposited in the Museum precisely in the same condition in which Captain Sabretash had found it; – that is to say, the coffin had not been disturbed. For eight years it had thus stood, subject only externally to public inspection. We had now, there-fore, the complete Mummy at our disposal; and to those who are aware how very rarely the unransacked antique reaches our shores, it will be evident, at once, that we had great reason to congratulate ourselves upon our good fortune.

Approaching the table, I saw on it a large box, or case, nearly seven feet long, and perhaps three feet wide, by two feet and a half deep. It was oblong – not coffin-shaped. The material was at first supposed to be the wood of the sycamore (*platanus*), but, upon cutting into it, we found it to be pasteboard, or more properly, *papier mâché*, composed of papyrus. It was thickly ornamented with paintings, repre-senting funeral scenes, and other mournful sub-jects, interspersed among which in every variety of position, were certain series of hieroglyphical characters intended, no doubt, for the name of the departed. By good luck, Mr Gliddon formed one of our party; and he had no difficulty in translating the letters, which were simply pho-netic, and represented the word, *Allamistakeo*.

We had some difficulty in getting this case open without injury, but, having at length accomplished the task, we came to a second, coffin-shaped, and very considerably less in size than the exterior one, but resembling it precisely in every other respect. The interval between the two was filled with resin, which had, in some degree, defaced the colors of the interior box.

Upon opening this latter (which we did quite easily,) we arrived at a third case, also coffin-shaped, and varying from the second one in no particular, except in that of its material, which was cedar, and still emitted the peculiar and highly aromatic odor of that wood. Between the second and the third case there was no interval; the one fitting accurately within the other.

Removing the third case, we discovered and took out the body itself. We had expected to find it, as usual, enveloped in frequent rolls, or bandages, of linen, but, in place of these, we found a sort of sheath, made of papyrus, and coated with a layer of plaster, thickly gilt and painted. The paintings represented subjects connected with the various supposed duties of the soul, and its presentation to different divinities, with numerous identical human figures, intended, very probably, as portraits of the persons embalmed. Extending from head to foot, was a columnar, or perpendicular inscription in phonetic hieroglyphics, giving again his name and titles, and the names and titles of his relations.

Around the neck thus ensheathed, was a collar of cylindrical glass beads, diverse in color, and so arranged as to form images of deities, of the scarabæus, etc., with the winged globe. Around the small of the waist was a similar collar, or belt.

Stripping off the papyrus, we found the flesh in excellent preservation, with no perceptible odor. The color was reddish. The skin was hard, smooth and glossy. The teeth and hair were in good condition. The eyes (it seemed) had been removed, and glass ones substituted, which were very beautiful and wonderfully life-like, with the exception of somewhat too determined a stare. The finger and toe nails were brilliantly gilded.

Mr Gliddon was of opinion, from the redness of the epidermis, that the embalmment had been effected altogether by asphaltum; but, on scraping the surface with a steel instrument, and throwing into the fire some of the powder thus obtained, the flavor of camphor and other sweet-scented gums became apparent.

We searched the corpse very carefully for the usual openings through which the entrails are extracted, but, to our surprise, we could discover none. No member of the party was at that period aware that entire or unopened mummies are not unfrequently met. The brain it was customary to withdraw through the nose; the intestines through an incision in the side; the body was then shaved, washed, and salted; then laid aside for several weeks, when the operation of embalming, properly so called, began.

As no trace of an opening could be found, Doctor Ponnonner was preparing his instruments for dissection, when I observed that it was then past two o'clock. Hereupon it was agreed to postpone the internal examination until the next evening; and we were about to separate for the present, when some one suggested an experiment or two with the Voltaic pile.

The application of electricity to a Mummy three or four thousand years old at the least, was an idea, if not very sage, still sufficiently original, and we all caught at it at once. About one tenth in earnest and nine tenths in jest, we arranged a battery in the Doctor's study, and conveyed thither the Egyptian.

It was only after much trouble that we succeeded in laying bare some portions of the temporal muscle which appeared of less stony rigidity than other parts of the frame, but which, as we had anticipated, of course, gave no indication of galvanic susceptibility when brought in contact with the wire. Thus the first trial, indeed, seemed decisive, and, with a hearty laugh at our own absurdity, we were bidding each other good night, when my eyes, happening to fall upon those of the Mummy, were there immediately riveted in amazement. My brief glance, in fact, had sufficed to assure me that the orbs which we had all supposed to be glass, and which were originally noticeable for a certain wild stare, were now so far covered by the lids that only a small portion of the *tunica albuginea* remained visible.

With a shout I called attention to the fact, and it became immediately obvious to all.

I cannot say that I was *alarmed* at the phenomenon, because 'alarmed' is, in my case, not exactly the word. It is possible, however, that, but for the Brown Stout, I might have been a little nervous. As for the rest of the company, they really made no attempt at concealing the downright fright which possessed them. Doctor Ponnonner was a man to be pitied. Mr Gliddon, by some peculiar process, rendered himself invisible. Mr Silk Buckingham, I fancy, will scarcely be so bold as to deny that he made his way, upon all fours, under the table.

After the first shock of astonishment, however, we resolved, as a matter of course, upon farther experiment forthwith. Our operations were now directed against the great toe of the right foot. We made an incision over the out-side of the exterior *os sesamoideum pollicis pedis*, and thus got at the root of the *abductor* muscle. Re-adjusting the battery, we now applied the fluid to the bisected nerves – when, with a movement of exceeding life-likeness, the Mummy first drew up its right knee so as to bring it nearly in contact with the abdomen, and then, straightening the limb with inconceivable force, bestowed a kick upon Doctor Ponnonner, which had the effect of discharging that gentleman, like an arrow from a catapult, through a window into the street below.

We rushed out *en masse* to bring in the mangled remains of the victim, but had the happiness to meet him upon the staircase, coming up in an unaccountable hurry, brimfull of the most ardent philosophy, and more than ever impressed with the necessity of prosecuting our experiments with rigor and with zeal.

It was by his advice, accordingly, that we made, upon the spot, a profound incision into the tip of the subject's nose, while the Doctor himself, laying violent hands upon it, pulled it into vehement contact with the wire.

Morally and physically – figuratively and literally – was the effect electric. In the first place, the corpse opened its eyes and winked very rapidly for several minutes, as does Mr Barnes in the pantomime; in the second place, it sneezed; in the third, it sat upon end; in the fourth, it shook its fist in Doctor Ponnonner's face; in the fifth, turning to Messieurs Gliddon and Buckingham, it addressed them, in very capital Egyptian, thus:

'I must say, gentlemen, that I am as much surprised as I am mortified, at your behaviour. Of Doctor Ponnonner nothing better was to be expected. He is a poor little fat fool who *knows* no better. I pity and forgive him. But you, Mr Gliddon – and you, Silk – who have travelled and resided in Egypt until one might imagine you to the manor born – you, I say, who have been so much among us that you speak Egyptian fully as well, I think, as you write your mother tongue – you, whom I have always been led to regard as the firm friend of the mummies – I really did anticipate more gentlemanly conduct from *you*. What am I to think of your standing quietly by and seeing me thus unhandsomely used? What am I to suppose by your permitting Tom, Dick and Harry to strip me of my coffins, and my clothes, in this wretchedly cold climate? In what light (to come to the point) am I to regard your aiding and abetting that miserable little villain, Doctor Ponnonner, in pulling me by the nose?'

It will be taken for granted, no doubt, that upon hearing this speech under the circumstances, we all either made for the door, or fell into violent hysterics, or went off in a general swoon. One of these three things was, I say, to be expected. Indeed each and all of these lines of conduct might have been very plausibly pursued. And, upon my word, I am at a loss to know how or why it was that we pursued neither the one or the other. But, perhaps, the true reason is to be sought in the spirit of the age, which proceeds by the rule of contraries altogether, and is now usually admitted as the solution of everything in the way of paradox and impossibility. Or, perhaps, after all, it was only the Mummy's exceedingly natural and matter-of-course air that divested his words of the terrible. However this may be, the facts are clear, and no member of our party betrayed any very particular trepidation, or seemed to consider that any thing had gone very especially wrong.

For my part I was convinced it was all right, and merely stepped aside, out of the range of the Egyptian's fist. Doctor Ponnonner thrust his hands into his breeches' pockets, looked hard at the Mummy, and grew excessively red in the face. Mr Gliddon stroked his whiskers and drew up the collar of his shirt. Mr Buckingham hung down his head, and put his right thumb into the left corner of his mouth.

The Egyptian regarded him with a severe countenance for some minutes, and at length, with a sneer, said:

'Why don't you speak, Mr Buckingham? Did you hear what I asked you, or not? *Do* take your thumb out of your mouth!'

Mr Buckingham, hereupon, gave a slight start, took his right thumb out of the left corner of his mouth, and, by way of indemnification, inserted his left thumb in the right corner of the aperture above-mentioned.

Not being able to get an answer from Mr B., the figure turned peevishly to Mr Gliddon, and, in a peremptory tone, demanded in general terms what we all meant.

Mr Gliddon replied at great length, in phonetics; and but for the deficiency of American printing-offices in hieroglyphical type, it would afford me much pleasure to record here, in the original, the whole of his very excellent speech.

I may as well take this occasion to remark, that all the subsequent conversation in which the Mummy took a part, was carried on in primitive Egyptian, through the medium (so far as concerned myself and other untravelled members of the company) – through the medium, I say, of Messieurs Gliddon and Buckingham, as interpreters. These gentlemen spoke the mother-tongue of the mummy with inimitable fluency and grace; but I could not help observing that (owing, no doubt, to the introduction of images entirely modern, and, of course, entirely novel to the stranger,) the two travellers were reduced, occasionally, to the employment of sensible forms for the purpose of conveying a particular meaning. Mr Gliddon, at one period, for example, could not make the Egyptian comprehend the term 'politics', until he sketched upon the wall, with a bit of charcoal, a little carbuncle-nosed gentleman, out at elbows, standing upon a stump, with his left leg drawn back, his right arm thrown forward, with the fist shut, the eyes rolled up toward Heaven, and the mouth open at an angle of ninety degrees. Just in the same way Mr Buckingham failed to convey the absolutely modern idea, 'wig', until, (at Doctor Ponnonner's suggestion,) he grew very pale in the face, and consented to take off his own.

It will be readily understood that Mr Gliddon's discourse turned chiefly upon the vast benefits accruing to science from the unrolling and disembowelling of mummies; apologizing, upon this score, for any disturbance that might have been occasioned *him*, in particular, the individual Mummy called Allamistakeo; and concluding with a mere hint (for it could scarcely be considered more,) that, as these little matters were now explained, it might be as well to proceed with the investigation intended. Here Doctor Ponnonner made ready his instruments.

In regard to the latter suggestions of the orator, it appears that Allamistakeo had certain scruples of conscience, the nature of which I did not distinctly learn; but he expressed himself satisfied with the apologies tendered, and, getting down from the table, shook hands with the company all round.

When this ceremony was at an end, we immediately busied ourselves in repairing the damages which our subject had sustained from the scalpel. We sewed up the wound in his temple, bandaged his foot, and applied a square inch of black plaster to the tip of his nose.

It was now observed that the Count, (this was the title, it seems, of Allamistakeo,) had a slight fit of shivering – no doubt from the cold. The doctor immediately repaired to his wardrobe, and soon returned with a black dress coat, made in Jennings' best manner, a pair of sky-blue plaid pantaloons with straps, a pink gingham *chemise*, a flapped vest of brocade, a white sack overcoat, a walking cane with a hook, a hat with no brim, patent-leather boots, straw-colored kid gloves, an eye-glass, a pair of whiskers, and a waterfall cravat. Owing to the disparity of size between the Count and the doctor, (the proportion being as two to one,) there was some little difficulty in adjusting these habiliments upon the person of the Egyptian; but when all was arranged, he might have been said to be dressed. Mr Gliddon, therefore, gave him his arm, and led him to a comfortable chair by the fire, while the doctor rang the bell upon the spot and ordered a supply of cigars and wine.

The conversation soon grew animated. Much curiosity was, of course, expressed in regard to the somewhat remarkable fact of Allamistakeo's still remaining alive.

'I should have thought,' observed Mr Buckingham, 'that it is high time you were dead.'

'Why,' replied the Count, very much aston-ished, 'I am little more than seven hundred years old! My father lived a thousand, and was by no means in his dotage when he died.'

Here ensued a brisk series of questions and computations, by means of which it became evident that the antiquity of the Mummy had been grossly misjudged. It had been five thousand and fifty years, and some months, since he had been consigned to the catacombs at Eleithias.

'But my remark,' resumed Mr Buckingham, 'had no reference to your age at the period of interment; (I am willing to grant, in fact, that you are still a young man,) and my allusion was to the immensity of time during which, by your own showing, you must have been done up in asphaltum.'

'In what?' said the Count.

'In asphaltum,' persisted Mr B.

'Ah, yes; I have some faint notion of what you mean; it might be made to answer, no doubt, – but in my time we employed scarcely anything else than the Bichloride of Mercury.'

'But what we are especially at a loss to understand,' said Doctor Ponnonner, 'is how it happens that, having been dead and buried in Egypt five thousand years ago, you are here to-day all alive, and looking so delightfully well.'

'Had I been, as you say, *dead*,' replied the Count, 'it is more than probable that dead I should still be; for I perceive you are yet in the infancy of Galvanism, and cannot accomplish with it what was a common thing among us in the old days. But the fact is, I fell into catalepsy, and it was considered by my best friends that I was either dead or should be; they accordingly

embalmed me at once – I presume you are aware of the chief principle of the embalming process?'

'Why, not altogether.'

'Ah, I perceive; – a deplorable condition of ignorance! Well, I cannot enter into details just now: but it is necessary to explain that to embalm, (properly speaking,) in Egypt, was to arrest indefinitely *all* the animal functions subjected to the process. I use the word 'animal' in its widest sense, as including the physical not more than the moral and *vital* being. I repeat that the leading principle of embalmment consisted, with us, in the immediately arresting, and holding in perpetual *abeyance, all* the animal functions subjected to the process. To be brief, in whatever condition the individual was, at the period of embalmment, in that condition he remained. Now, as it is my good fortune to be of the blood of the Scarabæus, I was embalmed *alive*, as you see me at present.'

'The blood of the Scarabæus!' exclaimed Doctor Ponnonner.

'Yes. The Scarabæus was the *insignium*, or the "arms", of a very distinguished and a very rare patrician family. To be "of the blood of the Scarabæus", is merely to be one of that family of which the Scarabæus is the *insignium*. I speak figuratively.'

'But what has this to do with your being alive?'

'Why it is the general custom, in Egypt, to deprive a corpse, before embalmment, of its bowels and brains; the race of the Scarabæi alone did not coincide with the custom. Had I not been a Scarabæus, therefore, I should have been without bowels and brains; and without either it is inconvenient to live.'

'I perceive that;' said Mr Buckingham, 'and I presume that all the *entire* mummies that come to hand are of the race of Scarabæi.'

'Beyond doubt.'

'I thought,' said Mr Gliddon very meekly, 'that the Scarabæus was one of the Egyptian gods.'

'One of the Egyptian *what*?' exclaimed the Mummy, starting to its feet.

'Gods!' repeated the traveler.

'Mr Gliddon I really am astonished to hear you talk in this style,' said the Count, resuming his chair. 'No nation upon the face of the earth has ever acknowledged more than *one god*. The Scarabæus, the Ibis, etc., were with us, (as similar creatures have been with others) the symbols, or *media*, through which we offered worship to the Creator too august to be more directly approached.'

There was here a pause. At length the colloquy was renewed by Doctor Ponnonner.

'It is not improbable, then, from what you have explained,' said he, 'that among the catacombs near the Nile, there may exist other mummies of the Scarabæus tribe, in a condition of vitality.'

'There can be no question of it,' replied the Count; 'all the Scarabæi embalmed accidentally while alive, are alive now. Even some of those *purposely* so embalmed, may have been overlooked by their executors, and still remain in the tombs.'

'Will you be kind enough to explain,' I said, 'what you mean by "purposely so embalmed?"'

'With great pleasure,' answered the Mummy, after surveying me leisurely through his eye-glass – for it was the first time I had ventured to address him a direct question.

With great pleasure,' said he. 'The usual duration of man's life, in my time, was about eight hundred years. Few men died, unless by most extraordinary accident, before the age of six hundred; few lived longer than a decade of centuries; but eight were considered the natural term. After the discovery of the embalming principle, as I have already described it to you, it occurred to our philosophers that a laudable curiosity might be gratified, and, at the same time, the interests of science much advanced, by living this natural term in instalments. In the case of history, indeed, experience demonstrated that something of this kind was indispensable. An historian, for example, having attained the age of five hundred, would write a book with great labor and then get himself carefully embalmed; leaving instructions to his executors *pro tem.*, that they should cause him to be revivified after the lapse of a certain period – say five or six hundred years. Resuming existence at the expiration of this time, he would invariably find his great work converted into a species of hap-hazard note-book – that is to say, into a kind of literary arena for the conflicting guesses, riddles, and personal squabbles of whole herds of exasperated commentators. These guesses, etc., which passed under the name of annotations or emendations, were found so completely to have enveloped, distorted, and overwhelmed the text, that the author had to go about with a lantern to discover his own book. When discovered, it was never worth the trouble of the search. After rewriting it throughout, it was regarded as the bounden duty of the historian to set himself to work, immediately, in correcting from his own private knowledge and experience, the traditions of the day concerning the epoch at which he had originally lived. Now this process of rescription and personal rectification, pursued by various individual sages, from time to time, had the effect of preventing our history from degenerating into absolute fable.'

'I beg your pardon,' said Doctor Ponnonner at this point, laying his hand gently upon the arm of the Egyptian – 'I beg your pardon, sir, but may I presume to interrupt you for one moment?'

'By all means, *sir*,' replied the Count, drawing up.

'I merely wished to ask you a question,' said the Doctor. 'You mentioned the historian's personal correction of *traditions* respecting his own epoch. Pray, sir, upon an average, what proportion of these Kabbala were usually found to be right?'

'The Kabbala, as you properly term them, sir, were generally discovered to be precisely on a par with the facts recorded in the un-re-written histories themselves; – that is to say, not one individual iota of either, was ever known, under any circumstances, to be not totally and radically wrong.'

'But since it is quite clear,' resumed the Doctor, 'that at least five thousand years have elapsed since your entombment, I take it for granted that your histories at that period, if not your traditions, were sufficiently explicit on that one topic of universal interest, the Creation, which took place, as I presume you are aware, only about ten centuries before.'

'Sir!' said Count Allamistakeo.

The Doctor repeated his remarks, but it was only after much additional explanation, that

the foreigner could be made to comprehend them. The latter at length said, hesitatingly:

'The ideas you have suggested are to me, I confess, utterly novel. During my time I never knew any one to entertain so singular a fancy as that the universe (or this world if you will have it so) ever had a beginning at all. I remember, once, and once only, hearing something remotely hinted, by a man of many speculations, concerning the origin *of the human race*; and by this individual the very word *Adam*, (or Red Earth) which you make use of, was employed. He employed it, however, in a generical sense, with reference to the spontaneous germination from rank soil (just as a thousand of the lower *genera* of creatures are germinated) – the spontaneous germination, I say, of five vast hordes of men, simultaneously upspringing in five distinct and nearly equal divisions of the globe.'

Here, in general, the company shrugged their shoulders, and one or two of us touched our foreheads with a very significant air. Mr Silk Buckingham, first glancing slightly at the occiput and then at the sinciput of Allamistakeo, spoke as follows: –

'The long duration of human life in your time, together with the occasional practice of passing it, as you have explained, in instalments, must have had, indeed, a strong tendency to the general development and conglomeration of knowledge. I presume, therefore, that we are to attribute the marked inferiority of the old Egyptians in all particulars of science, when compared with the moderns, and more especially with the Yankees, altogether to the superior solidity of the Egyptian skull.'

'I confess again,' replied the Count with much

suavity, 'that I am somewhat at a loss to comprehend you; pray, to what particulars of science do you allude?'

Here our whole party, joining voices, detailed, at great length, the assumptions of phrenology and the marvels of animal magnetism.

Having heard us to an end, the Count proceeded to relate a few anecdotes, which rendered it evident that prototypes of Gall and Spurzheim had flourished and faded in Egypt so long ago as to have been nearly forgotten, and that the manœuvres of Mesmer were really very contemptible tricks when put in collation with the positive miracles of the Theban *savans*, who created lice and a great many other similar things.

I here asked the Count if his people were able to calculate eclipses. He smiled rather contemptuously, and said they were.

This put me a little out, but I began to make other inquiries in regard to his astronomical knowledge, when a member of the company, who had never as yet opened his mouth, whispered in my ear that, for information on this head, I had better consult Ptolemy, (whoever Ptolemy is) as well as one Plutarch *de facie lunæ*.

I then questioned the Mummy about burning-glasses and lenses, and, in general, about the manufacture of glass; but I had not made an end of my queries before the silent member again touched me quietly on the elbow, and begged me for God's sake to take a peep at Diodorus Siculus. As for the Count, he merely asked me, in the way of reply, if we moderns possessed any such microscopes as would enable us to cut cameos in the style of the Egyptians. While I was thinking how I should answer this question, little Doctor Ponnonner committed himself in a very extraordinary way.

'Look at our architecture!' he explained, greatly to the indignation of both the travelers, who pinched him black and blue to no purpose.

'Look,' he cried with enthusiasm, 'at the Bowling-Green Fountain in New York! or if this be too vast a contemplation, regard for a moment the Capitol at Washington, D. C.!' – and the good little medical man went on to detail very minutely the proportions of the fabric to which he referred. He explained that the portico alone was adorned with no less than four and twenty columns, five feet in diameter, and ten feet apart.

The Count said that he regretted not being able to remember, just at that moment, the precise dimensions of any one of the principal buildings of the city of Aznac, whose foundations were laid in the night of Time, but the ruins of which were still standing, at the epoch of his entombment, in a vast plain of sand to the westward of Thebes. He recollected, however, (talking of porticoes) that one affixed to an inferior palace in a kind of suburb called Carnac, consisted of a hundred and forty-four columns, thirty-seven feet each in circumference, and twenty-five feet apart. The approach of this portico, from the Nile, was through an avenue two miles long, composed of sphinxes, statues and obelisks, twenty, sixty, and a hundred feet in height. The palace itself (as well as he could remember) was, in one direction, two miles long, and might have been, altogether, about seven in circuit. Its walls were richly painted all over, within and without, with hieroglyphics. He would not pretend to *assert* that even fifty or sixty of the Doctor's Capitols might have been built within these walls, but he was by no means sure that two or three hundred of them might not have been squeezed in with some trouble. That palace at Carnac was an insignificant little building after all. He, (the Count) however, could not conscientiously refuse to admit the ingenuity, magnificence, and superiority of the Fountain at the Bowling-Green, as described by the Doctor. Nothing like it, he was forced to allow, had ever been seen in Egypt or elsewhere.

I here asked the Count what he had to say to our rail-roads.

'Nothing,' he replied, 'in particular.' They were rather slight, rather ill-conceived, and clumsily put together. They could not be compared, of course, with the vast, level, direct, iron-grooved causeways, upon which the Egyptians conveyed entire temples and solid obelisks of a hundred and fifty feet in altitude.

I spoke of our gigantic mechanical forces.

He agreed that we knew something in that way, but inquired how I should have gone to work in getting up the imposts on the lintels of even the little palace at Carnac.

This question I concluded not to hear, and demanded if he had any idea of Artesian wells; but he simply raised his eye-brows; while Mr Gliddon winked at me very hard, and said, in a low tone, that one had been recently discovered by the engineers employed to bore for water in the Great Oasis.

I then mentioned our steel; but the foreigner elevated his nose, and asked me if our steel could have executed the sharp carved work seen on the obelisks, and which was wrought altogether by edge-tools of copper.

This disconcerted us so greatly that we thought it advisable to vary the attack to Metaphysics. We sent for a copy of a book called the 'Dial', and read out of it a chapter or two about something which is not very clear, but which the Bostonians call the Great Movement or Progress.

The Count merely said that Great Movements were awfully common things in his day, and as for Progress it was at one time quite a nuisance, but it never progressed.

We then spoke of the great beauty and importance of Democracy, and were at much trouble in impressing the Count with a due sense of the advantages we enjoyed in living where there was suffrage *ad libitum*, and no king.

He listened with marked interest, and in fact seemed not a little amused. When we had done, he said that, a great while ago, there had occurred something of a very similar sort. Thirteen Egyptian provinces determined all at once to be free, and so set a magnificent example to the rest of mankind. They assembled their wise men, and concocted the most ingenious constitution it is possible to conceive. For a while they managed remarkably well; only the habit of bragging was prodigious. The thing ended, however, in the consolidation of the thirteen states, with some fifteen or twenty others, in the most odious and insupportable despotism that ever was heard of upon the face of the Earth.

I asked what was the name of the usurping tyrant.

As well as the Count could recollect, it was *Mob*.

Not knowing what to say to this, I raised my voice, and deplored the Egyptian ignorance of steam.

The Count looked at me with much astonishment, but made no answer. The silent gentleman, however, gave me a violent nudge in the ribs with his elbows – told me I had sufficiently exposed myself for once – and demanded if I was really such a fool as not to know that the modern steam engine is derived from the invention of Hero, through Solomon de Caus.

We were now in imminent danger of being discomfited; but, as good luck would have it, Doctor Ponnonner, having rallied, returned to our rescue, and inquired if the people of Egypt would seriously pretend to rival the moderns in the all-important particular of dress.

The Count, at this, glanced downward to the straps of his pantaloons, and then, taking hold of the end of one of his coat-tails, held it up close to his eyes for some minutes. Letting it fall, at last, his mouth extended itself very gradually from ear to ear; but I do not remember that he said anything in the way of reply.

Hereupon we recovered our spirits, and the Doctor, approaching the Mummy with great dignity, desired it to say candidly upon its honor as a gentleman, if the Egyptians had comprehended, at *any* period, the manufacture of either Ponnonner's lozenges, or Brandreth's pills.

We looked, with profound anxiety, for an answer; – but in vain. It was not forthcoming. The Egyptian blushed and hung down his head. Never was triumph more consummate; never was defeat borne with so ill a grace. Indeed I could not endure the spectacle of the poor Mummy's mortification. I reached my hat, bowed to him stiffly, and took leave.

Upon getting home I found it past four o'clock, and went immediately to bed. It is now ten. I have been up since seven, penning these memoranda for the benefit of my family and of mankind. The former I shall behold no more. My wife is a shrew. The truth is, I am heartily sick of this life and of the nineteenth century in general. I am convinced that every thing is going wrong. Besides, I am anxious to know who will be President in 2045. As soon, therefore, as I shave and swallow a cup of coffee, I shall just step over to Ponnonner's and get embalmed for a couple of hundred years.

■ ◉ ■ ◉ ■ ◉

Bram Stoker's novel *The Jewel of Seven Stars* was first published in 1903, and was acclaimed by the critics as his finest mystery novel since *Dracula* (a book whose structure it resembles), six years before. The story of an ancient Egyptian queen called Tera whose mummy is transported from the Valley of the Sorcerer to England for resurrection – just as Count Dracula was transported to Whitby, in his Transylvanian coffin – was, according to Stoker's biographer Harry Ludlam, 'evolved from ideas begun more than thirty years before in talks with Sir William Wilde' in Merrion Square, Dublin. When the book was first published, by William Heinemann, the account in the final chapter of the raising of Queen Tera from the dead, in a cave by the sea in Cornwall, was thought to be so disturbing that Stoker was asked by the publishers to rewrite it for later editions, so as to provide a 'happier dénouement'. All subsequent British editions, from 1912 onwards, have indeed featured this 'happier denouement'.

This collection of stories about the curse of the mummy provides a perfect opportunity to return the original, hair-raising, Chapter 20 – called 'The Great Experiment' – to its rightful place.

BRAM STOKER
The Jewel of Seven Stars
(1903)

If any evidence had been wanted of how absolutely one and all of us had come to believe in the spiritual existence of the Egyptian Queen, it would have been found in the change which in a few minutes had been effected in us by the statement of voluntary negation made, we all believed, through Margaret. Despite the coming of the fearful ordeal, the sense of which it was impossible to forget, we looked and acted as though a great relief had come to us. We had indeed lived in such a state of terrorism during the days when Mr. Trelawny was lying in a trance that the feeling had bitten deeply into us. No one knows till he has experienced it, what it is to be in constant dread of some unknown danger which may come at any time and in any form.

The change was manifested in different ways, according to each nature. Margaret was sad. Doctor Winchester was in high spirits, and keenly observant; the process of thought which had served as an antidote to fear, being now relieved from this duty, added to his intellectual enthusiasm. Mr Corbeck seemed to be in a retrospective rather than a speculative mood. I was myself rather inclined to be gay; the relief from certain anxiety regarding Margaret was sufficient for me for the time.

As to Mr. Trelawny he seemed less changed than any. Perhaps this was only natural, as he had had in his mind the intention for so many years of doing that in which we were to-night engaged, that any event connected with it could only seem to him as an episode, a step to the end. His was that commanding nature which looks so to the end of an undertaking that all else is of secondary importance. Even now, though his terrible sternness relaxed under the relief from the strain, he never flagged nor faltered for a moment in his purpose. He asked us men to come with him; and going to the hall we presently managed to lower into the cave an oak table, fairly long and not too wide, which stood against the wall in the hall. This we placed under the strong cluster of electric lights in the middle of the cave. Margaret looked on for a while; then all at once her face blanched, and in an agitated voice she said:

'What are you going to do, Father?'

'To unroll the mummy of the cat! Queen Tera will not need her Familiar to-night. If she should want him, it might be dangerous to us; so we shall make him safe. You are not alarmed, dear?'

'Oh no! she answered quickly. 'But I was thinking of my Silvio, and how I should feel if he had been the mummy that was to be unswathed!'

Mr Trelawny got knives and scissors ready, and placed the cat on the table. It was a grim beginning to our work; and it made my heart sink when I thought of what might happen in that lonely house in the mid-gloom of the night. The sense of loneliness and isolation from the world was increased by the moaning of the wind which had now risen ominously, and by the beating of waves on the rocks below. But we had too grave a task before us to be swayed by external manifestations: the unrolling of the mummy began.

There was an incredible number of bandages; and the tearing sound – they being stuck fast to each other by bitumen and gums and spices – and the little cloud of red pungent dust that arose, pressed on the senses of all of us. As the last wrappings came away, we saw the animal seated before us. He was all hunkered up; his hair and teeth and claws were complete. The eyes were closed, but the eyelids had not the fierce look which I expected. The whiskers had been pressed down on the side of the face by the bandaging; but when the pressure was taken away they stood out, just as they would have done in life. He was a magnificent creature, a tiger-cat of great size. But as we looked at him, our first glance of admiration changed to one of fear, and a shudder ran through each one of us; for here was a confirmation of the fears which we had endured.

His mouth and his claws were smeared with the dry, red stains of recent blood!

Doctor Winchester was the first to recover; blood in itself had small disturbing quality for him. He had taken out his magnifying-glass and was examining the stains on the cat's mouth. Mr Trelawny breathed loudly, as though a strain had been taken from him.

'It is as I expected,' he said. 'This promises well for what is to follow.'

By this time Doctor Winchester was looking at the red stained paws. 'As I expected!' he said. 'He has seven claws, too! Opening his pocket-book, he took out the piece of blotting-paper marked by Silvio's claws, on which was also marked in pencil a diagram of the cuts made on Mr Trelawny's wrist. He placed the paper under the mummy cat's paw. The marks fitted exactly.

When we had carefully examined the cat, finding, however, nothing strange about it but its wonderful preservation, Mr Trelawny lifted it from the table. Margaret started forward, crying out:

'Take care, Father! Take care! He may injure you!'

'Not now, my dear!' he answered as he moved towards the stairway. Her face fell. 'Where are you going?' she asked in a faint voice.

'To the kitchen,' he answered. 'Fire will take away all danger for the future; even an astral body cannot materialise from ashes!' He signed to us to follow him. Margaret turned away with a sob. I went to her; but she motioned me back and whispered:

'No, no! Go with the others. Father may want you. Oh! it seems like murder! The poor Queen's pet . . .!' The tears were dropping from under the fingers that covered her eyes.

In the kitchen was a fire of wood ready laid. To this Mr Trelawny applied a match; in a few seconds the kindling had caught and the flames leaped. When the fire was solidly ablaze, he threw the body of the cat into it. For a few seconds it lay a dark mass amidst the flames, and the room was rank with the smell of burning hair. Then the dry body caught fire too. The inflammable substances used in embalming became new fuel, and the flames roared. A few minutes of fierce conflagration; and then we breathed freely. Queen Tera's Familiar was no more!

When we went back to the cave we found Margaret sitting in the dark. She had switched off the electric light, and only a faint glow of the evening light came through the narrow openings. Her father went quickly over to her and put his arms round her in a loving protective way. She laid her head on his shoulder for a minute, and seemed comforted. Presently she called to me:

"Malcolm, turn up the light!' I carried out her orders, and could see that, though she had been crying, her eyes were now dry. Her father saw it too and looked glad. He said to us in a grave tone:

'Now we had better prepare for our great work. It will not do to leave anything to the last!' Margaret must have had a suspicion of what was coming, for it was with a sinking voice that she asked:

'What are you going to do now?' Mr Trelawny too must have had a suspicion of her feelings, for he answered in a low tone:

'To unroll the mummy of Queen Tera!' She came close to him and said pleadingly in a whisper:

'Father, you are not going to unswathe her! All you men . . .! And in the glare of light!'

'But why not, my dear?'

'Just think, Father, a woman! All alone! In such a way! In such a place! Oh! it's cruel, cruel!' She was manifestly much overcome. Her cheeks were flaming red, and her eyes were full of indignant tears. Her father saw her distress;

and, sympathising with it, began to comfort her. I was moving off; but he signed to me to stay. I took it that after the usual manner of men he wanted help on such an occasion, and man-like wished to throw on some one else the task of dealing with a woman in indignant distress. However, he began to appeal first to her reason:

'Not a woman, dear; a mummy! She has been dead nearly five thousand years!'

'What does that matter? Sex is not a matter of years! A woman is a woman, if she had been dead five thousand centuries! And you expect her to arise out of that long sleep! It could not be real death, if she is to rise out of it! You have led me to believe that she will come alive when the Coffer is opened!'

'I did, my dear; and I believe it! But if it isn't death that has been the matter with her all these years, it is something uncommonly like it. Then again, just think; it was men who embalmed her. They didn't have women's rights or lady doctors in ancient Egypt, my dear! And besides,' he went on more freely, seeing that she was accepting his argument, if not yielding to it, 'we men are accustomed to such things. Corbeck and I have unrolled a hundred mummies; and there were as many women as men amongst them. Doctor Winchester in his work has had to deal with women as well as men, till custom has made him think nothing of sex. Even Ross has in his work as a barrister . . .' He stopped suddenly.

'You were going to help too!' she said to me, with an indignant look.

I said nothing; I thought silence was best. Mr Trelawny went on hurriedly; I could see that he was glad of interruption, for the part of his argument concerning a barrister's work was becoming decidedly weak:

'My child, you will be with us yourself. Would we do anything which would hurt or offend you? Come now! be reasonable! We are not at a pleasure party. We are all grave men, entering gravely on an experiment which may unfold the wisdom of old times, and enlarge human knowledge indefinitely; which may put the minds of men on new tracks of thought and research. An experiment,' as he went on his voice deepened, 'which may be fraught with death to any one of us – to us all! We know from what has been, that there are, or may be, vast and unknown dangers ahead of us, of which none in the house to-day may ever see the end. Take it, my child, that we are not acting lightly; but with all the gravity of deeply earnest men! Besides, my dear, whatever feelings you or any of us may have on the subject, it is necessary for the success of the experiment to unswathe her. I think that under any circumstances it would be necessary to remove the wrappings before she became again a live human being instead of a spiritualised corpse with an astral body. Were her original intention carried out, and did she come to new life within her mummy wrappings, it might be to exchange a coffin for a grave! She would die the death of the buried alive! But now, when she has voluntarily abandoned for the time her astral power, there can be no doubt on the subject.'

Margaret's face cleared. 'All right, Father!' she said as she kissed him. 'But oh! it seems a horrible indignity to a Queen, and a woman.'

I was moving away to the staircase when she called to me:

'Where are you going?' I came back and took her hand and stroked it as I answered:

'I shall come back when the unrolling is over!' She looked at me long, and a faint suggestion of a smile came over her face as she said:

'Perhaps you had better stay, too! It may be useful to you in your work as a barrister!' She smiled out as she met my eyes: but in an instant she changed. Her face grew grave, and deadly white. In a far away voice she said:

'Father is right! It is a terrible occasion; we need all to be serious over it. But all the same – nay, for that very reason you had better stay, Malcolm! You may be glad, later on, that you were present to-night!'

My heart sank down, down, at her words; but I thought it better to say nothing. Fear was stalking openly enough amongst us already!

By this time Mr Trelawny, assisted by Mr Corbeck and Doctor Winchester, had raised the lid of the ironstone sarcophagus which contained the mummy of the Queen. It was a large one; but it was none too big. The mummy was both long and broad and high; and was of such weight that it was no easy task, even for the four of us, to lift it out. Under Mr Trelawny's direction we laid it out on the table prepared for it.

Then, and then only, did the full horror of the whole thing burst upon me! There, in the full glare of the light, the whole material and sordid side of death seemed staringly real. The outer wrappings, torn and loosened by rude touch, and with the colour either darkened by dust or worn light by friction, seemed creased as by rough treatment; the jagged edges of the wrapping-cloths looked fringed; the painting was patchy, and the varnish chipped. The coverings were evidently many, for the bulk was great. But through all, showed that unhidable human figure, which seems to look more horrible when partially concealed than at any other time. What was before us was Death, and nothing else. All the romance and sentiment of fancy had disappeared. The two elder men, enthusiasts who had often done such work, were not disconcerted; and Doctor Winchester seemed to hold himself in a business-like attitude, as if before the operating-table. But I felt low-spirited, and miserable, and ashamed: and besides I was pained and alarmed by Margaret's ghastly pallor.

Then the work began. The unrolling of the mummy cat had prepared me somewhat for it; but this was so much larger, and so infinitely more elaborate, that it seemed a different thing. Moreover, in addition to the ever present sense of death and humanity, there was a feeling of something finer in all this. The cat had been embalmed with coarser materials; here, all, when once the outer coverings were removed, was more delicately done. It seemed as if only the finest gums and spices had been used in this embalming. But there were the same surroundings, the same attendant red dust and pungent presence of bitumen; there was the same sound of rending which marked the tearing away of the bandages. There were an enormous number of these, and their bulk when opened was great. As the men unrolled them, I grew more and more excited. I did not take a part in it myself; Margaret had looked at me gratefully as I drew back. We clasped hands, and held each other hard. As the unrolling went on, the wrappings became finer, and the smell less

laden with bitumen, but more pungent. We all, I think, began to feel it as though it caught or touched us in some special way. This, however, did not interfere with the work; it went on uninterruptedly. Some of the inner wrappings bore symbols or pictures. These were done sometimes wholly in pale green colour, sometimes in many colours; but always with a prevalence of green. Now and again Mr Trelawny or Mr Corbeck would point out some special drawing before laying the bandage on the pile behind them, which kept growing to a monstrous height.

At last we knew that the wrappings were coming to an end. Already the proportions were reduced to those of a normal figure of the manifest height of the Queen, who was more than average tall. And as the end drew nearer, so Margaret's pallor grew; and her heart beat more and more wildly, till her breast heaved in a way that frightened me.

Just as her father was taking away the last of the bandages, he happened to look up and caught the pained and anxious look of her pale face. He paused, and taking her concern to be as to the outrage on modesty, said in a comforting way:

'Do not be uneasy, dear! See! there is nothing to harm you. The Queen has on a robe. — Ay, and a royal robe, too!'

The wrapping was a wide piece the whole length of the body. It being removed, a profusely full robe of white linen had appeared, covering the body from the throat to the feet.

And such linen! We all bent over to look at it.

Margaret lost her concern, in her woman's interest in fine stuff. Then the rest of us looked with admiration; for surely such linen was never seen by the eyes of our age. It was as fine as the finest silk. But never was spun or woven silk which lay in such gracious folds, constrict though they were by the close wrappings of the mummy cloth, and fixed into hardness by the passing of thousands of years.

Round the neck it was delicately embroidered in pure gold with tiny sprays of sycamore; and round the feet, similarly worked, was an endless line of lotus plants of unequal height, and with all the graceful abandon of natural growth.

Across the body, but manifestly not surrounding it, was a girdle of jewels. A wondrous girdle, which shone and glowed with all the forms and phases and colours of the sky!

The buckle was a great yellow stone, round in outline, deep and curved, as if a yielding globe had been pressed down. It shone and glowed, as though a veritable sun lay within; the rays of its light seemed to strike out and illumine all round. Flanking it were two great moonstones of lesser size, whose glowing, beside the glory of the sun-stone, was like the silvery sheen of moonlight.

And then on either side, linked by golden clasps of exquisite shape, was a line of flaming jewels, of which the colours seemed to glow. Each of these stones seemed to hold a living star, which twinkled in every phase of changing light.

Margaret raised her hands in ecstasy. She bent over to examine more closely; but suddenly drew back and stood fully erect at her grand height. She seemed to speak with the conviction of absolute knowledge as she said:

'That is no cerement! It was not meant for the clothing of death! It is a marriage robe!'

Mr Trelawny leaned over and touched the linen robe. He lifted a fold at the neck, and I knew from the quick intake of his breath that something had surprised him. He lifted yet a little more; and then he, too, stood back and pointed, saying:

'Margaret is right! That dress is not intended to be worn by the dead! See! her figure is not robed in it. It is but laid upon her.' He lifted the zone of jewels and handed it to Margaret. Then with both hands he raised the ample robe, and laid it across the arms which she extended in a natural impulse. Things of such beauty were too precious to be handled with any but the greatest care.

We all stood awed at the beauty of the figure which, save for the face cloth, now lay completely nude before us. Mr Trelawny bent over, and with hands that trembled slightly, raised this linen cloth which was of the same fineness as the robe. As he stood back and the whole glorious beauty of the Queen was revealed, I felt a rush of shame sweep over me. It was not right that we should be there, gazing with irreverent eyes on such unclad beauty: it was indecent; it was almost sacrilegious! And yet the white wonder of that beautiful form was something to dream of. It was not like death at all; it was like a statue carven in ivory by the hand of a Praxiteles. There was nothing of that horrible shrinkage which death seems to effect in a moment. There was none of the wrinkled toughness which seems to be a leading characteristic of most mummies. There was not the shrunken attenuation of a body dried in the sand, as I had seen before in museums. All the pores of the body seemed to have been preserved in some wonderful way. The flesh was full and round, as in a living person; and the skin was as smooth as satin. The colour seemed extraordinary. It was like ivory, new ivory; except where the right arm, with shattered, bloodstained wrist and missing hand had lain bare to exposure in the sarcophagus for so many tens of centuries.

With a womanly impulse; with a mouth that drooped with pity, with eyes that flashed with anger, and cheeks that flamed, Margaret threw over the body the beautiful robe which lay across her arm. Only the face was then to be seen. This was more startling even than the body, for it seemed not dead, but alive. The eyelids were closed; but the long, black, curling lashes lay over on the cheeks. The nostrils, set in grave pride, seemed to have the repose which, when it is seen in life, is greater than the repose of death. The full, red lips, though the mouth was not open, showed the tiniest white line of pearly teeth within. Her hair, glorious in quantity and glossy black as the raven's wing, was piled in great masses over the white forehead, on which a few curling tresses strayed like tendrils. I was amazed at the likeness to Margaret, though I had had my mind prepared for such by Mr Corbeck's quotation of her father's statement. This woman – I could not think of her as a mummy or a corpse – was the image of Margaret as my eyes had first lit on her. The likeness was increased by the jewelled ornament which she wore in her hair, the 'Disk and Plumes,' such as Margaret, too, had worn. It, too, was a glorious jewel; one noble pearl of moonlight lustre, flanked by carven pieces of moonstone.

Mr Trelawny was overcome as he looked.

He quite broke down; and when Margaret flew to him and held him close in her arms and comforted him, I heard him murmur brokenly:

'It looks as if you were dead, my child!'

There was a long silence. I could hear without the roar of the wind, which was now risen to a tempest, and the furious dashing of the waves far below. Mr Trelawny's voice broke the spell:

'Later on we must try and find out the process of embalming. It is not like any that I know. There does not seem to have been any opening cut for the withdrawing of the viscera and organs, which apparently remain intact within the body. Then, again, there is no moisture in the flesh; but its place is supplied with something else, as though wax or stearine had been conveyed into the veins by some subtle process. I wonder could it be possible that at that time they could have used paraffin. It might have been, by some process that we know not, pumped into the veins, where it hardened!'

Margaret, having thrown a white sheet over the Queen's body, asked us to bring it to her own room, where we laid it on her bed. Then she sent us away, saying:

'Leave her alone with me. There are still many hours to pass, and I do not like to leave her lying there, all stark in the glare of light. This may be the Bridal she prepared for – the Bridal of Death; and at least she shall wear her pretty robes.'

When presently she brought me back to her room, the dead Queen was dressed in the robe of fine linen with the embroidery of gold; and all her beautiful jewels were in place. Candles were lit around her, and white flowers lay upon her breast.

Hand in hand we stood looking at her for a while. Then with a sigh, Margaret covered her with one of her own snowy sheets. She turned away; and after softly closing the door of the room, went back with me to the others who had now come into the dining-room. Here we all began to talk over the things that had been, and that were to be.

Now and again I could feel that one or other of us was forcing conversation, as if we were not sure of ourselves. The long wait was beginning to tell on our nerves. It was apparent to me that Mr Trelawny had suffered in that strange trance more than we suspected, or than he cared to show. True, his will and his determination were as strong as ever; but the purely physical side of him had been weakened somewhat. It was indeed only natural that it should be. No man can go through a period of four days of absolute negation of life, without being weakened by it somehow.

As the hours crept by, the time passed more and more slowly. The other men seemed to get unconsciously a little drowsy. I wondered if in the case of Mr Trelawny and Mr Corbeck, who had already been under the hypnotic influence of the Queen, the same dormance was manifesting itself. Doctor Winchester had periods of distraction which grew longer and more frequent as the time wore on.

As to Margaret, the suspense told on her exceedingly, as might have been expected in the case of a woman. She grew paler and paler still; till at last about midnight, I began to be seriously alarmed about her. I got her to come into the library with me, and tried to make her lie down on a sofa for a little while. As Mr Trelawny had decided that the experiment was

to be made exactly at the seventh hour after sunset, it would be as nearly as possible three o'clock in the morning when the great trial should be made. Even allowing a whole hour for the final preparations, we had still two hours of waiting to go through. I promised faithfully to watch her, and to awake her at any time she might name; but she would not hear of resting. She thanked me sweetly, and smiled as she did so. But she was quite able to bear up; that it was only the suspense and excitement of waiting that made her pale. I agreed perforce, but I kept her talking of many things in the library for more than an hour; so that at last, when she insisted on going back to her father, I felt that I had at least done something to help her pass the time.

We found the three men sitting patiently in the dining-room in silence. With man's fortitude they were content to be still, when they felt they had done all in their power

And so we waited.

The striking of two o'clock seemed to freshen us all up. Whatever shadows had been settling over us during the long hours preceding seemed to lift at once, and we all went about our separate duties alert and with alacrity. We looked first to the windows to see that they were closed; for now the storm raged so fiercely that we feared it might upset our plans which, after all, were based on perfect stillness. Then we got ready our respirators to put them on when the time should be close at hand. We had from the first arranged to use them, for we did not know whether some noxious fume might not come from the Magic Coffer when it should be opened. Somehow it never seemed to occur to any of us that there was any doubt as to its opening.

Then, under Margaret's guidance, we carried the body of Queen Tera, still clad in her Bridal robes, from her room into the cavern.

It was a strange sight, and a strange experience. The group of grave silent men carrying away from the lighted candles and the white flowers the white still figure, which looked like an ivory statue when through our moving the robe fell back.

We laid her in the sarcophagus, and placed the severed hand in its true position on her breast. Under it was laid the Jewel of Seven Stars, which Mr Trelawny had taken from the safe. It seemed to flash and blaze as he put it in its place. The glare of the electric lights shone cold on the great sarcophagus fixed ready for the final experiment – the Great Experiment, consequent on the researches during a lifetime of these two travelled scholars. Again, the startling likeness between Margaret and the mummy, intensified by her own extraordinary pallor, heightened the strangeness of it all.

When all was finally fixed, three-quarters of an hour had gone; for we were deliberate in our doings. Margaret beckoned me, and I went with her to her room. There she did a thing which moved me strangely, and brought home to me keenly the desperate nature of the enterprise on which we were embarked. One by one, she blew out the candles carefully, and placed them back in their usual places. When she had finished she said to me:

'They are done with! Whatever comes – Life or Death – there will be no purpose in their using now!'

We returned to the cavern with a strange thrill as of finality. There was to be no going back now!

We put on our respirators, and took our places as had been arranged. I was to stand by the taps of the electric lights, ready to turn them off or on as Mr Trelawny should direct. His last caution to me to carry out his instructions exactly was almost like a menace; for he warned me that death to any or all of us might come from any error or neglect on my part. Margaret and Doctor Winchester were to stand between the sarcophagus and the wall, so that they would not be between the mummy and the Magic Coffer. They were to note accurately all that should happen with regard to the Queen.

Mr Trelawny and Mr Corbeck were to see the lamps lighted; and then to take their places, the former at the foot, the latter at the head, of the sarcophagus.

When the hands of the clock were close to the hour, they stood ready with their lit tapers, like gunners in old days with their linstocks.

For the few minutes that followed, the passing of time was a slow horror. Mr Trelawny stood with his watch in his hand, ready to give the signal.

The time approached with inconceivable slowness; but at last came the whirring of wheels which warns that the hour is at hand. The striking of the silver bell of the clock seemed to smite on our hearts like the knell of doom. One! Two! Three!

The wicks of the lamps caught, and I turned out the electric light. In the dimness of the struggling lamps, and after the bright glow of the electric light, the room and all within it took weird shape, and everything seemed in an instant to change. We waited, with our hearts beating. I know mine did; and I fancied I could hear the pulsation of the others. Without, the storm raged; the shutters of the narrow windows shook and strained and rattled, as though something was striving for entrance.

The seconds seemed to pass with leaden wings; it was as though all the world were standing still. The figures of the others stood out dimly, Margaret's white dress alone showing clearly in the gloom. The thick respirators, which we all wore, added to the strange appearance. The thin light of the lamps, as the two men bent over the Coffer, showed Mr Trelawny's square jaw and strong mouth, and the brown, wrinkled face of Mr Corbeck. Their eyes seemed to glare in the light. Across the room Doctor Winchester's eyes twinkled like stars, and Margaret's blazed like black suns.

Would the lamps never burn up!

It was only a few seconds in all till they did blaze up. A slow, steady light, growing more and more bright; and changing in colour from blue to crystal white. So they stayed for a couple of minutes, without any change in the Coffer being noticeable. At last there began to appear all over it a delicate glow. This grew and grew, till it became like a blazing jewel; and then like a living thing, whose essence was light. Mr Trelawny and Mr Corbeck moved silently to their places beside the sarcophagus.

We waited and waited, our hearts seeming to stand still.

All at once there was a sound like a tiny muffled explosion, and the cover of the Coffer lifted right up on a level plane a few inches; there was no mistaking anything now, for the whole cavern was full of light. Then the cover, staying fast at one side, rose slowly up on the other, as though yielding to some pressure of balance. I could not see what was within, for

the risen cover stood between. The Coffer still continued to glow; from it began to steal a faint greenish vapour which floated in the direction of the sarcophagus as though impelled or drawn towards it. I could not smell it fully on account of the respirator; but, even through that, I was conscious of a strange, pungent odour. The vapour got somewhat denser after a few seconds, and began to pass directly into the open sarcophagus. It was evident now that the mummied body had some attraction for it; and also that it had some effect on the body, for the sarcophagus slowly became illumined as though the body had begun to glow. I could not see within from where I stood, but I gathered from the faces of all the four watchers that something strange was happening.

I longed to run over and take a look for myself; but I remembered Mr Trelawny's solemn warning, and remained at my post.

The storm still thundered round the house, and I could feel the rock on which it was built tremble under the furious onslaught of the waves. The shutters strained as though the screaming wind without would in very anger have forced an entrance. In that dread hour of expectancy, when the forces of Life and Death were struggling for the mastery, imagination was awake. I almost fancied that the storm was a living thing, and animated with the wrath of the quick!

All at once the eager faces round the sarcophagus were bent forward. The look of speechless wonder in the eyes, lit by that supernatural glow from within the sarcophagus, had a more than mortal brilliance.

My own eyes were nearly blinded by the

awful, paralysing light, so that I could hardly trust them. I saw something white rising up from the open sarcophagus. Something which appeared to my tortured eyes to be filmy, like a white mist. In the heart of this mist, which was cloudy and opaque like an opal, was something like a hand holding a fiery jewel flaming with many lights. As the fierce glow of the Coffer met this new living light, the green vapour floating between them seemed like a cascade of brilliant points – a miracle of light!

But at that very moment there came a change. The fierce storm, battling with the shutters of the narrow openings, won victory. With the sound of a pistol shot, one of the heavy shutters broke its fastening and was hurled on its hinges back against the wall. In rushed a fierce blast which blew the flames of the lamps to and fro, and drifted the green vapour from its course.

On the very instant came a change in the outcome from the Coffer. There was a moment's quick flame and a muffled explosion; and black smoke began to pour out. This got thicker and thicker with frightful rapidity, in volumes of ever-increasing density; till the whole cavern began to get obscure, and its outlines were lost. The screaming wind tore in and whirled it about. At a sign from Mr Trelawny, Mr Corbeck went and closed the shutter and jammed it fast with a wedge.

I should have liked to help; but I had to wait directions from Mr Trelawny, who inflexibly held his post at the head of the sarcophagus. I signed to him with my hand, but he motioned me back. Gradually the figures of all close to the sarcophagus became indistinct in the smoke which rolled round them in thick billowy clouds. Finally, I lost sight of them altogether. I

had a terrible desire to rush over so as to be near Margaret; but again I restrained myself. If the Stygian gloom continued, light would be a necessity of safety; and I was the guardian of the light! My anguish of anxiety as I stood to my post was almost unendurable.

The Coffer was now but a dull colour; and the lamps were growing dim, as though they were being overpowered by the thick smoke. Absolute darkness would soon be upon us.

I waited and waited, expecting every instant to hear the command to turn up the light; but none came. I waited still, and looked with harrowing intensity at the rolling billows of smoke still pouring out of the casket whose glow was fading. The lamps sank down, and went out; one by one.

Finally, there was but one lamp alight, and that was dimly blue and flickering. I kept my eyes fixed towards Margaret, in the hope that I might see her in some lifting of the gloom; it was for her now that all my anxiety was claimed. I could just see her white frock beyond the dim outline of the sarcophagus.

Deeper and deeper grew the black mist and its pungency began to assail my nostrils as well as my eyes. Now the volume of smoke coming from the Coffer seemed to lessen, and the smoke itself to be less dense. Across the room I saw a movement of something white where the sarcophagus was. There were several such movements. I could just catch the quick glint of white through the dense smoke in the fading light; for now even the last lamp began to flicker with the quick leaps before extinction.

Then the last glow disappeared. I felt that the time had come to speak; so I pulled off my respirator and called out:

'Shall I turn on the light?' There was no answer. Before the thick smoke choked me, I called again, but more loudly:

'Mr Trelawny, shall I turn on the light? Answer me! If you do not forbid me, I shall turn it on!'

As there was no reply, I turned the tap. To my horror there was no response; something had gone wrong with the electric light! I moved, intending to run up the staircase to seek the cause, but I could now see nothing, all was pitch dark.

I groped my way across the room to where I thought Margaret was. As I went I stumbled across a body. I could feel by her dress that it was a woman. My heart sank; Margaret was unconscious, or perhaps dead. I lifted the body in my arms, and went straight forward till I touched a wall. Following it round I came to the stairway, and hurried up the steps with what haste I could make, hampered as I was with my dear burden. It may have been that hope lightened my task; but as I went the weight that I bore seemed to grow less as I ascended from the cavern.

I laid the body in the hall, and groped my way to Margaret's room, where I knew there were matches, and the candles which she had placed beside the Queen. I struck a match; and oh! it was good to see the light. I lit two candles, and taking one in each hand, hurried back to the hall where I had left, as I had supposed, Margaret.

Her body was not there. But on the spot where I had laid her was Queen Tera's Bridal robe, and surrounding it the girdle of wondrous gems. Where the heart had been, lay the Jewel of Seven Stars.

Sick at heart, and with a terror which has no name, I went down into the cavern. My two candles were like mere points of light in the black, impenetrable smoke. I put up again to my mouth the respirator which hung round my neck, and went to look for my companions.

I found them all where they had stood. They had sunk down on the floor, and were gazing upward with fixed eyes of unspeakable terror. Margaret had put her hands before her face, but the glassy stare of her eyes through her fingers was more terrible than an open glare.

I pulled back the shutters of all the windows to let in what air I could. The storm was dying away as quickly as it had risen, and now it only came in desultory puffs. It might well be quiescent; its work was done!

I did what I could for my companions; but there was nothing that could avail. There, in that lonely house, far away from aid of man, naught could avail.

It was merciful that I was spared the pain of hoping.

◉ ▣ ◉ ▣ ◉ ▣

Sir Arthur Conan Doyle's short story *The Ring of Thoth* was first published in 1890, in *The Cornhill Magazine*. Its basic idea – that an ancient Egyptian priest returns to a modern exhibition of mummies to find an antidote to the elixir of life which has kept him going – has provided the basis for the plots of all the great mummy movies: from *The Mummy* (1932, with Boris Karloff) to *The Mummy* (1959, with Christopher Lee), and beyond. Conan Doyle was to be a key figure in the press

Conan Doyle was to be a key figure in the press reporting of the curse of the pharaohs, thirty-three years after the *The Ring of Thoth* first appeared.

SIR ARTHUR CONAN DOYLE
The Ring of Thoth
(1890)

Mr John Vansittart Smith, F.R.S., of 147a Gower Street, was a man whose energy of purpose and clearness of thought might have placed him in the very first rank of scientific observers. He was the victim, however, of a universal ambition which prompted him to aim at distinction in many subjects rather than pre-eminence in one. In his early days he had shown an aptitude for zoology and for botany which caused his friends to look upon him as a second Darwin, but when a professorship was almost within his reach he had suddenly discontinued his studies and turned his whole attention to chemistry. Here his researches upon the spectra of the metals had won him his fellowship in the Royal Society; but again he played the coquette with his subject, and after a year's absence from the laboratory he joined the Oriental Society, and delivered a paper on the Hieroglyphic and Demotic inscriptions of El Kab, thus giving a crowning example both of the versatility and of the inconstancy of his talents.

The most fickle of wooers, however, is apt to be caught at last, and so it was with John Vansittart Smith. The more he burrowed his way into Egyptology the more impressed he became by the vast field which it opened to the inquirer, and by the extreme importance of a subject which promised to throw a light upon the first germs of human civilization and the origin of the greater part of our arts and sciences. So struck was Mr Smith that he straightway married an Egyptological young lady who had written upon the sixth dynasty, and having thus secured a sound base of operations he set himself to collect materials for a work which should unite the research of Lepsius and the ingenuity of Champollion. The preparation of this *magnum opus* entailed many hurried visits to the magnificent Egyptian collections of the Louvre, upon the last of which, no longer ago than the middle of last October, he became involved in a most strange and noteworthy adventure.

The trains had been slow and the Channel had been rough, so that the student arrived in Paris in a somewhat befogged and feverish condition. On reaching the Hôtel de France, in the Rue Laffitte, he had thrown himself upon a sofa for a couple of hours, but finding that he was unable to sleep, he determined, in spite of his fatigue, to make his way to the Louvre, settle the point which he had come to decide, and take the evening train back to Dieppe. Having come to his conclusion, he donned his greatcoat, for it was a raw rainy day, and made his way across the Boulevard des Italiens and down the Avenue de l'Opéra. Once in the Louvre he was on familiar ground, and he speedily made his way to the collection of papyri which it was his intention to consult.

The warmest admirers of John Vansittart Smith could hardly claim for him that he was a handsome man. His high-beaked nose and prominent chin had something of the same acute and incisive character which distinguished his intellect. He held his head in a birdlike fashion, and birdlike, too, was the pecking motion with which, in conversation, he threw out his objections and retorts. As he stood, with the high collar of his greatcoat raised to his ears, he might have seen from the reflection in the glass case before him that his appearance was a singular one. Yet it came upon him as a sudden jar when an English voice behind him exclaimed in very audible tones, 'What a queer-looking mortal!'

The student had a large amount of petty vanity in his composition which manifested itself by an ostentatious and overdone disregard of all personal considerations. He straightened his lips and looked rigidly at the roll of papyrus, while his heart filled with bitterness against the whole race of travelling Britons.

'Yes,' said another voice, 'he really is an extraordinary fellow.'

'Do you know,' said the first speaker, 'one could almost believe that by the continual contemplation of mummies the chap has become half a mummy himself?'

'He has certainly an Egyptian cast of countenance,' said the other.

John Vansittart Smith spun round upon his heel with the intention of shaming his countrymen by a corrosive remark or two. To his surprise and relief, the two young fellows who had been conversing had their shoulders turned towards him, and were gazing at one of the Louvre attendants who was polishing some brass-work at the other side of the room.

'Carter will be waiting for us at the Palais Royal,' said one tourist to the other, glancing at his watch, and they clattered away, leaving the student to his labours.

'I wonder what these chatterers call an Egyptian cast of countenance,' thought John Vansittart Smith, and he moved his position slightly in order to catch a glimpse of the man's face. He started as his eyes fell upon it. It was indeed the very face with which his studies had made him familiar. The regular statuesque features, broad brow, well-rounded chin, and dusky complexion were the exact counterpart of the innumerable statues, mummy-cases, and pictures which adorned the walls of the apartment. The thing was beyond all coincidence. The man must be an Egyptian. The national angularity of the shoulders and narrowness of the hips were alone sufficient to identify him.

John Vansittart Smith shuffled towards the attendant with some intention of addressing him. He was not light of touch in conversation, and found it difficult to strike the happy mean between the brusqueness of the superior and the geniality of the equal. As he came nearer, the man presented his side face to him, but kept his gaze still bent upon his work. Vansittart Smith, fixing his eyes upon the fellow's skin, was conscious of a sudden impression that there was something inhuman and preternatural about its appearance. Over the temple and cheek-bone it was as glazed and as shiny as varnished parchment. There was no suggestion of pores. One could not fancy a drop of moisture upon that arid surface. From brow to chin, however, it was cross-hatched by a million delicate wrinkles, which shot and interlaced as though nature in some Maori mood had tried how wild and intricate a pattern she could devise.

'Où est la collection de Memphis?' asked the student, with the awkward air of a man who is devising a question merely for the purpose of opening a conversation.

'C'est là,' replied the man brusquely, nodding his head at the other side of the room.

'Vous êtes un Egyptien, n'est-ce pas?' asked the Englishman.

The attendant looked up and turned his strange dark eyes upon his questioner. They were vitreous, with a misty dry shininess, such as Smith had never seen in a human head before. As he gazed into them he saw some strong emotion gather in their depths, which rose and deepened until it broke into a look of something akin both to horror and to hatred.

'Non, monsieur; je suis français.' The man turned abruptly and bent low over his polishing. The student gazed at him for a moment in astonishment, and then turning to a chair in a retired corner behind one of the doors he proceeded to make notes of his researches among the papyri. His thoughts, however, refused to return into their natural groove. They would run upon the enigmatical attendant with the sphinx-like face and the parchment skin.

'Where have I seen such eyes?' said Vansittart Smith to himself. 'There is something saurian about them, something reptilian. There's the membrana nictitans of the snakes,' he mused, bethinking himself of his zoological studies. 'It gives a shiny effect. But there was something more here. There was a sense of power, of wisdom – so I read them – and of weariness, utter weariness, and ineffable despair. It may be all imagination, but I never

had so strong an impression. By Jove, I must have another look at them!' He rose and paced round the Egyptian rooms, but the man who had excited his curiosity had disappeared.

The student sat down again in his quiet corner, and continued to work at his notes. He had gained the information which he required from the papyri, and it only remained to write it down while it was still fresh in his memory. For a time his pencil travelled rapidly over the paper, but soon the lines became less level, the words more blurred and finally the pencil tinkled down upon the floor, and the head of the student dropped heavily forward upon his chest. Tired out by his journey, he slept so soundly in his lonely post behind the door that neither the clanking civil guard, nor the footsteps of sightseers, nor even the loud hoarse bell which gives the signal for closing, were sufficient to arouse him.

Twilight deepened into darkness, the bustle from the Rue de Rivoli waxed and then waned, distant Notre Dame clanged out the hour of midnight, and still the dark and lonely figure sat silently in the shadow. It was not until close upon one in the morning that, with a sudden gasp and an intaking of the breath, Vansittart Smith returned to consciousness. For a moment it flashed upon him that he had dropped asleep in his study-chair at home. The moon was shining fitfully through the unshuttered window, however, and as his eye ran along the lines of mummies and the endless array of polished cases, he remembered clearly where he was and how he came there. The student was not a nervous man. He possessed that love of a novel situation which is peculiar to his race. Stretching out his cramped limbs, he looked at his watch, and burst into a chuckle as he observed the hour. The episode would make an admirable anecdote to be introduced into his next paper as a relief to the graver and heavier speculations. He was a little cold, but wide awake and much refreshed. It was no wonder that the guardians had overlooked him, for the door threw its heavy black shadow right across him.

The complete silence was impressive. Neither outside nor inside was there a creak or a murmur. He was alone with the dead men of a dead civilization. What though the outer city reeked of the garish nineteenth century! In all this chamber there was scarce an article, from the shrivelled ear of wheat to the pigment-box of the painter, which had not held its own against four thousand years. Here was the flotsam and jetsam washed up by the great ocean of time from that far-off empire. From stately Thebes, from lordly Luxor, from the great temples of Heliopolis, from a hundred rifled tombs, these relics had been brought. The student glanced round at the long-silent figures who flickered vaguely up through the gloom, at the busy toilers who were now so restful, and he fell into a reverent and thoughtful mood. An unwonted sense of his own youth and insignificance came over him. Leaning back in his chair, he gazed dreamily down the long vista of rooms, all silvery with the moonshine, which extend through the whole wing of the widespread building. His eyes fell upon the yellow glare of a distant lamp.

John Vansittart Smith sat up in his chair with his nerves all on edge. The light was advancing slowly towards him, pausing from time to time, and then coming jerkily onwards. The bearer moved noiselessly. In the utter silence there was no suspicion of the pat of a footfall. An idea of robbers entered the Englishman's head. He snuggled up farther into the corner. The light was two rooms off. Now it was in the next chamber, and still there was no sound. With something approaching to a thrill of fear the student observed a face, floating in the air as it were, behind the flare of the lamp. The figure was wrapped in shadow, but the light fell full upon the strange, eager face. There was no mistaking the metallic, glistening eyes and the cadaverous skin. It was the attendant with whom he had conversed.

Vansittart Smith's first impulse was to come forward and address him. A few words of explanation would set the matter clear, and lead doubtless to his being conducted to some side-door from which he might make his way to his hotel. As the man entered the chamber, however, there was something so stealthy in his movements, and so furtive in his expression, that the Englishman altered his intention. This was clearly no ordinary official walking the rounds. The fellow wore felt-soled slippers, stepped with a rising chest, and glanced quickly from left to right, while his hurried, gasping breathing thrilled the flame of his lamp. Vansittart Smith crouched silently back into the corner and watched him keenly, convinced that his errand was one of secret and probably sinister import.

There was no hesitation in the other's movements. He stepped lightly and swiftly across to one of the great cases, and, drawing a key from his pocket, he unlocked it. From the upper shelf he pulled down a mummy, which he bore away with him, and laid it with much care and solicitude upon the ground. By it he placed his lamp, and then squatting down beside it in Eastern fashion he began with long, quivering fingers to undo the cerecloths and bandages which girt it round. As the crackling rolls of linen peeled off one after the other, a strong aromatic odour filled the chamber, and fragments of scented wood and of spices pattered down upon the marble floor.

It was clear to John Vansittart Smith that this mummy had never been unswathed before. The operation interested him keenly. He thrilled all over with curiosity, and his birdlike head protruded farther and farther from behind the door. When, however, the last roll had been removed from the four-thousand-year-old head, it was all that he could do to stifle an outcry of amazement. First, a cascade of long, black, glossy tresses poured over the workman's hands and arms. A second turn of the bandage revealed a low, white forehead, with a pair of delicately arched eyebrows. A third uncovered a pair of bright, deeply fringed eyes, and a straight, well-cut nose, while a fourth and last showed a sweet, full, sensitive mouth, and a beautifully curved chin. The whole face was one of extraordinary loveliness, save for the one blemish that in the centre of the forehead there was a single irregular coffee-coloured splotch. It was a triumph of the embalmer's art. Vansittart Smith's eyes grew larger and larger as he gazed upon it, and he chirruped in his throat with satisfaction.

Its effect upon the Egyptologist was as nothing, however, compared with that which it produced upon the strange attendant. He threw his hands up into the air, burst into a harsh clatter of words, and then, hurling himself down upon the ground beside the mummy, he threw his arms round her, and kissed her repeatedly upon the lips and brow. 'Ma petite!' he groaned in French. 'Ma pauvre petite!' His voice broke with emotion, and his innumerable wrinkles quivered and writhed, but the student observed in the lamp-light that his shining eyes were still dry and tearless as two beads of steel. For some minutes he lay, with a twitching face, crooning and moaning over the beautiful head. Then he broke into a sudden smile, and some words in an unknown tongue, and sprang to his feet with the vigorous air of one who has braced himself for an effort.

In the centre of the room there was a large, circular case which contained, as the student had frequently remarked, a magnificent collection of early Egyptian rings and precious stones. To this the attendant strode, and, unlocking it, threw it open. On the ledge at the side he placed his lamp, and beside it a small, earthenware jar which he had drawn from his pocket. He then took a handful of rings from the case, and with a most serious and anxious face he proceeded to smear each in turn with some liquid substance from the earthen pot, holding them to the light as he did so. He was clearly disappointed with the first lot, for he threw them petulantly back into the case and drew out some more. One of these, a massive ring with a large crystal set in it, he seized and eagerly tested with the contents of the jar. Instantly he uttered a cry of joy, and threw out his arms in a wild gesture which upset the pot and set the liquid streaming across the floor to the very feet of the Englishman. The attendant drew a red handkerchief from his bosom, and, mopping up the mess, he followed it into the corner, where in a moment he found himself face to face with his observer.

'Excuse me,' said John Vansittart Smith, with all imaginable politeness; 'I have been unfortunate enough to fall asleep behind this door.'

'And you have been watching me?' the other asked in English, with a most venomous look on his corpse-like face.

The student was a man of veracity. 'I confess,' said he, 'that I have noticed your movements, and that they have aroused my curiosity and interest in the highest degree.'

The man drew a long, flamboyant-bladed knife from his bosom. 'You have had a very narrow escape,' he said; 'had I seen you ten minutes ago, I should have driven this through your heart. As it is, if you touch me or interfere with me in any way you are a dead man.'

'I have no wish to interfere with you,' the student answered. 'My presence here is entirely accidental. All I ask is that you will have the extreme kindness to show me out through some side-door.' He spoke with great suavity, for the man was still pressing the tip of his dagger against the palm of his left hand, as though to assure himself of its sharpness, while his face preserved its malignant expression.

'If I thought –' said he. 'But no, perhaps it is as well. What is your name?'

The Englishman gave it.

'Vansittart Smith,' the other repeated, 'Are you the same Vansittart Smith who gave a paper in London upon El Kab? I saw a report of it. Your knowledge of the subject is contemptible.'

'Sir!' cried the Egyptologist.

'Yet it is superior to that of many who make even greater pretensions. The whole keystone of our old life in Egypt was not the inscriptions or monuments of which you make so much, but was our hermetic philosophy and mystic knowledge of which you say little or nothing.'

'Our old life!' repeated the scholar, wide-eyed; and then suddenly, 'Good god, look at the mummy's face!'

The strange man turned and flashed his light upon the dead woman, uttering a long, doleful cry as he did so. The action of the air had already undone all the art of the embalmer. The skin had fallen away the eyes had sunk inwards, the discoloured lips had writhed away from the yellow teeth, and the brown mark upon the forehead alone showed that it was indeed the same face which had shown such youth and beauty a few short minutes before.

The man flapped his hands together in grief and horror. Then mastering himself by a strong effort he turned his hard eyes once more upon the Englishman.

'It does not matter,' he said, in a shaking voice. 'It does not really matter. I came here tonight with the fixed determination to do something. It is now done. All else is as nothing. I have found my quest. The old curse is broken. I can rejoin her. What matter about her inanimate shell so long as her spirit is awaiting me at the other side of the veil!'

'These are wild words,' said Vansittart Smith. He was becoming more and more convinced that he had to do with a madman.

'Time presses, and I must go,' continued the other. 'The moment is at hand for which I have waited this weary time. But I must show you out first. Come with me.'

Taking up the lamp, he turned from the disordered chamber, and led the student swiftly through the long series of the Egyptian,

Assyrian, and Persian apartments. At the end of the latter he pushed open a small door let into the wall and descended a winding, stone stair. The Englishman felt the cold, fresh air of the night upon his brow. There was a door opposite him which appeared to communicate with the street. To the right of this another door stood ajar, throwing a spurt of yellow light across the passage. 'Come in here!' said the attendant shortly.

Vansittart Smith hesitated. He had hoped that he had come to the end of his adventure. Yet his curiosity was strong within him. He could not leave the matter unsolved, so he followed his strange companion into the lighted chamber.

It was a small room, such as is devoted to a *concierge*. A wood fire sparkled in the grate. At one side stood a truckle bed, and at the other a coarse, wooden chair, with a round table in the centre, which bore the remains of a meal. As the visitor's eye glanced round he could not but remark with an ever-recurring thrill that all the small details of the room were of the most quaint design and antique workmanship. The candlesticks, the vases upon the chimney-piece, the fire-irons, the ornaments upon the walls, were all such as he had been wont to associate with the remote past. The gnarled, heavy-eyed man sat himself down upon the edge of the bed, and motioned his guest into the chair.

'There may be design in this,' he said, still speaking excellent English. 'It may be decreed that I should leave some account behind as a warning to all rash mortals who would set their wits up against workings of Nature. I leave it with you. Make such use as you will

of it. I speak to you now with my feet upon the threshold of the other world.

'I am, as you surmised, an Egyptian – not one of the down-trodden race of slaves who now inhabit the Delta of the Nile, but a survivor of that fiercer and harder people who tamed the Hebrew, drove the Ethiopian back into the southern deserts, and built those mighty works which have been the envy and the wonder of all after generations. It was in the reign of Tuthmosis, sixteen hundred years before the birth of Christ, that I first saw the light. You shrink away from me. Wait, and you will see that I am more to be pitied than to be feared.

'My name was Sosra. My father had been the chief priest of Osiris in the great temple of Abaris, which stood in those days upon the Bubastic branch of the Nile. I was brought up in the temple and was trained in all those mystic arts which are spoken of in your own Bible. I was an apt pupil. Before I was sixteen I had learned all which the wisest priest could teach me. From that time on I studied Nature's secrets for myself, and shared my knowledge with no man.

'Of all the questions which attracted me there were none over which I laboured so long as over those which concern themselves with the nature of life. I probed deeply into the vital principle. The aim of medicine has been to drive away disease when it appeared. It seemed to me that a method might be devised which should so fortify the body as to prevent weakness or death from ever taking hold of it. It is useless that I should recount my researches. You would scarce comprehend them if I did. They were carried out partly upon animals, partly upon slaves, and partly on myself. Suffice it that their result was to furnish me with a substance which, when injected into the blood, would endow the body with strength to resist the effects of time, of violence, or of disease. It would not indeed confer immortality, but its potency would endure for many thousands of years. I used it upon a cat, and afterwards drugged the creature with the most deadly poisons. That cat is alive in Lower Egypt at the present moment. There was nothing of mystery or magic in the matter. It was simply a chemical discovery, which may well be made again.

'Love of life runs high in the young. It seemed to me that I had broken away from all human care now that I had abolished pain and driven death to such a distance. With a light heart I poured the accursed stuff into my veins. Then I looked round for someone whom I could benefit. There was a young priest of Thoth, Parmes by name, who had won my goodwill by his earnest nature and his devotion to his studies. To him I whispered my secret, and at his request I injected him with my elixir. I should now, I reflected, never be without a companion of the same age as myself.

'After this grand discovery I relaxed my studies to some extent, but Parmes continued his with redoubled energy. Every day I could see him working with his flasks and his distiller in the Temple of Thoth, but he said little to me as to the result of his labours. For my own part, I used to walk through the city and look around me with exultation as I reflected that all this was destined to pass away, and that only I should remain. The people would bow to me as they passed me, for the fame of my knowledge had gone abroad.

'There was war at this time, and the Great King had sent down his soldiers to the eastern boundary to drive away the Hyksos. A Governor, too, was sent to Abaris, that he might hold it for the King. I had heard much of the beauty of the daughter of this Governor, but one day as I walked out with Parmes we met her, borne upon the shoulders of her slaves. I was struck with love as with lightning. My heart went out from me. I could have thrown myself beneath the feet of her bearers. This was my woman. Life without her was impossible. I swore by the head of Horus that she should be mine. I swore it to the Priest of Thoth. He turned away from me with a brow which was as black as midnight.

'There is no need to tell you of our wooing. She came to love me even as I loved her. I learned that Parmes had seen her before I did, and had shown her that he, too, loved her, but I could smile at his passion, for I knew that her heart was mine. The white plague had come upon the city and many were stricken, but I laid my hands upon the sick and nursed them without fear or scathe. She marvelled at my daring. Then I told her my secret, and begged her that she would let me use my art upon her.

'"Your flower shall then be unwithered, Atma," I said. "Other things may pass away, but you and I, and our great love for each other, shall outlive the tomb of King Chefru."

'But she was full of timid, maidenly objections. "Was it right?" she asked, "was it not a thwarting of 'the will of the gods?' If the great Osiris had wished that our years should be so long, would he not himself have brought it about?"

'With fond and loving words I overcame her

doubts, and yet she hesitated. It was a great question, she said. She would think it over for this one night. In the morning I should know of her resolution. Surely one night was not too much to ask. She wished to pray to Isis for help in her decision.

'With a sinking heart and a sad foreboding of evil I left her with her tirewomen. In the morning, when the early sacrifice was over, I hurried to her house. A frightened slave met me upon the steps. Her mistress was ill, she said, very ill. In a frenzy I broke my way through the attendants, and rushed through hall and corridor to my Atma's chamber. She lay upon her couch, her head high upon the pillow, with a pallid face and a glazed eye. On her forehead there blazed a single angry, purple patch. I knew that hell-mark of old. It was the scar of the white plague, the sign-manual of death.

'Why should I speak of that terrible time? For months I was mad, fevered, delirious, and yet I could not die. Never did an Arab thirst after the sweet wells as I longed after death. Could poison or steel have shortened the thread of my existence, I should soon have rejoined my love in the land with the narrow portal. I tried, but it was of no avail. The accursed influence was too strong upon me. One night as I lay upon my couch, weak and weary, Parmes, the priest of Thoth, came to my chamber. He stood in the circle of the lamplight, and he looked down upon me with eyes which were bright with a mad joy.

'"Why did you let the maiden die?" he asked; "why did you not strengthen her as you strengthened me?"

'"I was too late," I answered. "But I had forgot. You also loved her. You are my fellow in misfortune. Is it not terrible to think of the centuries which must pass ere we look upon her again? Fools, fools, that we were to take death to be our enemy?"

'"You may say that," he cried with a wild laugh: "the words come well from your lips. For me they have no meaning."

'"What mean you?" I cried, raising myself upon my elbow. "Surely, friend, this grief has turned your brain." His face was aflame with joy, and he writhed and shook like one who hath a devil.

'"Do you know whither I go?" he asked.

'"Nay," I answered, "I cannot tell."

'"I go to her," said he. "She lies embalmed in the farther tomb by the double palm-tree beyond the city wall."

'"Why do you go there?" I asked.

'"To die!" he shrieked, "to die! I am not bound by earthen fetters."

'"But the elixir is in your blood," I cried.

'"I can defy it," said he; "I have found a stronger principle which will destroy it. It is working in my veins at this moment, and in an hour I shall be a dead man. I shall join her, and you shall remain behind."

'As I looked upon him I could see that he spoke words of truth. The light in his eye told me that he was indeed beyond the power of the elixir.

'"You will teach me!" I cried.

'"Never!" he answered.

'"I implore you, by the wisdom of Thoth, by the majesty of Anubis!"

'"It is useless," he said coldly.

'"Then I will find it out," I cried.

'"You cannot," he answered; "it came to me by chance. There is one ingredient which you can never get. Save that which is in the ring of Thoth, none will ever more be made."

'"In the ring of Thoth!" I repeated, "where then is the ring of Thoth?"

'"That also you shall never know," he answered. "You won her love. Who has won in the end? I leave you to your sordid earth life. My chains are broken. I must go!" He turned upon his heel and fled from the chamber. In the morning came the news that the Priest of Thoth was dead.

'My days after that were spent in study. I must find this subtle poison which was strong enough to undo the elixir. From early dawn to midnight I bent over the test-tube and the furnace. Above all, I collected the papyri and the chemical flasks of the Priest of Thoth. Alas! they taught me little. Here and there some hint or stray expression would raise hope in my bosom, but no good ever came of it. Still, month after month, I struggled on. When my heart grew faint I would make my way to the tomb by the palm-trees. There, standing by the dead casket from which the jewel had been rifled, I would feel her sweet presence, and would whisper to her that I would rejoin her if mortal wit could solve the riddle.

'Parmes had said that his discovery was connected with the ring of Thoth. I had some remembrance of the trinket. It was a large and weighty circlet, made, not of gold, but of a rarer and heavier metal brought from the mines of Mount Harbal. Platinum, you call it. The ring had, I remembered, a hollow crystal set in it, in which some few drops of liquid might be stored. Now, the secret of Parmes could not have to do with the metal alone, for there were many rings of that metal in the Temple. Was it

not more likely that he had stored his precious poison within the cavity of the crystal? I had scarce come to this conclusion before, in hunting through his papers, I came upon one which told me that it was indeed so, and that there was still some of the liquid unused.

'But how to find the ring? It was not upon him when he was stripped for the embalmer. Of that I made sure. Neither was it among his private effects. In vain I searched every room that he had entered, every box and vase and chattel that he had owned. I sifted the very sand of the desert in the places where he had been wont to walk; but, do what I would, I could come upon no traces of the ring of Thoth. Yet it may be that my labours would have overcome all obstacles had it not been for a new and unlooked-for misfortune.

'A great war had been waged against the Hyksos, and the Captains of the Great King had been cut off in the desert, with all their bowmen and horsemen. The shepherd tribes were upon us like the locusts in a dry year. From the wilderness of Shur to the great, bitter lake there was blood by day and fire by night. Abaris was the bulwark of Egypt, but we could not keep the savages back. The city fell. The Governor and the soldiers were put to the sword, and I, with many more, was led away into captivity.

'For years and years I tended cattle in the great plains by the Euphrates. My master died, and his son grew old, but I was still as far from death as ever. At last I escaped upon a swift camel, and made my way back to Egypt. The Hyksos had settled in the land which they had conquered, and their own King ruled over the country. Abaris had been torn down, the city had been burned, and of the great Temple there was nothing left save an unsightly mound. Everywhere the tombs had been rifled and the monuments destroyed. Of my Atma's grave no sign was left. It was buried in the sands of the desert, and the palm-trees which marked the spot had long disappeared. The papers of Parmes and the remains of the Temple of Thoth were either destroyed or scattered far and wide over the deserts of Syria. All search after them was vain.

'From that time I gave up all hope of ever finding the ring or discovering the subtle drug. I set myself to live as patiently as might be until the effect of the elixir should wear away. How can you understand how terrible a thing time is, you who have experience only of the narrow course which lies between the cradle and the grave! I know it to my cost, I who have floated down the whole stream of history. I was old when Ilium fell. I was very old when Herodotus came to Memphis. I was bowed down with years when the new gospel came upon earth. Yet you see me much as other men are, with the cursed elixir still sweetening my blood, and guarding me against that which I would court. Now, at last, at last I have come to the end of it!

'I have travelled in all lands and I have dwelt with all nations. Every tongue is the same to me. I learned them all to help pass the weary time. I need not tell you how slowly they drifted by, the long dawn of modern civilization, the dreary middle years, the dark times of barbarism. They are all behind me now. I have never looked with the eyes of love upon another woman. Atma knows that I have been constant to her.

'It was my custom to read all that the scholars had to say upon Ancient Egypt. I have been in many positions, sometimes affluent, sometimes poor, but I have always found enough to enable me to buy the journals which deal with such matters. Some nine months ago I was in San Francisco, when I read an account of some discoveries made in the neighbourhood of Abaris. My heart leapt into my mouth as I read it. It said that the excavator had busied himself in exploring some tombs recently unearthed. In one there had been found an unopened mummy with an inscription upon the outer case setting forth that it contained the body of the daughter of the Governor of the city in the days of Tuthmosis. It added that on removing the outer case there had been exposed a large platinum ring set with a crystal, which had been laid upon the breast of the embalmed woman. This, then, was where Parmes had hid the ring of Thoth. He might well say that it was safe, for no Egyptian would ever stain his soul by moving even the outer case of a buried friend.

'That very night I set off from San Francisco, and in a few weeks I found myself once more at Abaris, if a few sand-heaps and crumbling walls may retain the name of the great city. I hurried to the Frenchmen who were digging there and asked them for the ring. They replied that both the ring and the mummy had been sent to the Boulak Museum at Cairo. To Boulak I went, but only to be told that Mariette Bey had claimed them and had shipped them to the Louvre. I followed them, and there, at last, in the Egyptian chamber, I came, after close upon four thousand years, upon the remains of my Atma, and upon the ring for which I had sought so long.

'But how was I to lay hands upon them? How was I to have them for my very own? It chanced that the office of attendant was vacant. I went to the Director. I convinced him that I knew much about Egypt. In my eagerness I said too much. He remarked that a professor's chair would suit me better than a seat in the conciergerie. I knew more, he said, than he did. It was only by blundering, and letting him think that he had over-estimated my knowledge, that I prevailed upon him to let me move the few effects which I have retained into this chamber. It is my first and my last night here.

'Such is my story, Mr. Vansittart Smith. I need not say more to a man of your perception. By a strange chance you have this night looked upon the face of the woman whom I loved in those far-off days. There were many rings with crystals in the case, and I had to test for the platinum to be sure of the one which I wanted. A glance at the crystal has shown me that the liquid is indeed within it, and that I shall at last be able to shake off that accursed health which has been worse to me than the foulest disease. I have nothing more to say to you. I have unburdened myself. You may tell my story or you may withhold it at your pleasure. The choice rests with you. I owe you some amends, for you have had a narrow escape of your life this night. I was desperate man, and not to be baulked in my purpose. Had I seen you before the thing was done, I might have put it beyond your power to oppose me or to raise an alarm. This is the door. It leads into the Rue de Rivoli. Good night.'

The Englishman glanced back. For a moment the lean figure of Sosra the Egyptian stood framed in the narrow doorway. The next the door had slammed, and the heavy rasping of a bolt broke on the silent night.

It was on the second day after his return to London that Mr. John Vansittart Smith saw the following concise narrative in the Paris correspondence of *The Times*:

'*Curious Occurrence in the Louvre.* – Yesterday morning a strange discovery was made in the principal Eastern chamber. The *ouvriers* who are employed to clean out the rooms in the morning found one of the attendants lying dead upon the floor with his arms round one of the mummies. So close was his embrace that it was only with the utmost difficulty that they were separated. One of the cases containing valuable rings had been opened and rifled. The authorities are of opinion that the man was bearing away the mummy with some idea of selling it to a private collector, but that he was struck down in the very act by long-standing disease of the heart. It is said that he was a man of uncertain age and eccentric habits, without any living relations to mourn over his dramatic and untimely end.'

◻ ◉ ◻ ◉ ◻ ◉

Sax Rohmer, the pseudonym of Arthur Ward (the name was intended to mean 'free lance' in Anglo-Saxon), is best known today for his series of thirteen novels featuring the Chinese super-villain Dr Fu-Manchu. But at the time of the discovery of the tomb of Tutankhamun, he was equally well known for his mystery stories set in the world of Egyptian archaeology – stories such as *The Sins of Séverac Bablon* (1914), *The Brood of the Witch Queen* (1918), *Tales of Secret Egypt* (1918) and *The Green*

Eyes of Bast (1920). His only non-fiction work, *The Romance of Sorcery* (1914) – the title says it all – was centrally concerned with Egyptian magic, and his most prized possession was a copy of the so-called *Book of the Dead*, given to him by the music-hall comedian George Robey (for whom he regularly worked, and penned the hit song *Bang Went the Chance of a Lifetime*). Sax Rohmer visited Egypt on his honeymoon in 1913 and was shown around the Meydum pyramid by Rex Engelbach, curator at the Cairo Museum and assistant to Flinders Petrie. (The Dr Watson figure in Rohmer's Fu-Manchu stories, Dr Petrie, had in fact been named after the 'father of modern Egyptology' himself.) Rohmer subsequently wrote of Engelbach:

'Popular conception of a working Egyptologist is grotesquely wide of the mark. We must substitute a tough specimen of humanity with leather lungs and hardy frame, his skin baked by the sun to a dark copper colour; grain, nerve and muscle ready for any emergency. An absent-minded, flabby Egyptologist would be lucky if he lasted three months.'

This story is from the collection *Tales of Secret Egypt* and it was loosely adapted for the London stage in 1928 (with Leon M. Lion), where it played at the 'Q' Theatre – an attempt to cash in on Tutmania.

SAX ROHMER
The Valley of the Sorceress
(1918)

I

Condor wrote to me three times before the end (said Neville, Assistant-Inspector of Antiquities, staring vaguely from his open window at a squad drilling before the Kasr-en-Nîl Barracks). He dated his letters from the camp at Deir-el-Bahari. Judging from these, success appeared to be almost within his grasp. He shared my theories, of course, respecting Queen Hatasu, and was devoting the whole of his energies to the task of clearing up the great mystery of Ancient Egypt which centres around that queen.

For him, as for me, there was a strange fascination about those defaced walls and roughly obliterated inscriptions. That the queen under whom Egyptian art came to the apogee of perfection should thus have been treated by her successors; that no perfect figure of the wise, famous, and beautiful Hatasu should have been spared to posterity; that her very cartouche should have been ruthlessly removed from every inscription upon which it appeared, presented to Condor's mind a problem only second in interest to the immortal riddle of Gîzeh.

You know my own views upon the matter? My monograph, 'Hatasu, the Sorceress,' embodies my opinion. In short, upon certain evidences, some adduced by Theodore Davis, some by poor Condor, and some resulting from my own inquiries, I have come to the conclusion that the source – real or imaginary – of this queen's power was an intimate acquaintance with what nowadays we term, vaguely, magic. Pursuing her studies beyond the limit which is lawful, she met with a certain end, not uncommon, if the old writings are to be believed, in the case of those who penetrate too far into the realms of the Borderland.

For this reason – the practice of black magic – her statues were dishonoured, and her name erased from the monuments. Now, I do not propose to enter into any discussion respecting the reality of such practices; in my monograph I have merely endeavoured to show that, according to contemporary belief, the queen was a sorceress. Condor was seeking to prove the same thing; and when I took up the inquiry, it was in the hope of completing his interrupted work.

He wrote to me early in the winter of 1908, from his camp by the Rock Temple. Davis's tomb, at Bibân el-Mulûk, with its long, narrow passage, apparently had little interest for him; he was at work on the high ground behind the temple, at a point one hundred yards or so due west of the upper platform. He had an idea that he should find there the mummies of Hatasu – and another; the latter, a certain Sen-Mût, who appears in the inscriptions of the reign as an architect high in the queen's favour. The archæological points of the letter do not concern us in the least, but there was one odd little paragraph which I had cause to remember afterwards.

'A girl belonging to some Arab tribe,' wrote Condor, 'came racing to the camp two nights ago to claim my protection. What crime she had committed, and what punishment she feared, were far from clear; but she clung to me,

trembling like a leaf, and positively refused to depart. It was a difficult situation, for a camp of fifty native excavators, and one highly respectable European enthusiast, affords no suitable quarters for an Arab girl – and a very personable Arab girl. At any rate, she is still here; I have had a sort of lean-to rigged up in a little valley east of my own tent, but it is very embarrassing.'

Nearly a month passed before I heard from Condor again; then came a second letter, with the news that on the eve of a great discovery – as he believed – his entire native staff – the whole fifty – had deserted one night in a body! 'Two days' work,' he wrote, 'would have seen the tomb opened – for I am more than ever certain that my plans are accurate. Then I woke up one morning to find every man Jack of my fellows missing! I went down into the village where a lot of them live, in a towering rage, but not one of the brutes was to be found, and their relations professed entire ignorance respecting their whereabouts. What caused me almost as much anxiety as the check in my work was the fact that Mahâra – the Arab girl – had vanished also. I am wondering if the thing has any sinister significance.'

Condor finished with the statement that he was making tremendous efforts to secure a new gang. 'But,' said he, 'I shall finish the excavation, if I have to do it with my own hands.'

His third and last letter contained even stranger matters than the two preceding it. He had succeeded in borrowing a few men from the British Archæological camp in the Fáyûm. Then, just as the work was restarting, the Arab girl, Mahâra, turned up again, and entreated him to bring her down the Nile, 'at least as far as Dendera. For the vengeance of her tribesmen,' stated Condor, 'otherwise would result not only in her own death, but in mine! At the moment of writing I am in two minds about what to do. If Mahâra is to go upon this journey, I do not feel justified in sending her alone, and there is no one here who could perform the duty,' etc.

I began to wonder, of course; and I had it in mind to take the train to Luxor merely in order to see this Arab maiden, who seemed to occupy so prominent a place in Condor's mind. However, Fate would have it otherwise; and the next thing I heard was that Condor had been brought into Cairo, and was at the English hospital.

He had been bitten by a cat – presumably from the neighbouring village; and although the doctor at Luxor dealt with the bite at once, travelled down with him, and placed him in the hands of the Pasteur man at the hospital, he died, as you remember, on the night of his arrival, raving mad; the Pasteur treatment failed entirely.

I never saw him before the end, but they told me that his howls were horribly like those of a cat. His eyes changed in some way, too, I understand; and, with his fingers all contracted, he tried to *scratch* everyone and everything within reach.

They had to strap the poor beggar down, and even then he tore the sheets into ribbons.

Well, as soon as possible, I made the necessary arrangements to finish Condor's inquiry. I had access to his papers, plans, etc., and in the spring of the same year I took up my quarters near Deir-el-Bahari, roped off the approaches to the camp, stuck up the usual notices, and prepared to finish the excavation, which, I gathered, was in a fairly advanced state.

My first surprise came very soon after my arrival, for when, with the plan before me, I started out to find the shaft, I found it, certainly, but only with great difficulty.

It had been filled in again with sand and loose rock right to the very top!

II

All my inquiries availed me nothing. With what object the excavation had been thus closed I was unable to conjecture. That Condor had not reclosed it I was quite certain, for at the time of his mishap he had actually been at work at the bottom of the shaft, as inquiries from a native of Suefee, in the Fáyûm, who was his only companion at the time, had revealed.

In his eagerness to complete the inquiry, Condor, by lantern light, had been engaged upon a solitary night-shift below, and the rabid cat had apparently fallen into the pit; probably in a frenzy of fear, it had attacked Condor, after which it had escaped.

Only this one man was with him, and he, for some reason that I could not make out, had apparently been sleeping in the temple – quite a considerable distance from Condor's camp. The poor fellow's cries had aroused him, and he had met Condor running down the path and away from the shaft.

This, however, was good evidence of the existence of the shaft at the time, and as I stood contemplating the tightly packed rubble which alone marked its site, I grew more and more mystified, for this task of reclosing the cutting represented much hard labour.

Beyond perfecting my plans in one or two particulars, I did little on the day of my arrival.

I had only a handful of men with me, all of whom I knew, having worked with them before, and beyond clearing Condor's shaft I did not intend to excavate further.

Hatasu's Temple presents a lively enough scene in the daytime during the winter and early spring months, with the streams of tourists constantly passing from the white causeway to Cook's Rest House on the edge of the desert. There had been a goodly number of visitors that day to the temple below, and one or two of the more curious and venturesome had scrambled up the steep path to the little plateau which was the scene of my operations. None had penetrated beyond the notice boards, however, and now with the evening sky passing through those innumerable shades which defy palette and brush, which can only be distinguished by the trained eye, but which, from palest blue melt into exquisite pink, and by some magical combination form that deep violet which does not exist to perfection elsewhere than in the skies of Egypt, I found myself in the silence and the solitude of 'the Holy Valley.'

I stood at the edge of the plateau, looking out at the rosy belt which marked the course of the distant Nile, with the Arabian hills vaguely sketched beyond. The rocks stood up against that prospect as great black smudges, and what I could see of the causeway looked like a grey smear upon a drab canvas. Beneath me were the chambers of the Rock Temple, with those wall paintings depicting events in the reign of Hatasu which rank among the wonders of Egypt.

Not a sound disturbed my reverie, save a faint clatter of cooking utensils from the camp behind me – a desecration of that sacred solitude. Then a dog began to howl in the neighbouring village. The dog ceased, and faintly to my ears came the note of a reed pipe. The breeze died away, and with it the piping.

I turned back to the camp, and, having partaken of a frugal supper, turned in upon my campaigner's bed, thoroughly enjoying my freedom from the routine of official life in Cairo, and looking forward to the morrow's work pleasurably.

Under such circumstances a man sleeps well; and when, in an uncanny grey half-light, which probably heralded the dawn, I awoke with a start, I knew that something of an unusual nature alone could have disturbed my slumbers.

Firstly, then, I identified this with a concerted howling of the village dogs. They seemed to have conspired to make night hideous; I have never heard such an eerie din in my life. Then it gradually began to die away, and I realized, secondly, that the howling of the dogs and my own awakening might be due to some common cause. This idea grew upon me, and as the howling subsided, a sort of disquiet possessed me, and, despite my efforts to shake it off, grew more urgent with the passing of every moment.

In short, I fancied that the thing which had alarmed or enraged the dogs was passing from the village through the Holy Valley, upward to the Temple, upward to the plateau, and was approaching *me*.

I have never experienced an identical sensation since, but I seemed to be audient of a sort of psychic patrol, which, from a remote *pianissimo* swelled *fortissimo*, to an intimate but silent clamour, which beat in some way upon my brain, but not through the faculty of hearing, for now the night was deathly still.

Yet I was persuaded of some *approach* – of the coming of something sinister, and the suspense of waiting had become almost insupportable, so that I began to accuse my Spartan supper of having given me nightmare, when the tent-flap was suddenly raised, and, outlined against the paling blue of the sky, with a sort of reflected elfin light playing upon her face, I saw an Arab girl looking in at me!

By dint of exerting all my self-control I managed to restrain the cry and upward start which this apparition prompted. Quite still, with my fists tightly clenched, I lay and looked into the eyes which were looking into mine.

The style of literary work which it has been my lot to cultivate fails me in describing that beautiful and evil face. The features were severely classical and small, something of the Bisharîn type, with a cruel little mouth and a rounded chin, firm to hardness. In the eyes alone lay the languor of the Orient; they were exceedingly – indeed, excessively – long and narrow. The ordinary ragged, picturesque finery of a desert girl bedecked this midnight visitant, who, motionless, stood there watching me.

I once read a work by Pierre de l'Ancre, dealing with the Black Sabbaths of the Middle Ages, and now the evil beauty of this Arab face threw my memory back to those singular pages, for, perhaps owing to the reflected light which I have mentioned, although the explanation scarcely seemed adequate, those long, narrow eyes shone catlike in the gloom.

Suddenly I made up my mind. Throwing the blanket from me, I leapt to the ground, and in a flash had gripped the girl by the wrists. Confuting some lingering doubts, she proved to be substantial enough. My electric torch lay upon a box at the foot of the bed, and, stooping, I caught it up and turned its searching rays upon the face of my captive.

She fell back from me, panting like a wild creature trapped, then dropped upon her knees and began to plead – began to plead in a voice and with a manner which touched some chord of consciousness that I could swear had never spoken before, and has never spoken since.

She spoke in Arabic, of course, but the words fell from her lips as liquid music in which lay all the beauty and all the deviltry of the 'Sirens' Song.' Fully opening her astonishing eyes, she looked up at me, and, with her free hand pressed to her bosom, told me how she had fled from an unwelcome marriage; how, an outcast and a pariah, she had hidden in the desert places for three days and three nights, sustaining life only by means of a few dates which she had brought with her, and quenching her thirst with stolen water-melons.

'I can bear it no longer, *effendim*. Another night out in the desert, with the cruel moon beating, beating, beating upon my brain, with creeping things coming out from the rocks, wriggling, wriggling, their many feet making whisperings in the sand – ah, it will kill me! And I am for ever outcast from my tribe, from my people. No tent of all the Arabs, though I fly to the gates of Damascus, is open to me, save I enter in shame, as a slave, as a plaything, as a toy. My heart' – furiously she beat upon her breast – 'is empty and desolate, *effendim*. I am meaner than the lowliest thing that creeps upon the sand; yet the God that made that creeping thing made me also – and you, you, who are merciful and strong, would not crush any creature because it was weak and helpless.'

I had released her wrist now, and was looking down at her in a sort of stupor. The evil which at first I had seemed to perceive in her was effaced, wiped out as an artist wipes out an error in his drawing. Her dark beauty was speaking to me in a language of its own; a strange language, yet one so intelligible that I struggled in vain to disregard it. And her voice, her gestures, and the witch-fire of her eyes were whipping up my blood to a fever heat of passionate sorrow – of despair. Yes, incredible as it sounds, despair!

In short, as I see it now, this siren of the wilderness was playing upon me as an accomplished musician might play upon a harp, striking this string and that at will, and sounding each with such full notes as they had rarely, if ever, emitted before.

Most damnable anomaly of all, I – Edward Neville, archæologist, most prosy and matter-of-fact man in Cairo, perhaps – *knew* that this nomad who had burst into my tent, upon whom I had set eyes for the first time scarce three minutes before, held me enthralled; and yet, with her wondrous eyes upon me, I could summon up no resentment, and could offer but poor resistance.

'In the Little Oasis, *effendim*, I have a sister who will admit me into her household, if only as a servant. There I can be safe, there I can rest. O *Inglîsi*, at home in England you have a sister of your own! Would you see her pursued, a hunted thing from rock to rock, crouching for shelter in the lair of some jackal, stealing that she might live – and flying always, never

resting, her heart leaping for fear, flying, flying, with nothing but dishonour before her?'

She shuddered and clasped my left hand in both her own convulsively, pulling it down to her bosom.

'There can be only one thing, *effendim*,' she whispered. 'Do you not see the white bones bleaching in the sun?'

Throwing all my resolution into the act, I released my hand from her clasp, and, turning aside, sat down upon the box which served me as chair and table, too.

A thought had come to my assistance, had strengthened me in the moment of my greatest weakness; it was the thought of that Arab girl mentioned in Condor's letters. And a scheme of things, an incredible scheme, that embraced and explained some, if not all, of the horrible circumstances attendant upon his death, began to form in my brain.

Bizarre it was, stretching out beyond the realm of things natural and proper, yet I clung to it, for there, in the solitude, with this wildly beautiful creature kneeling at my feet, and with her uncanny powers of fascination yet enveloping me like a cloak, I found it not so improbable as inevitably it must have seemed at another time.

I turned my head, and through the gloom sought to look into the long eyes. As I did so they closed and appeared as two darkly luminous slits in the perfect oval of the face.

'You are an imposter!' I said in Arabic, speaking firmly and deliberately. 'To Mr Condor' – I could have sworn that she started slightly at sound of the name – 'you called yourself Mahâra. I know you, and I will have nothing to do with you.'

But in saying it I had to turn my head aside, for the strangest, maddest impulses were bubbling up in my brain in response to the glances of those half-shut eyes.

I reached for my coat, which lay upon the foot of the bed, and, taking out some loose money, I placed fifty piastres in the nerveless brown hand.

'That will enable you to reach the Little Oasis, if such is your desire,' I said. 'It is all I can do for you, and now – you must go.'

The light of the dawn was growing stronger momentarily, so that I could see my visitor quite clearly. She rose to her feet, and stood before me, a straight, slim figure, sweeping me from head to foot with such a glance of passionate contempt as I had never known or suffered.

She threw back her head magnificently, dashed the money on the ground at my feet, and, turning, leapt out of the tent.

For a moment I hesitated, doubting, questioning my humanity, testing my fears; then I took a step forward, and peered out across the plateau. Not a soul was in sight. The rocks stood up grey and eerie, and beneath lay the carpet of the desert stretching unbroken to the shadows of the Nile Valley.

III

We commenced the work of clearing the shaft at an early hour that morning. The strangest ideas were now playing in my mind, and in some way I felt myself to be in opposition to definite enmity. My excavators laboured with a will, and, once we had penetrated below the first three feet or so of tightly packed stone, it became a mere matter of shovelling, for apparently the lower part of the shaft had been filled up principally with sand.

I calculated that four days' work at the outside would see the shaft clear to the base of Condor's excavation. There remained, according to his own notes, only another six feet or so; but it was solid limestone – the roof of the passage, if his plans were correct, communicating with the tomb of Hatasu.

With the approach of night, tired as I was, I felt little inclination for sleep. I lay down on my bed with a small Browning pistol under the pillow, but after an hour or so of nervous listening drifted off into slumber. As on the night before, I awoke shortly before the coming of dawn.

Again the village dogs were raising a hideous outcry, and again I was keenly conscious of some ever-nearing menace. This consciousness grew stronger as the howling of the dogs grew fainter, and the sense of *approach* assailed me as on the previous occasion.

I sat up immediately with the pistol in my hand, and, gently raising the tent-flap, looked out over the darksome plateau. For a long time I could perceive nothing; then, vaguely outlined against the sky, I detected something that moved above the rocky edge.

It was so indefinite in form that for a time I was unable to identify it, but as it slowly rose higher and higher, two luminous eyes – obviously feline eyes, since they glittered greenly in the darkness – came into view. In character and in shape they were the eyes of a cat, but in point of size they were larger than the eyes of any cat I had ever seen. Nor were they jackal eyes. It occurred to me that some predatory beast from the Sûdan might conceivably have strayed thus far north.

The presence of such a creature would account for the nightly disturbance amongst the village dogs; and, dismissing the superstitious notions which had led me to associate the mysterious Arab girl with the phenomenon of the howling dogs, I seized upon this new idea with a sort of gladness.

Stepping boldly out of the tent, I strode in the direction of the gleaming eyes. Although my only weapon was the Browning pistol, it was a weapon of considerable power, and, moreover, I counted upon the well-known cowardice of nocturnal animals. I was not disappointed in the result.

The eyes dropped out of sight, and as I leapt to the edge of rock overhanging the temple a lithe shape went streaking off in the greyness beneath me. Its colouring appeared to be black, but this appearance may have been due to the bad light. Certainly it was no cat, was no jackal; and once, twice, thrice my Browning spat into the darkness.

Apparently I had not scored a hit, but the loud reports of the weapon aroused the men sleeping in the camp, and soon I was surrounded by a ring of inquiring faces.

But there I stood on the rock-edge, looking out across the desert in silence. Something in the long, luminous eyes, something in the sinuous, flying shape, had spoken to me intimately, horribly.

Hassan es-Sugra, the headman, touched my arm, and I knew that I must offer some explanation.

'Jackals,' I said shortly. And with no other word I walked back to my tent.

The night passed without further event, and in the morning we addressed ourselves to the work with such a will that I saw, to my satisfaction, that by noon of the following day the labour of clearing the loose sand would be completed.

During the preparation of the evening meal I became aware of a certain disquiet in the camp, and I noted a disinclination on the part of the native labourers to stray far from the tents. They hung together in a group, and whilst individually they seemed to avoid meeting my eye, collectively they watched me in a furtive fashion.

A gang of Moslem workmen calls for delicate handling, and I wondered if, inadvertently, I had transgressed in some way their iron-bound code of conduct. I called Hassan es-Sugra aside.

'What ails the men?' I asked him. 'Have they some grievance?'

Hassan spread his palms eloquently.

'If they have,' he replied, 'they are secret about it, and I am not in their confidence. Shall I thrash three or four of them in order to learn the nature of this grievance?'

'No, thanks all the same,' I said, laughing at this characteristic proposal. 'If they refuse to work to-morrow, there will be time enough for you to adopt those measures.'

On this, the third night of my sojourn in the Holy Valley by the Temple of Hatasu, I slept soundly and uninterruptedly. I had been looking forward with the keenest zest to the morrow's work, which promised to bring me within sight of my goal, and when Hassan came to awaken me, I leapt out of bed immediately.

Hassan es-Sugra, having performed his duty,

did not, as was his custom, retire; he stood there, a tall, angular figure, looking at me strangely.

'Well?' I said.

'There is trouble,' was his simple reply. 'Follow me, Neville Effendi.'

Wondering greatly, I followed him across the plateau and down the slope to the excavation. There I pulled up short with a cry of amazement.

Condor's shaft was filled in to the very top, and presented, to my astonished gaze, much the same aspect that had greeted me upon my first arrival!

'The men –' I began.

Hassan es-Sugra spread wide his palms.

'Gone!' he replied. 'Those Coptic dogs, those eaters of carrion, have fled in the night.'

'And this' – I pointed to the little mound of broken granite and sand – 'is their work?'

'So it would seem,' was the reply; and Hassan sniffed his sublime contempt.

I stood looking bitterly at this destruction of my toils. The strangeness of the thing at the moment did not strike me, in my anger; I was only concerned with the outrageous impudence of the missing workmen, and if I could have laid hands upon one of them it had surely gone hard with him.

As for Hassan es-Sugra, I believe he would cheerfully have broken the necks of the entire gang. But he was a man of resource.

'It is so newly filled in,' he said, 'that you and I, in three days, or in four, can restore it to the state it had reached when those nameless dogs, who regularly prayed with their shoes on, those devourers of pork, began their dirty work.'

His example was stimulating. *I* was not going to be beaten, either.

After a hasty breakfast, the pair of us set to work with pick and shovel and basket. We worked as those slaves must have worked whose toil was directed by the lash of the Pharaoh's overseer. My back acquired an almost permanent crook, and every muscle in my body seemed to be on fire. Not even in the midday heat did we slacken or stay our toils; and when dusk fell that night a great mound had arisen beside Condor's shaft, and we had excavated to a depth which it had taken our gang double the time to reach.

When at last we threw down our tools in utter exhaustion, I held out my hand to Hassan, and wrung his brown fist enthusiastically. His eyes sparkled as he met my glance.

'Neville Effendi,' he said, 'you are a true Moslem!'

And only the initiated can know how high was the compliment conveyed.

That night I slept the sleep of utter weariness, yet it was not a dreamless sleep, or perhaps it was not so deep as I supposed, for blazing cat-eyes encircled me in my dreams, and a constant feline howling seemed to fill the night.

When I awoke the sun was blazing down upon the rock outside my tent, and, springing out of bed, I perceived, with amazement, that the morning was far advanced. Indeed, I could hear the distant voices of the donkey-boys and other harbingers of the coming tourists.

Why had Hassan es-Sugra not awakened me?

I stepped out of the tent and called him in a loud voice. There was no reply. I ran across the plateau to the edge of the hollow.

Condor's shaft had been reclosed to the top!

Language fails me to convey the wave of anger, amazement, incredulity, which swept over me. I looked across to the deserted camp and back to my own tent; I looked down at the mound, where but a few hours before had been a pit, and seriously I began to question whether I was mad or whether madness had seized upon all who had been with me. Then, pegged down upon the heap of broken stones, I perceived, fluttering, a small piece of paper.

Dully I walked across and picked it up. Hassan, a man of some education, clearly was the writer. It was a pencil scrawl in doubtful Arabic, and, not without difficulty, I deciphered it as follows:

'Fly, Neville Effendi! This is a haunted place!'

Standing there by the mound, I tore the scrap of paper into minute fragments, bitterly casting them from me upon the ground. It was incredible; it was insane.

The man who had written that absurd message, the man who had undone his own work, had the reputation of being fearless and honourable. He had been with me before a score of times, and had quelled petty mutinies in the camp in a manner which marked him a born overseer. I could not understand; I could scarcely believe the evidence of my own senses.

What did I do?

I suppose there are some who would have abandoned the thing at once and for always, but I take it that the national traits are strong within me. I went over to the camp and prepared my own breakfast; then, shouldering pick and shovel, I went down into the valley and set to work. What ten men could not do, what two men had failed to do, one man was determined to do.

It was about half an hour after commencing my toils, and when, I suppose, the surprise and rage occasioned by the discovery had begun to wear off, that I found myself making comparisons between my own case and that of Condor. It became more and more evident to me that events – mysterious events – were repeating themselves.

The frightful happenings attendant upon Condor's death were marshalling in my mind. The sun was blazing down upon me, and distant voices could be heard in the desert stillness. I knew that the plain below was dotted with pleasure-seeking tourists, yet nervous tremors shook me. Frankly, I dreaded the coming of the night.

Well, tenacity or pugnacity conquered, and I worked on until dusk. My supper despatched, I sat down on my bed and toyed with the Browning.

I realized already that sleep, under existing conditions, was impossible. I perceived that on the morrow I must abandon my one-man enterprise, pocket my pride, in a sense, and seek new assistants, new companions.

The fact was coming home to me conclusively that a menace, real and not mythical, hung over the valley. Although, in the morning sunlight and filled with indignation, I had thought contemptuously of Hassan es-Sugra, now, in the mysterious violet dusk so conducive to calm consideration, I was forced to admit that he was at least as brave a man as I. And he had fled! What did that night hold in keeping for me?

*

I will tell you what occurred, and it is the only explanation I have to give of why Condor's shaft, said to communicate with the real tomb of Hatasu, to this day remains unopened.

There, on the edge of my bed, I sat far into the night, not daring to close my eyes. But physical weariness conquered in the end, and, although I have no recollection of its coming, I must have succumbed to sleep, since I remember – can never forget – a repetition of the dream, or what I had assumed to be a dream, of the night before.

A ring of blazing green eyes surrounded me. At one point this ring was broken, and in a kind of nightmare panic I leapt at that promise of safety, and found myself outside the tent.

Lithe, slinking shapes hemmed me in – cat shapes, ghoul shapes, veritable figures of the pit. And the eyes, the shapes, although they were the eyes and shapes of cats, sometimes changed elusively, and became the wicked eyes and the sinuous, writhing shapes of women. Always the ring was incomplete, and always I retreated in the only direction by which retreat was possible. I retreated from those cat-things.

In this fashion I came at last to the shaft, and there I saw the tools which I had left at the end of my day's toil.

Looking around me, I saw also, with such a pang of horror as I cannot hope to convey to you, that the ring of green eyes was now unbroken about me.

And it was closing in.

Nameless feline creatures were crowding silently to the edge of the pit, some preparing to spring down upon me where I stood. A voice seemed to speak in my brain; it spoke of capitulation, telling me to accept defeat, lest, resisting, my fate be the fate of Condor.

Peals of shrill laughter rose upon the silence. The laughter was mine.

Filling the night with this hideous, hysterical merriment, I was working feverishly with pick and with shovel filling in the shaft.

The end? The end is that I awoke, in the morning, lying, not on my bed, but outside on the plateau, my hands torn and bleeding and every muscle in my body throbbing agonisingly. Remembering my dream – for even in that moment of awakening I thought I had dreamed – I staggered across to the valley of the excavation.

Condor's shaft was reclosed to the top.

◼ ◉ ◼ ◉ ◼ ◉

Howard Phillips Lovecraft, the self-styled 'eccentric and recluse of Providence Rhode Island', ghosted this short story for the famous escapologist Harry Houdini (born Ehrich Weiss) in the magazine *Weird Tales* for May–June 1924. Houdini had told the editor of *Weird Tales* a story (which may or may not have been very loosely based on fact) about how he was thrown into 'an ancient subterranean temple at Gizeh' by two Arab guides and left to get out 'as best he might'. The editor thought it would make a successful tale, and asked Lovecraft to 'put this into a vivid narrative form'. It turned out to be Lovecraft's greatest commercial success to date, and he was offered the editorship of *Weird Tales* as a result. He seems to have gleaned the atmosphere of the piece from Sax Rohmer's *Brood of the Witch Queen*, and the background details from Baedeker's *Guide to Egypt and the Sudan*. The rest – including the extraordinary adjectives – he imagined as he went along. The story as reproduced here has been slightly abridged.

Houdini, an inveterate hunter of fake spiritualist mediums, was often in the news for this reason in the mid-1920s, and he had crossed swords with the more credulous Sir Arthur Conan Doyle on several occasions during Doyle's lecture-tour of the United States, which started in April 1923.

H. P. LOVECRAFT AND HARRY HOUDINI
Imprisoned with the Pharaohs
(1924)

I

Mystery attracts mystery. Ever since the wide appearance of my name as a performer of unexplained feats, I have encountered strange narratives and events which my calling has led people to link with my interests and activities. Some of these have been trivial and irrelevant, some deeply dramatic and absorbing, some productive of weird and perilous experiences and some involving me in extensive scientific and historical research. Many of these matters I have told and shall continue to tell very freely; but there is one of which I speak with great reluctance, and which I am now relating only after a session of grilling persuasion from the publishers of this magazine, who had heard vague rumors of it from other members of my family.

The hitherto guarded subject pertains to my non-professional visit to Egypt fourteen years ago, and has been avoided by me for several reasons. For one thing, I am averse to exploiting certain unmistakably actual facts and conditions obviously unknown to the myriad tourists who throng about the pyramids and apparently

secreted with much diligence by the authorities at Cairo, who cannot be wholly ignorant of them. For another thing, I dislike to recount an incident in which my own fantastic imagination must have played so great a part. What I saw – or thought I saw – certainly did not take place; but is rather to be viewed as a result of my then recent readings in Egyptology, and of the speculations anent this theme which my environment naturally prompted. These imaginative stimuli, magnified by the excitement of an actual event terrible enough in itself, undoubtedly gave rise to the culminating horror of that grotesque night so long past.

In January, 1910, I had finished a professional engagement in England and signed a contract for a tour of Australian theatres. A liberal time being allowed for the trip, I determined to make the most of it in the sort of travel which chiefly interests me; so accompanied by my wife I drifted pleasantly down the Continent and embarked at Marseilles on the P. & O. Steamer *Malwa*, bound for Port Said. From that point I proposed to visit the principal historical localities of lower Egypt before leaving finally for Australia.

The voyage was an agreeable one, and enlivened by many of the amusing incidents which befall a magical performer apart from his work. I had intended, for the sake of quiet travel, to keep my name a secret; but was goaded into betraying myself by a fellow-magician whose anxiety to astound the passengers with ordinary tricks tempted me to duplicate and exceed his feats in a manner quite destructive of my incognito. I mention this because of its ultimate effect – an effect I should have foreseen before unmasking to a

shipload of tourists about to scatter throughout the Nile valley. What it did was to herald
my identity wherever I subsequently went, and
deprive my wife and me of all the placid
inconspicuousness we had sought. Traveling to
seek curiosities, I was often forced to stand
inspection as a sort of curiosity myself!

We had come to Egypt in search of the picturesque and the mystically impressive, but
found little enough when the ship edged up to
Port Said and discharged its passengers in small
boats. Low dunes of sand, bobbing buoys in
shallow water, and a drearily European small
town with nothing of interest save the great De
Lesseps statue, made us anxious to get on to
something more worth our while. After some
discussion we decided to proceed at once to
Cairo and the Pyramids, later going to Alexandria for the Australian boat and for whatever
Greco-Roman sights that ancient metropolis
might present.

The railway journey was tolerable enough,
and consumed only four hours and a half. We
saw much of the Suez Canal, whose route we
followed as far as Ismailiya and later had a
taste of Old Egypt in our glimpse of the
restored fresh-water canal of the Middle
Empire. Then at last we saw Cairo glimmering
through the growing dusk; a winkling constel-
lation which became a blaze as we halted at the
great Gare Centrale.

But once more disappointment awaited us,
for all that we beheld was European save the
costumes and the crowds. A prosaic subway
led to a square teeming with carriages,
taxicabs, and trolley-cars and gorgeous with
electric lights shining on tall buildings; whilst
the very theatre where I was vainly requested to

play and which I later attended as a spectator,
had recently been renamed the 'American Cos-
mograph.' We stopped at Shepheard's Hotel,
reached in a taxi that sped along broad,
smartly built-up streets; and amidst the perfect
service of its restaurant, elevators and generally
Anglo-American luxuries the mysterious East
and immemorial past seemed very far away.

The next day, however, precipitated us
delightfully into the heart of the *Arabian
Nights atmosphere*; and in the winding ways
and exotic skyline of Cairo, the Bagdad of
Harun-al-Rashid seemed to live again. Guided
by our Baedeker, we had struck east past the
Ezbekiyeh Gardens along the Mouski in quest
of the native quarter, and were soon in the
hands of a clamorous cicerone who – notwithstanding later developments – was assuredly a
master at his trade.

Not until afterward did I see that I should
have applied at the hotel for a licensed guide.
This man, a shaven, peculiarly hollow-voice
and relatively cleanly fellow who looked like a
Pharaoh and called himself 'Abdul Reis el
Drogman,' appeared to have much power over
others of his kind; though subsequently the
police professed not to know him, and to suggest that *reis* is merely a name for any person in
authority, whilst 'Drogman' is obviously no
more than a clumsy modification of the word
for a leader of tourist parties – *dragoman* . . .

The red sun sank low, bringing the relentless
chill of Egyptian dusk; and as it stood poised
on the world's rim like that ancient god of
Heliopolis – Re-Harakhte, the Horizon-Sun –
we saw silhouetted against its vermeil holo-
caust the black outlines of the Pyramids of
Gizeh – the palaeogean tombs there were hoary

with a thousand years when Tut-Ankh-Amen mounted his golden throne in distant Thebes. Then we knew that we were done with Saracen Cairo, and that we must taste the deeper mysteries of primal Egypt – the black Kem of Re and Amen, Isis and Osiris . . .

That evening, the members of our party feeling somewhat tired after the strenuous program of the day, I went alone with Abdul Reis for a walk through the picturesque Arab quarter. Though I had seen it by day, I wished to study the alleys and bazaars in the dusk, when rich shadows and mellow gleams of light would add to their glamor and fantastic illusion. The native crowds were thinning, but were still very noisy and numerous when we came upon a knot of reveling Bedouins in the Suken-Nahhasin, or bazaar of the coppersmiths. Their apparent leader, an insolent youth with heavy features and saucily cocked tarbush, took some notice of us, and evidently recognized with no great friendliness my competent but admittedly supercilious and sneeringly disposed guide.

Perhaps, I thought, he resented that odd reproduction of the Sphinx's half-smile which I had remarked with amused irritation; or perhaps he did not like the hollow and sepulchral resonance of Abdul's voice. At any rate, the exchange of ancestrally opprobrious language became very brisk; and before long Ali Ziz, as I heard the stranger called when called by no worse name, began to pull violently at Abdul's robe, an action quickly reciprocated and leading to a spirited scuffle in which both combatants lost their sacredly cherished headgear and would have reached an even direr condition had I not intervened and separated them by main force.

My interference, at first seemingly unwelcome on both sides, succeeded at last in effecting a truce. Sullenly each belligerent composed his wrath and his attire, and with an assumption of dignity as profound as it was sudden, the two formed a curious pact of honor which I soon learned is a custom of great antiquity in Cairo – a pact for the settlement of their difference by means of a nocturnal fist fight atop the Great Pyramid, long after the departure of the last moonlight sightseer. Each duellist was to assemble a party of seconds, and the affair was to begin at midnight, proceeding by rounds in the most civilized possible fashion.

In all this planning there was much which excited my interests. The fight itself promised to be unique and spectacular, while the thought of the scene on that hoary pile overlooking the antediluvian plateau of Gizeh under the wan moon of the pallid small hours appealed to every fiber of imagination in me. A request found Abdul exceedingly willing to admit me to his party of seconds; so that all the rest of the early evening I accompanied him to various dens in the most lawless regions of the town – mostly northeast of the Ezbekiyeh – where he gathered one by one a select and formidable band of congenial cutthroats as his pugilistic background.

Shortly after nine our party, mounted on donkeys bearing such royal or tourist-reminiscent names as 'Rameses,' 'Mark Twain,' 'J. P. Morgan,' and 'Minnehaha,' edged through street labyrinths both Oriental and Occidental, crossed the muddy and mast-forested Nile by the bridge of the bronze lions, and cantered philosophically between the lebbakhs on the road to Gizeh. Slightly over two hours were consumed by the trip, toward the end of which we passed the last of the returning tourists, saluted the last inbound trolley-car, and were alone with the night and the past and the spectral moon.

Then we saw the vast pyramids at the end of the avenue, ghoulish with a dim atavistical menace...

As most travelers know, the actual apex of [the Great Pyramid] has long been worn away, leaving a reasonably flat platform twelve yards square. On this eery pinnacle a squared circle was formed, and in a few moments the sardonic desert moon leered down upon a battle which, but for the quality of the ringside cries, might well have occurred at some minor athletic club in America. As I watched it, I felt that some of our less desirable institutions were not lacking; for every blow, feint, and defense bespoke 'stalling' to my not inexperienced eye. It was quickly over, and despite my misgivings as to methods I felt a sort of proprietary pride when Abdul Reis was adjudged the winner.

Reconciliation was phenomenally rapid, and amidst the singing, fraternizing and drinking which followed, I found it difficult to realize that a quarrel had ever occurred. Oddly enough, I myself seemed to be more a center of notice than the antagonists; and from my smattering of Arabic I judged that they were discussing my professional performances and escapes from every sort of manacle and confinement, in a manner which indicated not only a surprising knowledge of me, but a distinct hostility and skepticism concerning my feats of escape. It gradually dawned on me that the elder magic of Egypt did not depart without leaving traces, and that fragments of a strange secret lore and priestly cult-practises have survived surreptitiously amongst the fellaheen to such an extent that the prowess of a strange *hahwi* or magician is resented and disputed. I thought of how much my hollow-voiced guide Abdul Reis looked like an old Egyptian priest or Pharaoh or smiling Sphinx ... and wondered.

Suddenly something happened which in a flash proved the correctness of my reflection and made me curse the denseness whereby I had accepted this night's events as other than the empty and malicious 'frame-up' they now showed themselves to be. Without warning, and doubtless in answer to some subtle sign from Abdul, the entire band of Bedouins precipitated itself upon me; and having produced heavy ropes, soon had me bound as securely as I was ever bound in the course of my life, either on the stage or off.

I struggled at first, but soon saw that one man could make no headway against a band of over twenty sinewy barbarians. My hands were tied behind my back, my knees bent to their fullest extent, and my wrists and ankles stoutly linked together with unyielding cords. A stifling gag was forced into my mouth, and a blindfold fastened tightly over my eyes. Then, as Arabs bore me aloft on their shoulders and began a bouncing descent of the pyramid, I heard the taunts of my late guide Abdul, who mocked and jeered delightedly in his hollow voice, and assured me that I was soon to have my 'magic powers' put to a supreme test which would quickly remove any egotism I might have gained through triumphing over all the tests offered by America and Europe. Egypt, he reminded me, is very old, and full of inner mysteries and antique powers not even conceivable to the experts of today, whose devices had so uniformly failed to entrap me.

How far or in what direction I was carried, I cannot tell; for the circumstances were all against the formation of any accurate judgment. I know, however, that it could not have been a great distance; since my bearers at no point hastened beyond a walk, yet kept me aloft a surprisingly short time. It is this perplexing brevity which makes me feel almost like shuddering whenever I think of Gizeh and its plateau – for one is oppressed by hints of the closeness to everyday tourist routes of what existed then and must exist still.

The evil abnormality I speak of did not become manifest at first. Setting me down on a surface which I recognized as sand rather than rock, my captors passed a rope around my chest and dragged me a few feet to a ragged opening in the ground, into which they presently lowered me with much rough handling. For apparent eons I bumped against the stony irregular sides of a narrow hewn well which I took to be one of the numerous burial-shafts of the plateau until the prodigious, almost incredible depth of it robbed me of all bases of conjecture.

The horror of the experience deepened with every dragging second. That any descent through the sheer solid rock could be so vast without reaching the core of the planet itself, or that any rope made by man could be so long as to dangle me in these unholy and seemingly fathomless profundities of nether earth, were beliefs of such grotesqueness that it was easier to doubt my agitated senses than to accept them. Even now I am uncertain, for I know how deceitful the sense of time becomes when one is removed or distorted. But I am quite sure that I preserved a logical consciousness that far; that at least I did not add any full-grown phantoms of imagination to a picture hideous enough in its reality, and explicable by a type of cerebral illusion vastly short of actual hallucination.

All this was not the cause of my first bit of fainting. The shocking ordeal was cumulative, and the beginning of the latter terrors was a very perceptible increase in my rate of descent. They were paying out that infinitely long rope very swiftly now, and I scraped cruelly against the rough and constricted sides of the shaft as I shot madly downward. My clothing was in tatters, and I felt the trickle of blood all over, even above the mounting and excruciating pain. My nostrils, too, were assailed by a scarcely definable menace: a creeping odor of damp and staleness curiously unlike anything I had ever smelled before, and having faint overtones of spice and incense that lent an element of mockery.

Then the mental cataclysm came. It was horrible – hideous beyond all articulate description because it was all of the soul, with nothing of detail to describe. It was the ecstasy of nightmare and the summation of the fiendish. The suddenness of it was apocalyptic and demoniac – one moment I was plunging agonizingly down that narrow well of million-toothed torture, yet the next moment I was soaring on bat-wings in the gulfs of hell; swinging free and swoopingly through illimitable miles of boundless, musty space; rising dizzily to measureless pinnacles of chilling ether, then diving gaspingly to sucking nadirs of ravenous, nauseous lower vacua … Thank God for the mercy that shut out in oblivion those clawing Furies of consciousness which half unhinged my faculties, and tore harpy-like at my spirit! That one respite, short as it was, gave me the strength and sanity to endure those still greater sublimations of cosmic panic that lurked and gibbered on the road ahead.

II

It was very gradually that I regained my senses after that eldritch flight through stygian space. The process was infinitely painful, and colored by fantastic dreams in which my bound and gagged condition found singular embodiment. The precise nature of these dreams was very clear while I was experiencing them, but became blurred in my recollection almost immediately afterward, and was soon reduced to the merest outline by the terrible events — real or imaginary — which followed. I dreamed that I was in the grasp of a great and horrible paw; a yellow, hairy, five-clawed paw which had reached out of the earth to crush and engulf me. And when I stopped to reflect what the paw was, it seemed to me that it was Egypt. In the dream I looked back at the events of the preceding weeks, and saw myself lured and enmeshed little by little, subtly and insidiously, by some hellish ghoul-spirit of the elder Nile sorcery; some spirit that was in Egypt before ever man was, and that will be when man is no more.

I saw the horror and unwholesome antiquity of Egypt, and the grisly alliance it has always had with the tombs and temples of the dead. I saw phantom processions of priests with the heads of bulls, falcons, cats, and ibises; phantom processions marching interminably through subterraneous labyrinths and avenues of titanic propylaea beside which a man is as a fly, and offering unnamable sacrifice to indescribable gods. Stone colossi marched in endless night and drove herds of grinning androspinxes down to the shores of illimitable stagnant rivers of pitch. And behind it all I saw the ineffable malignity of primordial necromancy, black and amorphous, and fumbling greedily after me in the darkness to choke out the spirit that had dared to mock it by emulation.

In my sleeping brain there took shape a melodrama of sinister hatred and pursuit, and I saw the black soul of Egypt singling me out and calling me in inaudible whispers; calling and luring me, leading me on with the glitter and glamor of a Saracenic surface, but ever pulling me down to the age-mad catacombs and horrors of its *dead* and abysmal pharaonic heart.

Then the dream faces took on human resemblances, and I saw my guide Abdul Reis in the robes of a king, with the sneer of the Sphinx on his features. And I knew that those features were the features of Khephren the Great, who raised the Second Pyramid, carved over the Sphinx's face in the likeness of his own and built that titanic gateway temple whose myriad corridors the archaeologists think they have dug out of the cryptical sand and the uninformative rock. And I looked at the long, lean, rigid hand of Khephren … and wondered that I had not shrieked when I saw it on Abdul Reis … That hand? It was hideously cold, and it was crushing me; it was the cold and cramping of the sarcophagus … the chill and constriction of unrememberable Egypt … It was nighted, necropolitan Egyptian itself . . . that yellow paw . . . and they whisper such things of Khephren . . .

But at this juncture I began to awake – or at least, to assume a condition less completely that of sleep than the one just preceding. I recalled the fight atop the pyramid, the treacherous Bedouins and their attack, my frightful descent by rope through endless rock depths, and my mad swinging and plunging in a chill void redolent of aromatic putrescence. I perceived that I now lay on a damp rock floor, and that my bonds were still biting into me with unloosened force. It was very cold, and I seemed to detect a faint current of noisome air sweeping across me. The cuts and bruises I had received from the jagged sides of the rock shaft were paining me woefully, their soreness enhanced to a stinging or burning acuteness by some pungent quality in the faint draft, and the mere act of rolling over was enough to set my whole frame throbbing with untold agony.

As I turned I felt a tug from above, and concluded that the rope whereby I was lowered still reached to the surface. Whether or not the Arabs still held it, I had no idea; nor had I any idea how far within the earth I was. I knew that the darkness around me was wholly or nearly total, since no ray of moonlight penetrated my blindfold; but I did not trust my senses enough to accept as evidence of extreme depth the sensation of vast duration which had characterized my descent.

Knowing at least that I was in a space of considerable extent reached from the surface directly above by an opening in the rock, I doubtfully conjectured that my prison was perhaps the buried gateway chapel of old Khephren – the Temple of the Sphinx – perhaps some inner corridor which the guides had not shown me during my morning visit, and from which I might easily escape if I could find my way to the barred entrance. It would be a labyrinthine wandering, but no worse than others out of which I had in the past found my way.

The first step was to get free of my bonds, gag, and blindfold; and this I knew would be no great task, since subtler experts than these Arabs had tried every known species of fetter upon me during my long and varied career as an exponent of escape, yet had never succeeded in defeating my methods.

Then it occurred to me that the Arabs might be ready to meet and attack me at the entrance upon any evidence of my probable escape from the binding cords, as would be furnished by any decided agitation of the rope which they probably held. This, of course, was taking for granted that my place of confinement was indeed Khephren's Temple of the Sphinx. The direct opening in the roof, wherever it might lurk, could not be beyond easy reach of the ordinary modern entrance near the Sphinx; if in truth it were any great distance at all on the surface, since the total area known to visitors is not at all enormous. I had not noticed any such opening during my daytime pilgrimage, but knew that these things are easily overlooked amidst the drifting sands.

Thinking these matters over as I lay bent and bound on the rock floor, I nearly forgot the horrors of abysmal descent and cavernous swinging which had so lately reduced me to a coma. My present thought was only to outwit the Arabs, and I accordingly determined to work myself free as quickly as possible, avoiding any tug on the descending line which might betray an effective or even problematical attempt at freedom.

This, however, was more easily determined than effected. A few preliminary trials made it clear that little could be accomplished without considerable motion; and it did not surprise me when, after one especially energetic struggle, I began to feel the coils of falling rope as they piled up about me and upon me. Obviously, I thought, the Bedouins had felt my movements and released their end of the rope; hastening no doubt to the temple's true entrance to lie murderously in wait for me.

The prospect was not pleasing – but I had faced worse in my time without flinching, and would not flinch now. At present I must first of all free myself of bonds, then trust to ingenuity to escape from the temple unharmed. It is curious how implicitly I had come to believe myself in the old temple of Khephren beside the Sphinx, only a short distance below the ground.

That belief was shattered, and every pristine apprehension of preternatural depth and demoniac mystery revived, by a circumstance which grew in horror and significance even as I formulated my philosophical plan. I have said that the falling rope was piling up about and upon me. Now I saw that it was continuing to pile, as no rope of normal length could possibly do. It gained in momentum and became an avalanche of hemp, accumulating mountainously on the floor and half burying me beneath its swiftly multiplying coils. Soon I was completely engulfed and gasping for breath as the increasing convolutions submerged and stifled me.

My senses tottered again, and I vainly tried to fight off a menace desperate and ineluctable. It was not merely that I was tortured beyond human endurance – not merely that life and breath seemed to be crushed slowly out of me – it was the knowledge of what those unnatural lengths of rope implied, and the consciousness of what unknown and incalculable gulfs of inner earth must at this moment be surrounding me. My endless descent and swinging flight through goblin space, then, must have been real, and even now I must be lying helpless in some nameless cavern world toward the core of the planet. Such a sudden confirmation of ultimate horror was insupportable, and a second time I lapsed into merciful oblivion.

When I say oblivion, I do not imply that I was free from dreams. On the contrary, my absence from the conscious world was marked by visions of the most unutterable hideousness. God! ... If only I had not read so much Egyptology before coming to this land which is the fountain of all darkness and terror! This second spell of fainting filled my sleeping mind anew with shivering realization of the country and its archaic secrets, and through some damnable chance my dreams turned to the ancient notions of the dead and their sojournings in soul and body beyond those mysterious tombs which were more houses than graves. I recalled, in dream-shapes which it is well that I do not remember, the peculiar and elaborate construction of Egyptian sepulchers; and the exceedingly singular and terrific doctrines which determined this construction.

All these people thought of was death and the dead. They conceived of a literal resurrection of the body which made them mummify it with desperate care, and preserve all the vital organs in canopic jars near the corpse; whilst besides the body they believed in two other elements, the soul, which after its weighing and approval by Osiris dwelt in the land of the blest, and the obscure and portentous *ka* or life-principle which wandered about the upper and lower worlds in a horrible way, demanding occasional access to the preserved body, consuming the food offerings brought by priests and pious relatives to the mortuary chapel, and sometimes – as men whispered – taking its body or the wooden double always buried beside it and stalking noxiously abroad on errands peculiarly repellent.

For thousands of years those bodies rested gorgeously encased and staring glassily upward when not visited by the *ka*, awaiting the day when Osiris should restore both *ka* and soul, and lead forth the stiff legions of the dead from the sunken houses of sleep. It was to have been a glorious rebirth – but not all souls were approved, nor were all tombs inviolate, so that certain grotesque *mistakes* and fiendish *abnormalities* were to be looked for. Even today the Arabs murmur of unsanctified convocations and unwholesome worship in forgotten nether abysses, which only winged invisible *kas* and soulless mummies may visit and return unscathed.

Perhaps the most leeringly blood-congealing legends are those which relate to certain perverse products of decadent priestcraft – *composite mummies* made by the artificial union of human trunks and limbs with the heads of animals in imitation of the elder gods. At all stages of history the sacred animals were mummified, so that consecrated bulls, cats, ibises,

crocodiles and the like might return some day to greater glory. But only in the decadence did they mix the human and animal in the same mummy – only in the decadence, when they did not understand the rights and prerogatives of the *ka* and the soul.

What happened to those composite mummies is not told of – at least publicly – and it is certain that no Egyptologist ever found one. The whispers of Arabs are very wild, and cannot be relied upon. They even hint that old Khephren – he of the Sphinx, the Second Pyramid and the yawning gateway temple – lives far underground, wedded to the ghoul-queen Nitocris and ruling over the mummies that are neither of man or of beast.

It was of these – of Khephren and his consort and his strange armies of the hybrid dead – that I dreamed, and that is why I am glad the exact dream-shapes have faded from my memory. My most horrible vision was connected with an idle question I had asked myself the day before when looking at the great carven riddle of the desert and wondering with what unknown depth the temple close to it might be secretly connected. That question, so innocent and whimsical then, assumed in my dream a meaning of frenetic and hysterical madness . . . *what huge and loathsome abnormality was the Sphinx originally carven to represent?*

My second awakening – if awakening it was – is a memory of stark hideousness which nothing else in my life – save one thing which came after – can parallel; and that life has been full and adventurous beyond most men's. Remember that I had lost consciousness whilst buried beneath a cascade of falling rope whose immensity revealed the cataclysmic depth of my present position. Now, as perception returned, I felt the entire weight gone; and realized upon rolling over that although I was still tied, gagged and blindfolded, *some agency had removed completely the suffocating hempen landslide which had overwhelmed me.* The significance of this condition, of course, came to me only gradually; but even so I think it would have brought unconsciousness again had I not by this time reached such a state of emotional exhaustion that no new horror could make much difference. I was alone . . . *with what?*

Before I could torture myself with any new reflection, or make any fresh effort to escape from my bonds, an additional circumstance became manifest. Pains not formerly felt were racking my arms and legs, and I seemed coated with a profusion of dried blood beyond anything my former cuts and abrasions could furnish. My chest, too, seemed pierced by a hundred wounds, as though some malign, titanic ibis had been pecking at it. Assuredly the agency which had removed the rope was a hostile one and had begun to wreak terrible injuries upon me when somehow impelled to desist. Yet at the time my sensations were distinctly the reverse of what one might expect. Instead of sinking into a bottomless pit of despair, I was stirred to a new courage and action; for now I felt that the evil forces were physical things which a fearless man might encounter on an even basis.

On the strength of this thought I tugged again at my bonds, and used all the art of a lifetime to free myself as I had so often done amidst the glare of lights and the applause of vast crowds. The familiar details of my escaping process commenced to engross me,

and now that the long rope was gone I half regained my belief that the supreme horrors were hallucinations after all, and that there had never been any terrible shaft, measureless abyss of interminable rope. Was I after all in the gateway temple of Khephren beside the Sphinx, and had the sneaking Arabs stolen in to torture me as I lay helpless there? At any rate, I must be free. Let me stand up unbound, ungagged, and with eyes open to catch any glimmer of light which might come trickling from any source, and I could actually delight in the combat against evil and treacherous foes!

How long I took in shaking off my encumbrances I cannot tell. It must have been longer than in my exhibition performances, because I was wounded, exhausted, and enervated by the experiences I had passed through. When I was finally free, and taking deep breaths of a chill, damp, evilly spiced air all the more horrible when encountered without the screen of gag and blindfolded edges, I found that I was too cramped and fatigued to move at once. There I lay, trying to stretch a frame bent and mangled, for an indefinite period, and straining my eyes to catch a glimpse of some ray of light which would give a hint as to my position.

By degrees my strength and flexibility returned, but my eyes beheld nothing. As I staggered to my feet I peered diligently in every direction, yet met only an ebony blackness as great as that I had known when blindfolded. I tried my legs, blood-encrusted beneath my shredded trousers, and found that I could walk; yet could not decide in what direction to go. Obviously I ought not to walk at random, and perhaps retreat directly from the entrance I sought; so I paused to note the direction of the cold, fetid, natron-scented air-current which I had never ceased to feel. Accepting the point of its source as the possible entrance of the abyss, I strove to keep track of this landmark and to walk consistently toward it.

I had a match-box with me, and even a small electric flashlight; but of course the pockets of my tossed and tattered clothing were long since emptied of all heavy articles. As I walked cautiously in the blackness, the draft grew stronger and more offensive, till at length I could regard it as nothing less than a tangible stream of detestable vapor pouring out of some aperture like the smoke of the genie from the fisherman's jar in the Eastern tale. The East ... Egypt ... truly, this dark cradle of civilization was ever the wellspring of horrors and marvels unspeakable!

The more I reflected on the nature of this cavern wind, the greater my sense of disquiet became; for although despite its odor I had sought its source as at least an indirect clue to the outer world, I now saw plainly that this foul emanation could have no admixture or connection whatsoever with the clean air of the Libyan Desert, but must be essentially a thing vomited from sinister gulfs still lower down. I had, then, been walking in the wrong direction.

After a moment's reflection I decided not to retrace my steps. Away from the draft I would have no landmarks, for the roughly level rock floor was devoid of distinctive configurations. If, however, I followed up the strange current, I would undoubtedly arrive at an aperture of some sort, from whose gate I could perhaps work round the walls to the opposite side of this Cyclopean and otherwise unnavigable

hall. That I might fail, I well realized. I saw that this was no part of Khephren's gateway temple which tourists know, and it struck me that this particular hall might be unknown even to archaeologists, and merely stumbled upon by the inquisitive and malignant Arabs who had imprisoned me. If so, was there any present gate of escape to the known parts or to the outer air?

What evidence, indeed, did I now possess that this was the gateway temple at all? For a moment all my wildest speculations rushed back upon me, and I thought of that vivid melange of impressions – the descent, suspension in space, the rope, my wounds, and the dreams that were frankly dreams. Was this the end of life for me? Or indeed, would it be merciful if this moment *were* the end? I could answer none of my own questions, but merely kept on, till Fate for a third time reduced me to oblivion.

This time there were no dreams, for the suddenness of the incident shocked me out of all thought either conscious or subconscious. Tripping on an unexpected descending step at a point where the offensive draft became strong enough to offer an actual physical resistance, I was precipitated headlong down a black flight of huge stone stairs into a gulf of hideousness unrelieved.

That I ever breathed again is a tribute to the inherent vitality of the healthy human organism. Often I look back to that night and feel a touch of actual humor in those repeated lapses of consciousness; lapses whose succession reminded me at the time of nothing more than the crude cinema melodramas of that period. Of course, it is possible that the repeated lapses never occurred; and that all the features of that underground nightmare were merely the dreams of one long coma which began with the shock of my descent into that abyss and ended with the healing balm of the outer air and of the rising sun which found me stretched on the sands of Gizeh before the sardonic and dawn-flushed face of the Great Sphinx.

I prefer to believe this latter explanation as much as I can, hence was glad when the police told me that the barrier to Khephren's gateway temple had been found unfastened, and that a sizeable rift to the surface did actually exist in one corner of the still buried part. I was glad, too, when the doctors pronounced my wounds only those to be expected from my falling some distance – perhaps into a depression in the temple's inner gallery – dragging myself to the outer barrier and escaping from it, and experiences like that ... a very soothing diagnosis. And yet I know that there must be more than appears on the surface. The extreme descent is too vivid a memory to be dismissed – and it is odd that no one has ever been able to find a man answering the description of my guide. Abdul Reis el Drogman – the tomb-throated guide who looked and smiled like King Khephren.

I have digressed from my connected narrative – perhaps in the vain hope of evading the telling of that final incident; that incident which of all is most certainly an hallucination. But I promised to relate it, and I do not break promises. When I recovered – or seemed to recover – my senses after that fall down the black stone stairs, I was quite as alone and in darkness as before. The windy stench, bad

enough before, was now fiendish; yet I had acquired enough familiarity by this time to bear it stoically. Dazedly I began to crawl away from the place whence the putrid wind came, and with my bleeding hands felt the colossal blocks of a mighty pavement. Once my head struck against a hard object, and when I felt it I learned that it was the base of a column – a column of unbelievable immensity – whose surface was covered with gigantic chiseled hieroglyphics very perceptible to my touch.

Crawling on, I encountered other titan columns at incomprehensible distances apart; when suddenly my attention was captured by the realization of something which must have been impinging on my subconscious hearing long before the conscious sense was aware of it.

From some still lower chasm in earth's bowels were proceeding certain *sounds*, measured and definite, and like nothing I had ever heard before. That they were very ancient and distinctly ceremonial I felt almost intuitively; and much reading in Egyptology led me to associate them with the flute, the sambuke, the sistrum, and the tympanum. In their rhythmic piping, droning, rattling and beating I felt an element of terror beyond all the known terrors of earth – a terror peculiarly dissociated from personal fear, and taking the form of a sort of objective pity for our planet, that it should hold within its depths such horrors as must lie beyond these aegipanic cacophonies. The sounds increased in volume, and I felt that they were approaching. Then – and may all the gods of all pantheons unite to keep the like from my ears again – I began to hear, faintly and afar off, the morbid and millennial tramping of the marching things.

It was hideous that footfalls so dissimilar should move in such perfect rhythm. The training of unhallowed thousands of years must lie behind that march of earth's inmost monstrosities ... padding, clicking, walking, stalking, rumbling, lumbering, crawling ... and all to the abhorrent discords of those mocking instruments. And then – God keep the memory of those Arab legends out of my head! – the mummies without souls ... the meeting-place of the wandering *kas* ... the hordes of the devil-cursed pharaonic dead of forty centuries ... the *composite mummies* led through the uttermost onyx voids by King Khephren and his ghoul-queen Nitocris....

The tramping drew nearer – Heaven save me from the sound of those feet and paws and hooves and pads and talons as it commenced to acquire detail! Down limitless reaches of sunless pavement a spark of light flickered in the malodorous wind and I drew behind the enormous circumference of a Cyclopic column that I might escape for a while the horror that was stalking million-footed toward me through gigantic hypostyles of inhuman dread and phobic antiquity. The flickers increased, and the tramping and dissonant rhythm grew sickeningly loud. In the quivering orange light there stood faintly forth a scene of such stony awe that I gasped from sheer wonder that conquered even fear and repulsion. Bases of columns whose middles were higher than human sight ... mere bases of things that must each dwarf the Eiffel Tower to insignificance ... hieroglyphics carved by unthinkable hands in caverns where daylight can be only a remote legend ...

I *would not* look at the marching things. That I desperately resolved as I heard their creaking joints and nitrous wheezing above the dead music and the dead tramping. It was merciful that they did not speak ... but God! *their crazy torches began to cast shadows on the surface of those stupendous columns. Hippopotami should not have human hands and carry torches ... men should not have the heads of crocodiles ...*

I tried to turn away, but the shadows and the sounds and the stench were everywhere. Then I remembered something I used to do in half-conscious nightmares as a boy, and began to repeat to myself, 'This is a dream! This is a dream!' But it was of no use, and I could only shut my eyes and pray ... at least, that is what I think I did, for one is never sure in visions – and I know this can have been nothing more. I wondered whether I should ever reach the world again, and at times would furtively open my eyes to see if I could discern any feature of the place other than the wind of spiced putrefaction, the topless columns, and the thaumatrophically grotesque shadows of abnormal horror. The sputtering glare of multiplying torches now shone, and unless this hellish place were wholly without walls, I could not fail to see some boundary or fixed landmark soon. But I had to shut my eyes again when I realized how many of the things were assembling – and when I glimpsed a certain object walking solemnly and steadily *without any body above the waist.*

A fiendish and ululant corpse-gurgle or death-rattle now split the very atmosphere – the charnel atmosphere poisonous with naftha and bitumen blasts — in one concerted chorus from the ghoulish legion of hybrid blasphemies. My eyes, perversely shaken open, gazed for an instant upon a sight which no human creature could even imagine without panic, fear and physical exhaustion. The things had filed ceremonially in one direction, the direction of the noisome wind, where the light of their torches showed their bended heads — or the bended heads of such as had heads. They were worshipping before a great black fetor-belching aperture which reached up almost out of sight, and which I could see was flanked at right angles by two giant staircases whose ends were far away in shadow. One of these was indubitably the staircase I had fallen down.

The dimensions of the hole were fully in proportion with those of the columns — an ordinary house would have been lost in it, and any average public building could easily have been moved in and out. It was so vast a surface that only by moving the eye could one trace its boundaries ... so vast, so hideously black, and so aromatically stinking ... Directly in front of this yawning Polyphemus-door the things were throwing objects — evidently sacrifices or religious offerings, to judge by their gestures. Khephren was their leader; sneering King Khephren *or the guide Abdul Reis*, crowned with a golden pshent and intoning endless formulae with the hollow voice of the dead. By his side knelt beautiful Queen Nitocris whom I saw in profile for a moment, noting that the right half of her face was eaten away by rats or other ghouls. And I shut my eyes again when I saw what objects were being thrown as offerings to the fetid

aperture or its possible local deity.

It occurred to me that, judging from the elaborateness of this worship, the concealed deity must be one of considerable importance. Was it Osiris or Isis, Horus or Anubis, or some vast unknown God of the Dead still more central and supreme? There is a legend that terrible altars and colossi were reared to an Unknown One before ever the known gods were worshipped ...

And now, as I steeled myself to watch the rapt and sepulchral adorations of those nameless things, a thought of escape flashed upon me. The hall was dim, and the columns heavy with shadow. With every creature of that nightmare throng absorbed in shocking raptures, it might be barely possible for me to creep past to the far-away end of one of the staircases and ascend unseen; trusting to Fate and skill to deliver me from the upper reaches. Where I was, I neither knew nor seriously reflected upon — and for a moment it struck me as amusing to plan a serious escape from that which I knew to be a dream. Was I in some hidden and unsuspected lower realm of Khephren's gateway temple — that temple which generations have persistently called the Temple of the Sphinx? I could not conjecture, but I resolved to ascend to life and consciousness if wit and muscle could carry me.

Wriggling flat on my stomach, I began the anxious journey toward the foot of the left-hand staircase, which seemed the more accessible of the two. I cannot describe the incidents and sensations of that crawl, but they may be guessed when one reflects on what I had to watch steadily in that malign, wind-blown torchlight in order to avoid detection. The bottom of the staircase was, as I have said, far away in shadow, as it had to be to rise without a bend to the dizzy parapeted landing above the titanic aperture. This placed the last stages of my crawl at some distance from the noisome herd, though the spectacle chilled me even when quite remote at my right.

At length I succeeded in reaching the steps and began to climb; keeping close to the wall, on which I observed decorations of the most hideous sort, and relying for safety on the absorbed, ecstatic interest with which the monstrosities watched the foul-breezed aperture and the impious objects of nourishment they had flung on the pavement before it. Though the staircase was huge and steep, fashioned of vast porphyry blocks as if for the feet of a giant, the ascent seemed virtually interminable. Dread of discovery and the pain which renewed exercise had brought to my wounds combined to make that upward crawl a thing of agonizing memory. I had intended, on reaching the landing, to climb immediately onward along whatever upper staircase might mount from there; stopping for no last look at the carrion abominations that pawed and genuflected some seventy or eighty feet below – yet a sudden repetition of that thunderous corpse-gurgle and death-rattle chorus, coming as I had nearly gained the top of the flight and showing by its ceremonial rhythm that it was not an alarm of my discovery, caused me to pause and peer cautiously over the parapet.

The monstrosities were hailing something which had poked itself out of the nauseous aperture to seize the hellish fare proffered it. It was something quite ponderous, even as seen from my height; something yellowish and hairy, and endowed with a sort of nervous motion. It was as large, perhaps, as a good-sized hippopotamus, but very curiously shaped. It seemed to have no neck, but five separate shaggy heads springing in a row from a roughly cylindrical trunk; the first very small, the second good-sized, the third and fourth equal and largest of all, and the fifth rather small, though not so small as the first.

Out of these heads darted curious rigid tentacles which seized ravenously on the excessively great quantities of unmentionable food placed before the aperture. Once in a while the thing would leap up, and occasionally it would retreat into its den in a very odd manner. Its locomotion was so inexplicable that I stared in fascination, wishing it would emerge farther from the cavernous lair beneath me.

Then it *did emerge* . . . it *did* emerge, and at the sight I turned and fled into the darkness up the higher staircase that rose behind me; fled unknowingly up incredible steps and ladders and inclined planes to which no human sight or logic guided me, and which I must ever relegate to the world of dreams for want of any confirmation. It must have been a dream, or the dawn would never have found me breathing on the sands of Gizeh before the sardonic dawn-flushed face of the Great Sphinx.

The Great Sphinx! God! – that idle question I asked myself on that sun-blest morning before . . . *what huge and loathsome abnormality was the Sphinx originally carven to represent?* Accursed is the sight, be it in dream or not, that revealed to me the supreme horror – the unknown God of the Dead, which licks its colossal chops in the unsuspected abyss, fed hideous morsels by soulless absurdities that should not exist. The five-headed monster that emerged . . . that five-headed monster as large as a hippopotamus . . . the five-headed monster

– and that of which it is the merest forepaw . . .

But I survived, and I know it was only a dream.

◼ ◉ ◼ ◉ ◼ ◉

Tutmania

These extracts are intended to illustrate various aspects of the craze called 'Tutmania', which started with the first press report of the great discovery, in *The Times* on 30 November 1922, and continued for the next five years; in the case of rumours about the curse of the pharaohs, they have continued right up to the present day.

The first extracts are from *Punch* magazine of the mid-1920s. Punch had a lot of twentysish fun with the replica of Tutankhamun's tomb on show in the Amusements Park of the British Empire Exhibition at Wembley and with the popular interest in Egyptology. The next three extracts concern the curse itself: a chapter from Arthur Weigall's *Tutankhamen and Other Essays* (rushed out in 1923, before Howard Carter had had a chance to issue his version); a section from *My Mysteries and My Story* (1927), a book on palmistry by the society palmist and 'seer' calling himself Velma, in which he claimed to have warned Lord Carnarvon about the dire consequences of his return to Luxor before his Lordship went back for the last time; and an extract from *Real Life Stories* by the well-known clairvoyant 'Cheiro' (or Count Louis Harmon), published in 1934 and making a similar claim – only this time with the aid of a mummified hand belonging to an ancient Egyptian sorceress called Princess Makitaten. The final extract concerns a bizarre phenomenon which was said to have first manifested itself in autumn 1927, when an English schoolteacher called 'Rosemary' began to speak in a strange tongue – a talent known as 'xenoglossy' – which her amanuensis, Dr Frederick H. Wood, a music teacher, finally concluded was a form of ancient Egyptian. Professional Egyptologists were far from convinced by this, and in the extract from *This Egyptian Miracle – or the Restoration of the Lost Speech of Ancient Egypt by Supernatural Means* (recorded and edited by Wood in 1940) the voice – which goes by the name of 'Nona', the Egyptian equivalent of 'the nameless one' – answers back, in no uncertain terms. The collision of popular 'xenoglossy' and academic Egyptology – on the astral plain – seems an appropriate ending to this selection on the wilder excesses of Tutmania.

Punch Reacts to Tutankhamun

Pharaoh's Furniture
I see thy knops and owches,
    Thy carved and inlaid woods,
    Thy lion-headed couches:
    O King, they are the goods!
From the song of the Queen of Sheba
'Egyptology, Sir. A mere bagatelle.'
    Boswell's 'Life of Johnson'

'I want to go to Luxor,' he said, 'to-day.'

'Why Luxor?' I asked. 'I thought we had just got to Hong-Kong. I had rather looked forward to Hong-Kong. In the Hong-Kong section, I see by the Wembley programme, one hundred-and-seventy-five Chinese will be found at work.'

'That's only the yellow streak in them,' he replied. 'They'll soon learn better in this country. The reason why I want to do Egypt –'

'When you come to think of it,' I interrupted,

'what *is* the imperial status of Egypt? Is it auto-nomous under a Khedive, or is it a British Protectorate under Howard Carter, or what?'

'At Wembley,' declared the Illustrator firmly, 'they are going to have the Tomb of Tut-ankh-Amen. Just at present it is in the Tottenham Court Road.'

I began to weave a rather pretty story about this, which I told the Illustrator in a loud voice as we rattled along in the Tube. How Tut-ankh-Amen was not really buried at Luxor at all, but only a nameless man in his stead, and the young king wandered off and found a boat and went down the Nile, and when he came to the sea there was a ship with grave Phœnician traders on the decks, and he went aboard and hid in the bales, and so came to Cornwall, and from the West Country right up to London along the traders' way –

There when they heard the horse-bells ring
   The ancient Britons dressed and rode
To see the dark Phœnicians bring
   Their goods along the Western road.

Thus Tut-ankh-Amen was the earliest of all the gipsies to come into this land, and taught men the art of working in metal and the making of furniture, having a little booth first of all not very far from Goodge Street Station. So that in the end one of the great streets of London was named after him.

'What street?' asked the Illustrator crossly, for by this time he was beginning to be a little bored.

'Tut-ankh-amen Court Road,' I said; and we got out.

*

Whenever a new section of the shrine in the Luxor tomb was opened, Mr Howard Carter, I seem to remember, used to say, 'Words fail me to describe my emotions as I gazed at the wonderful scene within.' And for two columns and a half or so they went on failing him. Nothing ever caused so much speechlessness as the sights of the Luxor tomb.

Even the journalists at home in commenting on Mr Carter's discoveries, nearly always began, 'Words fail us when we try to imagine the splendours of King Tut-ankh-Amen's Court, with all its triumphs of artistic work-manship.' And then they also suffered from aphasia for a column or two.

But the Artificer in the Tottenham Court Road was not affected by Tut-ankh-Amen in this way. He admired, no doubt, but his spirit was not broken within him. He did not worry about words at all. He simply set to work to fashion couches and thrones and chariot-wheels and images and ark-shaped boxes in the same similitude as Tut-ankh-Amen's own. Replicas, in short. It was these that the Illustrator had brought me to see.

On a raised daïs there was a throne or chair glittering with gold. Where the Egyptians used faïence the Artificer used enamel paint, and where the Egyptians used metal he laid on two layers of gold-leaf.

'I don't understand how you know the details,' I objected.

'We have the photographs and we have the measurements,' he said simply.

On the chair-back was an inlaid picture of Tut-ankh-Amen having his shoulder anointed by his Queen. She had an immense embroidered collar, and close to her on a stand was a second collar, in case the King didn't like

The Anubis trot.

her in the first. A good plan.

'Why,' asked the Illustrator, 'has the lady such enormously long feet?'

She had. They must have been about twenty-five inches. Apparently beauty amongst the ancient Egyptians was judged largely by length of foot. Very awkward, as the Illustrator crudely pointed out, for dancing the Anubis trot.

The Illustrator in fact had to be restrained. He seemed to find something intensely comic in the golden lions on which the couches of the Pharaohs were slung. I believe he would have liked to fit the gold-felloed wheels on to the golden axle of the golden cart and have trundled it up the Tottenham Court Road with the painted port-manteaux of the King on it. A man who can hang his bowler hat on the head of the god Hathor is in my eyes a man without a sense of reverence. He is a mere reincarnation of the Memphian Mut or Tum.

And then we caught sight of Tut-ankh-Amen himself. His image, I mean. The one that you have seen so often in the photographs; marvellously lifelike and boyish – an uncanny thing. Or rather I ought to say it was an image copied from the photograph of an image, and still looking interested and faintly amused amongst the lumber of his personal effects.

It is my belief, though I cannot prove it, and I could not get the Artificer to agree, that the ancient Egyptian kings and princes bought an entirely new set of furniture to start the after-life with, just as we do to set up house with here. I imagine that a Pharaoh prince and his wife would go into the great furniture shop at Thebes and say –

'Good morning, Mr Thoth. I am Mr Anyman. My wife and I are just going to get buried, and have bought a small tomb. Unfortunately all the furniture here is too expensive for our slender means.'

'Don't let that trouble you for a moment, Mr Anyman,' Mr Thoth would say. 'We greatly prefer to deal with people who have no money. Just select a few golden chariots and a throne or two, and we will have them sent round to your tomb at once. And shall we say five pounds as a deposit, if that is convenient to you, the rest to be paid in easy instalments during the next five dynasties?'

Something like that.

While the Artificer and I had been discussing serious Egyptology, I found that the Illustrator had fallen into a trance on the golden throne of the Pharaohs. It was necessary to strike him on the knee with the sacred staff of command before he could be aroused. 'I dreamed,' he said, 'that I was riding on a long golden lion, three thousand years ago, in the Luxor Point-to-Point, with Tut-ankh-Amen a bad second, and got disqualified because it was only gilt.'

We now took leave of the Artificer.

'Words absolutely fail me,' I said as I shook hands, 'to describe the emotions with which I have been filled by the sight of the glories of the Luxor tomb —'

The Artificer rather anxiously took out his watch.

'You can tell me the rest down at Wembley,' he said.   Evoe

The Outline of Egyptology
Do you wish to be able to discuss Tutankh-Amen intelligently at the dinner-table?
GET WISE ABOUT CNUPHIS AND PASHT.
GAIN A CLEAR VIEW OF THE MANNERS AND CUSTOMS OF THREE THOUSAND YEARS AGO?

Egyptology is the art especially created to deal with discoveries of every kind about the ancient Egyptians, and it is a very lucky thing indeed for Egyptologists that the ancient Egyptians spent most of their time building extremely solid memorial edifices, temples and tombs. Present-day Egyptians take so little interest in this fascinating study that in another three thousand years or so it may decay altogether, and Egyptologists, a most deserving class, will then become totally extinct.

The Sphinx, which broods (eternally) over the desert, which is made of sand, and the Pyramids, remarkable for their peculiarly pyramidical shape, are known to all: but the ancient Egyptians also carved tombs underground, in which they painted battle pictures and in which they placed the mummified bodies of their kings. These mummified bodies were called mummies, and the tombs in which they were placed were carved, as our newspapers quite rightly tell us, out of the living rock. No ancient Egyptian, whatever his temptations, was known to carve a tomb out of the dead rock. It was simply not done.

The reason for all this labour and care was that the Egyptians were far more preoccupied about what was going to happen to them in the shades of the other world than about what would happen to them on earth; and so, instead of enjoying themselves as we do, they devoted all their energies to decorating and improving their graves. There was a good deal of wisdom in this, as the Nile flooded its banks so frequently and so violently that they were far more often dead than alive. It seems a sad pity that a later and less religious age has contented itself with disregarding posterity and damming the Nile.

With all these virtues, however, it cannot be said that the ancient Egyptians were a thoroughly truthful people. Whether out of carelessness or, as seems more probable, out of deliberate intention to deceive us, they left behind them records which are confusing and perplexing in the extreme. Professor Flinders Petrie adopts the latter theory, that of a course of calculated hypocrisy, and in support of his contention instances the crafty hieroglyphic alphabet and the shameless chronology of the Egyptian dynasties. On the whole the present Outline is inclined to agree with this eminent authority.

To take the alphabet first. The series of funny pictures subjoined

occurs almost more frequently than any other upon Egyptian monuments, and has generally been taken to represent the two following combinations of letters:–

WH~T R~T

an expression signifying in the old Egyptian language severe disapproval and apparently applied to the vain-glorious boasting of the Hittite kings. So misleading, however, is this method of writing compared with an honest straightforward alphabet, such as modern peoples have, that certain experts place an entirely different interpretation upon the symbols, holding that they do not represent letters at all, but merely a wild-fowling scene on the waste marshes of the Upper Nile. If this were so, the fraud practised by the original writer would destroy the whole basis on which the art of Egyptology stands. We can only hope earnestly for the best.

We come now to the Dynasties. There were thirty of these, and the difficulty lies not so much in their number as in their dates. In our own English history no uncertainty exists as to the dates of the various dynasties. The dynasty, for instance, of the Norman Kings began in 1066; that of the STUARTS, 1603; that of Mr. LLOYD GEORGE in 1916. But with the Egyptian dynasties it is quite different. One historian will place a particular king in 5000 B.C., and another historian will place the same king in 3000 B.C. There are few more painful sights in the Clubs of London than that of two eminent Egyptologists discussing after lunch, often with flushed faces and raised fists, the exact date of Thothmes III. But the sight, alas, is not rare. And yet if the Egyptian hieroglyphists had not been so culpably inexact in their references to famines, earthquakes and the eclipses of the moon, these distressing scenes might easily have been avoided. And the early historians were even worse than the hieroglyphists or makers of hieroglyphs. The most rudimentary acquaintance with apiculture, for instance, should have prevented Manetho from stating that in the reign of Nephercheres the Nile flowed mixed with honey for eleven days; and as for some of the statements made by Herodotus, one can only account for them by the supposition that he was not really well when he wrote.

Even more distressing is the confusion which reigns about the Egyptian gods. At the lowest computation there were thirty-eight of these – eight more, that is to say, than the number of the dynasties; and since many of them had three or four hundred different names each they have always caused antiquaries considerably more annoyance and unpleasantness in the smoking-room than even the Egyptian kings. The chief difficulty experienced by the beginner is to discover what the particular powers, functions, provinces and capacities of these gods were. According to the statements made by the Egyptians themselves they were roughly as follows:–

Ra was the Sun. He was the supreme god.

Osiris was the Sun. He was the supreme creative force.

Men-Tu and *At-Mu* were the rising and setting of the Sun.

Shu was the Sunlight.

Seb was the head of the family of Osiris. He was the father of the gods.

Isis was the female form of Osiris.

Horus was the god of the Sun. He was the child of Osiris.

Apis was the living emblem of Osiris. He was a bull.

Anubis was the living emblem of Osiris. He was a dog.

Cnuphis was the creator.

Serapis was the defunct Apis, who became Osiris.

Ptah was the creative force.

Ammon was the Sun.

From this list it will be seen that the general notion of the ancient Egyptians was to worship the Sun. It will also be seen that they carried it out in an extremely disingenuous manner, reflecting the greatest discredit on the priests and kings, who were responsible for the whole arrangement. Once more, in this matter of the worship of the Sun, we seem to trace the calculated effort to baffle and deceive posterity, which runs like a sinister thread through the whole fabric of Egyptian history.

One man, however, stood out against this treacherous practice. This was Aken-Aten, the father-in-law of Tutankh-Amen. He has come down to us as the heretic king; and it is easy to understand why. At the time when he ascended the throne there was already such indescribable confusion on the Egyptian monuments that nobody could make head or tail of them. Aken-Aten decided that all this must go. Determined to smooth the path of Egyptology, he resolved to have one Sun-god with a new name – Aten, and make a clean sweep of all the rest. Very likely, if he had lived longer, he would have simplified the alphabet, abolished the chronology and destroyed the Pyramids; but the people and the priests rebelled. They were proud of having about twenty-two different kinds of Sun, including a bull and a dog. They liked being able to say, 'A living emblem of Osiris has just tossed our manifestation of the creator Ra.' They rose up against their king. So Aken-Aten failed and died.

Small wonder, therefore, that when Tutankh-Amen returned to the good old practice of confusing the papyri and meddling up the hieroglyhs and the dates of the dynasties with the heads of dogs and hawks, and carving beetles and serpents all over his furniture, the Egyptians gave him a splendid burial and a finer tomb than anyone had before.

So gorgeous is this monument to the dead King, so richly carved, and filled with so many relics of the remote past, that without a doubt, when the work of excavation and classification is complete, it will throw a greater flood of obscurity and confusion on Egyptian history and theology than has ever been cast on it by any previous discovery. But will the body of the deceased be found inside? Who can foretell? We can only say that it would be very like the ancient Egyptians if it were not.

Evoe

Respecting the Pharaohs

I don't know whether I am more pained or

bewildered by the familiarity with which writers of newspaper articles are beginning to talk about the habits of the old Egyptian kings. I cast no reflection on the good faith of these writers. I do not doubt, if you had asked them a couple of years ago, they would have alluded in just the same airy way to the life and character of Maneptah and Amenhotep IV. I only say that it is a surprise to me because I had always regarded Egyptology as an extremely obscure and difficult science, to be approached with a kind of reverent awe: something rather more like the Pentateuch or the Books of Chronicles than like Green's *Short History of England*, or the despatches of our correspondent at Lausanne.

Supposing, for instance, that I had had to write a brisk paragraph or two about Thothmes III, I should have hunted him up in an Encyclopædia and turned out something like this:—

'Thothmes III. was a mighty king, who made great wars and extended his dominion even unto the walls of Nineveh itself. And he fought a great battle on the Plain of Megiddo and overthrew the Prince of Ketesh there. And he built great monuments. And he reigned fifty-four years and eleven months in the City of Thebes and did that which was right in the sight of Amen. And the rest of the acts of King Thothmes, and all that he did, and the wars that he made, and the temples he builded, are they not written in the scarabaei, or whatever you call them, that he had scratched for him?'

Something of that kind. I should have felt that, if only because of his immense and mysterious antiquity, Thothmes III deserved a little respect. But does your erudite literary reviewer have that feeling? Not at all. This, more or less, is his manner: —

'Thothmes III., with his gay debonair smile and reckless personal bravado, behind which there lay nevertheless concealed the brain of an astute and cautious diplomat, captivated all hearts. His successful campaigns exacted immense reparations from the Hittite kings, whilst at the same time his lavish gifts to the Church secured for him the whole-hearted support of the ecclesiastical block in his Cabinet.'

Just as if they were talking about M. Poincaré or Henry V, instead of a man who died three thousand years ago.

In exactly the same way, when they come on to Aken-Aten, the so-called heretic king who turned away from the gods of his forefathers and bowed down and worshipped the sun, these breezy writers remark without a qualm: —

'Then came Amenhotep's son, Aken-Aten, a physical degenerate and a religious fanatic.'

Physical degenerate, indeed! How on earth do they know that? When I look at my Encyclopædia again, I find: —

'The type under which the King and his family and subjects are represented is unlike any other in Egyptian Art. They are all of emaciated and distended figure and surpassing ugliness.'

Well, that may be. Probably there was a new fashion in Art under Aken-Aten. One knows what modern artists can do in the way of distending and emaciating the figure, and early Egypt may have suffered under similar sorrows. But to talk about Aken-Aten as if he were a mere modern pathological case or the hero of a highbrow novel seems to me to be lacking in all reverence for age. There may be a record that Aken-Aten was ugly, but I don't believe there is any record of his being a physical degenerate. I don't even believe that there is any ancient Egyptian for 'physical degenerate'. You can't write that sort of phrase with a lot of birds and serpents, which are what the ancient Egyptians used instead of an alphabet. Anyhow, Aken-Aten had seven daughters, one of whom married Lord Carnarvon's venerable friend; and the way I like to put the wedding announcement is this:

'Now the third daughter that he had Aken-Aten gave unto Tutankh-Amen to wife. And Aken-Aten died and was gathered to his fathers, and Tutankh-Amen, who also is Tutankh-Aten, reigned in his stead.'

Instead of which I am probably told: –

'Aken-Aten was somehow or other persuaded to give his third daughter in marriage to Tutankh-Amen, no doubt a mere political nominee of the hierarchical caucus at Thebes.'

And later –

'The fact that Tutankh-Amen sometimes spelt his name Tutankh-Aten denotes that he was sitting on the fence, waiting to see which of the two gods would prove the stronger, and prepared to throw in his lot with the winner.'

Phrases like that seem to me to take all the gilt and jewels off the Pharaoh's throne, his suit-case and his fly-whisks and his walking-sticks and all that he had. Besides, when one begins this kind of conjecture, there is simply no end to it. One might just as well say 'the smaller chariots were probably those used by the sisters-in-law of King Tutankh-Amen to pay calls in when he did not think it in the least necessary that the girls should have out the large car.'

Or –

'The fact that some of the tables and chairs appear to belong to the XVIIth and XVIIIth rather than the XIXth Dynasty may be accounted for by the supposition that Tutankh-Amen collected antiques. Nor does it follow that the pieces are genuine specimens of these earlier periods, for the Pharaoh may have been deceived by the crafty handiwork of furniture-fakers.'

All this, as I say, is the merest guess work and, true or no, takes away from the dignity of these fine old mummified men. It may be a plausible theory that Aken-Aten, who worshipped the sun with flowers and with hymns, was the kind of man whom one meets walking about a Garden City in sandals; whilst Tutankh-Amen, on the other hand, stands for the retrograde power which prevented the development of pacifism, vegetarianism, Free Trade and the reform of the Egyptian divorce laws. But I think the time has come to let by-gones be by-gones. There may have been social and political problems of a modern kind in front of these ancient Egyptian kings, but I for one prefer not to theorise about them. I prefer to think of Aken-Aten as a man who did evil in the sight of Amen and good in the sight of Aten, for no particular reason except that he thought he jolly well would. Tutankh-Amen, on the other hand, did good and evil in the sight of both of them. He has had a long time now to meditate on whether by dividing his allegiance he did wisely or no. But I do not think that we ought to pursue him beyond the grave with acrimonious comments on his reaction towards Chauvinism or his failure to revise the Book of the Dead. No doubt there was a lot of good in Tutankh-Amen, as there is in the worst of us.

Personally I have no grudge whatsoever against the man.   Evoe

ARTHUR WEIGALL
The Malevolence of Ancient Egyptian Spirits
(1923)

During the recent excavations which led to the discovery of the tomb of Tutankhamen, Mr Howard Carter had in his house a canary which daily regaled him with its happy song. On the day, however, on which the entrance to the tomb was laid bare, a cobra entered the house, pounced on the bird, and swallowed it. Now, cobras are rare in Egypt, and are seldom seen in winter; but in ancient times they were regarded as the symbol of royalty, and each Pharaoh wore this symbol upon his forehead, as though to signify his power to strike and sting his enemies. Those who believed in omens, therefore, interpreted this incident as meaning that the spirit of the newly-found Pharaoh, in its correct form of a royal cobra, had killed the excavators' happiness symbolised by this song-bird so typical of the peace of an English home.

At the end of the season's work, Lord Carnarvon was stung mysteriously upon the face, and died.

Millions of people throughout the world have asked themselves whether the death of the excavator of this tomb was due to some malevolent influence which came from it, and the story has been spread that there was a specific curse written upon a wall of the royal sepulchre. This, however, is not the case.

There are very few such curses known during the Eighteenth and Nineteenth Dynasties in ancient Egypt, that is to say, during the century or two before and after the time of Tutankhamen, and they are not at all common at any Pharaonic period.

Whenever they do appear, their object is simply to terrify the would-be tomb-robbers of their own epoch, who might smash up the mummy in their search for jewellery, or damage the tomb, thereby causing that loss of the dead man's identity which the Egyptians thought would injure the welfare of his spirit in the underworld. The mummy and the tomb were the earthly home of the disembodied spirit, and to wreck either was to render the spirit homeless and nameless. On the other hand, to enter a tomb for the purpose of renewing the dead man's memory was always considered by the Egyptians to be a most praiseworthy proceeding; and inscriptions are often found on the wall of a sepulchre stating that some friendly hand had been at work there, setting things to rights after a lapse of many years.

As an example of one of these curses, I will give here the translation of an inscription which is written upon a mortuary-statue of a certain Ursu, a mining engineer who lived less than a hundred years before the time of Tutankhamen. 'He who trespasses upon my property,' he says, 'or who shall injure my tomb or drag out my mummy, the Sun-god shall punish him. He shall not bequeath his goods to his children; his heart shall not have pleasure in life; he shall not receive water (for his spirit to drink) in the tomb; and his soul shall be destroyed for ever.' On the wall of the tomb of Harkhuf, at Aswân, dating from the Sixth Dynasty, these words are written: 'As for any man who shall enter into this tomb ... I will pounce upon him as on a bird; he shall be judged for it by the great god.'

The fear is that the tomb or the body will be broken up; and thus the scientific modern excavators, whose object is to rescue the dead from that oblivion which the years have produced, might be expected to be blessed rather than cursed for what they do. Only the robber would come under the scope of the curse. If we are to treat these questions seriously at all, it may be said that in general no harm has come to those who have entered these ancient tombs with reverence, and with the sole aim of saving the dead from native pillage and their identity from the obliterating hand of time.

The large number of visitors to Egypt and persons interested in Egyptian antiquities who believe in the malevolence of the spirits of the Pharaohs and their dead subjects, is always a matter of astonishment to me, in view of the fact that of all ancient peoples the Egyptians were the most kindly and, to me, the most loveable. Sober and thoughtful men, and matter-of-fact matrons, seem to vie with the lighter-minded members of society in recording the misfortunes which have befallen themselves or their friends as a consequence of their meddling with the property of the dead. On all sides one hears tales of the trials which have come upon those who, owing to their possession of some antiquity or ancient relic, have given offence to the spirits of the old inhabitants of the Nile Valley. These stories are generally open to some natural explanation, and those tales which I can relate at first hand are not necessarily to be connected with black magic. I will therefore leave it to the reader's taste to find an explanation for the incidents which I will here relate.

In the year 1909 Lord Carnarvon, who was then conducting excavations in the necropolis of the nobles of Thebes, discovered a hollow wooden figure of a large black cat, which we recognised, from other examples in the Cairo Museum, to be the shell in which a real embalmed cat was confined. The figure looked more like a small tiger as it sat in the sunlight at the edge of the pit in which it had been discovered, glaring at us with its yellow painted eyes and bristling its yellow whiskers. Its body was covered all over with a thick coating of smooth, shining pitch, and we could not at first detect the line along which the shell had been closed after it had received the mortal remains of the sacred animal within; but we knew from experience that the joint passed completely round the figure – from the nose, over the top of the head, down the back, and along the breast – so that, when opened, the two sides would fall apart in equal halves.

The sombre figure was carried down to the Nile and across the river to my house, where, by a mistake on the part of my Egyptian servant, it was deposited in my *bedroom*.

Returning home at dead of night, I here found it seated in the middle of the floor directly in my path from the door to the matches; and for some moments I was constrained to sit beside it, rubbing my shins and my head.

I rang the bell, but receiving no answer, I walked to the kitchen, where I found the servants grouped distractedly around the butler, who had been stung by a scorpion and was in the throes of that short but intense agony. Soon he passed into a state of delirium and believed himself to be pursued by a large grey cat, a fancy which did not surprise me since he had so lately assisted in carrying the figure to its ill-chosen resting-place in my bedroom.

At length I retired to bed, but the moonlight which now entered the room through the open French windows fell full upon the black figure of the cat; and for some time I lay awake watching the peculiarly weird creature as it stared past me at the wall. I estimated its age to be considerably more than three thousand years, and I tried to picture to myself the strange people who, in those distant times, had fashioned this curious coffin for a cat which had been to them half pet and half household god. A branch of a tree was swaying in the night breeze outside, and its shadow danced to and fro over the face of the cat, causing the yellow eyes to open and shut, as it were, and the mouth to grin. Once, as I was dropping off to sleep, I could have sworn that it had turned its head to look at me; and I could see the sullen expression of feline anger gathering upon its black visage as it did so. In the distance I could hear the melancholy wails of the unfortunate butler imploring those around him to keep the cat away from him, and it seemed to me that there came a glitter into the eyes of the figure as the low cries echoed down the passage.

At last I fell asleep, and for about an hour all was still. Then, suddenly, a report like that of a pistol rang through the room. I started up, and as I did so a large grey cat sprang either from or on to the bed, leapt across my knees, dug its claws into my hand, and dashed through the window into the garden. At the same moment I saw by the light of the moon that the two sides of the wooden figure had fallen apart and were rocking themselves to a standstill upon the floor, like two great empty shells. Between them sat the mummified figure of a cat, the bandages which swathed it round being ripped open at the neck, as though they had been burst outward.

I sprang out of bed and rapidly examined the divided shell; and it seemed to me that the humidity in the air here on the bank of the Nile had expanded the wood which had rested in the dry desert so long, and had caused the two halves to burst apart with the loud noise which I had heard. Then, going to the window, I scanned the moonlit garden; and there in the middle of the pathway I saw, not the grey cat which had scratched me, but my own pet tabby, standing with arched back and bristling fur, glaring into the bushes, as though she saw ten feline devils therein.

I will leave the reader to decide whether the grey cat was the malevolent spirit which, after causing me to break my shins and my butler to be stung by a scorpion, had burst its way through the bandages and woodwork and had fled into the darkness; or whether the torn embalming cloths represented the natural destructive work of Time, and the grey cat was a night-wanderer which had strayed into my room and had been frightened by the easily-explained bursting apart of the two sides of the ancient Egyptian figure. Coincidence is a factor in life not always sufficiently considered; and the events I have related can be explained in a perfectly natural manner, if one be inclined to do so.

My next story tells how a little earthenware lamp once in my possession brought misfortune upon at least two persons.

It sometimes happens that people who have visited Egypt and have there purchased a few trifling antiquities are suddenly seized with the fear that these relics are bringing them bad luck; and, in a moment of frenzy, they pack up their Egyptian purchases, and post them back to the Nile. When I was Inspector-General of Antiquities they not infrequently used to address these parcels to me or to my office at Luxor; and without further consideration the objects were laid away on the shelves of the store-room, where soon the dust gathered upon them and they were forgotten.

Now it chanced that a little earthenware lamp was once returned to me in this manner; and, happening to mention the fact to some friends, I learnt that it had been returned by a lady who declared herself dogged by misfortune ever since it came into her possession, and who had often stated that she intended to get rid of it by sending it back to the unoffending official in charge of antiquities. I cannot now recall the series of misfortunes which had occurred to the owner of the lamp, but I remember that they included little incidents such as the spilling of a bottle of ink over her dress. I paid, of course, small attention to the matter, and the lamp lay unnoticed on the shelf for a year or more.

One day, a certain royal lady who was travelling in Egypt asked me to give her some trifle as a souvenir of her visit; and, without recalling its history to my mind, I gave her the unlucky lamp, which, so far as I know, did not bring any particular ill-fortune to its owner. There the matter would have tamely ended, had it not been for a chance conversation on the subject of unlucky antiquities, which occurred one night at a dinner-party in London. One of the ladies present told me a long story of the ill-luck from which she had suffered during the whole time in which she was the owner of a little earthenware lamp which came from Egypt. To such a state of apprehension had she been brought, she said, by the intuitive feeling that this little antiquity was the cause of her troubles, that at last she went down to the Embankment and hurled it into the Thames.

Vague recollections of the story of the unlucky lamp which I had given to our illustrious visitor began to stir in my mind, and I asked with some interest how she came into possession of the malevolent object. Her reply confirmed my suspicions. The lamp had been given to her by the royal lady to whom I had presented it as a souvenir!

Most people have heard the story of the malevolent 'mummy' in the British Museum. As a matter of fact, it is not a mummy at all, but simply a portion of the lid of a coffin. It was bequeathed to the museum after it had wrought havoc wherever it went, but now it is said to confine its dangerous attentions to those visitors who are disrespectful to it. A lady of my acquaintance told me that she had 'been rude' to it, with the startling result that she fell headlong down the great staircase and sprained her ankle. There is also the well-known case of a journalist who wrote about it in jest, and was dead in a few days.

The originator of the whole affair was the late Mr Douglas Murray, who told me the following facts. He purchased the coffin some time in the 'sixties, and no sooner had he done so than he lost his arm, owing to the explosion of his gun. The ship in which the coffin was sent home was wrecked, as also was the cab in which it was driven from the docks; the house in which it was deposited was burnt down; and the photographer who made a picture of it shot himself. A lady who had some connection with it suffered great family losses, and was wrecked at sea shortly afterwards, her life being saved, so she told me, only by the fact that she clung to a rock for the greater part of a night. The list of accidents and misfortunes charged to the spirit which is connected with this coffin is now of enormous length, a fact which is not surprising, since persons who have seen the coffin attribute all their subsequent troubles to its baneful influence, and misfortunes in this life are not so rare that they can be counted on the five fingers. Personally, I think that, if these matters are to be considered at all, we should attempt rather to incur this restless spirit's benediction by refusing to credit it with an evil purpose.

The veracity of the next story cannot be questioned. A photograph in my possession about which there is no fake, tells the tale more accurately than could any words of mine; and there can be no getting away from the fact that a shadowy human face has come between the camera and the object which was being photographed. The facts are as follows.

Some years ago we were making excavations in the tomb of a Grand Vizir of about 1350 BC, when we came upon a highly decorated coffin of a certain priest, which, by the style of the workmanship, appeared to date from some two hundred years later, and evidently must have been buried there by unscrupulous undertakers who opened up the original tomb for its reception in order to save themselves the trouble of making a new sepulchre. Now this act of desecration might be thought to have called down upon the intruding mummy the wrath of the Vizir's spirit, whose body was probably ousted to make room for the newcomer; but, whether this be so or not, those who believe in these powers might have reason to suppose that the priestly usurper lay restlessly in his coffin, retaining, in place of the usual quiescence of the dead, a continued activity which caused an atmosphere of malignity to linger around his mortal remains.

As soon as the coffin and mummy were deposited in my store-room, I began to feel an unaccountable sense of apprehension whenever I stood in its presence; and every time I opened the door of the room to enter its dark recesses I glanced uneasily at the embalmed figure which lay in the now lidless coffin, as though expecting it to do me some injury. This appeared to me to be remarkable, for I had long been accustomed to the presence all around me of the embalmed dead. I had slept night after night in the tombs, sharing their comfortable shelter with the human remains which still lay therein; I had, during a *dahabiyeh* trip in the south, filled the cabin bunkers with the skulls and bones of the dead and had worked and slept contentedly in their company; I had eaten many a luncheon on the lid of a not empty coffin. But this particular mummy seemed to draw my eyes towards it, so that when I was at work in the room in which it lay, I caught myself glancing over my shoulder in its direction.

At length I decided to unwrap the bandages in which the mummy was rolled, and to look upon the face of the dead man who had now begun to haunt my thoughts, after which I proposed to send both it and the coffin down to the Cairo Museum. The process of unwrapping was lengthy, for of course many notes had to be taken and photographs made at the different stages of the proceedings; but at last it was completed, and the body was placed in the packing-case in which it was to travel. Some of the linen cloths which had covered the face were of such beautifully fine texture that I took them into the house to show them to the friends who were staying with me at the time; and one of the servants shortly afterwards placed them upon a shelf in a bedroom wardrobe.

Now it happened that this room was occupied by a lady and her little girl, and a day or two later, while the body still lay in the portico outside the house, and the ancient linen still rested upon the shelf inside the room, the child was seized with violent illness. There followed some days of anxiety, and at length one morning, when the doctor's visit had left us distraught with anxiety, the mother of the invalid came to me with a haggard face, holding in her hands the embalmer's linen. 'Here,' she cried, with an intensity which I shall not soon forget, 'take this horrible stuff and burn it; and for goodness' sake send that mummy away, or the child will die.'

The mummy and its linen went down to Cairo that night, and the little girl in due course recovered; but when, a month or two later, I developed the photographs which I had taken of the unwrapped body, there, between it and my camera, stared a shadowy face. It is possible that I took two photographs upon one plate; I do not remember, but that, and the state of my nerves, due to overwork, may account for all that happened.

I am minded now to relate an experience which befell me when I was conducting excavations in the desert behind the ancient city of Abydos. The tale does not deal with any very particular malevolence of any spirit of the past, but it bears sufficiently closely upon that subject to be recorded here. We were engaged in clearing out a vertical tomb-shaft which had been cut through the rock underlying the sandy surface of the desert. The shaft was about ten foot square; and by the end of the second day's work we had cleared out the sand and stones, wherewith it was filled, to the depth of some twenty feet. At sunset I gave the order to stop work for the night, and I was about to set out on my walk back to the camp when the foreman came to tell me that, with the last strokes of the pick, a mummied hand had been laid bare, and it was evident that we were about to come upon an interred body.

By lamplight, therefore, the work was continued; and presently we had uncovered the sand-dried body of an old woman, who by her posture appeared to have met with a violent death. It was evident that this did not represent the original burial in the tomb, the bottom of the shaft not yet having been reached; and I conjectured that the corpse before us had been thrown from above at some more recent date — perhaps in Roman times — when the shaft was but half full of debris, and in course of time had become buried by blown sand and natural falls of rock.

The workmen were now waiting for their evening meal, but I, on the other hand, was anxious to examine the body and its surroundings carefully, in order to see whether any objects of interest were to be found. I therefore sent all but one of the men back to the camp, and descended into the shaft by means of a rope ladder, carrying with me a hurricane lamp to light my search. In the flickering rays of the lamp the body looked particularly gruesome. The old woman lay upon her back, her arms outstretched upwards, as though they had stiffened thus in some convulsion, the fingers being locked together. Her legs were thrust outwards rigidly, and the toes were cramped and bent. The features of the face were well preserved, as was the whole body; and long black hair descended to her bony shoulders in a tangled mass. Her mouth was wide open, the two rows of teeth gleaming savagely in the uncertain light, and the hollow eye-sockets seemed to stare upwards, as though fixed upon some object of horror. I do not suppose that it is often man's lot to gaze upon so ghastly a spectacle, and it was only the fact of the extreme antiquity of the body which made it possible for me to look with equanimity upon it; for the centuries that had passed since the occurrence of this woman's tragedy seemed to have removed the element of personal affinity which sets the living shuddering at the dead.

Just as I was completing my search I felt a few drops of rain fall, and at the same time realised that the wind was howling and whistling above me and that the stars were shut out by dense clouds. A rain storm in Upper Egypt is a very rare occurrence, and generally it is of a tropical character. If I left the body at the bottom of the shaft, I thought to myself, it would be soaked and destroyed; and since, as a specimen, it was well worth preserving, I decided to carry it to the surface, where there was a hut in which it could be sheltered. I lifted the body from the ground, and found it to be quite light, but at the same time not at all fragile. I called out to the man whom I had told to wait for me on the surface, but received no reply. Either he had misunderstood me and gone home, or else the noise of the wind prevented my voice from reaching him. Large spots of rain were now falling, and there was no time for hesitation. I therefore lifted the body on to my back, the two outstretched arms passing over my shoulders and the linked fingers clutching, as it were, at my chest. I then began to climb up the rope ladder, and as I did so I noticed with something of a qualm that the old woman's face was peeping at me over my right shoulder and her teeth seemed about to bite my right ear.

I had climbed about half the distance when my foot dislodged a fragment of rock from the side of the shaft, and, as luck would have it, the stone fell right upon the lamp, smashing the glass and putting the light out. The darkness in which I found myself was intense, and now the wind began to buffet me and to hurl the sand into my face. With my right hand I felt for the woman's head and shoulder, in order to hitch the body more firmly on to my back, but to my surprise my hand found nothing there. At the same moment I became conscious that the hideous face was grinning at me over my *left* shoulder, my movements, I suppose, having shifted it; and, without further delay, I blundered and scrambled to the top of the shaft in a kind of panic.

No sooner had I reached the surface than I attempted to relieve myself of my burden. The wind was now screaming past me and the rain was falling fast. I put my left hand up to catch hold of the corpse's shoulder, and to my dismay found that the head had slipped round once more to my right, and the face was peeping at me from that side. I tried to remove the arms from around my neck, but, with ever increasing horror, I found that the fingers had caught in my coat and seemed to be holding on to me. A few moments of struggle ensued, and at last the fingers released their grip. Thereupon the body swung round so that we stood face to face, the withered arms still around my neck, and the teeth grinning at me through the darkness. A moment later I was free, and the body fell back from me, hovered a moment, as it were, in mid air, and suddenly disappeared from sight. It was then that I realised that we had been struggling at the very edge of the shaft, down which the old woman had now fallen, and near which some will say that she had been wildly detaining me.

Fortunately the rain soon cleared off, so there was no need to repeat the task of bringing the gruesome object to the surface. Upon the next morning we found the body quite unin- jured lying at the bottom of the shaft, in almost precisely the position in which we had discovered it; and it is now exhibited in the museum of one of the medical institutes of London.

Most people who have visited Upper Egypt will be familiar with the lioness-headed statue of Sekhmet which is to be seen in the small temple of Ptah, at Karnak. Tourists usually make a point of entering the sanctuary in which it stands by moonlight or starlight, for then the semi-darkness adds in an extraordinary manner to the dignity and mystery of the figure, and one feels disposed to believe the goddess not yet bereft of all power. Sekhmet was the agent employed by the Sun-God, Ra, in the destruction of mankind; and she thus had a sinister reputation in olden times. This has clung to her in a most persistent manner, and to this day the natives say that she has the habit of killing little children. When the statue was discovered a few years ago, a fall of earth just in front of her terminated the lives of two of the small boys who were engaged in the work, a fact which, not surprisingly, has been quoted as an indication of the malevolence of the spirit which resides in this impressive figure of stone. One hears it now quite commonly said that those who offend the goddess when visiting her are pursued by ill-fortune for weeks afterwards.

It actually became the custom for English and American ladies to leave their hotels after dinner and to hasten into the presence of the goddess, there to supplicate her and to appease her with fair words. On one of these occasions, a few years ago, a well-known lady threw herself upon her knees before the statue, and rapturously holding her hands aloft, cried out, 'I believe, I believe!' while a friend of hers passionately kissed the stone hand and patted the somewhat ungainly feet. On other occasions lamps were burnt before the goddess and a kind of ritual was mumbled by an enthusiastic gentleman; while a famous French lady of letters, who was a victim of the delusion that she possessed ventriloquial powers, made mewing noises, which were supposed to emanate from the statue, and which certainly added greatly to the barbaric nature of the scene. So frequent did these séances become that at last I had to put an official stop to them, and thereafter it was deemed an infringement of the rules to placate the malevolent goddess in this manner. There she stands alone, smiling mysteriously at her visitors, who are invariably careful not to arouse her anger by smiling back. A native, who probably believed himself to be under her ban, burgled his way, one summer's night, into the sanctuary and knocked her head and shoulders off; but the archæologist in charge cemented them on again, and thus she continues as before to dole out misfortune to those who credit her with that ill desire.

During the winter of 1908–9 the well-known Bostonian painter and pageant-master, Joseph Lindon Smith, and his wife, were staying with my wife and myself in our house on the banks of the Nile, at Luxor, the modern town which has grown up on the site of the once mighty 'hundred gated Thebes,' the old capital of Egypt. It was our custom to spend a great part of our time amongst the ruins on the western side of the Nile, for my work made it necessary for me to give constant attention to the excavations which were there being conducted, and

to supervise the elaborate system of policing and safeguarding, which is nowadays in force for the protection of the many historical and artistic treasures there on view. Mr Smith, also, had painting work to do amongst the tombs; while the ladies of our party amused themselves in the hundred different ways which are so readily suggested in these beautiful and romantic surroundings.

Sometimes we used to camp the night amongst the tombs, the tents pitched on the side of the hill of Shêkh abd'el Gurneh in the midst of the burial-place of the great nobles; and at sunset, after the tourists had all disappeared along the road back to Luxor, and our day's occupations were ended, we were wont to set out for long rambling walks in the desert ravines, over the rocky hills, and amongst the ruined temples; nor was it until the hour of dinner that we made our way back to the lights of the camp. The grandeur of the scenery when darkness had fallen is indescribable. In the dim light reflected from the brilliant stars, the cliffs and rocky gorges assumed the most wonderful aspect. Their shadows were full of mystery, and the broken pathways seemed to lead to hidden places barred to man's investigation. The hills, and the boulders at their feet, took fantastic shape; and one could not well avoid the thought that the spirits of Egypt's dead were at that hour roaming abroad, like us, amongst these illusory scenes.

It was during one of these evening walks that we found ourselves in the famous Valley of the Tombs of the Queens, a rock-strewn ravine in which some of Egypt's royal ladies were buried. At the end of this valley the cliffs close in, and an ancient torrent, long ago dried up, has scooped out a cavernous hollow in the face of the rock, into which, as into a cauldron, the waters must have poured as they rushed down from the hills at the back. The sides of the hollow form two-thirds of a circle, and overhead the rock somewhat overhangs. In front it is quite open to the valley, and as the floor is a level area of hard gravel, about twenty-five feet at its greatest breadth and depth, the hollow at once suggests to the mind a natural stage with the rocky valley which lies before it as the theatre. The place was well known to us, and in the darkness we now scrambled up into the deep shadows of the recess, and, sitting upon the gravel, stared out into the starlit valley, like ghostly actors playing to a deserted auditorium. The evening wind sighed quietly around us, and across the valley the dim forms of two jackals passed with hardly a sound. Far away over the Nile we could see, framed between the hills on either side of the mouth of the ravine, the brilliant lights of Luxor shining in the placid water; and these added the more to the sense of our remoteness from the world and our proximity to those things of the night which belong to the kingdom of dreams.

Presently I struck a match, in order to light my pipe, and immediately the rough face of the rocks around us was illuminated and made grotesque. As the flame flickered, the dark shadows fluttered like black hair in the wind, and the promontories jutted forward like great snouts and chins. An owl, startled by the light, half tumbled from its roost upon a deep ledge high above us and went floundering into the darkness, hooting like a lost soul. The match burnt out, and immediately blackness and silence closed once more about us.

'What a stage for a play!' exclaimed the amateur actor-manager; and a few moments later we were all eagerly discussing the possibility of performing a ghostly drama here amongst the desert rocks. By the time that we had reached our camp a plot had been evolved which was based on the historical fact that the spirit of the above-mentioned Pharaoh Akhnaton was, so to speak, excommunicated by the priests and was denied the usual prayers for the dead, being thus condemned to wander without home or resting-place throughout the years. Akhnaton, the son of the powerful and beautiful Queen Tiy, reigned from 1375 to 1358 B.C.; and being disgusted with the barbarities perpetrated at Thebes in the name of the god Amon, and believing that the only true god was Aton, the life-giving 'Energy of the Sun,' overthrew the former religion and preached a wonderfully advanced doctrine of peace and love, which he associated with the worship of Aton. He removed his capital from Thebes to 'The City of the Horizon of Aton,' and there reigned with his wife and children, devoting his whole energy to his religion and to the demonstration of his lofty teaching. He died at the age of about thirty years; and thereupon the nation unanimously returned, under Tutankhamen, to the worship of Amon and the old gods, whose priests erased the dead king's name from the book of life.

Here, then, was a ghost ready to hand, and here was our stage. The part of the young Akhnaton should be assigned to my wife, for his gentle character and youthful voice could better be rendered by a woman than by a man. Then we must bring in the beautiful Queen Tiy, who could well be impersonated by Mrs. Lindon Smith. Mr. Smith could take the part of the messenger of the gods, sent from the underworld to meet the royal ghost. And as for myself, I would be kept busy enough, managing the lights, prompting the actors, and doing the odd jobs. There would have to be some weird music at certain moments; and for this purpose our friend, Mr. F. F. Ogilvie, that painter of Anglo-Egyptian fame, might be commandeered together with his guitar.

On our return to Luxor we busied ourselves during all our spare hours in designing and making the costumes and properties; and it fell to me to write as fast as I could the lines of the play. They have no merit in themselves; but when a few days later they were read over in our desert theatre, beneath the starlit heavens, the quiet, earnest diction of the two ladies, and the strange, hawk-like tones of our celebrated amateur, caused them to sound very mysterious and full of meaning.

We now fixed the date for the performance and invited our friends to come by night to the Valley of the Tombs of the Queens to see the expected appearance of the ghost of the great Pharaoh, and a few days before that date we moved over once more to our desert camp.

We rehearsed the play a few nights later, but alas! hardly had Mrs. Smith finished her introductory lines, when she was struck down by agonising pains in her eyes, and in less than two hours she had passed into a raving delirium. The story of how at midnight she was taken across the deserted fields and over the river to our house at Luxor, would read like the narration of a nightmare. Upon the next day it was decided that she must be sent down immediately to Cairo, for there was no doubt that she was suffering from ophthalmia in its most virulent form, and there were grave fears that she might lose her sight. On this same day my wife was smitten down with violent illness, she being ordered also to proceed to Cairo immediately. On the next morning, Mr. Smith developed a low fever, and shortly afterwards, I myself was laid low with influenza. Mr. Ogilvie, returning to his headquarters by train, came in for a nasty accident in which his mother's leg was badly injured. And thus not one of us could have taken part in the production of the play on the date announced.

For the next two or three weeks Mrs. Smith's eyes and my wife's life hung in the balance and were often despaired of. Mercifully, however, they were both restored in due time to perfect health; but none of us entertained any desire to undertake the rehearsals a second time. Many of our friends were inclined to see in our misfortunes the punishing hand of the gods and spirits of ancient Egypt; but they must not forget that the play was to be given in all solemnity and without the smallest suggestion of burlesque. For my own part, as I have said, I do not think that the possibilities of that much under-rated factor in life's events, coincidence, have been exhausted in the search for an explanation of our tragedy; but far from me be it to offer an opinion upon the subject. I have heard the most absurd nonsense talked in Egypt by those who believe in the malevolence of the ancient dead; but at the same time, I try to keep an open mind on the subject.

VELMA
The Fatal Curse from the Tomb
(1927)

Some time ago the long arm of a dead Pharaoh reached down through the centuries and took its revenge on the man who had disturbed the security of a royal tomb.

To the world at large Lord Carnarvon, the great Egyptologist who discovered the tomb of Tutankhamen, died from the effects of a mosquito bite. Yet there are those who believe that his tragic end at his hour of triumph was brought about by much more subtle means.

They believe that he was the victim of the ancient curse of the Pharaohs for violating the tomb of their mighty dead.

When the body of Tutankhamen was revealed to those who entered his tomb in the fateful Valley of Kings, a mark was found on his face. The mark left by the fatal mosquito bite on the face of the Earl of Carnarvon was in exactly the same position!

To-day I am able to throw a new light on the mystery which lends curious support to the theory that Lord Carnarvon was the victim of powerful occult forces.

Not long before he embarked upon the final quest which resulted in the discovery of Tutankhamen's tomb he allowed me to read his hands on the way out to Egypt.

What I saw led me to warn him of the deadly peril he was running in meddling with the secrets of the dead kings.

All sorts of hands have come my way in my time – strong hands, tragic hands, weak hands – hands that told of unpleasant things in store for their owner; but never had I had to read a

more mysterious future than that written in the hands of Lord Carnarvon.

Here, marked so plainly that it might have been stamped into the skin, was the warning signboard of danger and the foreshadowing of his fate.

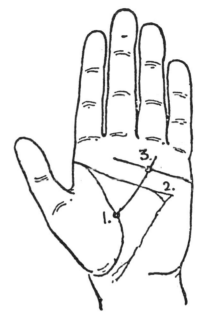

Lord Carnarvon's hand

Lord Carnarvon had more than an ordinary interest in the occult. He was keen that I should keep nothing back.

I found a fairly long Life Line, but thin in the centre, where there was an ominous spot which – given other combinations in the hand – might indicate death. This spot I have marked 1 on the accompanying diagram.

Unfortunately, it seemed that the confirming signs were there also, for there was a spot at the junction of the lines of Heart and Apollo (marked 3). This indicated a great peril which probably the possessor of the hand would not permit his head to turn him from.

The line of Apollo denoted great glory and success. More than ordinary interest in occult matters was indicated by the fact that the Health Line was forked at the Head Line. This is shown clearly on the diagram, marked 2.

'I see great peril for you,' I told Lord Carnarvon. 'Most probably – as the indications of occult interest are so strong in your hand – it will arise from such a source.'

His interest aroused, he discussed the excavations in the Valley of the Kings.

'Whatever happens,' he said, 'I will see to it that my interest in things occult never gets so strong as to affect either my reason or my health.'

Not long afterwards I met Lord Carnarvon again. Our conversation once more turned on occult matters. 'I've been thinking over what you told me,' he said. 'I wonder if you could discover more?'

We sat down and I took his hand.

To my horror I saw that the spots had greatly increased in density and that the one on his Life Line was perilously near his present age.

Eager to discover more, I suggested he might look into the crystal.

What he saw was not very clear. 'I see something like a temple, Velma,' he said. 'And there seem to be people, but it is all so cloudy that I can't make it out.'

I took the crystal and looked . . .

It was like looking back across the centuries at a scene in ancient Egypt.

There, as clear as a reflection in a mirror, was a great Egyptian temple thronged with people divided into three parties. Picture after picture made this clear, and as they passed through the sphere I described them to Lord Carnarvon.

He listened with tense interest.

There was an old man robed as a dignitary of the Goddess Isis, who seemed to be wrangling with a party of younger men who held aloft a banner with hieroglyphics upon it. From the mist which kept shrouding the figures came out the words in English – 'To Aton . . . only god . . . Universal Father . . .'

The mystery was heightened when the scene changed to a spectacle of huge sacred bulls and priests singing a dirge while the old dignitary placed a mask of gold over the face of a young man in a coffin.

There was no explanation, yet somehow I felt that I was watching the burial of Tutankhamen.

Suddenly the picture changed again, and I saw a party of men, led by Lord Carnarvon, working in the vicinity. From a mysterious tomb began to come vivid flashes betokening occult influences. As Lord Carnarvon and his party continued their work the flashes increased in vividness.

The series of pictures ended in an amazing spectacle.

I saw the old dignitary again, surrounded by a great concourse of people, who demanded vengeance against the disturbers of the tomb. Then, finally, I saw Lord Carnarvon standing alone in the very storm-centre of a hurricane of occult flashes.

That was all. The picture grew dim and faded away . . .

For a few moments Lord Carnarvon and I regarded one another without speaking. He was the first to break the silence.

'Of course, it all sounds ridiculous,' he said, 'but I have actually experienced some strange influence during the earlier stages of the work. I cannot say it was actually an impulse to stop, but it was something like that.

'But no one would jib at an adventure even if there was danger. Having gone so far with the work my curiosity and interest must be satisfied now.'

'If I were you,' I answered gravely, 'I should make some excuse to the public, and finish. I can only see disaster to you without any adequate gain to humanity to justify the sacrifice.'

Lord Carnarvon shook his head resolutely. 'No, no,' he replied. 'That is out of the question. Why, if I were to give up, there are a hundred men waiting to step into my shoes. Oh, no, I must finish what I have begun.

'But tell me, Velma, what do you think is the real answer to all this mysterious business? Is it preposterous rot to think of the influence of all these old priests still surviving to-day?'

'I have seen too many strange demonstrations of the occult not to believe in it,' I said. 'Wherever you get a place which has been the focus of tremendous emotion there is not the slightest doubt that something – I don't now what – persists. Votaries may feel its beneficial influence. Those who would destroy or harm have felt its baneful power.'

'I rather incline to agree with you, Velma,' Lord Carnarvon said seriously. Then with a shrug of his shoulders and a smile, he added:

'But what an adventure! A challenge to the psychic powers of the ages, Velma! What a challenge!'

Not long afterwards he was dead . . .

CHEIRO
A Mummy's Hand That Came to Life
(1934)

In this chapter I relate a strange but true story of a mummy's hand that after some thousands of years showed remarkable signs of coming back to life . . .

During the eighteen months that Professor von Heller and I were engaged in taking wax casts of hieroglyphics in the Tombs of the Kings, [our] old guide never left us for one moment. In the day-time he carried our instruments, cooked our meals, and when night came he slept on a rug just outside our door.

In the end, the time came when our work was accomplished and we prepared to return to England. As the professor and I one night retired for the last time, the old Egyptian whispered in my ear that he wanted me to accompany him back into one of the ruined temples. 'There, is something I want to give you,' he said. 'But I must give it *to you alone.*'

It was getting close to midnight but I went with him without any fear. We went together in silence towards a part of the ruins known as the 'Hall of Columns.' It was such a night as one can see only in Egypt, and that only during certain seasons of the year. In the deep purple sky a large pallid moon hung like the ghost of some dead world – unrested, and alone. A brooding silence pervaded the place. No sound of man or beast could be heard, our footsteps alone roused echoes that seemed to mock us among the ruins.

The old man left me for a few moments and entered an excavation that lay under the body of a broken Sphinx. When he returned he was carrying something in his hands, something wrapped up in one of those bandages that are found bound round the limbs of mummies.

Without speaking he sat down by my side and slowly undid the parcel he was carrying. As the last cloth fell away he held up before my face the right hand of a mummy *in a magnificent state of preservation.* I started back in astonishment – it was a long beautifully shaped hand, evidently that of a woman. The nails were perfect in shape, even the gold-leaf that the ancient Egyptians used instead of the red paint that ladies employ to-day was as good as when it had first been put on.

This small, delicate-looking hand had evidently been severed from the arm at the wrist and the bones of the joint stood out white and clear as the rays of the moon fell upon them. The hand had evidently been mummified by some extraordinary process. There were no linen wrappings round the fingers or any part of it. It just looked as if it were carved out of some piece of hard wood of a dark brown colour. On the first finger a ring of Egyptian gold shone out clear and distinct. In the brilliant moonlight I could see hieroglyphics carved on it like there are on every Egyptian cartouche.

Holding it tenderly in his hands, the old man told me the following story:

'This was the right hand,' he went on almost in a whisper, 'of the seventh daughter of the King Atennaten. He forsook the religion of his fathers, created a new religion at Tel-el-Amarna. At his death he was succeeded on the throne by Tut-Ankh-Amen, who returned to the old faith and restored the power of the priests here in the Temples of Thebes.

'King Atennaten's daughter, the Princess Makitaten, whose hand you are looking at, remained faithful to the religion of her father. At his death she raised an army, marched against Thebes, but was killed in the first battle. The priests had her hand, that held the sword, cut off at the wrist, embalmed by some secret process impervious to decay and placed it here in their principal temple as a warning to others.

'I heard the story,' he went on, 'from my father who was a descendant of the line of priests who served these temples. He and I alone knew where this hand was concealed, and now, my dear friend and Master,' he added sadly, '*I give this hand to you.*'

'But why to me?' I asked. 'You should give it to some Museum that would preserve it forever.'

'That cannot be,' he answered almost sternly. 'The curse that was placed on that hand *has not yet been fulfilled.* Listen carefully for you are *the one selected to carry out its purpose.*'

'Impossible!' I almost gasped. 'What can I have to do with it?'

'The ways of Fate are strange,' he smiled grimly. 'Listen and you will understand.'

He drew himself up to his full height. He was no longer the subservient guide that obeyed me as a dog would its master. Standing erect in the moonlight, his Arab bournouse hanging loosely from his shoulders, his dark eyes blazing with some inner fire, *he became the Master and I the slave to do his bidding.*

'Listen,' he said in a still more commanding voice, 'you are leaving in the morning for England, for what you call home. You dream you are going to settle there. You think you have travelled enough. You are looking forward to a quiet life in which you can carry on your occult studies. I am compelled to tell you there is no such destiny before you. Let me map out the pathway you are fated to follow.'

Like a person inspired or in a trance he went on rapidly, 'You are not going to settle down. There is no home before you for many long years – if ever. On your return to what you think is home,' and he laughed bitterly, 'you will find, during your absence in Egypt, your money has been taken from you. You will not be able to find any occupation, in the end you will become a teacher of occult studies. The one you are fated to take up will be the most abused and despised of all. You will raise it out of the mire of ignorance and superstition. Through it you will meet Kings, Rulers, and the great ones of the earth; through it and for it, you will travel without cease. Every country and clime will call and you will obey. We are all servants of Fate *and you are more markedly so than many others.*

'The curse placed on the hand before you has only been partly fulfilled. It is true, her mummy found a resting place by the Tomb of her father, King Atennaten, and *will some day be brought to light.* The part of the curse unfulfilled is, that her right hand would sooner or later be carried and exhibited in all the principal countries of the earth and would find no rest until after the end of a great war, when the lost tomb of her brother-in-law, the King Tut-Ankh-Amen, would be discovered.

'You are the person selected to carry out the latter part of the curse.'

'Impossible!' I again exclaimed.

'No, no,' he said. 'The word "impossible" does not exist. In less than a year from now you will commence your own wanderings. You will first visit North America, and from there Fate will take you to every principal nation of the earth. You will carry this hand with you. You will show it to Kings and Rulers as well as to the common people of the world. It will preach a lesson to all – more than any words that can be used.

'At the end of a great war in which Egypt will play some part, although what that may be I cannot see clearly, but on the very eve of the discovery of the lost tomb of her relative, Tut-Ankh-Amen, I am told by some power that seems to speak through me, this hand will for the first time endeavour to get free from your custody and the "Ka" or spirit imprisoned in it will return to its own.

'While it is with you it will be your protector. In your travels you will meet with many dangers. You will escape all as long as you keep your promise to guard this hand always with you. Will you give me that promise?'

Overawed by the man's solemn words, over-mastered by his will and overcome by the mystery of the scene around me, I bowed my head in assent.

'I demand more than that,' the old man went on. 'Promises may be undertaken lightly, but an oath before the God of All can never be forgotten. Go down on your knees in this broken temple of Amen, raise your right hand to heaven and vow before your own God that *you will keep your promise.*'

As I arose from my knees he placed the mummy's hand within my own. Folding it carefully in some of the linen wrappings that had fallen at my feet, I made my way back to the Arab hut where I lived.

The professor who was still busily engaged in packing up for our journey, did not notice the small parcel I carried. He also did not notice that I unpacked a valise of my personal belongings and placed the mummy's hand carefully on the top of the other things.

I had taken a vow never to let it out of my possession. *Already that vow had taken hold of my senses* and that night I slept for the first time with my valise containing the hand under my pillow.

Early the next morning we boarded the boat for the first stage of our homeward journey. The old Egyptian was at the wharf to say goodbye. Only a few words passed – he looked me straight in the face and said, 'I know you will keep your promise.' As the boat swung out into the river he stood there to the last. As I recall the scene I see him even now – a tall commanding figure of mystery that I shall never forget as long as I live . . .

I will now tell in as brief a way as possible some of the experiences I had while the mummy's hand was in my keeping . . .

Wherever I travelled the mummy hand of the Princess went with me. I never forgot my vow made under those weird conditions in Egypt. Resting on a purple cushion, it always occupied an honoured position by my side, and the thousands who came to consult me heard her story.

The Egyptian, as you may remember, had told me that the hand would be my protector and save me in moments of danger. I have not space in a book of this kind to tell how often escapes from death and other things appeared to happen, but I will give a few instances. On one occasion, a man concealed in my rooms in the Auditorium Hotel in Chicago attempted to rob me in the dead of night. He had already grasped my watch and a wallet of money lying on the table, when his hand in the dark, came in contact with that of the mummy. *With a gasp of fright, he dropped everything and fled.*

On another occasion, when travelling in South America, the hotel I was in took fire. People rushed from their rooms and so did I. As I had in my fright forgotten the hand I hesitated, the elevator started without me; I ran back to my room to get my prized possession – as I did so the ropes of the elevator burned in the roof – it *fell with a crash, and everyone in it was killed.*

But I must hurry on to my final experience. Before I do so I feel it is only fair to state quite frankly that every word I am writing is not only true, but has been substantiated by witnesses and sworn affidavits.

Before the end of the Great War, exactly as the old Egyptian had, some thirty-odd years before, predicted, I found myself living in the middle of Ireland where I was engaged in converting peat into activated carbon for gas-masks for the troops by a special process I had invented myself. For the time being I thought I had made a home in that 'dear, distressful country,' forgetting that the Egyptian had also said 'Fate had decreed that I would never have a home for any length of time.'

My wife and I had safely passed through that troublesome period when the Sinn Feiners were in active fighting against England, leading up to the formation of the Irish Free State and the Treaty of 1922. All had been well until the Irish began fighting among themselves, when the Republican section burned down my factory in order to force my employees to join their side.

As there was no reason for us to remain longer, we commenced dismantling our house, sending the furniture and chattels back to London. Almost everything had gone except a few packing cases and trunks left lying in the hall, and last but no means least, the mummy's hand still resting on its purple velvet cushion in the salon.

Curiously enough this mysterious companion of my thirty years of wandering had become my greatest difficulty. Some months previous to the factory being destroyed, the hand, that had been hard as a piece of ebony, had begun to alter in appearance. The fingers that had always been rigid as iron had become supple and soft.

One morning as I looked at it I started back with horror. Small drops of what looked *like blood were glistening on the knuckles*, larger drops were oozing from the finger tips. I could hardly believe my senses. I called in an English chemist employed at the factory. My first question to him was, 'Have you ever heard of a mummy's hand, or any part of a mummy showing signs of bleeding after having been embalmed for over 3,000 years?'

'Never!' he answered quickly. 'Such a thing would be impossible and absolutely unbelievable.'

'Well,' I said, 'you see this mummy's hand lying on that cushion. You will remember, that when you came here in 1920, it was as hard and rigid as if carved out of a piece of oak. You see now the flesh has become soft and the fingers supple, and what appears to be dark red blood is now oozing from the fingers. Take it into the laboratory, analyse a drop of the blood

under the microscope and give me your opinion. After that, use every means you may have at your disposal to restore the hand to its former hardness and rigid condition.'

A few hours later the chemist reported that there could be no doubt but that *it was human blood that was oozing from the fingers*. He added that the only thing he could do to stop the bleeding and restore it to its former rigid state was to dip the entire hand in a solution of pitch and shellac.

I hold a sworn affidavit from this chemist to prove this statement, also one from the Manager of the Factory who witnessed his experiments in his efforts to restore the hand.

For some time after the solution of pitch and shellac had stopped the bleeding, the hand appeared as it was before and rested as it always had done, on its velvet cushion on a table in the salon.

Later *the blood again began to ooze*, and this time forced its way through the coating of pitch and shellac and the hand itself became soft and showed signs of melting away. I was in despair. I wanted to keep it with me but I did not dare to pack it up on account of the condition it was in.

One night when nothing remained in the salon but the hand, we were terrified by four robbers forcing their way into this very room. As they switched on the electric light the ring of Egyptian gold on the first finger, which I mentioned previously, attracted the leader's attention. He snatched the hand up but dropped it at once on seeing his own covered with blood. With a curse of fear he rushed out of the house followed by his companions.

A few nights later, as we could not take the

hand with us on account of its condition, we decided to light a large fire in the chimney of the hall and cremate what had been my faithful companion for more than thirty years . . .

Without paying attention to the date, we had planned to carry out our purpose on the last night of October, which is called Hallowe'en. The night when, more than all others it is believed the spirits of the dead come back to visit their friends and relations.

While waiting for the fire in the hall to burn up, my wife and I took advantage of the night being clear and warm to walk up and down the garden in front of the old-fashioned house. The place being situated on a hill we could, on that radiant moonlit night, see for upwards of twenty miles towards the south to where the mountains of Tipperary appeared to lose themselves in the sky.

As our thoughts were full of what we were about to do the conversation naturally turned to Egypt – a land where my wife had also lived for many years. We pictured in our minds what such a night would be among the ruined Temples of Thebes, and I again recalled the scene when the Egyptian guide gave me the mummy's hand that we were now about to cremate.

Again I repeated his words: 'At the end of a great war this hand will endeavour to get free from your custody and the "Ka," or spirit, imprisoned in it will return to its own.'

It had indeed endeavoured to get free. For months it was slowly and steadily dissolving. There was nothing I could do to hold it longer in my possession. The time *had come when we had to separate.*

As we entered the house, close on midnight, we noticed the servants had left the dining-room windows open with a supper on the table following the quaint Irish custom of bidding welcome to the spirits of the departed on that one night of the year.

For the first time we remembered it was Hallowe'en – and with a strange feeling in our hearts we closed and bolted the door of the outer porch and the heavy oak doors of the inner hall. The fire had burned up and was so bright that we had no necessity to switch on the electric lamps. We made ourselves as comfortable as was possible on the empty packing cases. I went into the salon and brought out the hand.

It may have been only sentiment, if one wishes to call it that, but an intense feeling of sadness overwhelmed me. It was as if I were about to say farewell to some dear old friend. Almost reverently I took the little ebony stand and approached the fire.

'Wait one moment,' my wife said. 'Surely we should say some prayer before consigning it to the flames. This little hand may have been lifted so often in prayer to her own God in Egypt, that it seems only right for us to do so. Her God for all we know, many have been our own – only under a different name.'

'Yes,' I said, 'but prayers we know, do not seem suitable.'

'Strangely enough,' my wife answered, 'a verse from the Egyptian Book of the Dead seems forcing itself across my memory.' Softly and with great emphasis, she repeated the following lines:

Thy flesh have I given unto thee,
Thy bones have I kept for thee,

Thy members have I collected,
Thou art set in order;
Thou seest the Gods,
Thou settest out on thy way,
Thine hand reaches beyond the horizon and
    unto the holy place where thou wouldst be.

As her words died away I opened the heart of
the fire, slipped into the flames the ebony stand,
the velvet cushion and – the hand.

And now I come to the final part of this story
that is still more strange, in fact to many it may
be unbelievable. I assure my readers, however,
on my word of honour, that what I have
related is true in every particular and can be
supported by evidence and by sworn affidavits.
This latter part is equally true although it may
sound still more fantastic and impossible.

Well, to resume, the moment the hand
reached the heart of the fire long white flames
of intense brilliancy shot upward while the perfume of the spices by which it had been
embalmed floated out and pervaded the whole
place.

We sat there watching until all had disappeared – until only the red glow of the fire
and ashes on the hearth remained. Finally we
tore ourselves away to go to our rooms, but
had scarcely put our feet on the first step of the
stairs when *something happened that made us
stand still with fright.*

I have mentioned that the night was warm
and calm. There was not enough breeze to
move the leaves on the trees. Yet at the doors of
the outer porch, a noise like a whirlwind
seemed to force them open and to our horror
we saw the oak doors of the inner hall yielding
to some pressure behind them. Only thinking

of raids in that disturbed part of Ireland, and
having more than once seen armed men force
their way into the house, we realized our
absolutely defenceless position and turned and
faced what we believed would prove to be the
revolvers of the raiders.

The split in the centre where the folding
doors came together was already widening –
the force pressing against them was steady and
continuous – *with a crash they were flung wide
open*!

No armed men entered. There was nothing
to be seen but the rays of brilliant moonlight
that flooded the hall almost to where we stood.
We became cold with a strange feeling of dread
that words cannot describe. I am sure we
would have preferred the sight of armed men
rather than those wide open doors and the
uncanny stillness that seemed to enter.

We were, however, totally unprepared for
what was about to follow. Far out in the glass
porch, where a large 'Passion flower' formed
an arch of dark green leaves, *something* was
taking place – *something was taking shape.*

It was impossible to believe our eyes. A form
seemed shaping itself into a resemblance of a
spirit trying to materialize. As this undefined
shape slowly moved towards the inside doors it
appeared to gather more substance. Then suddenly, in the deeper shadow of the hall, it
assumed both shape and figure until we
actually saw before us the form of a woman,
with head, shoulders, and body down to the
hips, *clearly outlined and every moment
growing clearer.*

It was a very beautiful and remarkable face
that finally looked toward us. Nobility, grandeur, and pride of race seemed marked in every

line, while the eyes – no words of mine can describe them. Large, deep-set, lustrous eyes that shone with a radiance of their own.

Slowly and majestically the figure moved farther into the hall, becoming, as it did, still more clear and distinct.

The head-dress appeared like leaves of beaten gold formed like the wings of beetles, the ends resting gracefully on slender shoulders. In the centre of the forehead was a golden asp, the emblem of Egyptian royalty, while an enormous scarab held together, round the waist, a girdle of jewels or precious stones.

We felt rooted to the spot. We dared not move as the figure reached the fireplace where the dying embers were still glowing. For a moment it appeared inclining towards where the fire had been, then faced us again with *both hands clasped together as if in a moment of ecstasy.*

For a second her lips seemed to move; we thought she was going to speak; her eyes looked into ours. Then throwing her head back she lifted her hands slowly in the form of an arch over her head, and bowing towards where we poor trembling mortals stood, the figure glided backward through the hall and out into the porch where it had first appeared.

As if hypnotized, we followed – we could not help ourselves. We had nearly reached the inner doors when the figure began to float out into the night – the wonderful eyes alone remaining for a few seconds looking straight into our own. Like frightened children awakened from some dream we stood at the porch of that lonely house we were soon ourselves to leave.

It was no use trying to go to our rooms. We knew we could not sleep. As the dawn came our courage returned. We raked out the ashes of the fire and finding the calcined bones of the hand, we carefully gathered them together, vowing as we did so, that we some day would take them back to Egypt and place them in one of the tombs in the Valley of the Kings.

The last thing I found was the ring of Egyptian gold that had always been on her first finger. It was untarnished by the fire. I rubbed the ashes gently from it. It seemed, to my mind, a legacy from the hand I prized so much, and *I have kept it with me ever since.*

I must now relate the terrible experience we went through on the Irish train on our journey to catch the midnight boat from Kingstown Harbour.

In this experience I cannot help but come to the conclusion that the spirit of the Princess in some way played an important rôle.

The night before we left our house we were warned by some men from the rebel Army to leave the next afternoon, as they intended to destroy the railway bridges and no more trains would be running to Dublin for some time.

We hastily took our valises and hand-luggage with us and boarded the train on the following day. The only carriage we could get into was a Pullman behind the engine, full of officers and soldiers belonging to the new Irish Free State. They were 'armed to the teeth' as the expression goes, and rifles and revolvers were all over the car. These men told us they were being drafted to Dublin, as an attack by the rebels on the barracks there was expected to take place that very night.

In order to make as much room for us as possible the soldiers packed our valises in the luggage racks over our heads. In one valise directly over my wife was the glass jar containing the bones of the mummy's hand.

The train pulled out of the station. There were some sixty-odd miles to go, so we all made ourselves as comfortable as possible – under the circumstances. The long train was packed with soldiers. The few passengers on it were, like ourselves, leaving Ireland. The soldiers from time to time varied the monotony of the journey by singing Irish songs interspaced with verses of 'It's a long way to Tipperary, It's a long way to go.'

I had almost dropped off to sleep when my eyes were suddenly attracted to the luggage label on the valise directly over my wife's head, in which the bones of the mummy's hand were packed. The label had *suddenly become agitated* while other labels were just wagging with the movement of the carriage.

As I looked, there came into my mind an irresistible desire to take those valises from the rack and place them on the floor. I had scarcely obeyed the impulse to do this in spite of the protests from the soldiers, and got back into my seat, when the train came to such a violent stop that all the other luggage was thrown from the racks and many of the men were severely injured.

The confusion that followed in the crowded car was indescribable, but we quickly realized what had happened when from the windows we saw that the station we were entering was on fire and portions of the roof were already falling on the engine.

This place, Liffey Junction, was the last station on the line before we entered the Terminus.

But there was still a greater danger before us. Far away in the distance one could hear the roar of an engine rushing towards us on the same track. In another second we saw it in the distance, tearing like a mad thing , under full head of steam, directly towards where our train was standing – a head-on collision was inevitable. Men threw themselves on their knees and prayed; others white as death seemed turned into stone.

Quick as a flash the same thought passed through everyone's mind – and it was *the true one* – the rebels had uncoupled the express engine of the Galway Mail waiting in the Terminus, pulled open the throttle and hurled it, the biggest locomotive of the company, against the soldiers and passengers on our train.

Escape was impossible. All were paralysed with fear – and then the miracle happened – the railway points, we shall call it – by chance, were closed only a hundred yards ahead – the swaying monster swung over to the Liffey track, crashed through a freight train on the siding, finally smashing itself against a concrete wall some ten miles away at the end of the line.

Taking our valises and getting some of the soldiers to help us we walked into Dublin, took a cab across the city to the Kingstown train and caught the boat for England that night – and we were the only passengers that did so.

I will now come to the last message I got from the Princess, or perhaps I should say, from the Mummy's Hand.

On arrival in London we found the papers full of Howard Carter's discovery of the steps leading to the Tomb of Tut-Ankh-Amen in the Valley of the Kings. The date of this remarkable 'find' was *the day after we had cremated the hand in our house in Ireland*. This struck us as a remarkable coincidence and we spoke of it to many of our friends.

A few weeks later the newspapers rang with the tidings that the tomb itself had been found and that Lord Carnarvon who had financed the search was himself going to Egypt for the opening ceremony.

The night the news was printed in the papers I was writing in my study in London with my wife sitting opposite me finishing a pencil sketch she had made of the Princess as she had appeared to us in the hall of the old Irish house.

We were talking over our strange experience and reviewing notes, when we both remarked that in spite of a good fire the room had suddenly become extremely cold. Then another curious thing happened. The electric lamp on my writing table began to burn dim and then went down to a dull red glow.

We looked at one another without speaking. At the other side of my writing table a shadowy form was already taking on shape. Then, as quickly as I am now writing, the figure of the Princess appeared before us exactly as we had seen her on the previous occasion – her right hand was raised and seemed to be pointing to the scribbling pad lying before me. I seized a pencil and rapidly wrote down words that came into my mind – it was as if I was acting under dictation.

As the vision faded away the electric lamp again burned normally and I read aloud what I had written on the pad. It was nothing more or less than a warning to Lord Carnarvon.

It was to the effect that on his arrival at the tomb of Tut-Ankh-Amen he was not to allow any of the relics found in it to be removed or taken away. The ending of the message was 'that if he disobeyed the warning he would suffer an injury while in the Tomb – a sickness from which he would never recover, and that death would claim him in Egypt.'

Rightly or wrongly I sent this warning to Lord Carnarvon. The letter reached him as he was leaving England. He read it over to one of his companions, the Hon. Richard Bethell, and to a close friend of Admiral Smith Dorrien, whose letter relating these facts I have still in my possession.

Lord Carnarvon, as all his friends know, was an extremely strong-headed obstinate type of an Englishman. Although he admitted to his companion that he was deeply impressed by the warning, he added, 'If at this moment of my life all the mummies in Egypt were to warn me I would go on with my project just the same.'

It is common knowledge what happened. Lord Carnarvon took numerous relics out of the tomb and sent them on to England. He would probably have taken still more if the Egyptian Government had not interfered.

Then, in the highest moment of his triumph, with every newspaper in England praising him for his enterprise, in the Tomb one day a simple little insect stung him on the cheek, blood poisoning set in and in spite of everything doctors could do, death claimed Lord Carnarvon in Egypt and he died within a short distance of the Tomb his money and wealth had enabled him to find.

FREDERICK H. WOOD
A Message from Ancient Egypt
(1940)

The next day I sent a second batch of xeno-glossy to Professor Gunn, who had written a disparaging review of *Ancient Egypt Speaks* in a journal of which he was Editor. I sent it as raw material which I did not then understand . . .

It was a sporting risk of course; but I had faith in Nona. As events proved, my faith was justified.

Professor Gunn, however, was good enough to reply that it seemed to him 'to have no connection with real Egyptian.' He also declined my invitation to a personal sitting with Rosemary, or to hear the First I.P.R. [Institute of Psychical Research] record, and closed the correspondence, 'since there was no evidence that the xenoglossy was Egyptian.' . . .

Eight months later I publicly challenged him in Oxford to a debate on the Nona-Rosemary Xenoglossy. This was on the occasion of my second lecture to the Oxford S.P.R., on March 8, 1938. He had referred to my first lecture in his review of *Ancient Egypt Speaks*. This time, however, he declined the local secretary's invitation to attend my lecture on the ground that he was 'not interested in mediumship.' Finally, although the Oxford papers reported my lecture and published my challenge, Professor Gunn made no reply.

After that I put him out of mind. I do not think Rosemary ever gave him a second thought. We both considered the controversy closed; but in this we reckoned without Nona.

Four months later, on July 14, she gave him *her* answer, unexpectedly, on a gramophone record made in ten minutes at I.P.R., London . . .

[On 14 July] the experiment was carried out under Dr. Nandor Fodor's courteous supervision. Mr. H. Day, of W. Day Ltd., the gramophone recording experts, was in attendance with his apparatus in an adjoining room, which was linked with a microphone standing on a table in the lecture hall. Rosemary and I took our seats at this table, as in our usual sittings. I borrowed a small pad from Dr. Fodor, for any script Nona might wish to write. Neither of us had any other notes, nor any idea of what might happen, or even that anything *would* happen, for that matter.

The sitting opened, as usual, with prayer, and Nona wrote at once: '*It is very strange here this morning. I will tap when I am ready.*'

Rosemary quietly passed under control, and her hand gave three taps. I then spoke the prearranged word, 'Ready,' into the microphone, as a signal to Dr. Fodor and the operator outside the room to start the machine.

A few moments later, Rosemary gave a deep sigh – audible on the record – and the xenoglossy began in slow, detached phrases. In numbering them here, in the exact order in which they may be heard on the gramophone disc, I have numbered them, as always, according to the pauses between. In some cases the sense of the phrase is complete, but in others it runs into the next phrase and even as far as the third phrase. The text had evidently been carefully prepared by Nona, for the substance of her message is continuous, as will be seen from my general translation . . . Once she stumbled slightly, as a foreigner might, in pronouncing the English word 'Institute'; otherwise, her control of her nervous medium was perfect. Here is the sequence of phrases on the first side:

LT

1135   *a(r) náda di hêv-en* ... We come to record ...

1136   *di geem a(r) oo ént* ... speech. It is evidence...

1137   ... *sa dán: oo nêda* ... ... to satisfy the ear. It will state ...

1138   ... *di(h) eém* ... and place on record (lit. 'put in') (that) ...

1139   ... *vée-st a seelêta*. ... it bears indeed a message.

1140   *Nahéemahón* ... Assuredly ...

1141   ... *teevéen di (h)éiran* ... ... (this) was done beforehand ...

1142   ... *a(r) nóus*. ... by a metal object (gramophone).

1143   *See vên dihóona* ... This came to facilitate, indeed ...

1144   ... *donse*. ... (what is) difficult;

1145   *Vee nées ta dów dan*. to bring the spoken language to the ear.

1146   *oo vékee eéna!* It has not yet broken through!

1147   *Da zéet!* That is so!

1148   *Da zéet oo nêdan!* That is it, as has been stated!

1149   *Vrong vée-st* ... The force it carries ...

1150   ... *ístia, tiya nóoda!* ... lo, indeed, is lost!

1151   *Di zeém!* Give assistance!

1152   *Kon têsta!* Amplify (make perfect) this declaration!

1153   *Dóo-a (h)éfan eém* ... Those in the Spirit-World,

1154   ... *aránta* ... inasmuch as ...

1155   ... *dsee ców dan*: ... they have observed what is lacking to the ear,

1156   ... *di ê féran héem* ... ... give me then authority ...

1157   ... *óos ta*. ... to remove this (handicap).

1158   *Aránta di hêv-en* ... Seeing that, we come ...

1159   ... *déeza khêd-en oónt!* ... to express our disappointment, indeed!

1160   *Aránta*, Seeing that ...

1161   *oo vékee quónta di s ta* ... it is to break through this misfortune, she (Rosemary) gives this ...

1162   *a nêda*. ... statement.

1163   *ar-éf an éftee*: Now as to the reckoning:

1164   *a zóodan di héenti* ... Make straight, authorize ...

1165   ... *vee nee zéest* ... ... and support, therefore, what has been written ...

1166   ... *a nóon ta*. ... this time.

1167   *Asee (h)éfan ef* ... These observations are calculated ...

1168   ... *a(r) gúa-anta. Di têsta!* ... to frustrate opposition. Give this declaration!

1169   *Vee nee zóo!* Testify of him!

1170   *Vee nee zóo!* (Nona repeated this for emphasis). Testify of him!

1171   *Di zéem!* Give assistance!

1172   *Di têsta, (h)aróonta ef*. Issue a connected statement, because it will count.

1173   *Seena (h)ésta!* Pass the report!

1174   *Arq ántee têma!* Finish the whole thing!

1175   *a dóng!* Give a hand! (Imperative).

1176   *Zeen éftee!* Look into (his) judgments!

1177   *oo (h)éfan véet* ... These (statements) are to crush ...

1178 ... *gonn záma* ... the defects (weak points) and correct ...

1179 ... *a vrá-ntee* ... indeed, that which goes forth (in) ...

1180 ... *vee ʄ nêda.* ... the statement *he* bears.

1181 *Zeéna (h)éiran née ʄ.* Have a copy (of this record) made for him.

1182 *oo zen-tee oo éiran.* It will follow up (what) has been done.

This completed the first side of the gramophone disc. As on the former occasion, Nona appeared to know just when to stop, and did so several seconds before Dr Fodor's knock on the door gave us the prearranged signal that one side of the disc was full, and about to be reversed.

While this was being done in the adjoining room, the now deeply entranced medium placed her left hand over the microphone, turned slightly towards me, and spoke three interim phrases in a much deeper, more masculine tone than had been used hitherto. They were clearly meant to be an 'aside' to me, as my subsequent translations proved:

1225 '*Kòn-tee-sêna!*' 'You will amplify (make perfect), brother!

1226 (With a gesture) '*Azéen-ta!*' 'Look into this!' (Imperative.)

1227 '*Veen ist Féran(g).*' 'Testified, lo, has Pharaoh.' (Pharaoh has spoken.)

These three phrases are not on the gramophone disc, which was being reversed as they were spoken. Dr Fodor, however, wrote afterwards to say that he had heard them, indistinctly, through the headphones he was using while Mr. Day reversed the disc. The second was accompanied by an expressive gesture of the medium's right hand towards the small writing-pad in front of me, lent by Dr Fodor. I had already recorded a few notes at the beginning of the experiment, but Nona had restrained me with a movement of Rosemary's right hand, from continuing. I recorded these three interim phrases, however, in my usual way.

Dr Fodor's second knock having indicated that the disc was now reversed, and the machine once more in motion, Nona resumed her statement, with the voice at its usual pitch:

1183 '*ésti néeda téen.* "Take charge of this statement.

1184 *Don zeéma. Khêna* ... Cause to be published the facts. Ask ...

1185 *Doctor Fodor* ... Dr. Fodor ...

1186 ... *vá na (h)éstee.* ... to carry (retain in his possession) these records.

1187 *Aróoma, eest.* ... A responsible man, ... lo, ...

1188 ... *efn gérra!* ... has chosen to run away!

1189 *ésti néeda!* Make a note of it! (lit. 'Take charge of the statement.')

1190 *Di a hêd an véen* ... I will punish (cause defeat) to this (statement) ...

1191 ... *voo ʄ éiran!* ... that *he* made!

1192 *Di zóng-tee a(r) gúa la.* You will keep an account in order to refute calumny.

1193 *Di a éfan a(r) náza* ... I give these (statements) to tally (for reference);

1194 ... *di zêna,* ... and to place on record (lit. 'put in a box'),

1195   ... *erra góntee* ... ... to make angry (literal translation here) ...

1196   ... *óona. A-zéena!* ... the mistaken man. Make a copy! (Imperative).

1197   *Vee nee (h)ésta. A-dóon!* Testify of the report. Cause it to be (done).

1198   *Zeest a(r) néentee!* Write about these things!

1199   *Soot af éiran* ... It is a gramophone record (lit. 'plaque') made by ...

1200   ... *eenst–eenstitute:* ... the Institute:

1201   *nésa(t) a(r) gés ta: oo fées;* attached to the seal of, and in the presence of this (Institute); it is *hers* (Rosemary's);

1202   *oo fées af éiran nátee* ... It is *her* gramophone record, made to vanquish ...

1203A   ... *gésa qu ántee di véen a* ... uncertainty; and to attack that which has been testified, indeed ...

1203B   ... *nee éfan aróont.* .... of this, and to that effect.

1204   *Téka!* See ...

1205   ... *an(g)see véen a!* ... this retribution, indeed!

1206   *Di see péf ar ént.* Let his come (retribution) by evidence.

1207   *Nás tiya (h)óona!* Name, forsooth, the mistaken man!

1208   *a(r) hóoma véen* ... Verily, this gramophone disc (lit. 'circular object') ...

1209   ... *vée-st-ee* ... ... it will carry (it) and ...

1210   *Ver n ánt!* ... see to that!

1211   *o (h)ésta di kón.* Let this Report be amplified (made perfect).

1212   *Lêkha!* Learn!

1213   *Lêkha di déen!* Let understanding be given! (or, 'Understand and put this:')

1214   *Asée-foon?* What was it, indeed? ...

1215   ... *a(r) vésti di f éiran?* ... as to the substance (lit. 'backbone') of what he did?((or, 'What does it amount to?')

1216   *Vessta!* A mere bite, indeed!

1217   *Aróoma* ... (N.B.—Out of consideration for our critic, phrases 1217 to the end will not be translated here, but they are absolutely correct and forceful Egyptian. – F.H.W.)

1218   *Aróoma di Gúnn* ...

1219   ... *oo-ê-ga.*

1220   *ása!*

1221   *ása fónn* ...

1222   ... *toot a féren déen* ...

1223   ... *istia Gúnn! Kon!*

At this point listeners will hear my 'Thank you, Nona!' spoken into the microphone on hearing Nona's familiar closing signal. It was spoken to indicate that the experiment was over, and that the operators outside the room might stop the machine.

A hint of the bi-lingual was given by Rosemary as she returned to the normal: 'That message refers to the Institute in one place, and to our own case in particular,' she said. 'There is also a note of indignation at the difficulties you have had to encounter.' As the reader will have noticed, my subsequent translation – which took a fortnight to complete – confirmed these statements.

◼ ◉ ◼ ◉ ◼ ◉

Tutankhamun Today

The blockbusting exhibitions of the treasures of Tutankhamun's tomb which toured the world between 1961 and 1967 (USA, Canada, Japan, France) and especially between 1972 and 1981 (England, USSR, USA, Canada, West Germany) did a great deal to restimulate popular interest in the discovery itself. Most of the symptoms of Tutmania, which had last been diagnosed in the 1922–5 period, returned with a vengeance: 'Egyptian revivals' in fashion design, interior design and architecture; replicas, both expensive and cheap; books (this time round with colour pictures) by Egyptologists; mummy movies which were basically Technicolor remakes of the Universal Studios version of 1932; and assorted manifestations of the curse of the pharaohs – sometimes involving the airline pilots, manual attendants or curators who were involved in the transportation of exhibits.

Just before the grand opening of the 'Wonderful Things' (or 'Treasures of Tutankhamun') show at the Metropolitan Museum, in December 1978, the *New Yorker* magazine published a satirical 'interview' with His Royal Highness Tutankhamun, Pharaoh of the Eighteenth Dynasty, in which he was asked what he thought all the fuss and the hype were about. He was interviewed, said the *Notes and Comment* column, 'in the pale pink sitting room of his suite [at the Stanhope] ... sipping Perrier'. During the conversation the delicate sadness on his mask-like face was gradually transformed into something that looked like 'opening -night fever', and he began to come on like a post-Woodstock rock musician (quoting Shelley – like Mick Jagger in Hyde Park – as if he were the first rock 'n' roller):

'We did very well out of town,' he said. 'A million three in Seattle. A million four, give or take, in Chicago. Total US attendance may break seven mil. I'm nervous, of course – New York is *the* experience. But they've booked us into a class place. I stand outside the Met and think, Zowie! Look on my works, ye Mighty! I mean, they've got one of our temples *under glass*, man. It's amazing.'

What, asked the interviewer, was the main theme of the show?

'It's about gold, man. Heavy metal. I mean, I'm quite comfortable with gold ... But I'm not most people. Most people, they see a little gold that's not in a *wristwatch* or something – and they begin *shedding skin*, man ... Gold is the *main thing* but not the *whole* thing. This stuff is *old*, man. Time abolished ... and then of course there's the mummy thing, and the *curse* thing. We've got quite a lot going for us, really.'

But was the curse thing still functioning? In *1978*? King Tut replied:

'Well, when I walk down the street, I don't step on the cracks myself. The old let-the-hand raised-against-my-form-be withered. You understand, *I* placed no curse. You always have a panel of priests around wanting to slam a curse on this, a curse on that, I guess it keeps them off the streets.'

And what about the revival of Tutmania, and all the newspaper hype? Did these get on his nerves?

'They say that there's a Tut madness ... that the show has been overcommercialized. Sure, we're peddling a few little items. But they're class knockoffs, man – beautifully reproduced for the most part . . . The Frisbees, the T-shirts, the Tut beer mugs – I just regard those as kind of light, kind of kicky. I think of the show as sort of an ambassadorial sort of thing, don't you know. Sort of a goodwill sort of thing.'

Apart from the streetwise 1970s expressions, the satire could almost as well be applied to the 1920s as to the era of Gamal Abdal Nasser (whose government negotiated the original tours) and Anwar Sadat (whose government turned them into 'an ambassadorial sort of thing'). But unlike in the 1920s, in the late 1970s the whole question of the relationship of the cult of Tutankhamun to *contemporary* politics began explicitly to enter the agenda – in large part because of Edward Said's very influential book *Orientalism* (1978). As Said wrote:

'We mustn't accept the notion that the fascination with what is Egyptian is merely perennial and stable. In fact, the taste for Egypt and the images that derive from it are part of the political history of our time, as changeable and shifting in their meaning as any other of the icons with which our perspectives are propped up.'

Orientalism also encouraged a more questioning attitude towards the often-told story of the discovery itself. 'The nature of Egyptology is less about Egypt than it is about Europe,' declared Said, highlighting notably the discipline's tendencies to leave its own assumptions unexamined, to 'ignore the Islamic present' as it searched for the comfortably distant 'Phar-

aonic past', and to preserve a living Egyptian heritage (albeit a confusing one) in museum galleries devoted to the birth of *Western* civilization. Although Egypt joined the Arab and Muslim world in AD 639, none of the archaeologists of the 'golden age' (from Petrie to Carter) seemed to be aware of the fact, or, if they were, to be particularly interested in it.

Such controversial social and political questions were part of the reason why Tutmania was different second time around. Another was that the story of the discovery itself had become controversial, with the publication in 1978 of *Tutankhamun: The Untold Story* by Thomas Hoving, then director of the Metropolitan Museum. With great relish Hoving's book drew attention to what it claimed were the less savoury aspects of the story: the clandestine re-entry of Carter and Carnarvon into the tomb shortly after the antechamber had first been opened; Carter's difficult personality – at its worst when dealing with the press, the Egyptian government, and his own colleagues in the profession; the illicit removal of a handful of small objects from the tomb – some of which found their way, by a circuitous route, into the Metropolitan's collection (via Howard Carter, who was said to have removed them) and one of which was found near the site of the tomb in a wooden Fortnum & Mason's wine box; and the scandalous neglect of the Americans' role in the project in favour of the English Milord and his short-fused partner. The book became a best-seller, and more balanced accounts of the story are still busy replying to it. Yes, Carter and Carnarvon *did* re-enter the tomb (as Lucas publicly admitted in 1942 and 1947), but that was surely understandable in the circumstances. Yes, Carter *could* be very difficult at times, but he was working under considerable pressure, there had always been social tensions between him and the British Egyptological establishment, and in any case there were plenty of others behaving equally badly: the press and visitors to the tomb, the French administrators of the Antiquities organization and representatives of the Egyptian government of the day, for example. Yes, certain objects *do* appear to have been removed, but the likelihood (no stronger) is that they went into the *Carnarvon* collection and thence, eventually, to New York, rather than to Carter himself; in any case, the whole issue of 'partage' (as it was euphemistically called), or the sharing out of objects, became more and more confused between November 1922 and January 1925. As to the Americans' role in the project, yes, it was quite true that the important contributions made by the team of specialists generously provided by Albert Lythgoe of the Metropolitan had been downplayed in the interests of a more dramatic adventure story (as indeed had Mace's contribution to the writing of the first volume of *The Discovery*). And so on.

This heady combination of blockbusting exhibitions, high-temperature controversy and global politics, not to mention 'heavy metal', is examined in Peter Green's article 'The Treasures of Egypt' (extracted from his book *Classical Bearings*, 1989), and in Edward Said's article about 'the battle to depict Egypt', called 'Egyptian Rites' (from the *Village Voice*, August 1983).

Meanwhile, the issue of the *conservation* of the artefacts excavated by European arch-aeologists in the last 130 years or so, and exhibited or left *in situ* in Egypt – of how the international community can help with this staggeringly complex problem – has been promoted on to the public agenda. The team responsible for the clearance of the tomb in 1922–32 was, in fact, very concerned about conservation and preservation (Lucas and Mace were specialists, and very effective too), but the subject did not capture the public imagination then to anything like the same degree it has since the 1970s. And according to Dennis C. Forbes's article 'Abusing Pharaoh' (extracted from *KMT* magazine, a modern journal of ancient Egypt, spring 1992), this concern about conservation during the clearance itself does not always appear to have been extended to the mummy itself. As F. Filce Leek has written, in *The Human Remains from the Tomb of Tutankhamun*, from the field-notes and diary Howard Carter wrote at the time:

'It is easy to follow Carter's devouring passion for all the many treasures and artefacts found in the tomb and within the sarcophagus. It is also possible to feel his lack of interest in the human remains . . . This lack of interest is further emphasised by the unemotional entry in his daily diary for 23 October 1926, which reads, "the first outermost coffin containing the King's Mummy, finally rewrapped, was lowered into the sarcophagus this morning. We are now ready to begin upon the investigation of the Store Room [or Treasury]" '

The problem was that the physical condition of Tutankhamun's body – after it had been unwrapped and closely examined – made 'rewrapping' very difficult indeed.

It seems appropriate to end this section with an essay about the sorry state of the pharaoh's mummy, for amid all the hype and the glamour and the tall stories, it is easy to forget that beneath a plate-glass top and gilded coffin-lid, inside a quartzite sarcophagus in tomb number 62 in the Valley of the Kings lies the body (or what is left of it) of a boy who died at about eighteen years old – just as his wisdom-teeth were about to break through – in *c.* 1323 BC. The priests did not say 'rest in peace' in those days, but even if they had the interests of the science of archaeology – not to mention the press of the Western world – would no doubt have ensured that the wish was not granted.

PETER GREEN
The Treasures of Egypt
(1989)

By the time that the Tutankhamun exhibition closed in San Francisco, it had been seen by more than eight million people, almost all of whom had to apply for reserved tickets: the potential audience was probably twice as large again. Museum directors and their PR men have, in the past decade or two, become experts at what one critic nicely terms 'the techniques of hype and hoopla', the hard sell of cultural packages, from the Chinese show of 1973 to 1978's 'Pompeii AD 79': not surprisingly, since the windfalls that such happenings generate can be immense. The 'Tut craze' provided the biggest money-spinner of the lot. The New Orleans Museum of Art, for instance, let it be known that a 'minimum of $69.4 million was pumped into the New Orleans economy' in no more than four months, as a direct result of the Tutankhamun exhibition being on view there.

In the *New Yorker*'s 'Talk of the Town' column for 25 December 1978 there was an interview with Tutankhamun himself ('We found the boy king in the pale pink sitting room of his suite, wearing a Turnbull and Asser djellabah and sipping Perrier'), in which he was asked if his spectacle had a theme, and replied, with commendable bluntness: 'Yes, it's about gold, man, heavy metal.' So it was, and in more ways than one. When Robert Hughes characterised the art world as 'the last refuge for nineteenth-century laissez-faire capitalism' he was not indulging in mere idle hyperbole. The Egyptian government alone made about $7 million out of Tut's peregrinations around the USA and Canada, all altruistically earmarked (despite rumours to the contrary) for revamping the somewhat tacky display facilities of the Cairo Museum.

Yet this, clearly, was not an exorbitant slice of the cake. Ahmed Abushadi, press counsellor to the Egyptian Embassy, described it as 'peanuts', and is on record as saying: 'We didn't bring the show here for the money, or we'd have demanded a fair share of the millions made by cities around the country on it.' Heavy metal, indeed. It is interesting, too, that a large amount of the cash-flow came from what was labelled 'Tutsploitation' or the 'Tut glut': Tut beer mugs, T-shirts, tote-bags, stationery, posters, paper dolls, whiskey decanters, and, at a slightly more pretentious level, the replicas of Egyptian artifacts marketed, as an exclusive monopoly, by the Metropolitan Museum of Art. These ranged from simple ankh pendants or crook-and-flail pins to a slap-up gold-surfaced copy of the exquisite statuette of the goddess Selket, going for a mere $1,850, and unkindly described by Frank Schulze as 'neo-sleazo'. Museum boutiquefication in itself strikes me as a comparatively harmless trend, which has the advantage of bringing attractive historical designs within reach of almost anyone who can appreciate them. No one is forced to buy the grungier items, much less go broke in pursuit of limited-edition exotica. *Caveat emptor.* But a large market exists, and as long as it does, laissez-faire commercialisers will continue, quite legitimately, to milk it for their own benefit.

Attempting to film a 'Tutmania' sequence for BBC2's *The Face of Tutankhamun.*

This, of course, raises the far more intriguing question of just *why* a collection of grave-goods from the tomb of a minor, and in his own day little esteemed, New Kingdom pharaoh (*c.* 1343–1325 BC; dates disputed) should have 'managed to agitate almost the entire surface of American culture'. Not all the hoopla,

obviously, can be put down to clever hype and promotion. You need an intrinsically magnetic commodity to market in the first place. The stunning artistic quality of the Tutankhamun material has to be one major factor in the exhibition's success: but another, perhaps even more potent, is the prodigal use of what has always been the rare, royal, and ornamental metal *par excellence*, lustrous, indestructible, untarnishing, infinitely malleable and ductile, its smooth, soft, almost liquid yellow sheen a never-failing visual and tactile delight. *It's about gold, man.*

No accident, then, that the exhibition catalogue, *Treasures of Tutankhamun* (1976), the Met's more elaborate survey *Tutankhamun: His Tomb and His Treasure* (1976), and two publications sponsored by *Newsweek*, *Treasures of the Egyptian Museum* (1969) and *The Gold of Tutankhamun* (1978) – the latter the most sumptuous, scholarly, and exquisitely produced art-book to have come my way in years: lucky the coffee-table that gets it – all blazon the young king's famous gold-and-lapis mask across their dust-jackets, and give pride of place, in full seductive colour, to the other golden artifacts that cluttered his burial-chamber in more-than-royal abundance: statuettes, shrine-panels, daggers, sandals, and, above all, coffin-cases, of which one – the innermost of Tutankhamun's three – weighs no less than 2,448 lbs of pure beaten 22-carat gold. Two of these volumes even have golden end-papers. Their cumulative impact is undeniable. The contents of the Shaft Graves at Mycenae – gold masks and daggers there, too – look like mere provincial *Edelkitsch* by comparison. An art-book such as *Egyptian*

Treasures from the Collections of the Brooklyn Museum (1978), which has only one gold piece to offer – an admittedly exquisite fly necklace – and a limited range of other material, is, in a sense, subsidised by the Tutankhamun treasure-trove. This kind of cultural surf-boarding has also, inevitably, spilt over into popular fiction, complete with antiquities-smuggling, sexy female Egyptologists, and variations on the obligatory Mummy's Curse. Among more sensational finds, the Valley of Kings has also given the world a barrelful of romantic clichés.

The effect is all the more arresting, in historical terms, when we reflect that Tutankhamun died young, and that by royal Egyptian standards his burial was (it seems safe to say) a cut-price and makeshift affair: he had had little time to accumulate heavenly treasure. If *his* tomb yielded such wealth, what must have gone into those, say, of Chefren, or Amenhotep III, or Rameses II, the self-styled victor of Kadesh (1300 BC), the grandiose builder of Karnak and Abu Simbel? The depredations of tomb-robbers, mostly ancient, who made an almost clean sweep of the royal burials at Thebes, ensure that such a question must remain for ever rhetorical (though from tomb-paintings and documents we can glimpse something of that lost splendour): there is a nice eschatological paradox here, since the more visibly magnificent preparations an Egyptian made to ensure his own ultimate survival, the more liable he was to have his mummy destroyed – and with it, his chance of life hereafter – by ruthless thieves in pursuit of fabulously rich pickings.

A convicted tomb-robber was impaled through the anus; but the long catalogue of rifled burial-chambers makes it clear that many felt the enormous rewards more than justified the risk (which was, in any case, much reduced by the systematic bribery and collusion of court officials). Indeed, it is by pure luck that Tutankhamun's own burial survived intact. At least two near-successful attempts were made to rifle it soon after the boy-king's death: the thieves penetrated the antechamber but missed the inner sanctum. Then Rameses VI (d. 1134 BC), excavating his own tomb slightly above and to one side of Tutankhamun's, blocked the entrance of the latter with rubble, leaving it hidden – and forgotten – for three millennia. The sheer antiquity of this funeral treasure-trove, the dazzling glimpse that its priceless wealth and artistry offered into a lost world of wholly alien power and privilege, and – by no means least – the archaeological drama associated with its recovery from the silent earth; all these factors combined to ensure a powerful, and continuing, public fascination, not only with Tutankhamun (who, his relation to the 'heretic pharaoh' Akhenaten apart, was historically negligible), but with the whole enigmatic, yet extraordinarily well-documented, civilisation to which he belonged.

Even a cursory acquaintance with the diffuse modern literature on ancient Egypt makes it clear that the so-called 'Tut craze' forms part of a far wider, and older, phenomenon than mere gold-mania or archaeological romanticism, let alone the hype generated by a well-publicised travelling exhibition. Such

The author with American archaeologist Dr Donald Ryan, in the Theban necropolis – Indiana Jones lives!

Fagan as a 'surge of nationalistic lust for the precious and exotic' led to an orgy of looting, a series of treasure-hunts thinly disguised as 'scientific investigation' and carried out under the aegis of gunboat diplomacy. Private purchase became a well-organised and corrupt racket, surreptitious excavations and smuggling abroad of finds were a commonplace. Museums, too, carried on a brisk under-the-counter traffic in stolen antiquities, justifying themselves with the familiar argument that at least they were rescuing priceless material from oblivion.

Filming a facsimile of the well-known Camel cigarette pack for *The Face of Tutankhamun*.

things, of course, have their place in the overall picture: they are symptomatic of that persistent, acquisitive process of exploitation that began with the tomb-robbers of the Twentieth Dynasty and has continued almost to our own day, a colourful saga of amateur eccentrics, quirky obsessional scholars, con-men and rip-off artists. Sometimes, indeed, we find all these qualities united in the same person: Giovanni Battista Belzoni (1778–1822) is a nice case in point. It was Napoleon's savants who not only opened the way for the first scientific Egyptologists, men such as Champollion and Mariette, but also, at the same time, made ancient Egypt fashionable, with quite horrendous results. What has been well described by Brian

The excavation of Tutankhamun's burial in 1922 by Howard Carter becomes a good deal more comprehensible when viewed against this louche background: it is entirely appropriate that the latest, and liveliest, account of it – stressing the shady private manoeuvres as well as the public success story – should be by none other than Thomas Hoving, ex-director of the Met, main begetter of the Tut exhibition, master publicist, and (as several reviewers have pointed out, with heavy-handed implications) an entrepreneur whose own personality strikingly resembles that of his hero Carter (if hero is the right word in this context). Hoving reveals, *inter alia*, that Carter and his patron Lord Carnarvon privately, and illegally, 'cased' the inner chamber before bringing in any official representatives of the Egyptian Antiquities Service; that they were, to say the least, high-handed in their disposal of artifacts (what may be described as 'The Affair of the Lotus Head in the Fortnum and Mason Wine Case' is instructive here); and that they had, for some time, been involved in the clandestine sale of Egyptian antiquities to American museums. The minor inaccuracies scattered through Hoving's text are irksome, but do not invalidate his main point: that such behaviour was commonplace rather than anomalous. In obeying, all too literally, the Biblical injunction to spoil the Egyptians, Carter and Carnarvon were simply doing what all their predecessors had taken for granted; indeed, they were far more scrupulous than most. It is sad, but perhaps not surprising, that Carter, a prickly maverick who never learnt the art of compromise, was denied in his lifetime the academic recognition he so richly deserved; another minor scandal to add to the rest.

Archaeological curiosity, then, laced with a dash of romance and scandal, and floated on the Tut revival, may partly – but by no means entirely – have accounted for this recent Egyptological craze, and consequent publishing boom. *Publishers Weekly* at the time estimated a total of almost fifty Tut-related titles in print. To judge from a personal sampling, I would guess the overall tally to have been, in fact, far larger, much of it, significantly, in paperback. You could find titles galore (often reprints of works fifty and more years old) on Egyptian temples, archaeology, medicine, civilisation, daily life, art, chronology, hieroglyphics (and language generally), literature, religion, and magic: a lot of this material was both arcane and technical, including facsimile reproductions that looked marvellous and cost the earth. Who bought such books, and why?

At one level the attraction is obvious enough. Both the culture itself and those who rediscovered it constitute a powerful natural draw for the large audience of amateurs who insist on having their past perspectives dramatic, vivid, and larger than life. The process of rediscovery contains its own special lure. Not all Victorian Egyptologists were mere rapacious treasure-hunters, and the development of scientific archaeology on the Nile, in the hands of great pioneers such as Flinders Petrie of University College London, and J. H. Breasted of the Oriental Institute at Chicago, is in itself as fascinating and romantic a saga as one could hope to find. Today, moreover, refinements of technique are available that would have been way beyond even Petrie's wildest dreams, of which he had not a few.

Scholars today are even ready to bombard the pyramids with cosmic ray muons in search of hidden chambers and galleries: and there can be few more brilliant examples of scientific skills implementing archaeological retrieval than the use of the computer to reconstitute

Akhenaten's totally demolished and dispersed temple to Amun-Re at Karnak by matching up almost 40,000 recycled building blocks (and, incidentally, the reliefs carved on them). In a less spectacular, but no less effective, use of multidisciplinary scientific techniques, contemporary Egyptologists are expanding our hitherto sketchy knowledge of predynastic Egypt into the palaeolithic period, far beyond the Badarian and Merimden cultures of 5–4000 BC. Hence the attraction of books such as T. G. H. James's *The Archaeology of Ancient Egypt* (1972), an excellent piece of *haute vulgarisation* done by a first-class scholar for the general public, and primarily concerned, again, with the physical recovery of Egypt's past.

For anyone like myself, brought up in the classical tradition, where before 750 BC the literary pickings are nil, and even the archaeological evidence (despite show-pieces such as Mycenae, Pylos, Cnossos and Troy) tends to be sporadic, the sheer mass and variety of Egyptian material available from the third and second millennia almost defy belief: it reaches right back to the dynasties of the Archaic or Thinite Period (*c.* 3100–2778 BC). Scholars may debate whether Narmer and Menes (the traditional uniter of Upper and Lower Egypt, the first pharaoh of the First Dynasty) were one and the same man: but we have Narmer's personal cosmetic palette, and much besides, including ivory gaming sets, inlaid ebony boxes, alabaster vases, copper tools, and some surprisingly realistic portraiture, too soon thereafter to be fixed and stylised.

Perhaps more important, from the Fifth Dynasty onwards, *c.* 2400 BC, we have a considerable literary record for the Old Kingdom: funerary prayers, autobiographical testaments, royal decrees, the famous 'pyramid texts', other theological and didactic poems. When we move on into the Middle and New Kingdoms, the evidence multiplies to a staggering degree. Frescoes, bas-reliefs, statues, furniture, exquisite *objets d'art*, elaborate games and toys are reinforced by a wealth of military records, hymns, harpers' songs, school texts, love lyrics, and prose tales somewhat akin to those in the *Arabian Nights*. Nothing, it's true, even approaches the creative or intellectual achievements of Greek literature, and the prevailing tone – bureaucratic where not theological – in fact suggests a Near Eastern tradition much closer to the world of the Old Testament or the Hittite and Eblaite archives. But the age of this material alone makes it noteworthy; almost all of it predates the collapse of the Mycenaean kingdoms in Greece (*c.* 1150 BC).

The author musing on the implications of a 'Tutankhamun Theme Park', scheduled for tourists in Cairo.

Thus one most seductive aspect of Egyptian civilisation is the vivid, rich, and uniquely bountiful manner in which it opens up for our bemused inspection a world as far removed in time from, say, the Rome of Augustus as Augustus' Rome is from contemporary New York. The sheer hoary antiquity of Egypt was already impressing tourists in Herodotus' day, when Pharaonic culture was virtually a spent force. The initial appeal, of course, is that incredulous sense of kinship one feels across the centuries with these cheerful, humorous, energetic, and erotically inclined people, whose religion never got in the way of their pleasure, and indeed seems in many ways designed to enhance it. The beer-swilling artisans, the per-nickety letter-writers, the elegant, svelte, fashionable ladies, the ambitious bureaucrats and dedicated hunters, all come across (we delude ourselves) as the sort of people we know, and have met.

There is something a little factitious about such an attitude, as Didcrot saw during the brouhaha over the first discoveries at Her-culaneum. He commented, ironically, on the astonishment generated in an antiquarian, M. Fougeroux, by the fact that these first-century Italians actually used cooking-pots and table-utensils, just like modern men. ('Que ne s'étonnait-il aussi qu'ils eussent une bouche et un derrière?' he enquired waspishly.) In any case, it very soon becomes apparent that with Egypt the differences far outweigh the simi-larities; that this was an exotic (not to say freakish) culture, which demands a real effort of the imagination on our part to comprehend; totally conditioned by its surroundings, rooted in concrete particularities, indifferent to abstractions or theories as to the outside world, deeply suspicious of change, an early Shangri-La dedicated, with unswerving hedonism, to the preservation of the status quo up to, and above all beyond, the grave, at whatever cost.

To begin with, the country's geography and ecology were, and remain, unique. From Aswan to the Delta, Egypt's existence is wholly predicated on the Nile and its annual inunda-tion. South of Memphis the country is simply one long narrow oasis, never more than twelve miles wide, between burning desert wastes: an enclave in every sense. Rain is rare, and in Upper Egypt almost unheard-of. The sun beats down daily out of a cloudless sky; Akhenaten's attempt to create a kind of solar monotheism was logical enough. Control of the Nile – essential for human survival – demanded, and got, centralised, efficient, conservative govern-ment. A natural symbiosis grew up between Upper and Lower Egypt, between the red land of the desert and the rich black soil of the Delta. The predictability of the Nile flood pro-duced a stable agricultural pattern, together with a relatively advanced, but non-theoretical technology. The existence of the desert meant that Egypt evolved, at least to begin with, in virtual isolation.

The ever-visible, sharply drawn contrast between that narrow, luxuriant, unbelievably fertile strip and the barren sun-scorched land-scape encroaching on it must have given these Nile-dwellers a proto-Manichaean cast of mind. Their ideal life was, surely, seen as an oasis – all brightness and shade, music, cool-ness, good food and drink, love-making, the teeming bird-life of the marshes, colour, sensa-tion. Death, by contrast, will have been envisaged as the negation of all this; the parching waterless desert, bare burnt rock, the mirage at noon. We might have expected such a dichotomy to produce something more akin to the Horatian *carpe diem* philosophy of hedonism rather than the complex and *outré* Egyptian attempt to beat death at its own game; and indeed the trend existed. The famous harper's song from the Middle Kingdom tomb of King Intef advised men to eat and drink their fill, to make love, to 'follow your heart and your happiness', since death is the irreversible end of all men: you can't take your good things with you, so make the most of them while you're still here. This scepticism regarding both the reality of the afterlife and the effectiveness (for those who hoped to achieve it) of tomb-building – a scepticism shared, we may assume, by generations of tomb-robbers if by no one else – came in for some sharp criticism from more orthodox later poets: not surprisingly, since it ran flat counter to the whole observable pattern of Egyptian belief.

There are two options available to the dedicated hedonist. He can accept this life as a one-shot, and squeeze it for all it's worth on the grounds that he won't get a second chance; or, alternatively, he can predicate an afterlife that continues, indeed possibly improves on, this world's pleasures, and do all he can to ensure that he makes the transition with as little change to his enjoyable mundane existence as possible. The ancient Egyptians went, with quite extraordinary thoroughness, for the second approach. As has often been pointed out, they were not so much possessed by death as obsessed with life, and determined to pro-

long it, or a semblance of it, in any way open to them. Hence, *inter alia*, the mummification of corpses: the body must be preserved as nearly as possible as it was before death.

The contrast between the pathetic physical remains of Tutankhamun (the embalmers botched their job) and that magnificent funeral mask, one of the very finest surviving portraits from antiquity, or indeed from any period, is instructive: the true immortality, as some writers were aware even at the time, is that conferred by art. Yet from the age of the pyramid-builders on, a seemingly illimitable amount of time, money and skill was expended on the business of projecting this world's investments into the next: mummification became more elaborate, coffin-texts multiplied, complex ritual was reinforced by posthumous offerings. To an outsider all this must have looked very odd. The afterworld itself was endowed with all the functions of this life, work and sex included. Most of the gods seemed to be animals or birds: Ptolemaic Greeks had a derisive saying, 'Like an Egyptian temple, magnificent to look at, and inside a priest singing a hymn to a cat or a crocodile.' Egyptian myths contradicted each other at every turn, and no one cared to rationalise or reconcile them: it was all enough to drive a logical Greek mind to drink.

The Greeks in fact reveal two standard reactions to Egypt: derision and awe. These have more in common than is generally supposed, being both based upon profound ignorance. There was the potent mystery of the unknown, an awareness of dim and alien antiquity that suggested superhuman wisdom, the sheer colossal scale of Karnak or Memphis or the pyramids. There was also that astonishing theocratic conservatism which so appealed to moral authoritarians like Plato, and is most apparent in the visual arts: not only were painting and sculpture (and music, it would appear) wholly subsumed to a didactic-religious function, but for centuries their formal conventions remained fixed and immutable, with a firm ban on innovation of any sort. Such absolutism has by no means lost its appeal in some quarters even today: one more element of attraction to add to the rest.

Early Greek mercenaries, on the other hand, made a conscious effort not to be impressed. (No accident, I feel, that those Greeks who succumbed to the lure of Mysterious Egypt always had some pretensions to intellect, whereas the common man remained immune, if not actively contemptuous.) They cut graffiti on the legs of Rameses II's giant statues at Abu Simbel ('written by Archon son of Amoibichos, and Hatchet son of Nobody'). To the strange outsize creatures and gigantic monuments they saw they gave names designed to scale such conceits down to size. The very word 'pyramid' is Greek for a small bun of that shape. An 'obelisk' was a kitchen skewer or spit, a 'crocodile' a garden lizard. Ostriches they called *strouthoi*, i.e. 'sparrows'. The theriomorphic cults of cat, ibis or baboon were still attracting derisive comment in Juvenal's day.

But in earlier times a great deal of this reductionist nomenclature was, I suspect, mere whistling in the dark to keep up one's courage. For Herodotus, as for many later Greek writers, Egypt remained a place of marvels and magic, and a fertile source of fictional anecdote (e.g. visits supposedly made there, in search of arcane wisdom, by such figures as Solon, Thales, or Pythagoras). Behind the great temples, the sphinxes and pylons and elaborate religious ritual, lay (they were convinced) the immemorial wisdom, and more than human powers, of the mysterious East, expressed in hieroglyphs as potently symbolic, to a Greek eye, as they were incomprehensible. The quasi-occult myth thus generated has proved singularly resistant to progress or knowledge. Since Champollion's day, after all, scholars have been deciphering the hieroglyphic, hieratic and demotic scripts with increasing assurance and accuracy.

Today we have a very fair notion, based on extensive literary and iconographic evidence, of what these people knew as well as what they believed; and about the former, at least, there is nothing mysterious or arcane at all. Their medical records show the same mixture of common sense and sympathetic magic as we find in the Greek tradition a thousand years later. Their mathematical knowledge, far from being ahead of its time, was both primitive and pragmatic – though, as such, quite adequate to construct a pyramid with accurate mensuration. They were indifferent astronomers, far inferior in this respect to the Babylonians. They reveal themselves as masters of no lost transcendental philosophy: since they were unacquainted with the zodiacal system even their reputation as astrologers has been overblown. The mystical sounding *Book of the Dead* reads in places more like a Baedeker to the underworld than anything else, and its eschatological symbolism, though complex, is amenable to patient analysis. No great hidden truths there – and some remarkably silly spells.

Yet over a century of increasing scholarly light in dark places has completely failed to destroy the myth of Egyptian hermetic wisdom. A remarkable succession of occultists, numerologists, Pythagoreans and the like (satirised memorably by Samuel Butler in *Hudibras*, and known to Egyptologists, unkindly, as 'Pyramidiots') continues to promote any number of arcane theories, most prominent among them being the notion that the Great Pyramid of Giza was a kind of 'gigantic prophecy in stone, built by a group of ancient adepts in magic'. What is more, these fantasies command a large and apparently insatiable market. Another profitable element in the current Egyptological boom at once falls into place.

Whatever scientific critics may say – and most of it is pretty scathing – about such professional bagmen of fantasy as Immanuel Velikovsky or Erich von Däniken, there can be no doubt that these popular purveyors of pseudoscience – '*paradoxers*', as Carl Sagan calls them – have touched a most responsive nerve in the public psyche, and can therefore (like anyone else in that rewarding position) ignore their detractors while laughing all the way to the bank. The putatively transcendental qualities of the Great Pyramid are equally big business: one reason, perhaps, why paperbacks on Egyptology tend to wind up in bookstores among titles dealing with such topics as I Ching numerology, Zen, Vedanta, UFOs, the Bermuda Triangle, or works like Ouspensky's *Tertium Organum*. A half-educated age that questions all established beliefs will inevitably create its own crop of synthetic absolutes and instant folk-dogma. These are then sold to the unwary, packaged in a pseudo-scientific format that apes the external trappings of scholarship.

It's an ill wind that blows no one any good, and genuine Egyptologists probably have this trend to thank for the republication of many classic works that would otherwise be unobtainable – or, at best, prohibitively expensive. Who would have thought to find Budge's exemplary interlinear edition and translation of *The Book of the Dead* – or, even less probably, his invaluable, but highly technical, *Egyptian Hieroglyphic Dictionary* – available in paperback? It would be over-optimist to deduce from such phenomena a renaissance in formal Egyptological studies. The real giveaway is the absence from the paperback lists of Sir Alan Gardiner's monumental *Egyptian Grammar*: indispensable for all serious students, it offers nothing to the pseudoscientific fringe. A trickle of linguists doesn't float glossy reprints. The real market for these publications, it seems clear, lies with the would-be adepts who hope to tap ancient Egypt for anything from hyperkinetic energy to prophetic wisdom and, for all I know, the music of the spheres: for anything, in fact, rather than the fascinating culture that the scholars have actually unravelled. But then, for such devotees of the arcane, what kind of fun is public, non-hermetic knowledge?

The entertaining notion of the Great Pyramid as a predictive code-matrix in stone, to be cracked by enterprising numerologists, got a great boost in the nineteenth century from Piazzi Smyth, the then Astronomer Royal for Scotland, whose work on the subject – a masterpiece of misconceived mathematical ingenuity – was, ironically enough, responsible for Petrie's first youthful investigations at Giza. Brilliant scientists, like other men, can have their dotty obsessions: Sir Isaac Newton's astrological notebooks are quite an eye-opener. The trouble is that their reputations sometimes induce unwary readers to take the nonsense on trust. Mystical mathematics, as Pythagoras and Sir Thomas Browne knew, can be horribly attractive: in such cases reason is no deprogrammer. It took Petrie very little time to check, and refute, Smyth's theories: but as he said afterwards, 'It is useless to state the real truth of the matter, as it has no effect on those who are subject to this sort of hallucination.' I suspect that there are more of the latter around than one thinks (it would be interesting to inspect the sales figures of those publishers who specially cater to them), and that their perennial hunger for such esoterica constitutes a major factor in the recurrent 'Tut craze.'

Certainly the trade for the converted remains as brisk as ever. The Great Pyramid is still being touted as a 'blueprint for human destiny' (the Egyptians, of all people, cared not a jot for human destiny apart from their own, but no matter), while Egyptian culture emerges as (what else?) the heir to Atlantis, another splendid catch-all for dotty speculation; and the vulgar notion, so unaccountably popular with serious Egyptologists, that the pyramids were simply what their builders claimed them to be, i.e. monumental sepulchres for great pharaohs, is stigmatised as 'crankier than all the fantasising of the pyramidologists and the UFO freaks'. (Here we detect a characteristically modern obtuseness: it's assumed without question that to channel infinite energy, capital and ingenuity into such superstitious flummery as

tomb-building is the mark of a 'primitive' or 'barbarian' mentality irreconcilable with the Egyptians' supposed superior wisdom.) The collateral notion of the pyramids, or pyramidal objects generally, as a source of mysterious energy is also flourishing. Special pyramidally-shaped tents are very popular: their inherent forces can be harnessed, one gathers from the literature, to do anything from dehydrate meat to sharpen razor-blades (provided the latter are laid along a north–south axis). One adept even claims that half an hour or so in a pyramid converted his cat to vegetarianism. Tom Hoving had to fend off a character who wanted to embrace Chefren's statue outside its glass case, his object being to test the power of the life-giving rays that 'most assuredly emanated from the ancient divinity-being and would beyond doubt cure most, if not all, maladies of mankind's oppressed and feeble bodies'.

So it goes: every generation gets the nonsense it needs and deserves. One merit this material certainly possesses is that of drawing attention to the persistence, irrational optimism, and almost infinite elasticity of human belief. The otherwise sensible authors of *Egypt Observed* still cherish the old chimera of a 'mummy's curse' operating out of Tutankhamun's tomb, even though its prime disturber, Howard Carter, lived on till 1939; and the apotropaic furore over Skylab – with hundreds of apparently sane people making a concerted effort to raise its orbit by willpower – showed that the market for instant magic has scarcely been touched by the progress of science.

This is all a great pity, since the culture of Egypt was quite extraordinary enough in sober fact; to credit the Egyptians, in addition, with being the guardians, if not the inventors, of every sort of hermetic wisdom, arcane science, prophetic skill, and perennial philosophy merely detracts from what they *did* do. (The collected works of Bacon are an impressive achievement in their own right: why over-egg the pudding by throwing in those of Shakespeare too?) It is also seriously misleading, since it implies a gift for conceptualisation which was the one thing, notoriously, that the Egyptians lacked, and which constitutes their most fundamental distinction from natural generalisers like the Greeks, who couldn't rub two facts together without coming up with a hot universal theory. Jon Manchip White puts the case with admirable concision:

'The Egyptians were devotees of the concrete object: they did not traffic in speculations or abstractions. They were not metaphysicians but practical men. Just as they failed to appreciate the fundamental principles underlying their building, engineering, mathematics, astronomy or medicine, so they failed to interest themselves in the principles and possibilities of hieroglyphic writing. It would hardly be going too far to say that the ancient Egyptian dreaded theorizing and abstract thinking. He felt at home only with what he could experience with his five senses. Even his attitude to so nebulous an experience as death or survival after death was practical and positive. It is therefore not surprising that the Egyptian language contains no words of a truly abstract nature.'

It is easy to forget that Egypt's omnipresent bureaucracy got on very well without a coin-age; that surviving Egyptian literature contains nothing identifiable, in our terms, as philosophy, hermetic or otherwise; that the proliferation of irreconcilable Egyptian myths (which bothered no one in Egypt) strongly suggests the pre-Hesiodic localism of Greece before rationalising intellectuals got at it; and that the quarrelling of Egyptian gods (e.g. over the struggle between Horus and Set) makes Homer's Olympus look a model of genteel decorum by comparison. Horus at one point decapitates his mother Isis in a fit of pique, a fact eventually noticed by Ra: 'Who is this headless woman?' he enquires. Even Ares and Aphrodite manage a little better than that. No accident that Akhenaten's aberrant excursion (as his successors saw it) into monotheism and realistic art provoked so violent a reaction: both are symptoms of a nascent capacity, and inclination, for independent intellectual thought.

The natural focus of Egyptian civilisation (as the Akhenaten case forcibly reminds us) was not intellectual but theological, indeed theocentric. The power inherent in the god-king achieved its peak of faith during the Old Kingdom (2778–2300 BC), a faith that built pyramids not only as a memorial of great rulers, but as a 'palace of eternity' for the occupant. A spell on the wall of one Fifth Dynasty pyramid declares: 'A staircase to heaven is laid for Pharaoh, that he may ascend to heaven thereby' – an interesting gloss on Zoser's early Step Pyramid. The diorite statue of Chefren (Fourth Dynasty, *c.* 2580 BC) from Giza reveals this consciousness of absolute divine power in all its unquestioning majesty.

Originally, it was believed, only Pharaoh

made the crucial transition to a life hereafter. However, as time went on, and the aristocracy multiplied, and something resembling a middle class of craftsmen and scribes and other officials developed, eligibility for eternal life soon became general, while Pharaoh's own role, though as autocratic and theophanic as ever, grew increasingly politicised by a series of historical conflicts, including periods of anarchy and foreign rule, such as that of the 'shepherd kings', the Hyksos (c. 1730–c. 1580 BC). Yet despite such inroads of temporal interest, throughout Egyptian history almost all the surviving monuments and writings – the pyramids, the huge temples, the tomb paintings, the jewellery, the literature, whether imaginative or didactic – were designed for one single, dominant, all-obsessional purpose: to ensure that the dead continued to enjoy, in a paradise as like their previous existence as possible, all the amenities and pleasures of this world.

It is entirely typical of the Egyptians that, having once opened up a potential afterlife to anyone who could afford the necessary preparations – mummification, elaborate ritual, coffin-texts and so on – they seem to have applied only the most perfunctory moral sanctions over the actual business of admission. True, there was what the Greeks called a *psychostasia*, at which the dead man's soul or heart was weighed against the feather of truth, *maat*, with a hybrid monster known as the Devourer ready to put away anyone who failed the test: but there is no evidence to suggest that in fact anyone did fail it. Hell-fire had no takers in the Nile Valley. A written profession of innocence was an adequate substitute for the thing itself: bureaucracy triumphed even in

death. No other culture – except perhaps our own – has ever manifested so intense, persistent, and physically sensuous an addiction to the simple fact of being alive. The most common prayer for the departed is 'bread, beer, and prosperity'.

How many people got the pleasure? If we visualise ancient Egyptian society (appropriately enough) as a pyramid, how far down did the privileges extend? Further, certainly, as time went on: after the revolutionary upheavals of the First Intermediate Period (2300–2065 BC) the peasantry got at least an embryonic bill of rights, while the easygoing Egyptian temperament shielded workers from the grosser forms of exploitation. The myth of pyramid workers driven on under the lash is a myth only, reinforced in recent times by Goldwyn and De Mille: during the months of inundation peasants were only too glad of public employment. It remains true, nevertheless, that then, as in later ages, Egypt was essentially a monolithic two-class society, with the aristocracy, the priesthood, the court bureaucracy and some skilled functionaries forming a *de facto* elite, and the fellahin a toiling invisible majority, about whose lives and feelings we know very little.

The afterlife was a privilege that came expensive, a club with an enormous entrance fee. No elaborate burial awaited the peasant, but a shallow pit in the hot sand – and thus, natural mummification at no cost. Perhaps this was how the practice originated. The little *ushabti* figures in the graves of the rich, 'answerers' who substituted for the dead man when he was called upon to do menial work in the hereafter, are socially eloquent: we know the faceless underlings who gave such a notion currency. For the ambitious a certain upward mobility was possible. 'Be a scribe', boys are advised again and again. 'You will not be like a hired ox. You are in front of others.' Ancient Egypt had no monopoly of such attitudes. The *apparatchik*, the *petit fonctionnaire*, are perennial and ubiquitous: any strong bureaucracy offers them rich soil in which to flourish.

Perhaps what fascinates most today about Egyptian civilisation is, paradoxically, its static self-assurance. To an age of transient governments and crumbling creeds it presents the spectacle of massive energy, absolute faith, and virtually limitless resources harnessed, for almost three millennia, to a unique, unswerving vision of immortality and the good life. Further, what Eliot called the 'strong brown god' remains perennial, outlasting creeds and dynasties. Nothing can change the rhythms of the life-giving Nile, though ingenuity continues, as always, to exploit and conserve its gifts: the great pharaohs of the Old and Middle Kingdoms, who believed that bigger was better, and embodied that belief in memorable achievements, would surely have approved the building of the Aswan High Dam. Islamic Egypt is Egypt still: Nasser's funeral has a place beside Tutankhamun's, and we sense the continuum between them. When the last cache of pharaohs' mummies was shipped downriver to Cairo by the archaeologists, the banks of the Nile were lined with wailing women, and men fired off their rifles in salute.

By emphasising this sense of continuity, finely illustrated general surveys of Egypt serve a really useful purpose. Photographs of mosques, minarets, potters' kilns, *souks*, feluccas, desert tanks, and the crowded polyglot streets of Cairo and Alexandria are interleaved in a diachronic simultaneity with those of gravegoods, temples and hieroglyphs. Sometimes a modern picture, e.g. threshing spice crops, will gloss an ancient one – it is Egyptian tombpaintings, characteristically, that give us our fullest record of ancient daily life – stressing the changeless quality of Nilotic culture. 'To subsist in bones,' sniffed Sir Thomas Browne, 'and to be but Pyramidally extant, is a fallacy in duration', thus brushing aside the monolithic faith that could – and did – move mountains, and boasted a longer run for its money than Christianity has yet notched up. Here, surely, is the key to the current – and perennial – obsession with Egypt of the pharaohs. Nothing, in the last resort, not even gold is more insidious than unshakeable belief.

EDWARD W. SAID
Egyptian Rites
(1983)

Egypt isn't just another foreign country; it is special. Everyone has some acquaintance with it, whether through photographs of Abu Simbel, busts of Nefertiti, school courses in ancient history, or images of Anwar Sadat on television. Historical characters – Cleopatra, Ramses, Tutankhamen, among many – have been drafted for service in mass culture, and they continue to exist and function as symbols of passion, conquest, and wealth complicated by an exotic remoteness that remains attractive in the late 20th century. Yet curiously, because these figures have such a clearly outlined yet eccentric status, in their isolated distance from anything truly familiar, they also remind us how small and selective is our knowledge of Egypt which, after all, is a real place with real people possessing a real history. Nevertheless, Western representations of Egypt have a history too, one that doesn't always coincide with Egyptian representations of Egypt.

This is to be kept in mind as we try to unravel the dense symbolic web encircling the Metropolitan Museum's new Egyptian wing and the film series that has accompanied its opening ... Much has been written and said about these pharaonic treasures. Yet what hasn't been articulated is just as significant and certainly as telling. Above all we mustn't accept the notion that the fascination with what is Egyptian is merely perennial and stable. In fact, the taste for Egypt and the images that derive from it are part of the political history of our time, as changeable and shifting in their meaning as any other of the icons with which our ideological perspectives are propped up.

Egypt's astonishing historical continuity of thousands of years of recorded existence has regularly attracted European travelers, visionaries, artists, and conquerors, from Herodotus, Caesar, and Alexander to Shakespeare, Napoleon, and Flaubert. Then came the Americans – Cecil B. De Mille, David Rockefeller, Henry Kissinger. Its strategic closeness to Europe and the East has made Egypt a highly prized and much sought after imperial possession: the roll call of civilizations that constructed foreign policies around Egypt is virtually unparalleled in world history, although the Atlantic West and the Arab world together have played the dominant part in this continuing drama.

As a result, then, we can speak intelligibly and correctly of a battle not only *for* Egypt, but also for the right to depict Egypt. On the one hand, there is the Egypt whose symbolic, cultural, and political identity while African is nevertheless essentially Western, in which the country's ancient grandeur and modern significance come together in ways that are British, French, German, Italian, or American. On the other, there is the Egypt whose Islamic and Arab roles are in frequent conflict with its Western representations, which have often stressed the country's remote (therefore more attractive) past at the expense of its actual present. In the contemporary phase of this conflict Egyptians themselves have been divided in ways that are both surprising and interesting, since in the age of mass international communications they too have become participants in the contest over Egypt's identity.

Yet everyone who has ever been to Egypt or, without actually going there, has thought about it somewhat is immediately struck by its coherence, its unmistakable identity, its powerful unified presence. All sorts of reasons have been put forward for Egypt's millennial integrity, but they can all be characterized as aspects of the battle to represent Egypt, which somehow remains itself, aloof and yet inviting, distant and still accessible. To contemporary Arabs, for example, Egypt is quite simply the only *real* Arab country, society, people; in comparison, all the others are an odd assortment of badly put together postcolonial countries sorely lacking in the kind of genuine nationality that Egypt has. For in Egypt, it is argued, there are real institutions, real traditions, real civil dynamics; the crude posturings of puerile colonels and mafialike political parties are not long tolerated there, as much because Egyptian history instantly makes them look silly as because the celebrated Egyptian ironic wit – flowing confidently from the country's assumed historical continuity – wears them down. To Egypt has therefore gone the role of leader, naturally and irresistibly. It is one index of Gamal Abdal Nasser's Arab success and Anwar Sadat's failure that the former understood and exploited Egypt's Arab role, whereas the latter rejected it totally. And so in the Arab world the efforts made to regain (or shun) Egypt since Nasser's death in 1970 are implicit in daily political life.

But these matters are tangential where Egyptology and Egyptological interests are concerned. These are usually portrayed as European, Western activities. This is of course true up to a point, but it is also true that the nature of Egyptology is to some degree less about Egypt than it is about Europe. Consider that for almost two millennia European scientists, philosophers, painters, musicians, and poets created a fantastic myth about Egypt – its hieratic mysteries, its fabulous gods, its age-old wisdom – without even being able to decipher hieroglyphics, the language in which ancient Egypt recorded its own history. Mozart's masonic fantasies about Egyptian rites in *The Magic Flute*, for example, were no more inaccurate than the disquisitions of all the philologists and scholars who pronounced on the secrets of Egypt's past. Then in 1822, using the Rosetta Stone as text and guide , Champollion decoded hieroglyphics in one of the most brilliant cryptographic discoveries of all time. From then on Egyptology was put on a more scientific basis which, it must immediately be added, corresponded exactly with the era of high European imperialism. Thus it is perfectly fitting that the most readable and interesting of recent books on the history of Egyptology should be entitled *The Rape of the Nile* (by Brian Fagan).

As it emerges from the pages of Fagan's book, Egyptology's past is not an attractive one, and gives new meaning to Walter Benjamin's aphorism that 'there is no document of civilization which is not at the same time a document of barbarism, [barbarism that] also taints the manner in which it was transmitted from one owner to another.' For whereas Egypt joined the Arab and Muslim world with its conquest by Amr ibn-As in AD 639, none of the great 19th century European archaeological pioneers had anything but contempt or ignorance to show for that aspect of Egypt. During this period, however, some European scholars and travelers also developed an interest in modern Egypt, the greatest cultural result of which was Edward Lane's classic *The Manners and Customs of the Modern Egyptians* (1836). Nevertheless, the country was mainly available as a place to be ransacked for treasures and imposing ruins, a great many of which found their way into the major European museums. Although it was part of the Ottoman Empire, for most of the 19th century Egypt was in everything but name a European annex, traveled and raided – scientifically and enterprisingly – at will. Men like Belzoni and Mariette (Verdi's librettist for *Aida*) were heroic workers who endured unimaginable hardships in Upper Egypt as they unearthed, traded in, and transported a vast number of important finds; and Mariette in addition was a genuine scholar who, in the words of the catalogue for the huge Egyptian exhibit at the 1867 Paris Exposition, rescued ancient Egypt for Europe.

Nonetheless, their methods were those of marauding pirates encouraged both by a string of feeble and corrupt Macedonian Circassian–Albanian viceroys (whose last fruit was King Farouk) and by a profitable network of European museums, speculators, traders, and scholarly societies. Thus Egypt was bankrupt and lost title to the Suez Canal, as well as to an enormous bulk of its archaeological treasure by the time it was occupied by England in 1882. In stark contrast, the major European cities were decorated with imposing ancient Egyptian monuments showing off a languid imperial splendor, their museums exhibiting Egyptian materials that ranged from the minuscule to the gigantic. Yet, at the same time, an air of melancholy seemed to hang over those splendid Egyptological fragments. Somehow their funerary tone and the fact that their aesthetic was a neutralizing combination of embalmment and aggrandizement seemed also to highlight, or at least comment on, 19th century archaeology's inability to integrate rapacity with human interest. There is no more concrete equivalent of the inability than Flaubert's novel *Salammbô*.

And still the passion for ancient Egypt continued, given additional impetus by Howard Carter's discovery of Tutankhamen's tomb in 1922. To Europeans and Arabs, Egypt at midcentury was, however, becoming a more problematic place. It was a palimpsest of conflicting actualities, overlapping cultural spheres, tense political rivalries.

I spent a good part of my youth there and I can recall more vividly than any of my other early experiences the sense of a dangerously rich environment in which the whole place was steeped. The British occupation was nearing its end, Arab nationalism was beginning its big postwar rise, the currents of Islamic resistance were frequently and violently in evidence, and interfused with them all was Egypt's ungraspably long past, pharaonic, Hellenistic, Coptic, Fatimid, Mameluke, Ottoman, European. Cairo then was a wonder of places to grow up in, with spacious European boulevards and manicured suburbs – the products of what seemed to be a harmonious imperial vision drawing out responses from the city's innate majesty – adjoining colorful Arab and Islamic vistas populated by a rich variety of human types that spilled out of Egypt into the neighbouring region. To the south the pyramids hovered, visible in delicate outline on the horizon. I saw my first *Aida* in the very same Cairo Opera House for which Verdi wrote it, an ornate small-scale model of the Garnier Opéra in Paris; a traveling Italian company did an annual winter season in Cairo and Alexandria to a mixed audience of Europeans, smart Egyptians, and adaptable Levantines. Hardly half a mile away lay the great treasures of the Cairo Museum, supervised in its construction by Mariette and Maspero, a hulk so overcrowded and dusty as inevitably to suggest the irrelevance into which Ramses, Horus, and Isis (who lived on in modern Egypt only as Coptic first names), Akhnaton and Hatshepsut had fallen.

America's Egypt has very little in common with all this. Egypt is of course a polar opposite, an Old World with which the early American connections were at bottom romantic, mythological, or, if you prefer, ideological – not colonial, historical, or political in an ongoing concrete sense. While the British and French were excavating the Nile Valley, the Americans (among them Emerson, Melville, and Whitman) appropriated Egypt and its hieroglyphic culture as a mythical emblem which, the scholar John Irwin has written, was 'various enough to sustain almost any interpretation that man projected on it in the act of knowing.' The Metropolitan Museum of course acquired (and during the early 1960s flooded the buyers' market with) a large collection of miscellaneous objects, the biggest of which is the Temple of Dendur, entire. Until the postwar period, American travelers, some archaeologists, scholars, missionaries, and merchants were in Egypt, but there was never the large-scale investment there that characterized the centuries-old European presence.

This was to change, as the British and French ceded their Eastern empires to the U.S., which now embarked on an on-again, off-again romance with Egypt that the Met's exhibition halls – more neutral, minus the national context provided by European excavations – and its feature film series curiously but accurately symbolize. Cecil B. De Mille's *Cleopatra* (1934), an odd amalgam of one Shaw and two Shakespeare plays, was shot in Hollywood: Claudette Colbert was ill throughout the shooting, but, as if that wasn't enough of a problem, the historical models used for the film are unclear, improvised, stylistically unin-

tegrated. Little attempt seemed to have been made to ground *Cleopatra* in anything particularly Egyptian, or for that matter, historical, and the verbal idiom seems always to be alluding to rather than saying something. As one character puts it impatiently to Mark Anthony. 'You and your "friends, Romans, and countrymen"!'

Unbearably heavy, earnest, and long, *The Ten Commandments* (1956) emanates from a different world altogether. There is first neither the loose suggestiveness of *Cleopatra*, nor the floating but quite effective atmospherics of another 'Egyptian' '30s film, *The Mummy*. Every statement in *The Ten Commandments* is italicized; its scenes are soggy with significance and authenticity, so much so that one spill-off from the film was a book, *Moses and Egypt* (1956), purporting to show how all of the film's details were 'true' and historical, firmly anchored in the Bible and other unimpeachable sources: 'to accomplish the vast research work for the film, 950 books, 984 periodicals, 1,286 clippings and 2,964 photographs were studied.' It is difficult to know how much of this is bad faith, how much naiveté. For, secondly, *The Ten Commandments* is saturated with an ideology that no amount of sources and historical accuracy can dispel. De Mille himself was an ultraconservative literalist whose penchant for vulgar spectacle and titillating fleshiness served to promote a world view perfectly in harmony with John Foster Dulles's. Certainly his biblical films were an aspect of the American passion for origins, historical myths by which we explain ourselves with reference to a past that dignifies and makes sense of us. But the fact that Moses is played by the emphatically American Charlton Heston herds the Bible into line with an American national ego whose source is no less than God. It is perhaps worth recalling that whereas European countries sought their national myths of origin in Greco-Roman or Norse mythology, we have sought ours, like the Founding Fathers, in selected portions of the Old Testament, whose bloodthirsty righteousness and unselfconscious authoritarianism are both powerful and (to me at least) deeply unattractive.

Charlton Moses is also the American abroad, telling the devious wogs of the third world that 'our' way is the right way, or there'll be hell to pay. Two years before *The Ten Commandments* was released, the Egyptian revolution had occurred and, in its early days, it teetered between the Soviet bloc and the U.S. as arms suppliers; this was also the period when Egypt's new rulers (headed by General Naguib, who figureheaded the government whereas Gamal Abdal Nasser was really in control) were seeking some sort of working relationship with the U.S. Perhaps inadvertently De Mille's vision posed the issues with a realism that so angered the Egyptian government that it banned the film, which had been shot on location. On the one hand, there was a WASP Old Testament prophet who led his people following God and Conscience into a Promised Land conveniently empty of any inhabitants; on the other stood his scheming, vaguely Oriental foster brother (Yul Brynner) who had it in for Hebrews (and by extension Americans). Egypt was an oppressor, Hebrews were heroes. In the context of the time, with the creation of Israel barely eight years old and

the Suez invasion a few months in the future, De Mille, like Dulles, seemed to be warning Egypt that nationalism not vindicated by God and America was evil and would therefore be punished. Moreover, by some quick telescoping of history, America *included* Israel, and if that meant that Egypt was therefore excluded, then so much the worse for Egypt. The fact that Charlton Moses returns from his sojourn in the desert equipped with all sorts of technological tricks (a magic staff, the ability to work miracles, parting the Red Sea) simply underlined the point to contemporary Egyptians that Israel and America possessed modern techniques for dominating nature and other societies.

Like *The Egyptian*, another film of the same period shown in the Met's current series, *The Ten Commandments* is a historico-biblical epic at serious cross-purposes with itself, designed to render history beyond politics, yet undercut by both history and politics. The blaring trumpets, the vast scale, the cast of thousands, the insufferably posturing characters are made to coexist both with a dialogue that is hopelessly flat, dull, and spoken with a variety of different accents, as well as with a series of scenes designed to show audiences that people back then were human, small scale, 'like us.' Clearly these attempts at familiarity and hominess carry over into one of the Met's catalogues for the Egyptian exhibits, organized around the notion that everyday life in the ancient world actually did occur, and we can identify with it. Yet the overall effect is that of history rendered by displacement, not by accuracy, memory produced as a branch of forgetting and not as genuine recollection. This is an attitude to the past that makes sense only as an attitude of the present, an imperial view of reality that is unlike classical European colonialism, based instead on an imagined view of how the Other can be interpreted, understood, manipulated. It derives from an imperial power that is still at a very great distance from the realities it seeks to control, and while in a sense it removes from the past much of its inaccessibility and strangeness, it also imparts to the world out there a peculiar, if hypnotic, unreality.

Underlying the contemporary American interest in ancient Egypt is therefore, I think, a persistent desire to bypass Egypt's Arab identity, to reach back to a period where things were assumed to be both simple and amenable to the always well-intentioned American will. It is not an exaggeration to view the media, government, and public love affair with Sadat as part of the same desire; for as Mohamed Heikal says in his brilliant new book about Sadat, *Autumn of Fury*, the assassinated president-for-life of Egypt aspired to the role of contrite and reformed pharaoh which America was all too prepared for him to play. His policies, after all, were a vindication of *The Ten Commandments*' ideology: make peace with Israel, acknowledge its existence, and all will be well. If, in the process, Sadat lifted Egypt out of the present into an imagined timelessness, like an inspired moviemaker (or a dutiful provincial who believed in history as De Mille wished it), it would be 'the Arabs' (as in fact Sadat used to say) who would be the losers. Never was such an attitude more dearly bought. He was assassinated by men who thought they represented the true, i.e., Islamic and Arab, Egypt, and he was unmourned by

the vast majority of his compatriots who, Heikal says, were part of his lost constituency, 'the constituency which was naturally his as President of Egypt – the Arab world.' Heikal continues:

'Sadat was the first Egyptian Pharaoh to come before his people armed with a camera; he was also the first Egyptian Pharaoh to be killed by his own people. He was a hero of the electronic revolution, but also its victim. When his face was no longer to be seen on the television screen it was as if the eleven years of his rule had vanished with a switch of the control knob.'

Not surprisingly then, the Met's Egyptian wing and its film series silently illustrate a larger phenomenon – the difficulty of dealing with Arab and Islamic Egypt. This is an Egypt represented by Abdal Nasser, a third world leader and popular nationalist who, unlike Gandhi, has not yet found a place in the canon of acceptable nonwhite heroes. He governed Egypt and, in a sense, the Arab world from 1952 till his death in 1970, and although he had many opponents in the region (not least the Saudi Arabians) it is ruefully and quite uselessly acknowledged that much of the mediocrity, corruption, and degeneration of the Arabs today exists because he hasn't been around to prevent it.

Nasser was never popular in the West and indeed could be considered its archetypal foreign devil. To some this is a true index of how successfully he stood up to imperialism, despite his disastrous military campaigns, his suppression of democracy at home, his over-rhetorical performances as maximum leader.

Nasser was the first modern Egyptian leader to make no claims for himself on the basis of caste or blood, and the first to transform Egypt into the major Arab and third world country. He sheltered the Algerian FLN, he was a leader at the Bandung Conference, and along with Nehru, Tito, and Sukarno, a pioneer of the Non-Aligned Movement. Above all, he changed Egypt irrevocably, a fact that Sadat seemed incapable of contending with. How much of this history has never reached the mass Western audience can be gauged by looking at the films dealing with Egypt that come from the period. Apart from the pharaonic and biblical epics, Egypt serves as a backdrop for a Western suspense story (*Death on the Nile*), or a location for European love stories (*Valley of the Kings*), and World War II history (*The Desert Fox*); I know of only one film that tried to reconcile itself to modern Egypt, Gregory Ratoff's *Abdullah's Harem*, an amusing, somewhat coarse caricature of Farouk's last days, which it is said was produced with the active encouragement of Egypt's new revolutionary government.

Excluded from mass culture except as political events dictated its presence, contemporary Egypt was – like so much of the third world – fixed within an ideological consensus. Its appearances were regulated accordingly: Egyptians were warlike, their leaders bloodthirsty, their existence a collective anonymous mass of ugly, poverty-stricken, and fanatical mobs. Sadat of course changed all that, to his credit, although it is highly arguable that the present media fix on Egypt as big and peace-loving (otherwise a cipher) is much of an improvement. True, Egyptian political rhetoric and propaganda under Nasser were strident and, true also, the state dominated life to a very great extent, as it still does. But things were going on that one should be prepared to admit might be of some interest to an American audience not completely brainwashed of transistorized. There is the tiniest suggestion of this other Egypt in the Met's current series, Shadi Abdelsalam's *The Night of Counting Years* (1969), which is presented anomalously as a film if not about ancient Egypt, then about Egyptology.

Abdelsalam's film is deeply political and utterly topical and, I am afraid, will be dismissed as a rather heavy and brooding film about life among the monuments of the Upper Nile. The plot is simple: alarmed at the trade in antiquities, the government's archaeological commission, under Maspero, a Frenchman, sends an expeditionary force up the Nile headed by a young native archaeologist whose job is to investigate and put an end to the thefts. The time is 1881. Meanwhile we are introduced to a tribe of austere Upper Egyptians whose traditional livelihood depends on their knowledge of secret pharaonic burial places, from which they extract treasure that is sold to a middleman. When the film opens, one of the tribe's elders has just died, and his two sons are initiated into the secret. Both are repelled by their people's complicity in this sordid trade. One of the brothers is assassinated when his protests threaten the tribe; the other, Salim, finally communicates the secret to the Cairo archaeologist who thereupon removes the cache of mummies and treasure for transport to Cairo. Salim is terrifyingly alone when the film closes.

If they are looking for insights into archaeology, viewers of this film will be disappointed, just as it is likely that they will miss the connection between the film's gloomy atmosphere and the last years of Nasser's regime, a period of disenchantment, introverted pessimism, and, in the arts, a good deal of oblique political criticism. Abdelsalam said in a 1971 interview that when he made the film he was given much trouble by the Egyptian central state bureaucracy, and certainly the sense of hostility and alienation felt by the film's tribespeople towards the 'effendis' from Cairo seems to duplicate the director's own feelings. But in addition, there are several forces in conflict throughout the film; all of them are highlighted by the date of the film's setting, just one year before the British occupation, which transposed to 1969 prefigures the end of Nasser's fiery anti-imperialism and the onset of an American domination of Egypt consummated by Sadat.

First is the presence of foreign experts, like Maspero, whose ideas about Egyptian priorities (museum artifacts rather than peasant livelihoods) are dominant. Second, the Cairo class of modernizing elites – archaeologists, traders, policemen – who live in collaboration with Europe, and against their own people. Third, the population of piously Islamic peasants; their traditional occupation is conducted with ritual dignity, but it happens to be nothing less than grave robbery. Fourth, of course, is the consciousness represented by Salim, acutely aware of what is wrong and right, but unable to make any decisions that do not also bring unfortunate consequences; thus for him to live as a dutiful son is to break the law, but to turn his people in is to collaborate with the hated Cairo authorities. The fact that everyone speaks a deliberate classical Arabic, rather than any of the spoken dialects, transforms the dialogue from a language of communication into a language of impersonal exhibition.

This, Abdelsalam seems to be saying, is the Egypt that goes on under its official rhetorical blanket of Arabism. His film therefore is like a matrix of the major problems in which modern Egypt is involved, and out of which many more questions arise than answers. The country's European heritage doesn't jibe with its Arab actuality, its pharaonic past is too remote from its modern Islamic culture for it to be any more than an object of trade, the state's allegedly principled loyalty to the splendors of ancient Egypt is brutal in its effect upon daily life, and if, like Salim, one tries sincerely to reconcile the demands of conscience with the social realities of modern life the results are going to be disastrous. Questions: can Egypt's Arab role – during the 1967 war or the Yemen campaign – be of much relevance either to the country's impoverished majority or to its incredibly old pharaonic past? Which Egypt is, so to speak, the right one? How can modern Egyptians disentangle themselves enough from the world system commanded by the West (symbolized by Maspero and his Cairo associates) to pay attention to their own prerogatives without at the same time living in a fossilized pattern of arid, unnourishing barter?

These are some of the things suggested by the film, but the point I'd like to conclude with is that in its New York setting, as one of the items celebrating the Met's new Egyptian wing, *The Night of Counting Years* will probably seem like an odd and perhaps dismissable bit of local color. During the amiable lecture that preceded the Met's screening of *The Egyptian*, the presiding curator remarked that the 14th century BC courtesan Nefer, played in the film by Bella Darvi, anachronistically addressed her servants in Armenian. This drew a titter from the audience. But in a sense a solitary Egyptian film about Egypt – presented at the Met alongside Cecil B. De Mille's extravaganzas and row after row of mute archaeological specimens – might in fact be the same kind of intrusion as Nefer's inappropriate Armenian jabberings. On the other hand, it might serve to allude to another reality, only barely evident elsewhere in the commemorative exercises . . .

DENNIS FORBES
Abusing Pharoah
(1992)

Most everyone who, in their youth, discovered and devoured all three volumes of Howard Carter's *The Tomb of Tut·ankh·Amen* probably also pondered the full-face and left-profile double portrait of the head of the boy-king's mummy, attempting to reconcile the desiccated and crackled empty-eyed husk in the two photographs with the remarkably handsome features of the youthful ruler in life, as idealized on his golden inner coffin, the famous gold mummy mask, and numerous large and small representations of him from the tomb and elsewhere.

Looking at these two official portraits of Tutankhamen's mummified face published by Carter, one had no reason to suspect that the

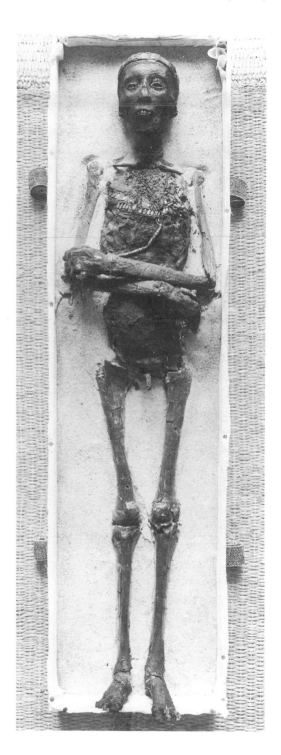

cotton batting framing the young king's mortal features in the Harry Burton photos carefully masked a hard fact: This head was not attached to the mummy's body. Tutankhamen had been decapitated – by none other than his modern-day discoverer and by a certain Dr. Douglas Derry, who assisted in the November 1925 complete dismemberment of the royal remains, in the course of the official scientific 'dismantling' of all-but-intact Tomb 62 in the Valley of the Kings.

The general world-public in the mid-1920s also had no reason to question the state of Tutankhamen's pathetic near-skeletal mummy, as seen in the official Burton full-figure photograph taken prior to the boy-king's October 1926 reinterment in KV62 – wherein the young ruler lies supine upon a shallow tray of fine grained sand, arms folded across his torso, stripped quite unregally naked, save for remnants of a crumbled bead-collar on his narrow chest and what remained of a beaded skullcap. Few who saw this photo at the time probably bothered to notice that the white sand in the tray – in which the mummy was partially submerged – mostly camouflaged the fact that Tutankhamen's head and limbs were detached from his trunk. Cosmetic retouching by Carter and Derry also hid the reality that the king's severed hands and feet had been reattached with resin to his wrists and ankles.

Sad though he was in this final official view, the last male of the Eighteenth Dynasty Thutmosid bloodline was then seemingly reverently rewrapped and returned to his outermost gilded-wood coffin, this placed once again in the great brown-quartzite sarcophagus left in situ in his modestly scaled sepulcher, still being emptied by Carter of its staggeringly rich treasure. There King Tutankhamen was to remain undisturbed for another forty-two years.

In 1968 the occupied sarcophagus in Valley of the Kings Tomb 62 was freed of its modern plate-glass covering and the first gilded coffin of Tutankhamen was reopened, to reveal the boy-king's pathetic mummy inside. A British expedition headed by R. G. Harrison, professor of anatomy at the University of Liverpool, had been given permission by Egyptian authorities to conduct the disinterment for the purpose of taking x-rays of the royal remains, which had not been done during the initial autopsy of Tutankhamen's mummy by Carter and Dr. Derry in 1925. Harrison's purpose in examining the mummy was to attempt to determine a cause for the young ruler's premature death. He and his team of Egyptian observers made a rather startling discovery.

First, the royal remains had *not* been rewrapped as Carter had recorded in his diary, but still lay on the sand tray employed to disguise their true state in Tutankhamen's official postautopsy full-length portrait recorded by photographer Burton in 1926. Secondly, it was clearly evident to all present – from the disarticulated condition of the mummy on the tray – that the boy-king had been decapitated and further divided into several parts: his arms removed at the shoulders; separated at the elbows and hands severed; his legs separated at the hip and knee joints, the feet severed; and his torso cut from the pelvis at the illiac crest. Harrison's subsequent x-ray of the trunk of the body revealed yet a further, truly puzzling fact: The sternum and frontal rib cage were missing!

Such condition had apparently escaped Dr. Derry's observation in 1925, inasmuch as the mummy's chest was thickly impasted with hardened resin, this embedded with minute fragments from a beaded floral-collar, which Carter did not attempt to remove.

World-press reaction to the decapitated state of 'King Tut' was predictably strident, Carter being accused by Kamal Al Malakh, archaeological editor of the Cairo daily *Al Ahram* of 'having cut off the king's head and packed it with other remains in a cheap sugar box.' Malakh was an official observer of the Harrison examination, although how he confused Carter's sand tray with a 'cheap sugar box' is not clear.

Following Professor Harrison's skeletal examination and x-raying of the head and trunk, Tutankhamen's fragmented corpse was reinterred a second time in his original outer coffin – still resting without dignity on Carter's sand tray – and the sarcophagus's plate-glass cover was replaced. There – hidden from the prying eyes of countless thousands of tourists who, season after season, pilgrimaged to his famous burial site as if to some saint's shrine – the sad earthly remains of the last Thutmosid male rested until officially visited one more time a decade later, in 1978.

In 1972 the Griffith Institute of the Ashmolean Museum, Oxford (recipient of Howard Carter's personal papers, notes and sketches, and Harry Burton's hundreds of glass negatives from the Tomb 62 clearance), published the fifth slim monograph in its 'Tut'Ankhamun Tomb Series', *The Human Remains from the Tomb of Tut'Ankhamun* by F. Flice Leek. Leek had been a member of the Harrison investigating team in 1968, assisting with the x-raying. His terse study includes extracts from Carter's diary, Dr. Derry's manuscript anatomical report on the royal mummy (with Leek's commentary) and, most significantly, numerous plates from Burton's photographic record of the remains, including fourteen unpublished views of the severed head and other anatomical details of the revealed and then disarticulated remains (one cropped, retouched view of the bodiless head had been published in 1963, but more on that below). These scientific 'record shots' prove to any of the interested general public who see them in Leek's volume that, indeed, the mummy of young 'Tut' had been thoroughly taken apart by Carter and Derry in 1925. The only New Kingdom ruler to have been found undisturbed in his coffins, Tutankhamen's is also the only royal mummy to have suffered so severely in the name of modern science and morbid curiosity.

The indifferent (some might even say sacrilegious) treatment of Tutankhamen's mortal remains went unremarked in the many popular book-length accounts of the discovery and clearance of his tomb, which were prompted by the traveling exhibition of choice KV62 treasures in Europe, the U.S. and Canada throughout the 1970s. It was not until 1990 that Carter's and Derry's deeds were attacked in print again, this time at length with specifics by a French physician, Dr. Maurice Bucaille, in his book, *Mummies of the Pharaohs, Modern Medical Investigations* (St. Martin's Press, New York). Dr. Bucaille not only details the Carter–Derry dismemberment of the king's mummy, he also attacks the blind eye which world Egyptologists and others in the know have cast towards the treatment of the royal corpse for over sixty-five years, even charging efforts of a cover-up on the part of renowned French Egyptologist and author (*Life and Death of a Pharaoh, Tutankhamen*, 1963), Mme. Christiene Desrouches-Noblecourt.

Bucaille charges that, because Carter realized his treatment of the royal mummy would be discovered by the public eventually (there were all Burton's incriminating photographs, after all), the English archaeologist,

'. . . exaggerated the damage to the outermost wrappings [of the mummy] by asserting in all of his writings that the wrappings and, by a false extension, the mummy itself, had spontaneously suffered from the attack of fatty acids supposedly contained in the ointments poured onto the wrappings [in antiquity] . . .'

The French physician purposes, instead, that the spontaneous combustion which allegedly carbonized the mummy in its bandages, was caused not by the unguents liberally applied in the ancient burial-rites, but rather because Carter had exposed Tutankhamen's unwrapped corpse directly to the Egyptian sun for several hours on two consecutive days (November 1st and 2nd, 1925), when the temperature reached sixty-five degrees centigrade, in an unsuccessful attempt to melt the pitch-like material cementing the body and gold mummy-mask to the bottom of the solid-gold innermost coffin. Bucaille writes,

'There can be little doubt that serious damage was caused to the mummy by subjecting it to such intense heat, as was seen when the wrappings were removed. It is now a well-known fact that heat causes mummified tissue to burst.'

He goes on to show how Carter and Derry – forced to 'unwrap' Tutankhamen within the close confines of his second and third coffins – found it expedient to separate the charred and cracked pelvis and lower limbs from the body's trunk at the iliac crest and remove these from the coffin, so that the thorax could be more easily cleared of the numerous funerary objects and jewelry covering it in several layers. To further facilitate this, the forearms were then detached (the many bracelets, encircling each forearm – eleven in all – could not have been slipped off otherwise). Because the back of the king's cranium was stuck fast to the inside of the golden mummy mask, archaeologist and anatomist next severed the head at the seventh cervical vertebra, leaving it inside the mask when the trunk (with the upper arms still attached) was freed from the cementing pitch on its backside by the application of 'hot knives.' This same hot-knife treatment was subsequently used to free the boy-king's head from the pitch adhering it to the backside of the mask. In the process the nape of the mummy's neck was pulled away, revealing the cervical vertebrae. What ultimately became of this royal tissue is not recorded by Carter/Derry (nor, in fact, commented on by Dr. Bucaille).

In his cataloguing of the physical indignities to which Tutankhamen's mummy was subjected during the 1925 'unwrapping' procedure, Maurice Bucaille overlooks the apparent damage to the king's ears. In the left-profile view of the head published in Carter's

The Tomb of Tut·ankh·Amen, it is apparent that the pierced left ear is fully intact. In later views by Burton (where the head is clearly totally separated from the body and held upright by a dowel-strut and nails driven into a wooden plank), the top half of the same ear is obviously missing. Did it, perhaps, come away accidentally when the gold temple-band was removed? And, if so, was this small bit of Tutankhamen simply tossed out with the mummy-wrapping refuse? (Or possibly pocketed as a bizarre souvenir?) The right ear in Burton's photos seems inexplicably mostly gone (the top portion and lobe are missing); and, when the king's severed head was photographed most recently, in 1978, this right ear appeared to be gone altogether.

In his controversial 1978 exposé, *Tutankhamun, The Untold Story*, Thomas Hoving waxed over Carter's reaction to the young king's countenance when this was finally revealed:

'To Howard Carter, the royal visage was placid, the features well-formed. The King must have been handsome beyond belief. As he held the head in his hands, Carter was suddenly transported to the time when the young, vibrant King still lived. He was profoundly shaken by the experience.'

Since Carter himself did not write that he was 'transported' or 'profoundly shaken,' on beholding the royal visage, one wonders how Hoving determined this. (But then, the credibility of the former director of the Metropolitan Museum of Art is suspect, when he informs his readers that the 'body [of Tutankhamen] was naked but for three decorations: the toes were encased in gold sheaths, as were the fingers and the King's penis.' Why did Carter not mention this gold penis sheath? And where is it today, if it existed at all in 1925? Another 'souvenir' perhaps?)

For Maurice Bucaille, Thomas Hoving is but one of many knowledgeable commentators 'in Egyptological circles' who have glossed over the evident Carter–Derry abuse of Tutankhamen's corpse. He holds a special grudge towards French Egyptologist Christiene Desrouches-Noblecourt, however, blaming her for having advanced Carter's 'false thesis' regarding the so-called ointment-ruined mummy 'in a spectacular manner.' Since Desrouches-Noblecourt had full access to the Griffith Institute materials concerning the mummy's examination (including Burton's telltale photographs) when she was researching her own work on Tutankhamen, Bucaille is persuaded that she knew very well 'that Carter had blatantly lied' about his slicing up of the boy-king's remains. Bucaille is particularly incensed by the 'reproduction of the head of the pharaoh, carefully faked in her book,' as Figure 134 in *Life and Death of a Pharaoh* is cleverly cropped to hide the fact of decapitation and the dowel propping up the head in Burton's original photo has been retouched out of existence.

Returning now to the official British re-examination of the Tutankhamen remains in 1968, R. G. Harrison's x-rays of the head and thorax revealed that the young king had, in fact, been treated somewhat unkindly by his ancient embalmers (Carter and Derry had earlier noted that Tutankhamen's scalp was most peculiarly shaven, covered with a white 'fatty' substance overlaid by a beaded skullcap). The broad, flat-topped, longish skull was found to be empty (the brain having been removed in the embalming process, as was normal procedure), except for two thick deposits of opaque material, probably solidified liquid resin which had likely been introduced into the skull cavity through the nasal passage. One of these was at the back of the skull, as would have naturally occurred with the king's corpse lying supine at the time of the resin's injection. The other deposit was at the top of the skull, however, causing Leek to speculate that the king had been suspended upside down when this resinous liquid was introduced. A strange way to treat a god-king, even a teenaged dead one!

Stranger still, however, is the fact of the missing sternum and frontal ribs, removed apparently at the time Tutankhamen was embalmed. But why? Was the young ruler's chest somehow crushed accidentally, resulting in his death? What would have become of this extracted boney material, its removal disguised by the thick impasto of resin coating the mummy's frontal thorax. As part of the sacred body of a god-king, whose 'anatomic integrity' (to quote Dr. Bucaille) was all important for his eternal existence, these bones would surely not have been simply discarded along with the royal brain and other nonessential internal tissues. Might they remain separately secreted still in some unknown Kings Valley cache?

Although it is apparently common knowledge among professional Egyptologists, it has never been published (that this writer can determine) that when Professor Harrison and team examined poor Tutankhamen in 1968, they were particularly surprised to note an ulti-mate desecration of the royal remains: The boy-king's penis was missing! As its presence is clearly evident in Burton's final full-length photo-portrait on the sand tray, it has to be surmised that someone snapped off the mummified member before Tutankhamen was reinterred the first time, in 1926. Does a collector somewhere secretly show off this ghoulish pharaonic trophy?

Because the Harrison–Leek x-ray of Tutankhamen's skull was of somewhat inferior quality – especially in clearly displaying the young ruler's dentition – American orthodontist and royal-mummy expert James E. Harris (*X-Raying the Pharaohs* and *X-Ray Atlas of the Royal Mummies*) was granted permission by the Egyptian Antiquities authorities to disinter Tutankhamen for yet a third time, in 1978. Photographs taken during this one-day mission (with Egyptian officials and other observers in attendance) show still further damage to the battered last Thutmosid: The King's eyesockets have collapsed (or been pushed in?), so that the once-open lids (with long lashes originally still visible) are now gone; and, as mentioned above, the right ear is entirely missing. Also, the remains generally seem ever blacker, more charred-looking (Derry's report described the mummy's skin as grayish in color). Perhaps Nebkheprure Tutankhamen is slowly self-destructing.

With the numerous royal mummies housed today in the Egyptian Museum, Cairo, so carefully guarded that removal of even miniscule tissue samples for the purpose of DNA testing is not allowed – and with several of the more attractively preserved individuals hermetically sealed now in new Getty Conservation

Institute-designed glass display cases – it is most ironic (and not a little sad) that the one New Kingdom pharaoh who – through luck of the draw – escaped the tomb robbers of antiquity lies today carbonized, denuded, dismembered, emasculated and disintegrating in his downscale rock-cut sepulcher emptied by modern dismantlers in the name of knowledge and science.

A New Hypothesis for Tutankhamen's Early Demise

There has been much speculation over the past seventy years as to why Nebkheprure Tutankhamen died prematurely, as a senior teenager according to most modern medical-opinion. Although life expectancy was not great in ancient Egypt (one was fortunate to survive past the mid-thirties), and young Tutankhamen came at the end of a long dynasty whose gene pool may have been somewhat depleted by his day (he was clearly not a robust individual), it is 'unromantic' to accept that he expired from 'natural causes.'

The political turmoil of the time was ripe for this son of the Aten Heresy to have been conveniently eliminated through palace intrigue and quiet coup – with Tutankhamen's first successor, the aged non-royal courtier Ay, and the next-in-line, ambitious regent Horemheb, as best candidates for the guilty parties if the teenage ruler was murdered.

Because the young king's mummy evidences a large roundish lesion on the left cheek, over the jawbone near the ear, it has been frequently suggested that he was victim of some pointed instrument being driven into his head (while sleeping, as one novelist had it). Fine and good, except that the jawbone seems an unlikely spot to inflict a fatal wound; a temple or anywhere else on the cranium would be a far better target if attempting to dispatch an unresisting victim by thrusting a spike into his head. Besides, the lesion contains scabious material, indicating that, whatever its cause, this 'wound' was healing at the time Tutankhamen died.

More intriguing as a probable cause for the king's early demise is the fact – learned in 1968, when his torso was x-rayed for the first time – that the mummy lacks a sternum (breastbone) and the frontal ribcage. Since one does not reach his teenage years with such a congenital deformity, it has to be assumed that these bones and cartilage were removed after Tutankhamen's death, during the embalming process. Why would this be done, however, unless they were severely damaged (and thus imperfect)? And how would they be damaged, unless the young king's chest had been crushed, presumably accidentally (it is hard to imagine either Ay or Horemheb dropping a boulder on the royal youth's chest while he slept)? If crushed accidentally, under what circumstances? is the next question.

Judging from the several extant representations of Tutankhamen in a speeding hunting chariot, it is thought that (like his twice-removed predecessor, Amenhotep III, in the latter's own youth) Nebkheprure was an avid sportsman and charioteer – driving his team himself, reins wrapped around his waist to free up his hands for use of a bow, boomerang or javelin, as appropriate to the game pursued.

The following scenario is, therefore, proposed: Tutankhamen and a group of equally chase-avid courtiers are racing their light hunting chariots across the desert plateau near the northern capital, Mennufer (Memphis), in hot pursuit of fleeing prey (let it be a lion pride for drama's sake). As the royal sportsman closes on his selected target, the beast abruptly changes course. In attempting to correct his chariot team's thundering trajectory, the king loses his footing and is suddenly thrown from his vehicle, the reins around his waist restraining his catapult, so that he is dragged alongside the speeding chariot, and then, struggling to free himself, under the moving wheel. Before horrified courtiers and attendents can overtake and bring the royal team to a halt, Tutankhamen has been repeatedly run over by the floundering lightweight chariot, his narrow chest crushed beneath the mail corslet he is wearing. Still alive, though undoubtedly unconscious, Horus Nebkheprure is carried back to the Royal Residence, where he languishes in a coma (distraught Great Royal Wife Ankhesenamen at his beside) long enough before finally expiring to permit a cheek wound sustained in the accident to begin to heal. Far fetched? I think not.

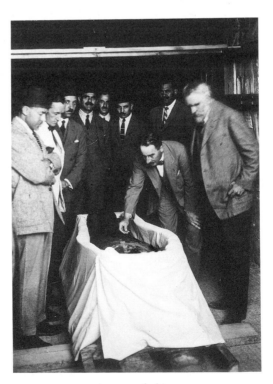

Autopsy of a king.

SELECT BIBLIOGRAPHY

Primary Sources

Howard Carter's unpublished 'notes towards an autobiography' (John Carter collection); Lord Carnarvon's unpublished account of the opening of the tomb (Metropolitan Museum, New York); Minnie Burton's diary (Rosalind Berwald collection); *The Times, New York Times, Morning Post, Daily Express, Daily Mail, Illustrated London News, Vogue, Punch*; notes and records (mainly by Carter and Mace) held by the Griffith Institute, Oxford; Harry Burton's and Arthur Weigall's photographs (also in the Griffith Institute).

Secondary Sources

The Discovery and Clearance of the Tomb of Tutankhamun

Aldred, C., *Tutankhamun's Egypt* (London, 1972)

Andrews, C., *Egyptian Mummies* (London, 1984)

Bernal, M., *Black Athena* (London, 1987)

Breasted, C., *Pioneer to the Past: The Story of James H. Breasted* (New York, 1943)

Breasted, J. H., 'Some Experiences in the Tomb of Tutankhamon' (*Art and Archeology*, XVII, January–February 1924)

Budge, E. A. W., *The Egyptian Book of the Dead* (London, 1895)

– *Egyptian Magic* (London, 1901)

Tutankhamen, Amenism, Atenism and Egyptian Monotheism (London, 1923)

Burton, H., 'The Late Theodore Davis's Excavations at Thebes' (*Bulletin of the Metropolitan*, XI, 1916)

Capart, J., *The Tomb of Tutankhamen* (London, 1923)

Carnarvon, Lord, and H. Carter, *Five Years' Exploration at Thebes: A Record of Work Done, 1907–1911* (Oxford, 1912)

Carter, H., 'A Tomb Prepared for Queen Hatshepsuit and Other Recent Discoveries at Thebes' (*Journal of Egyptian Archaeology*, IV, 1917)

– *The Discovery of the Tomb of Tutankhamen*, Vol. 3 (London, 1933)

Carter, H. and A. C. Mace, *The Discovery of the Tomb of Tutankhamen*, Vol. 1, (London, 1923)

Carter, H. and P. White, *The Discovery of the Tomb of Tutankhamen*, Vol. 2 (London, 1927)

Ceram, E. W., *Gods, Graves and Scholars* (London, 1967)

Cone, P. (ed.), *The Discovery of Tutankhamun's Tomb* (New York, 1976)

Cromer, Earl of, *Modern Egypt*, 2 vols.

(London, 1908)

Davis, T. *et. al.*, *The Tombs of Harmhabi and Touatånkhamanou* (London, 1912)

Desroches-Noblecourt, C., *Tutankhamen: Life and Death of a Pharaoh* (London, 1963)

Drower, M., *Flinders Petrie: A Life in Archaeology* (London, 1985)

Edwards, A. E., *One Thousand Miles up the Nile* (London, 1877)

– *Pharaohs, Fellahs and Explorers* (London, 1892)

Edwards, I. E. S., *Treasurers of Tutankhamun* (London, 1978)

Field, H., *The Track of Man* (London, 1955)

Gardiner, A. H., *My Working Years* (London, 1962)

Harrison, R. G., 'Post-mortem on Two Pharaohs' (*Buried History*, 1972)

– 'Tutankhamun's Post-mortem' (*Lancet*, 1973)

Hoving, T., *Tutankhamun: The Untold Story* (New York, 1978)

James, T. G. H., *The British Museum and Ancient Egypt* (London, 1983)

– *Howard Carter: The Path to Tutankhamun* (London, 1992)

James, T. G. H. (ed.), *Excavating in Egypt* (London, 1982)

Lee, C. C., *The Grand Piano Came by Camel: The Story of Arthur Mace and His Family* (Lochwinnock, 1989)

Leek, F. F., *The Human Remains from the Tomb of Tut'Ankhamun* (Oxford, 1972)

Lucas, A., 'Notes on Some Objects from the Tomb of Tutankhamen' (*Annales du Service des Antiquités de l'Egypte*, 42, 1942)

– 'Notes on Some Objects from the Tomb of Tutankhamen' (*Annales du Service des Antiquités de l'Egypte*, 45, 1947)

Mace, A. C., 'Work at the Tomb of Tutenkamon' (*Bulletin of the Metropolitan*, supplement, December 1923)

Macquoid, K. S., *Julia Kavanagh and Amelia Edwards* (London, 1897)

Maspero, G., *Egyptian Archaeology* (London, 1887)

– *Egypt: Ancient Sites and Modern Scenes* (London, 1910)

Metropolitan Museum, 'The Carnarvon Egyptian Collection' (*Bulletin of the Metropolitan*, 22, 1927)

– *Wonderful Things: The Discovery of Tutankhamun's Tomb* (New York, 1976)

Reeves, N., *Tutankhamun: A Pocket Guide* (London, 1987)

– *Ancient Egypt at Highclere Castle* (Highclere, 1989)

– *The Complete Tutankhamun* (London, 1990)

– *Valley of the Kings* (London, 1990)

Romer, J., *Valley of the Kings* (London, 1981)

Ryan, D., 'Who is Buried in KV60?' (*KMT Journal*, 1989)

– 'Return to Wadi Biban El Moluk' (*KMT Journal*, 1991)

– 'The Valley Again' (*KMT Journal*, spring 1992)

Smith, G. Elliot, *Tutankhamem and the Discovery of His Tomb* (London, 1923)

Weigall, A., *The Life and Times of Akhnaton* (London, 1922)

– *Tutankhamen and Other Essays* (London, 1923)

– *A History of the Pharaohs* (New York, 1925)

Winstone, A. V. F., *Howard Carter and the Discovery of Tutankhamun* (London, 1991)

The Reception of the Discovery

Achad, F., *The Egyptian Revival* (Illinois, 1926)

Albrecht, D., *Designing Dreams* (London, 1987)

Ash, C. van and E. S. Rohmer, *Master of Villainy* (London, 1972)

Atwell, D., *Cathedrals of the Movies* (London, 1980)

Battersby, M., *The Decorative Twenties* (London, 1969)

– *The Decorative Thirties* (London, 1971)

Beaver, H. (ed.), *The Science Fiction Stories of Edgar Allan Poe* (London, 1976)

Blackwood, A., *Tales of the Supernatural* (Suffolk, 1985)

Boschot, A., *Le Roman de la Momie de Théophile Gautier* (Paris, 1955)

Brownlow, K., *Hollywood: The Pioneers* (London, 1979)

Brunton, P., *A Search in Secret Egypt* (London, 1935)

Bullock, G., *Marie Corelli* (London, 1940)

Carter, L., *Lovecraft* (London, 1972)

'Cheiro', *Real Life Stories* (London, 1934)

Cohen, M., *Rider Haggard: His Life and Work* (London, 1968)

Conner, P., *Oriental Architecture in the West* (London, 1979)

– *The Inspiration of Egypt* (Brighton, 1983)

Crowley, A., *Confessions* (London, 1979)

Curl, J. S., *The Egyptian Revival* (London, 1982)

– *The Art and Architecture of Freemasonry* (London, 1991)

Dalby, R., *Bram Stoker: A Bibliography of First Editions* (London, 1983)

Deslandres, Y., *Poiret* (London, 1987)

El Mahdy, C., *Mummies, Myth and Magic* (London, 1989)

Fagan, B., *The Rape of the Nile* (New York, 1975)

Fitzsimons, R., *Death and the Magician* (London, 1980)

Forman, M., 'Tutmania' (*Dress*, 4, 1978)

Frayling, C., 'Sax Rohmer and the Devil Doctor' (*London Magazine*, June–July 1973)

– *Dreams of Dead Names*, in *Necronomicon*, ed. G. Hay (Jersey, 1978)

Gabardi, M., *Art Deco Jewellery* (Suffolk, 1989)

Gautier, T. (tr. F. G. Monkshood), *The Mummy's Romance* (London, 1908)

Gibson, W. B., *Houdini's Escapes* (New Jersey, 1931)

Gifford, D., *Movie Monsters* (London, 1969)

Graves, R. and A. Hodge, *The Long Weekend* (London, 1940)

Green, P., *Classical Bearings* (London, 1989)

Haining, P., *The Mummy* (London, 1988)

Halliwell, L., *The Dead that Walk* (London, 1986)

Hammerton, J. (ed.), *Wonders of the Past*, 3 vols. (London, 1925)

Haslam, M. (ed.), *The Amazing Bugattis* (London, 1979)

Higgins, D. S. (ed.), *The Private Diaries of Sir Henry Rider Haggard* (London, 1980)

Hillier, B., *The World of Art Deco* (New York, 1971)

– *Art Deco* (London, 1985)

Howell, G., *In Vogue* (London, 1975)

Hughes-Hallett, L., *Cleopatra* (London, 1990)

Hulme, A. J. H. and F. H. Wood, *Ancient Egypt Speaks* (London, 1937)

Klein, D. and N. McClelland, *In the Deco Style* (London, 1987)

Knight, D. R. and A. D. Sabey, *The Lion Roars at Wembley* (Barnet, 1984)

Lant, A., 'The Curse of the Pharaoh' (*October*, spring 1992)

Lindon Smith, J., *Tombs, Temples and Ancient Art* (Oklahoma, 1956)

Ludlam, H., *A Biography of Dracula* (London, 1962)

Mandelbaum, H., *Screen Deco* (Kent, 1985)

Mitchell, T., *Colonising Egypt* (Cambridge, 1988)

Mullen, C., *Cigarette Pack Art* (London, 1979)

Nelson, E. H., *Out of the Silence: The Story of 'Cheiro'* (London, c. 1940)

Nevins, F. M. (ed.), *The Mystery Writer's Art* (Bowling Green, 1970)

Nochlin, L., *The Imaginary Orient* in *The Politics of Vision* ed. L. Nochlin (London, 1991)

Nordon, P., *Conan Doyle* (London, 1966)

Praz, M., *The Romantic Agony* (Oxford, 1970)

Richardson, J., *Théophile Gautier: His Life and Times* (London, 1958)

Riley, P. J., (ed.), *Universal Pictures' 'The Mummy'* (New Jersey, 1989)

Rohmer, S., *The Romance of Sorcery* (New York, 1970)

Said, E., *Orientalism* (London, 1978)

Sattin, A., *Lifting the Veil: British Society in Egypt* (London, 1988)

Sprague de Camp, L. and C., *Citadels of Mystery* (London, 1965)

Tompkins, P., *The Magic of Obelisks* (New York, 1981)

Tudor, A., *Monsters and Mad Scientists* (Oxford, 1989)

Vandenburg, P., *The Curse of the Pharaohs* (London, 1973)

'Velma', *My Mysteries and My Story* (London, 1927)

Vyer, B., *Memories of Marie Corelli* (London, 1930)

Waugh, E., *Labels* (London, 1929)

Webb, J., *The Occult Establishment* (Glasgow, 1981)

– *The Occult Underground* (Illinois, 1988)

Wembley (British Empire Exhibitions), *Official Guides 1924 and 1925*

–Wood, F. H., *The Rosemary Records* (London, 1932)

– *This Egyptian Miracle* (London, 1940)

Woodham, J., 'Design and Empire–British Design in the 1930s (*Art History*, 3, June 1980)

– *Twentieth-Century Ornament* (London, 1990)

Wyndham Lewis, D. B., 'The Dithyrambic Spectator' (*Calendar of Modern Letters*, April 1925)

Wynne, B., *Behind the Mask of Tutankhamen* (London, 1972)

LIST OF ILLUSTRATIONS